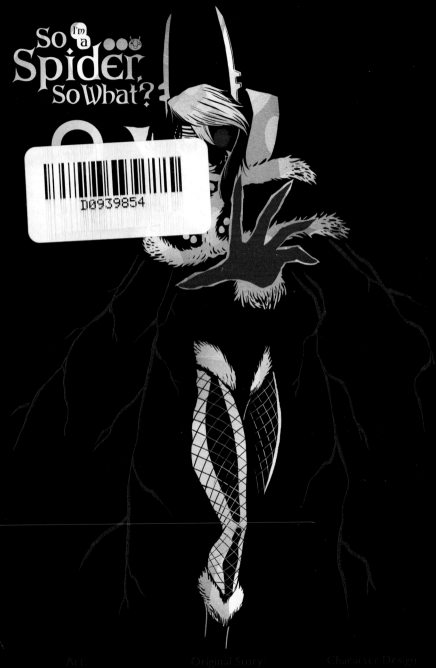

So I'm a Spider, So What?

Art:
Asahiro Kakashi

Original Story:
Okina Baba

Character Design:
Tsukasa Kiryu

So I'm a Spider, So What?

CONTENTS

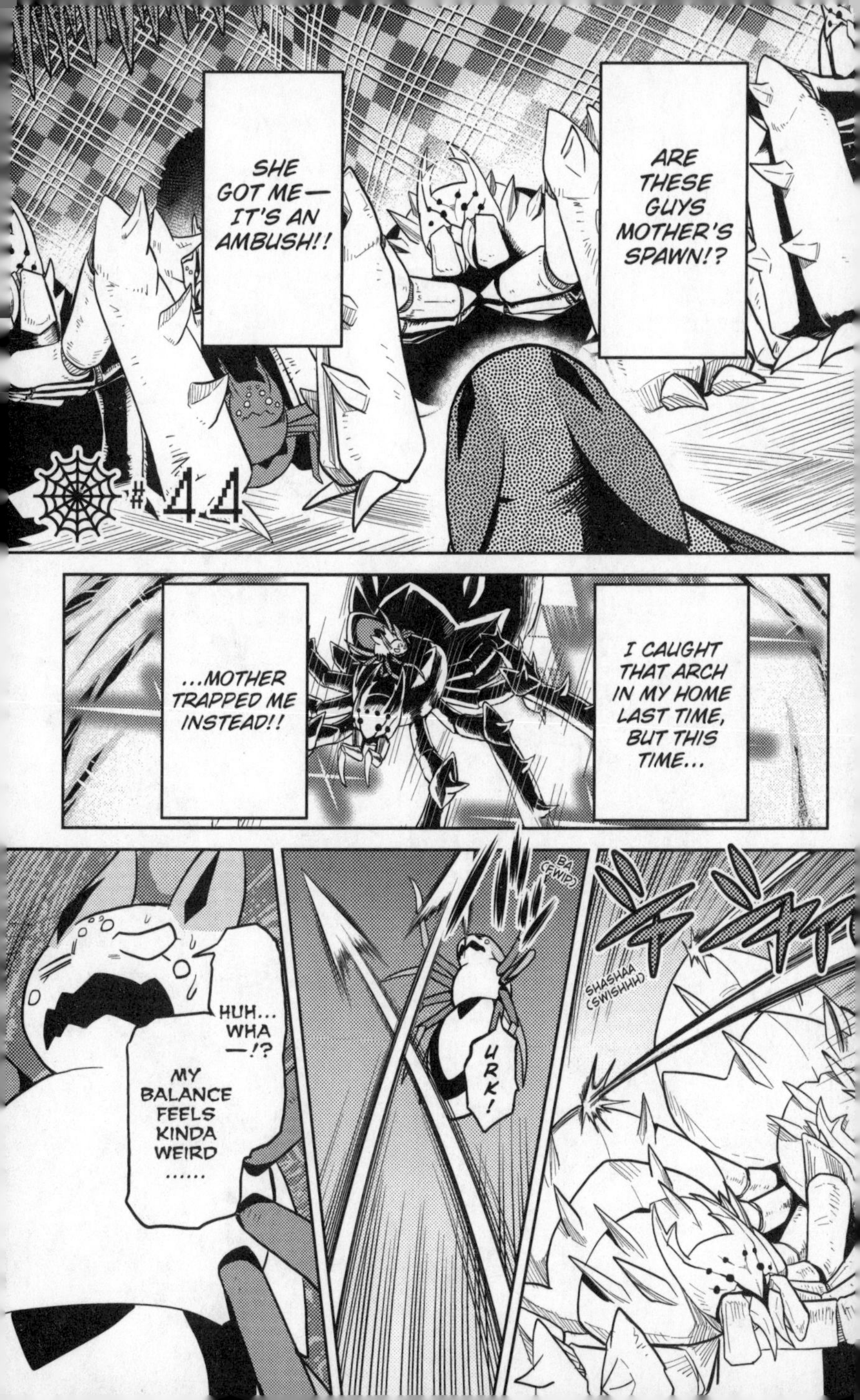
ARE THESE GUYS MOTHER'S SPAWN!?
SHE GOT ME—IT'S AN AMBUSH!!
#44
I CAUGHT THAT ARCH IN MY HOME LAST TIME, BUT THIS TIME...
...MOTHER TRAPPED ME INSTEAD!!
SHASHAA (SWISHHH)
BA (FWIP)
URK!
HUH... WHA—!?
MY BALANCE FEELS KINDA WEIRD......

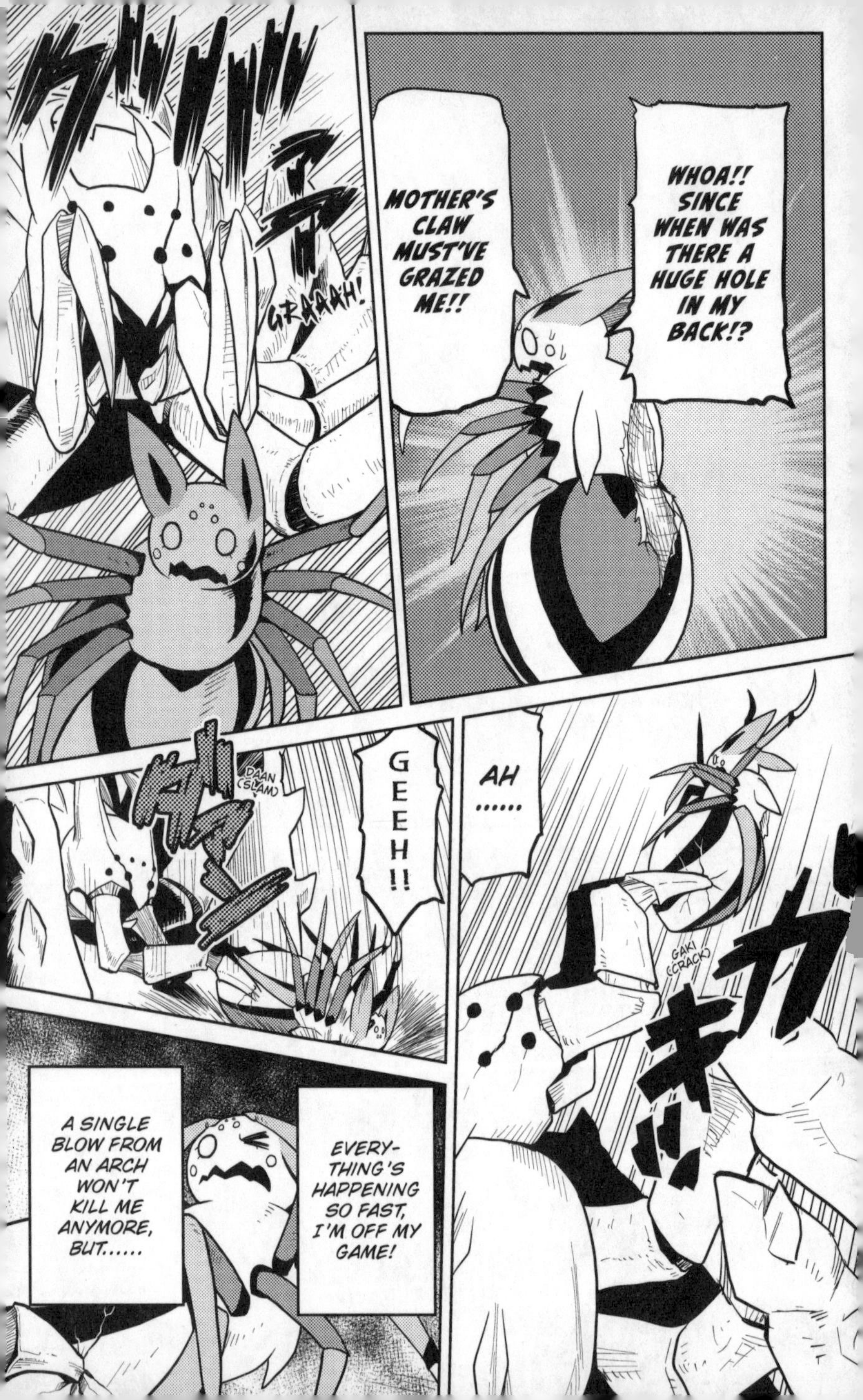
WHOA!! SINCE WHEN WAS THERE A HUGE HOLE IN MY BACK!?
MOTHER'S CLAW MUST'VE GRAZED ME!!
GRAAAH!
AH ......
GAKI (CRACK)
GEEEH!!
DAAN (SLAM)
EVERY-THING'S HAPPENING SO FAST, I'M OFF MY GAME!
A SINGLE BLOW FROM AN ARCH WON'T KILL ME ANYMORE, BUT......

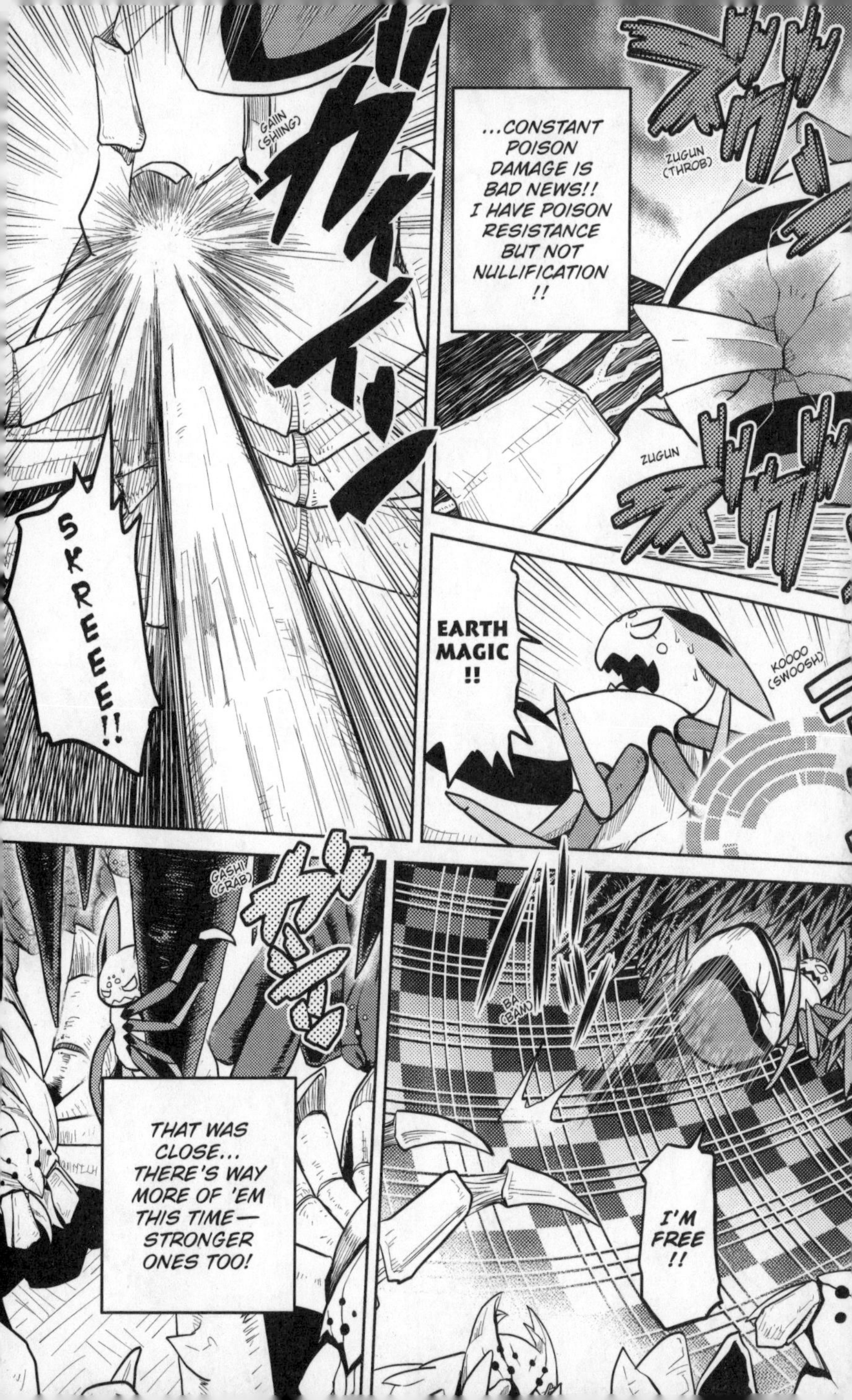
ZUGUN (THROB)
...CONSTANT POISON DAMAGE IS BAD NEWS!! I HAVE POISON RESISTANCE BUT NOT NULLIFICATION!!
ZUGUN
KOOOO (SWOOSH)
EARTH MAGIC!!
GAIIN (SHIING)
SKREEEE!!
BA (BAM)
I'M FREE!!
GASHI (GRAB)
THAT WAS CLOSE... THERE'S WAY MORE OF 'EM THIS TIME—STRONGER ONES TOO!

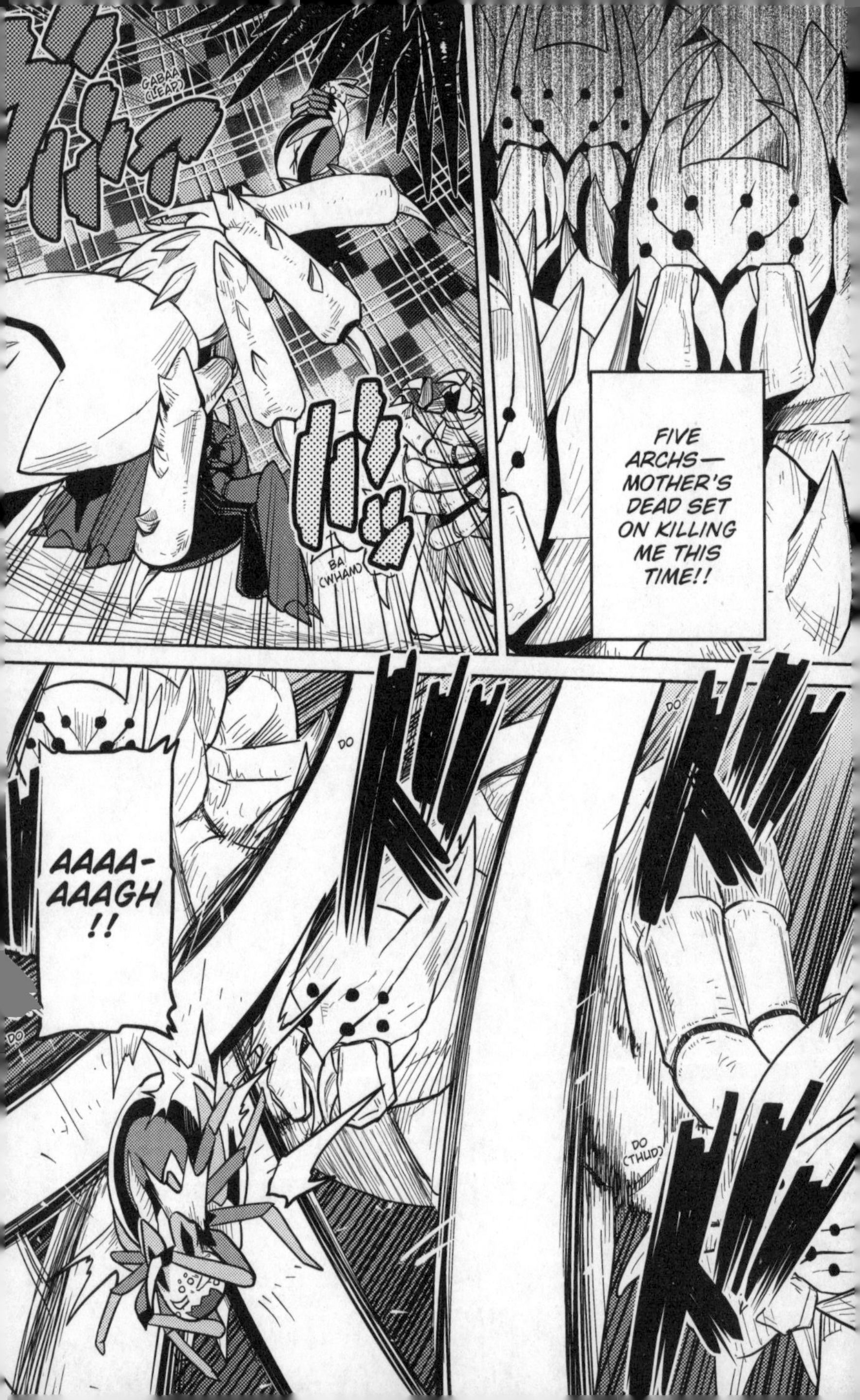
FIVE ARCHS—MOTHER'S DEAD SET ON KILLING ME THIS TIME!!
GABAA (LEAP)
BA (WHAM)
DO
DO
AAAA-AAAGH!!
DO
DO (THUD)

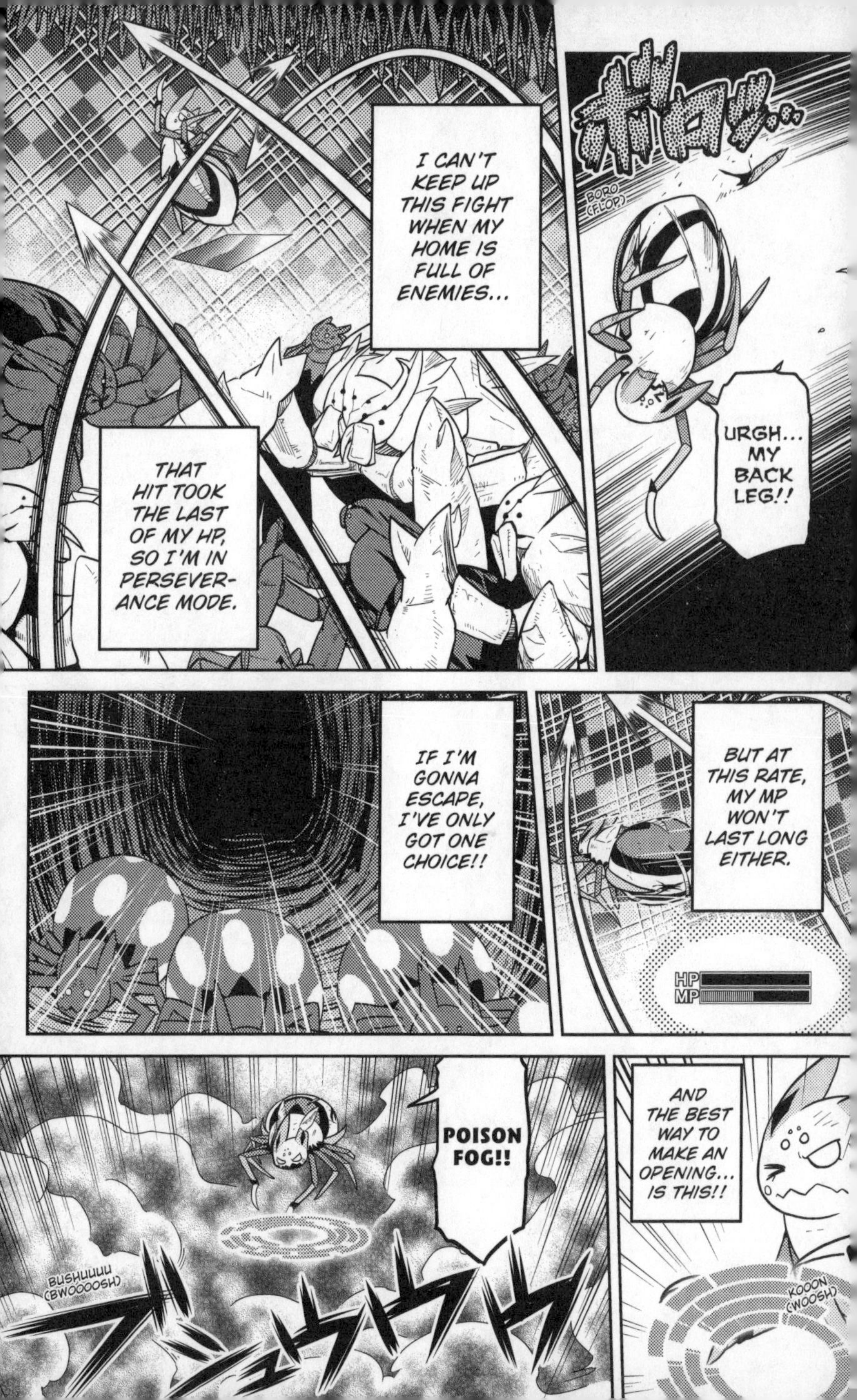
BORO (FLOP)
URGH... MY BACK LEG!!
I CAN'T KEEP UP THIS FIGHT WHEN MY HOME IS FULL OF ENEMIES...
THAT HIT TOOK THE LAST OF MY HP, SO I'M IN PERSEVERANCE MODE.
BUT AT THIS RATE, MY MP WON'T LAST LONG EITHER.
HP
MP
IF I'M GONNA ESCAPE, I'VE ONLY GOT ONE CHOICE!!
AND THE BEST WAY TO MAKE AN OPENING... IS THIS!!
KOOON (WOOSH)
POISON FOG!!
BUSHUUUU (BWOOOOSH)

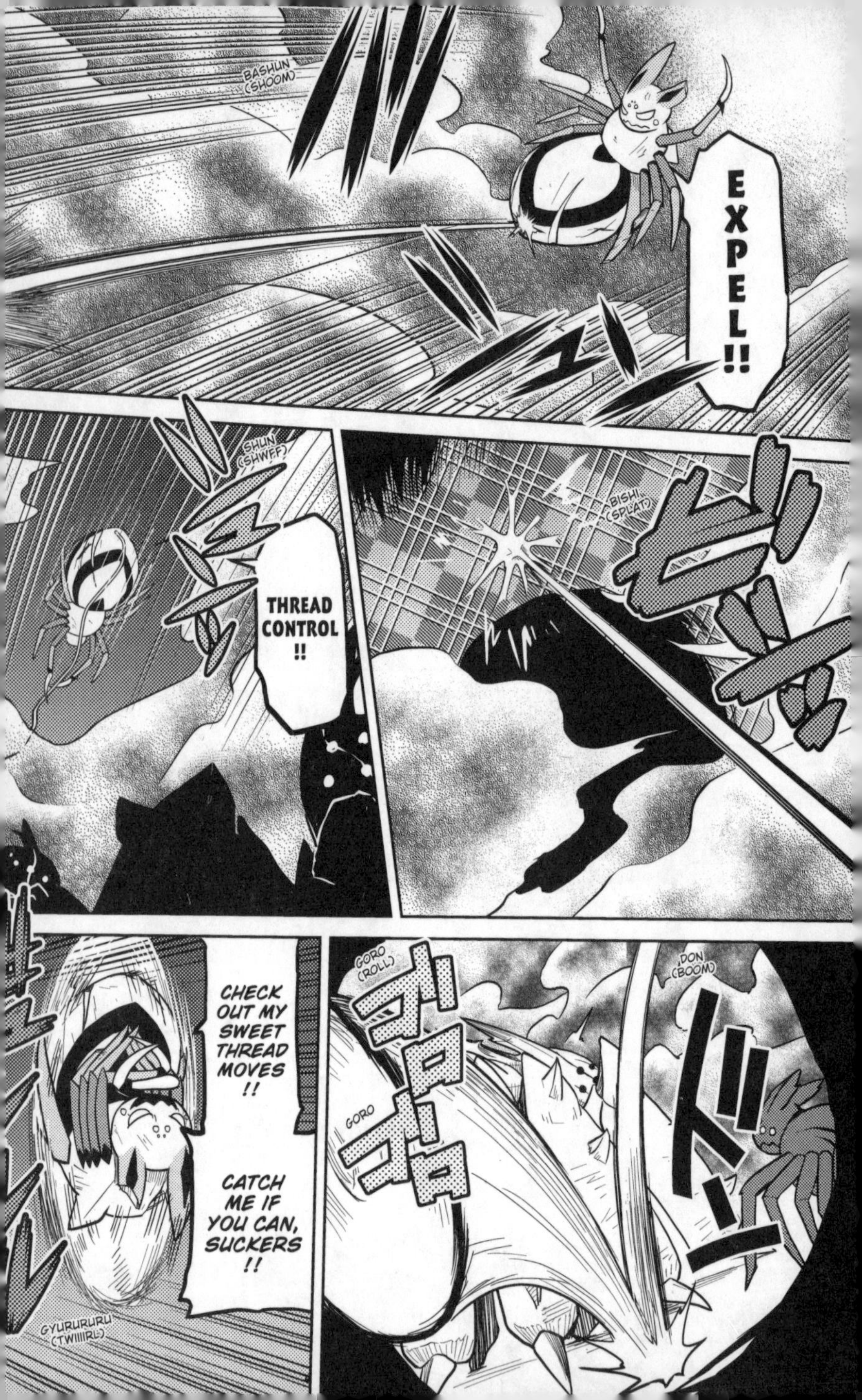
BASHUN (SHOOM)
EXPEL!!
BISHI (SPLAT)
SHUN (SHWFF)
THREAD CONTROL!!
GORO (ROLL)
DON (BOOM)
GORO
CHECK OUT MY SWEET THREAD MOVES!!
CATCH ME IF YOU CAN, SUCKERS!!
GYURURURU (TWIIIRL)

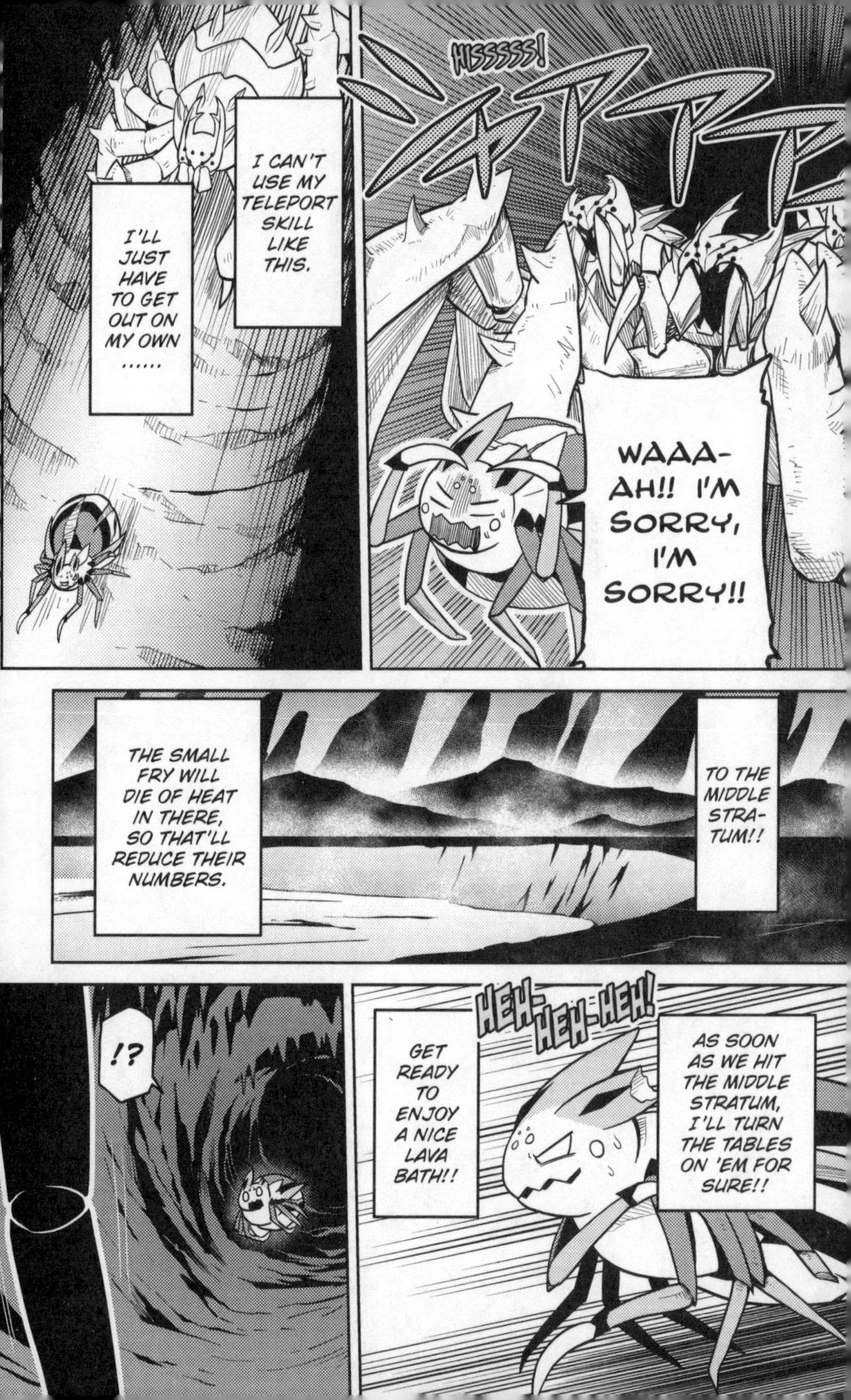
HISSSSS!
WAAA-AH!! I'M SORRY, I'M SORRY!!
I CAN'T USE MY TELEPORT SKILL LIKE THIS.
I'LL JUST HAVE TO GET OUT ON MY OWN......
TO THE MIDDLE STRA-TUM!!
THE SMALL FRY WILL DIE OF HEAT IN THERE, SO THAT'LL REDUCE THEIR NUMBERS.
HEH-HEH-HEH!
AS SOON AS WE HIT THE MIDDLE STRATUM, I'LL TURN THE TABLES ON 'EM FOR SURE!!
GET READY TO ENJOY A NICE LAVA BATH!!
!?

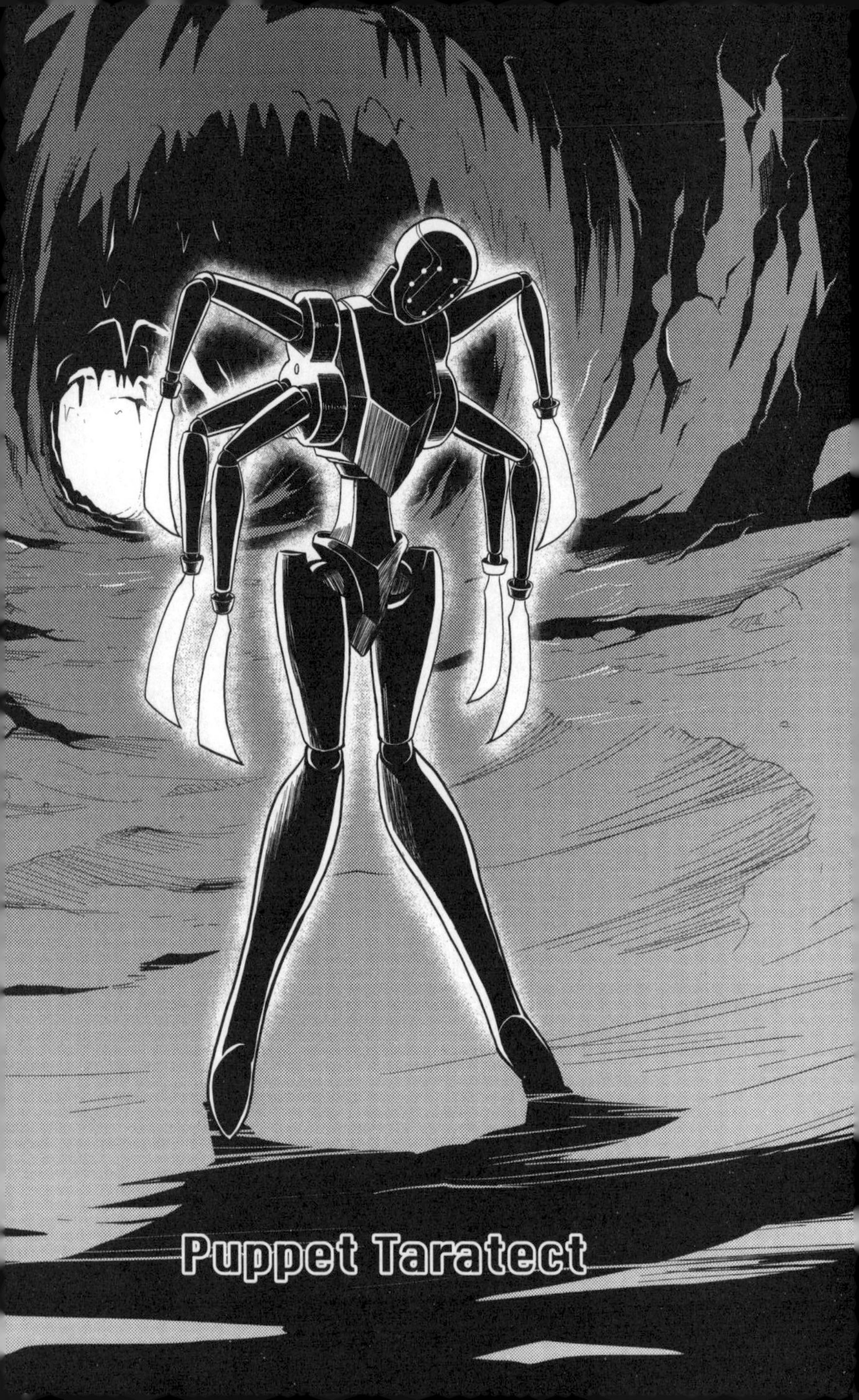
Puppet Taratect

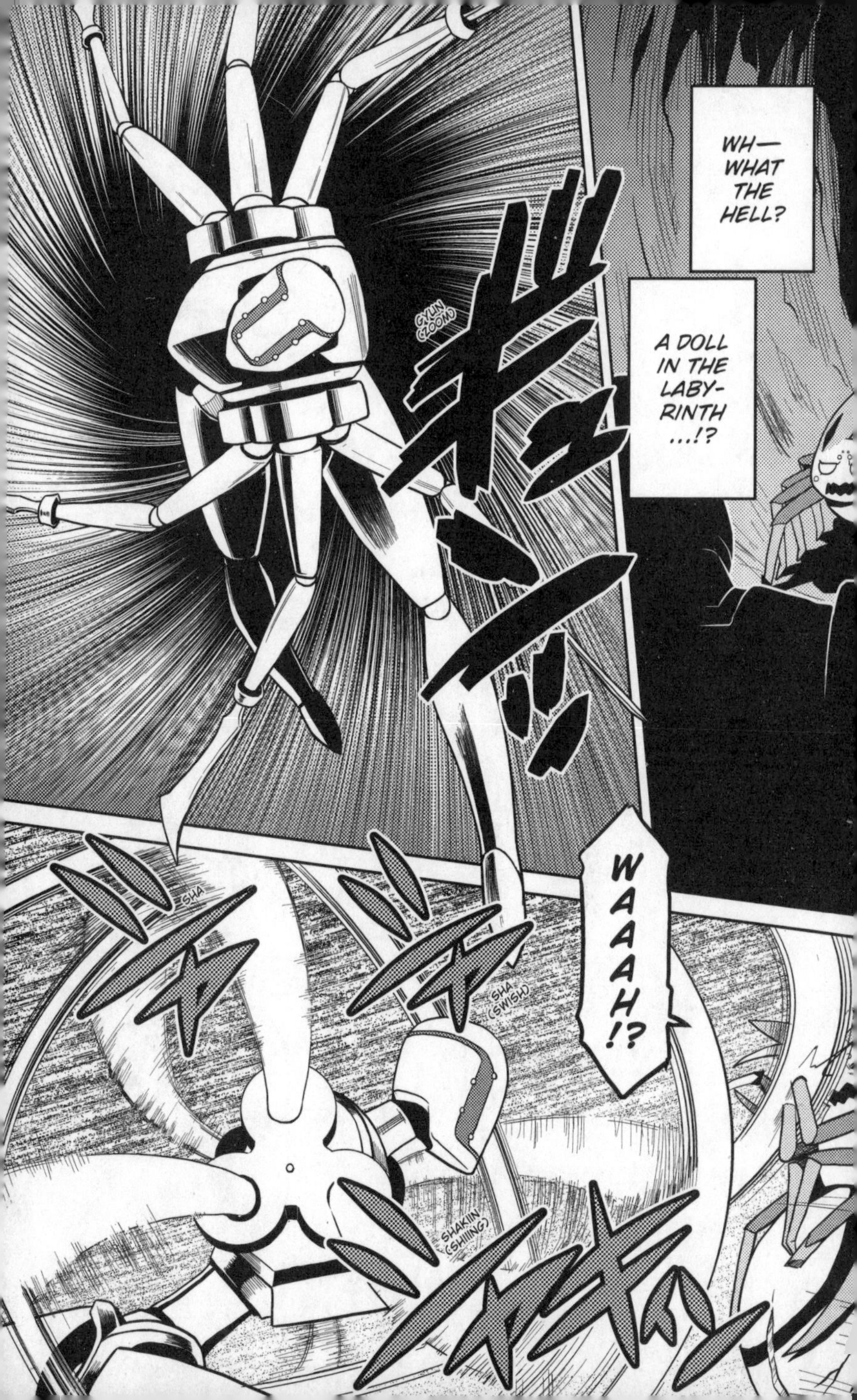
WH—WHAT THE HELL?
A DOLL IN THE LABYRINTH...!?
GYUN (ZOOM)
WAAAAH!?
SHA (SWISH)
SHA
SHAKIN (SHIIING)

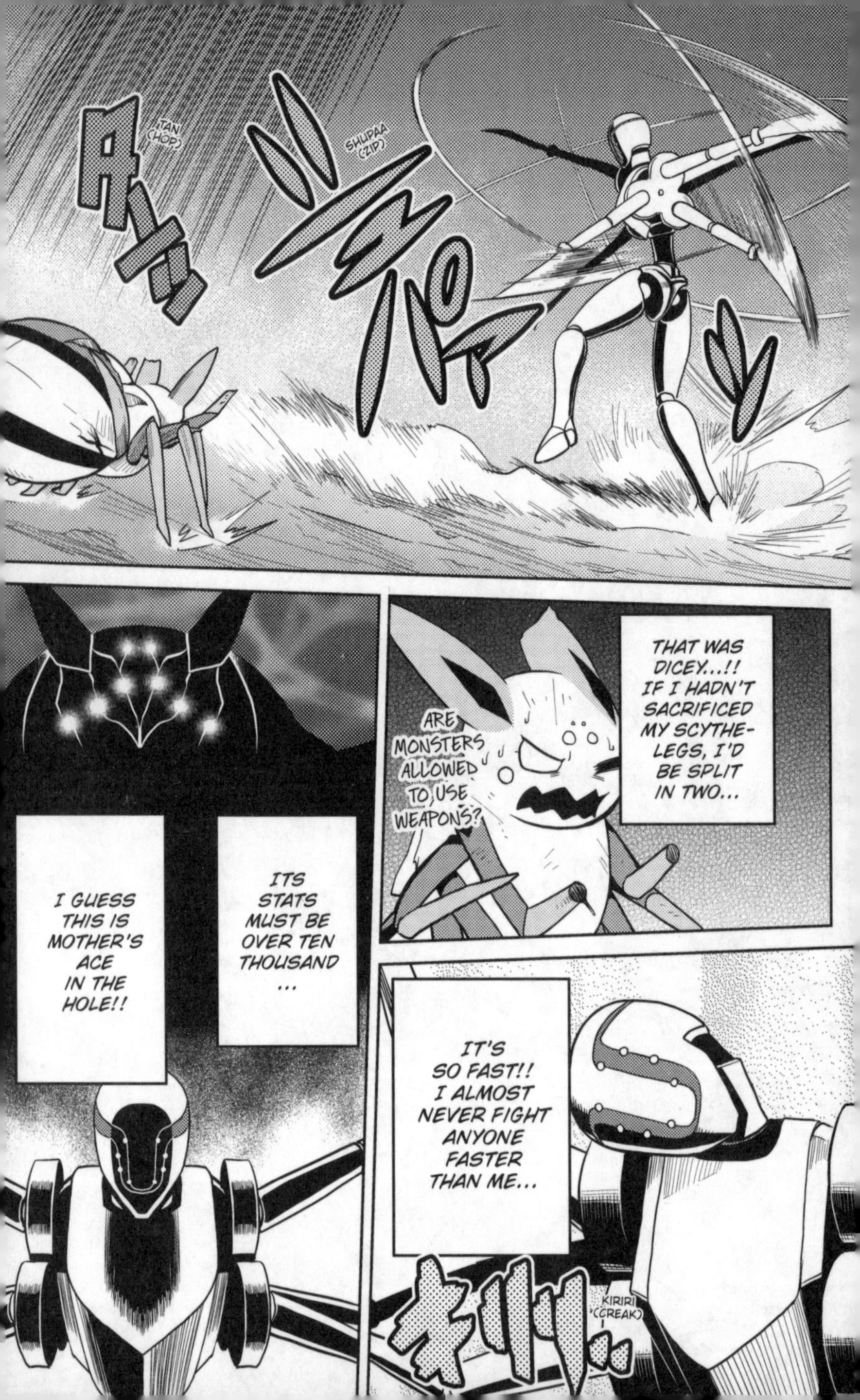
SHUPAA (ZIP)
TAN (HOP)
THAT WAS DICEY...!! IF I HADN'T SACRIFICED MY SCYTHE-LEGS, I'D BE SPLIT IN TWO...
ARE MONSTERS ALLOWED TO USE WEAPONS?
IT'S SO FAST!! I ALMOST NEVER FIGHT ANYONE FASTER THAN ME...
KIRIRI (CREAK)
ITS STATS MUST BE OVER TEN THOUSAND...
I GUESS THIS IS MOTHER'S ACE IN THE HOLE!!

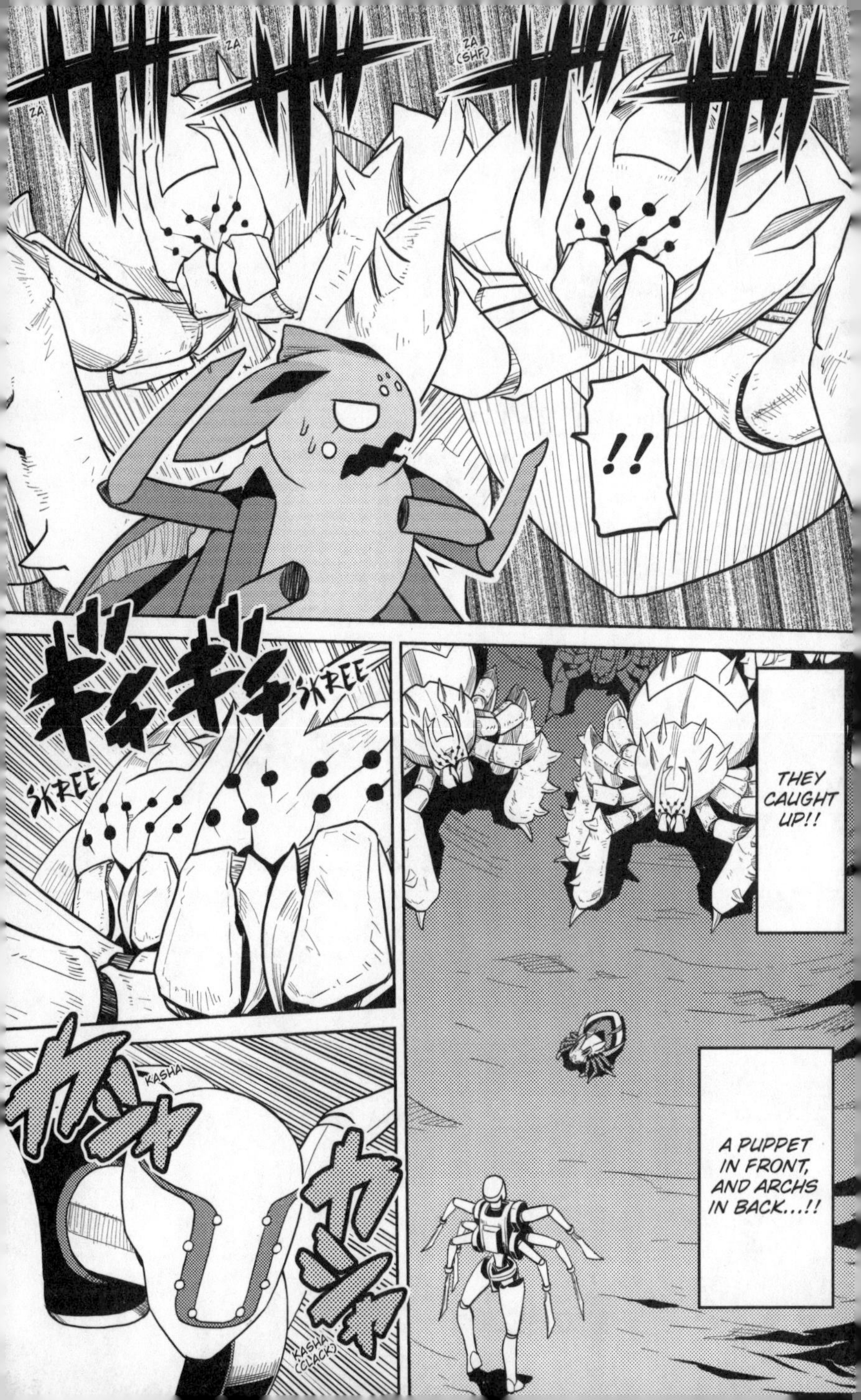
ZA
ZA (SHF)
ZA
ZA
!!
THEY CAUGHT UP!!
A PUPPET IN FRONT, AND ARCHS IN BACK...!!
SKREE
SKREE
KASHA
KASHA (CLACK)

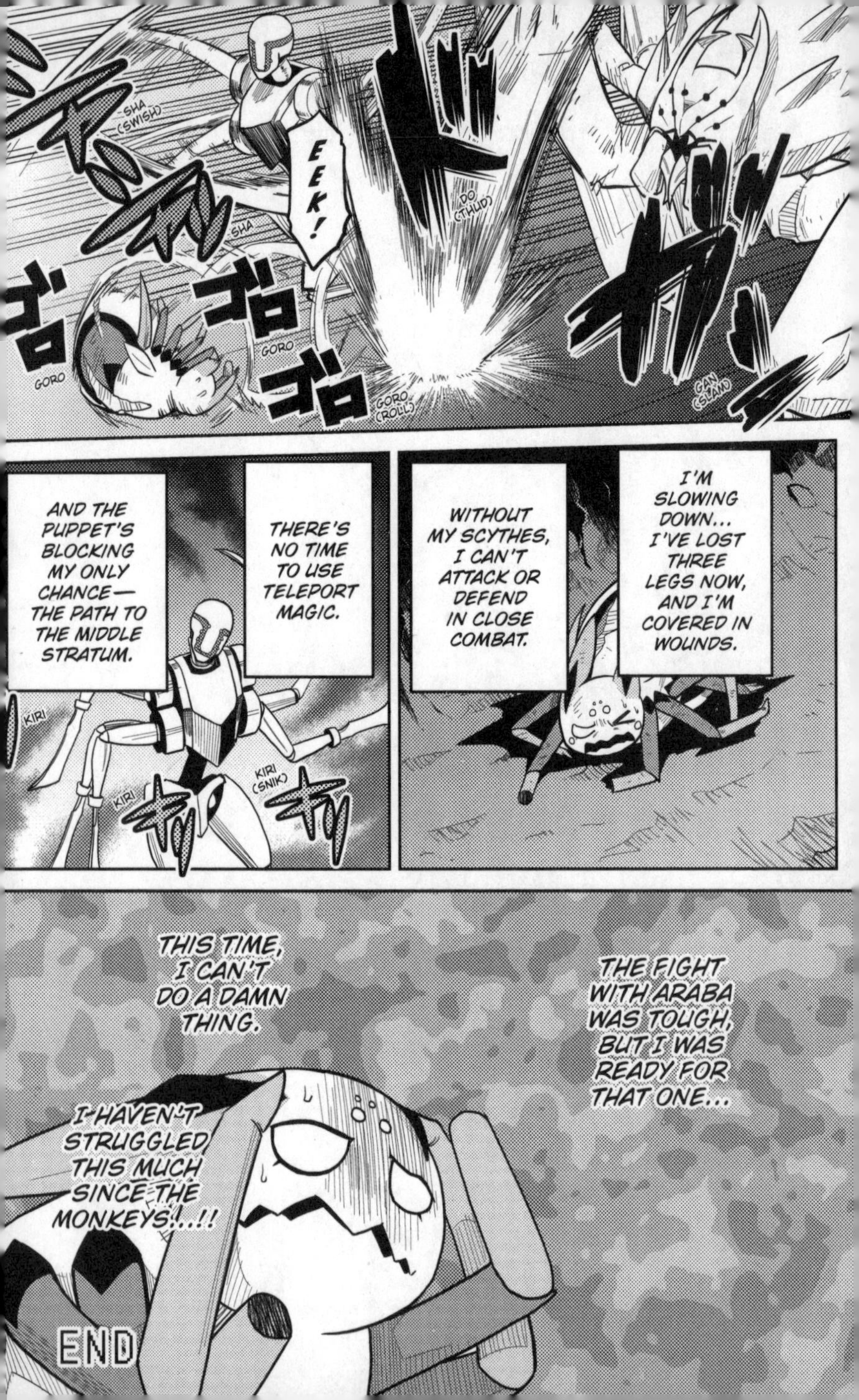
DO (THUD)
GAN (SLAM)
EEK!
SHA (SWISH)
SHA
GORO (ROLL)
GORO
GORO
I'M SLOWING DOWN... I'VE LOST THREE LEGS NOW, AND I'M COVERED IN WOUNDS.
WITHOUT MY SCYTHES, I CAN'T ATTACK OR DEFEND IN CLOSE COMBAT.
THERE'S NO TIME TO USE TELEPORT MAGIC.
AND THE PUPPET'S BLOCKING MY ONLY CHANCE—THE PATH TO THE MIDDLE STRATUM.
KIRI (SNIK)
KIRI
KIRI
THE FIGHT WITH ARABA WAS TOUGH, BUT I WAS READY FOR THAT ONE...
THIS TIME, I CAN'T DO A DAMN THING.
I HAVEN'T STRUGGLED THIS MUCH SINCE THE MONKEYS!..!!
END

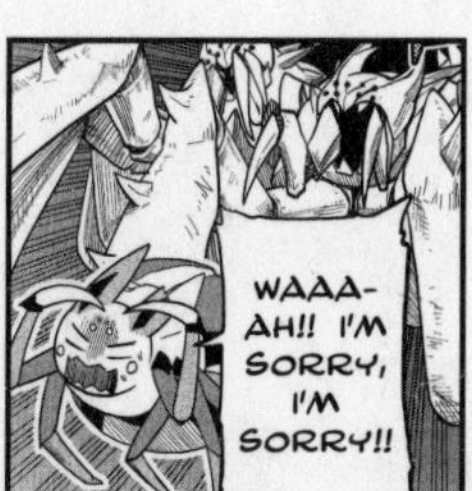
WAAA-AH!! I'M SORRY, I'M SORRY!!

So I'm a Spider, So What?

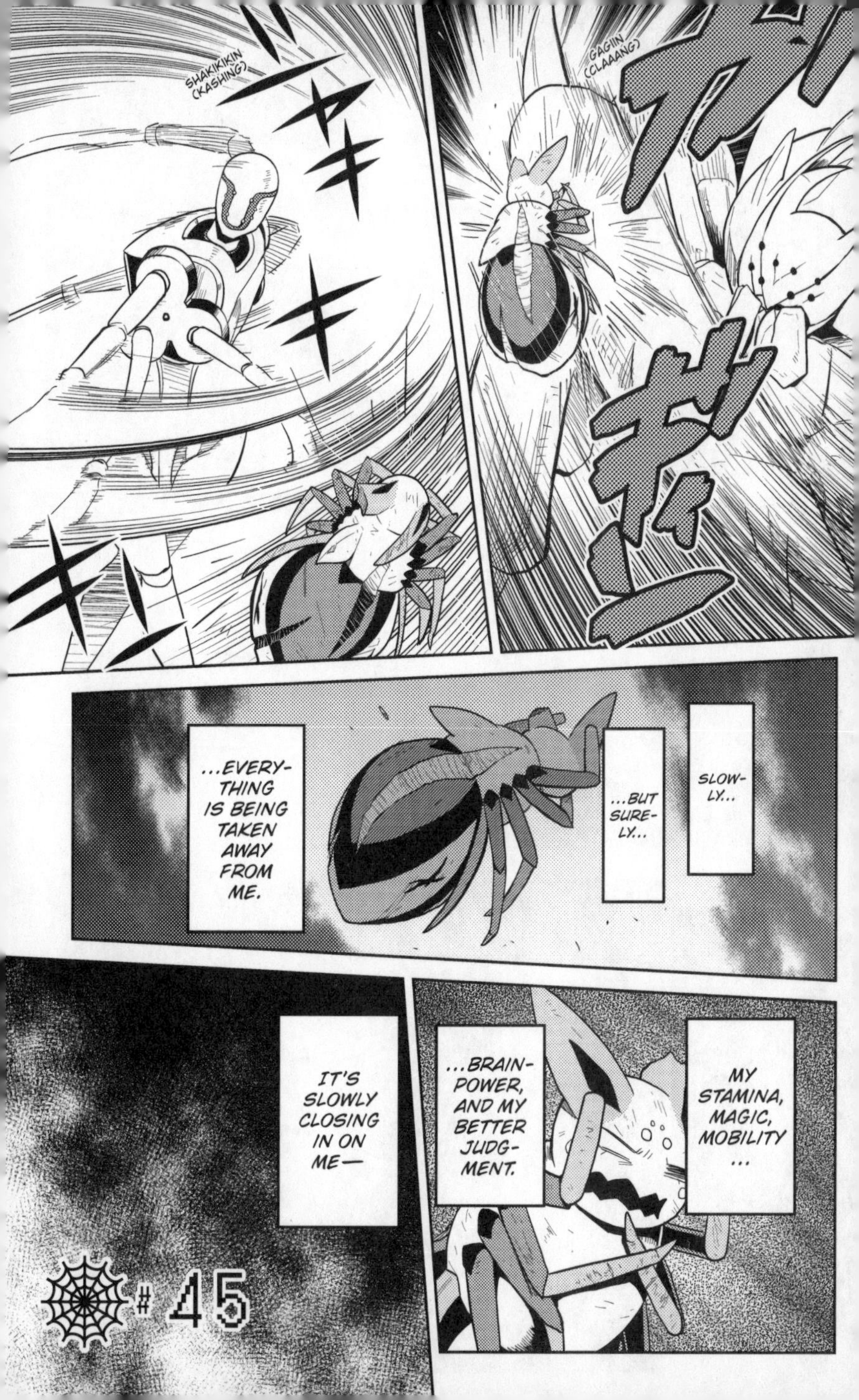
GAGIIN (CLAAANG)
SHAKIKIKIN (KASHING)
SLOWLY...
...BUT SURELY...
...EVERYTHING IS BEING TAKEN AWAY FROM ME.
MY STAMINA, MAGIC, MOBILITY...
...BRAINPOWER, AND MY BETTER JUDGMENT.
IT'S SLOWLY CLOSING IN ON ME—
#45

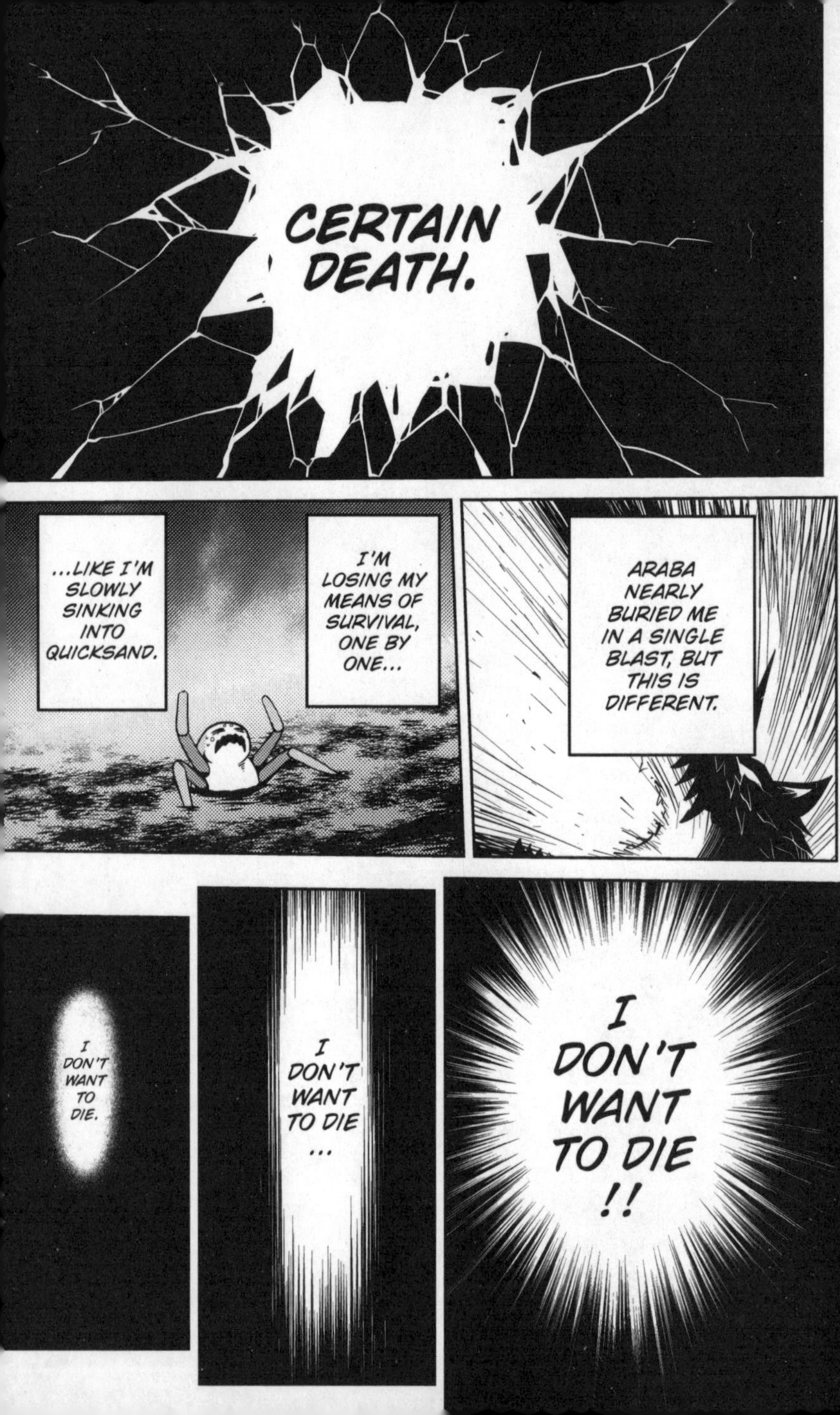
CERTAIN DEATH.
ARABA NEARLY BURIED ME IN A SINGLE BLAST, BUT THIS IS DIFFERENT.
I'M LOSING MY MEANS OF SURVIVAL, ONE BY ONE…
…LIKE I'M SLOWLY SINKING INTO QUICKSAND.
I DON'T WANT TO DIE !!
I DON'T WANT TO DIE …
I DON'T WANT TO DIE.

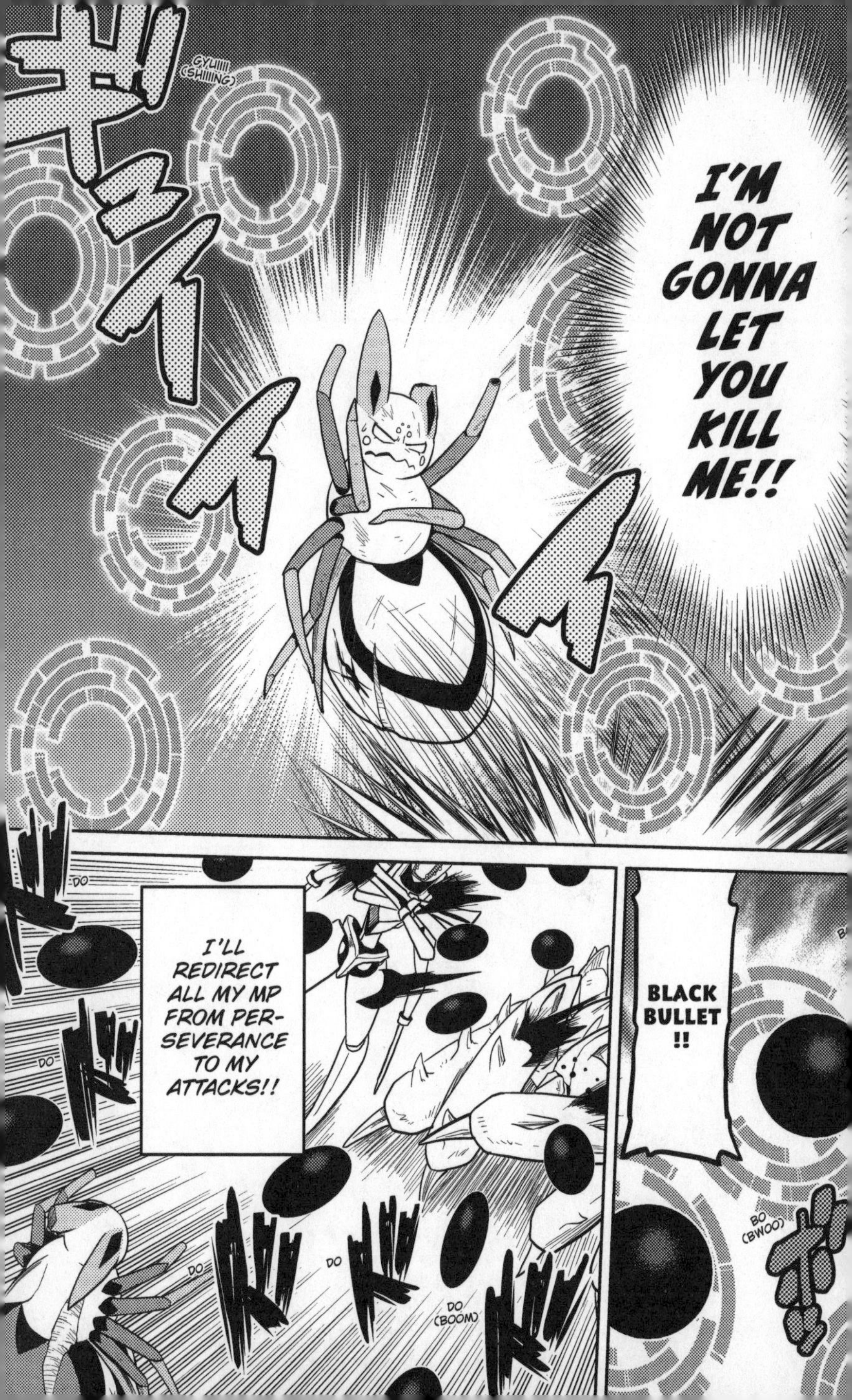
I'M NOT GONNA LET YOU KILL ME!!
GYUIIII (SHIIING)
BLACK BULLET!!
BO (BWOO)
I'LL REDIRECT ALL MY MP FROM PER-SEVERANCE TO MY ATTACKS!!
DO
DO
DO
DO
DO (BOOM)

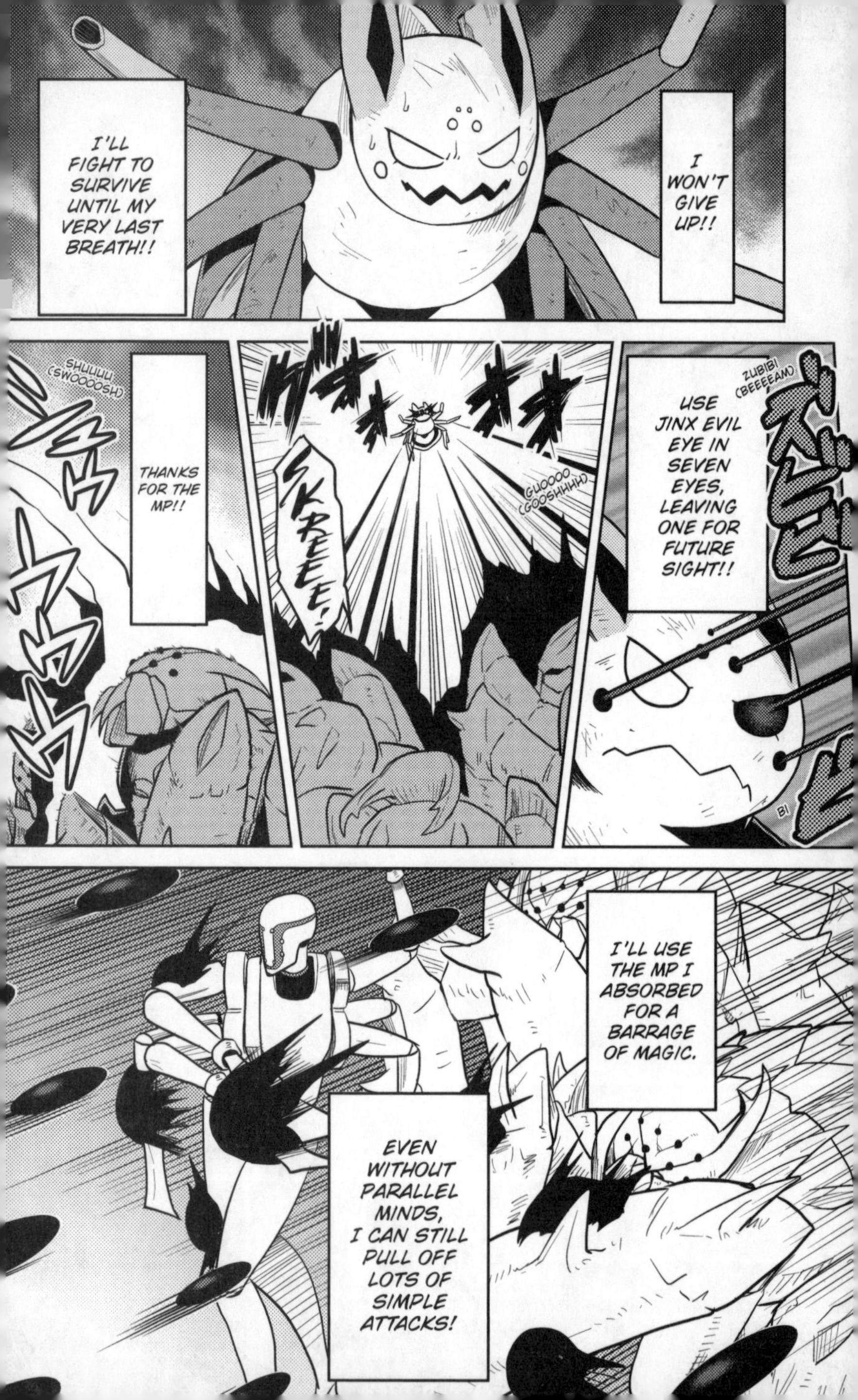
I WON'T GIVE UP!!
I'LL FIGHT TO SURVIVE UNTIL MY VERY LAST BREATH!!
ZUBIBI (BEEEEAM)
USE JINX EVIL EYE IN SEVEN EYES, LEAVING ONE FOR FUTURE SIGHT!!
BI
GUOOOO (GOOSHHHH)
SKREEEE!
SHUUUUU (SWOOOOSH)
THANKS FOR THE MP!!
I'LL USE THE MP I ABSORBED FOR A BARRAGE OF MAGIC.
EVEN WITHOUT PARALLEL MINDS, I CAN STILL PULL OFF LOTS OF SIMPLE ATTACKS!

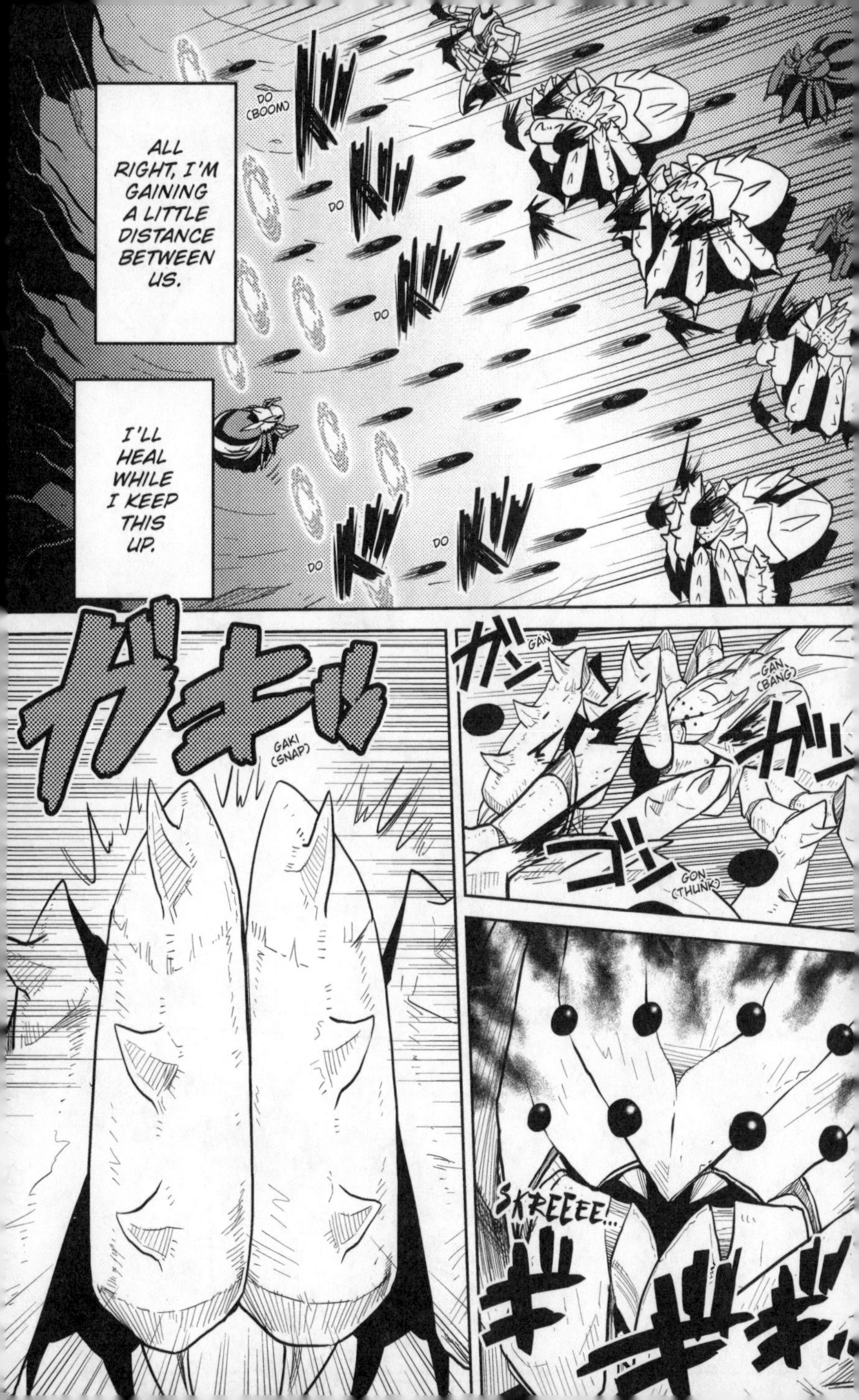
DO (BOOM)
DO
DO
ALL RIGHT, I'M GAINING A LITTLE DISTANCE BETWEEN US.
I'LL HEAL WHILE I KEEP THIS UP.
DO
DO
GAN
GAN (BANG)
GON (THUNK)
SKREEEE...
GAKI (SNAP)

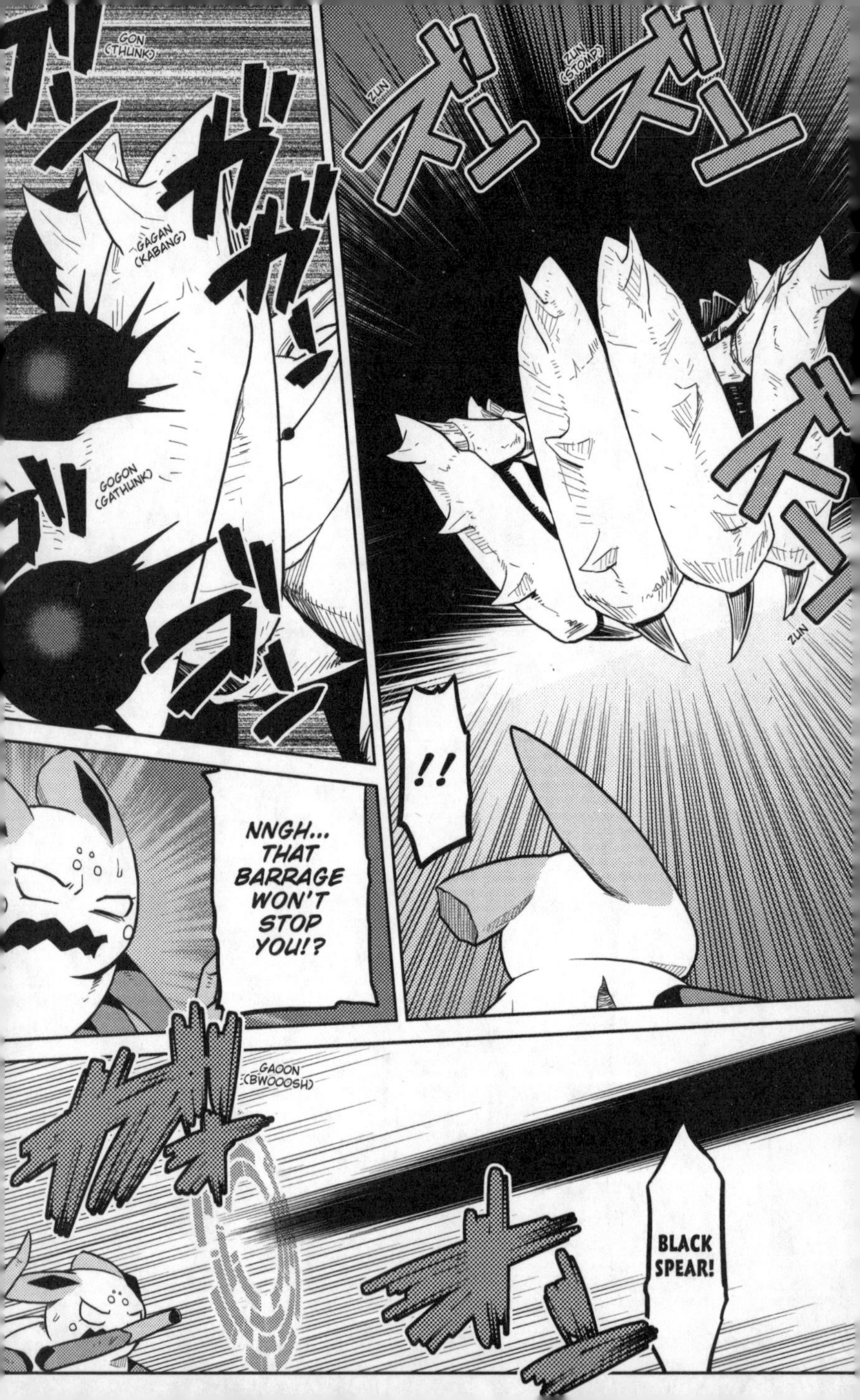

ZUN
ZUN (STOMP)
ZUN
!!
GON (THUNK)
GAGAN (KABANG)
GOGON (GATHUNK)
NNGH... THAT BARRAGE WON'T STOP YOU!?
GAOON (BWOOOSH)
BLACK SPEAR!

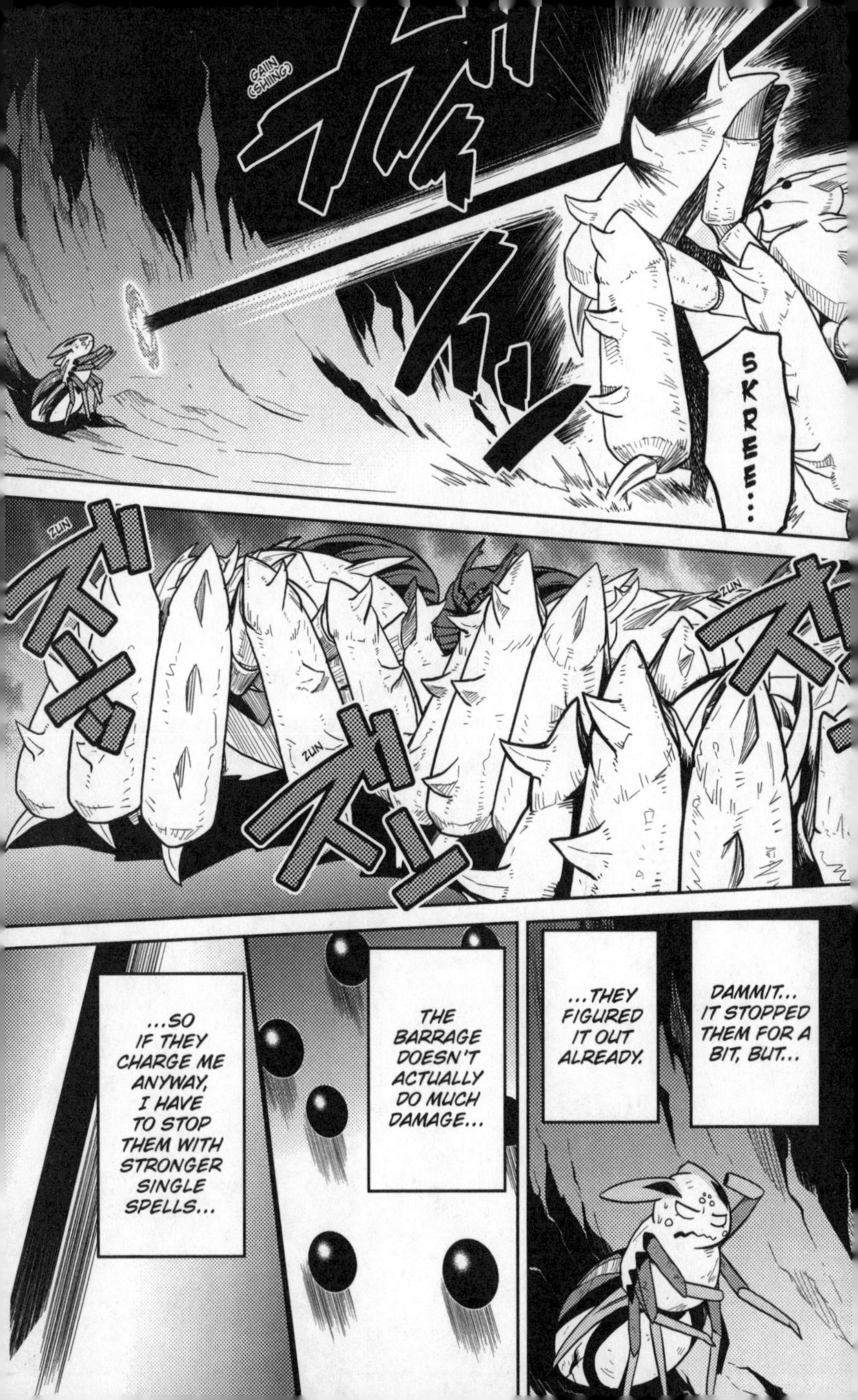
GAIN (SHIING)
SKREE...
ZUN
ZUN
ZUN
DAMMIT... IT STOPPED THEM FOR A BIT, BUT...
...THEY FIGURED IT OUT ALREADY.
THE BARRAGE DOESN'T ACTUALLY DO MUCH DAMAGE...
...SO IF THEY CHARGE ME ANYWAY, I HAVE TO STOP THEM WITH STRONGER SINGLE SPELLS...

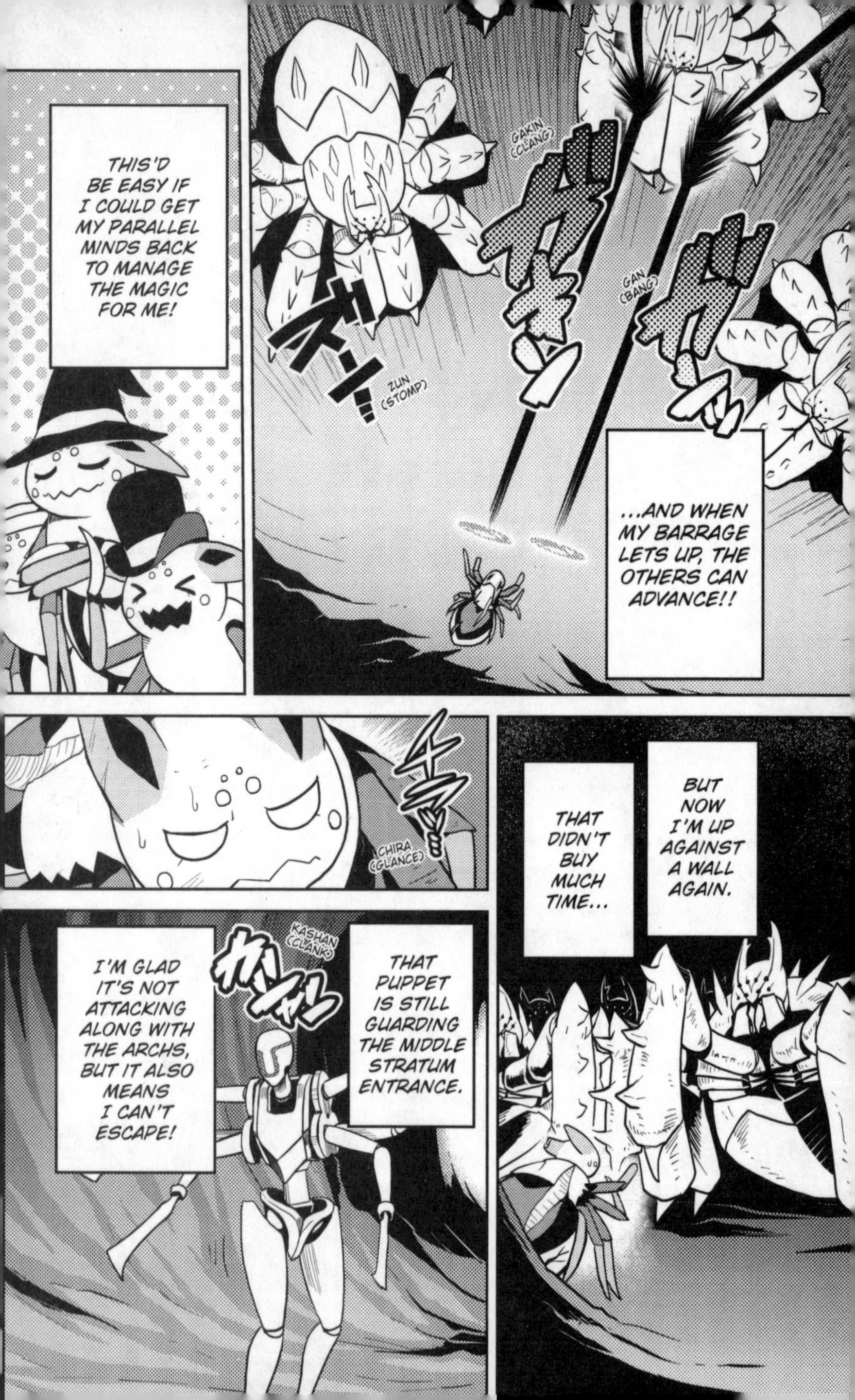
GAKIN (CLANG)
GAN (BANG)
ZUN (STOMP)
...AND WHEN MY BARRAGE LETS UP, THE OTHERS CAN ADVANCE!!
THIS'D BE EASY IF I COULD GET MY PARALLEL MINDS BACK TO MANAGE THE MAGIC FOR ME!
BUT NOW I'M UP AGAINST A WALL AGAIN.
THAT DIDN'T BUY MUCH TIME...
CHIRA (GLANCE)
THAT PUPPET IS STILL GUARDING THE MIDDLE STRATUM ENTRANCE.
KASHAN (CLANK)
I'M GLAD IT'S NOT ATTACKING ALONG WITH THE ARCHS, BUT IT ALSO MEANS I CAN'T ESCAPE!

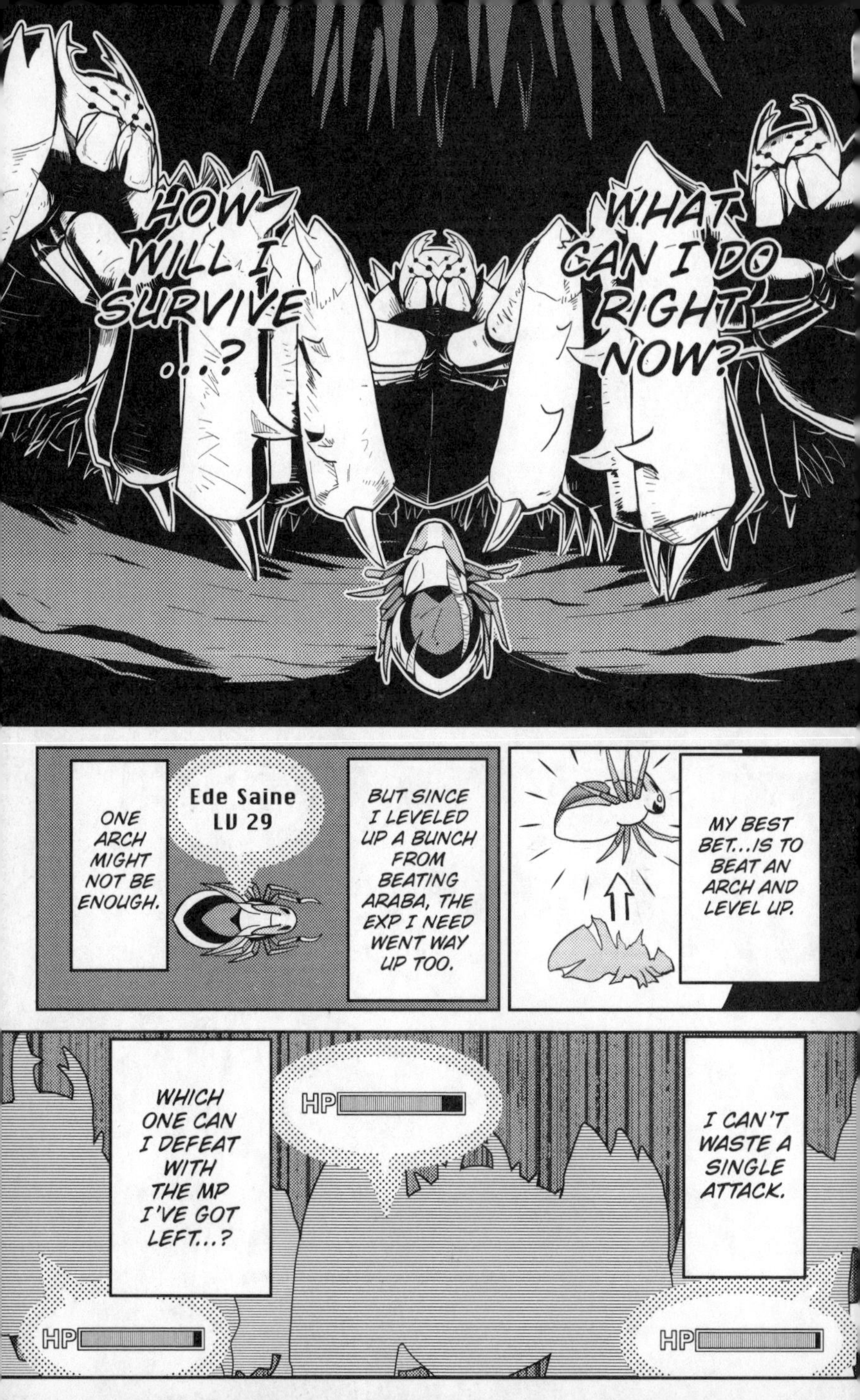
WHAT CAN I DO RIGHT NOW?
HOW WILL I SURVIVE...?
MY BEST BET...IS TO BEAT AN ARCH AND LEVEL UP.
BUT SINCE I LEVELED UP A BUNCH FROM BEATING ARABA, THE EXP I NEED WENT WAY UP TOO.
Ede Saine LV 29
ONE ARCH MIGHT NOT BE ENOUGH.
I CAN'T WASTE A SINGLE ATTACK.
HP
WHICH ONE CAN I DEFEAT WITH THE MP I'VE GOT LEFT...?
HP
HP

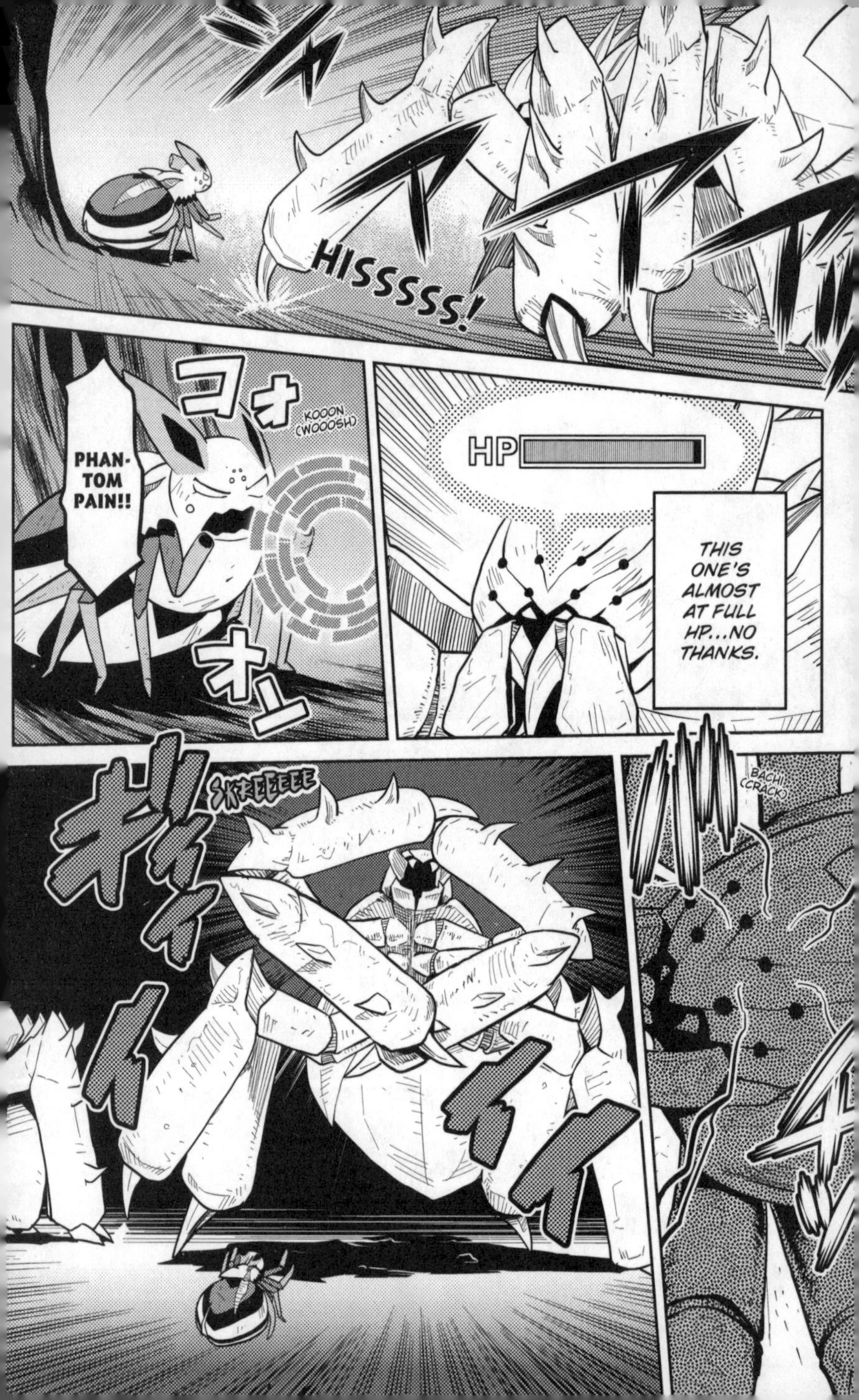
HISSSSS!
HP
THIS ONE'S ALMOST AT FULL HP...NO THANKS.
KOOON (WOOOSH)
PHAN-TOM PAIN!!
BACHI (CRACK)
SKREEEEE

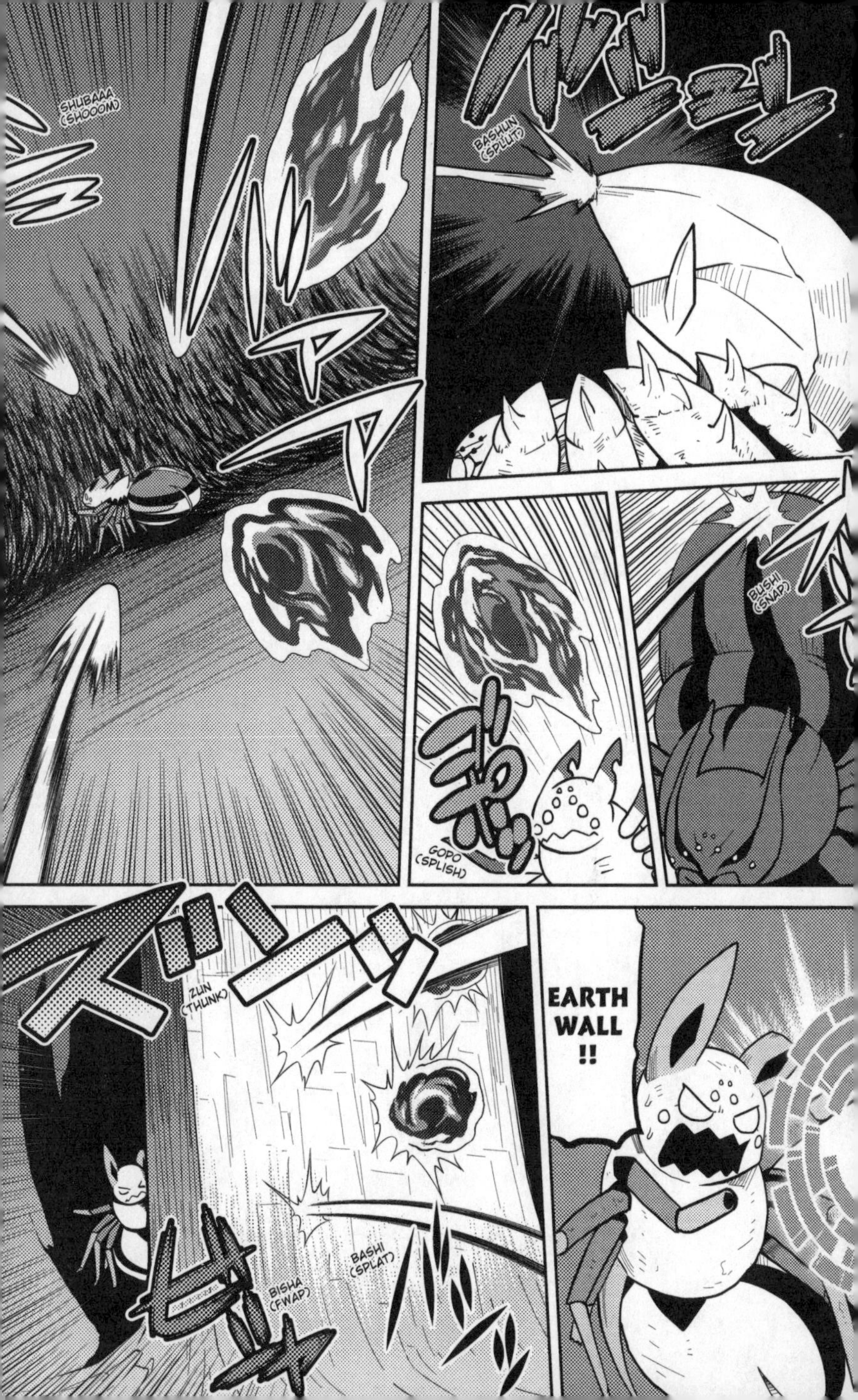
BASHUN (SPLUT)
BUSHI (SNAP)
GOPO (SPLISH)
SHUBAAA (SHOOOM)
EARTH WALL !!
ZUN (THUNK)
BASHI (SPLAT)
BISHA (F'WAP)

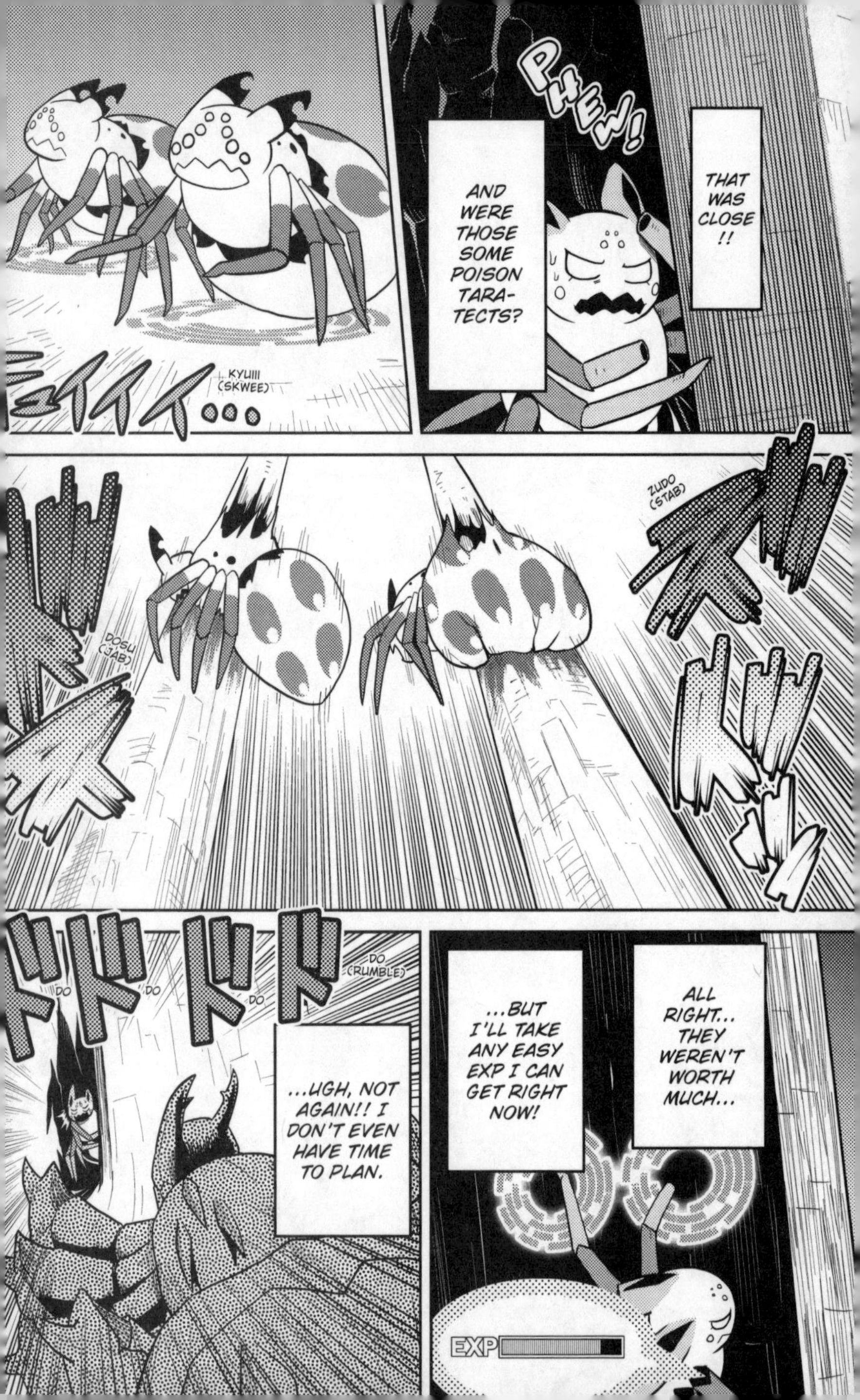

PHEW!
THAT WAS CLOSE!!
AND WERE THOSE SOME POISON TARA-TECTS?
KYUIII (SKWEE)
ZUDO (STAB)
DOSU (JAB)
ALL RIGHT... THEY WEREN'T WORTH MUCH...
...BUT I'LL TAKE ANY EASY EXP I CAN GET RIGHT NOW!
EXP
DO (RUMBLE)
DO
DO
DO
...UGH, NOT AGAIN!! I DON'T EVEN HAVE TIME TO PLAN.

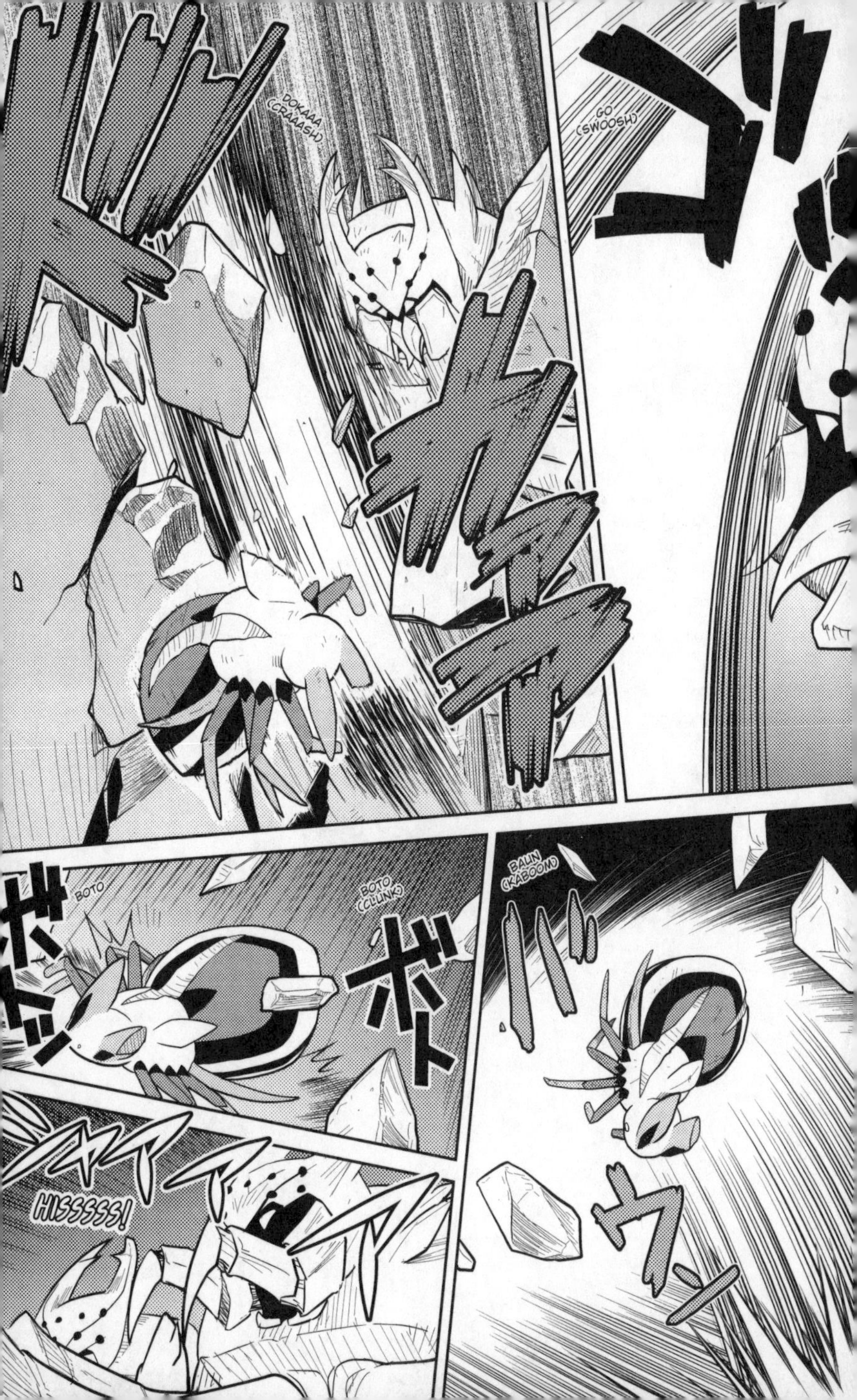
GO (SWOOSH)
DOKAAA (CRAAASH)
BAUN (KABOOM)
BOTO (CLLINK)
BOTO
HISSSSS!

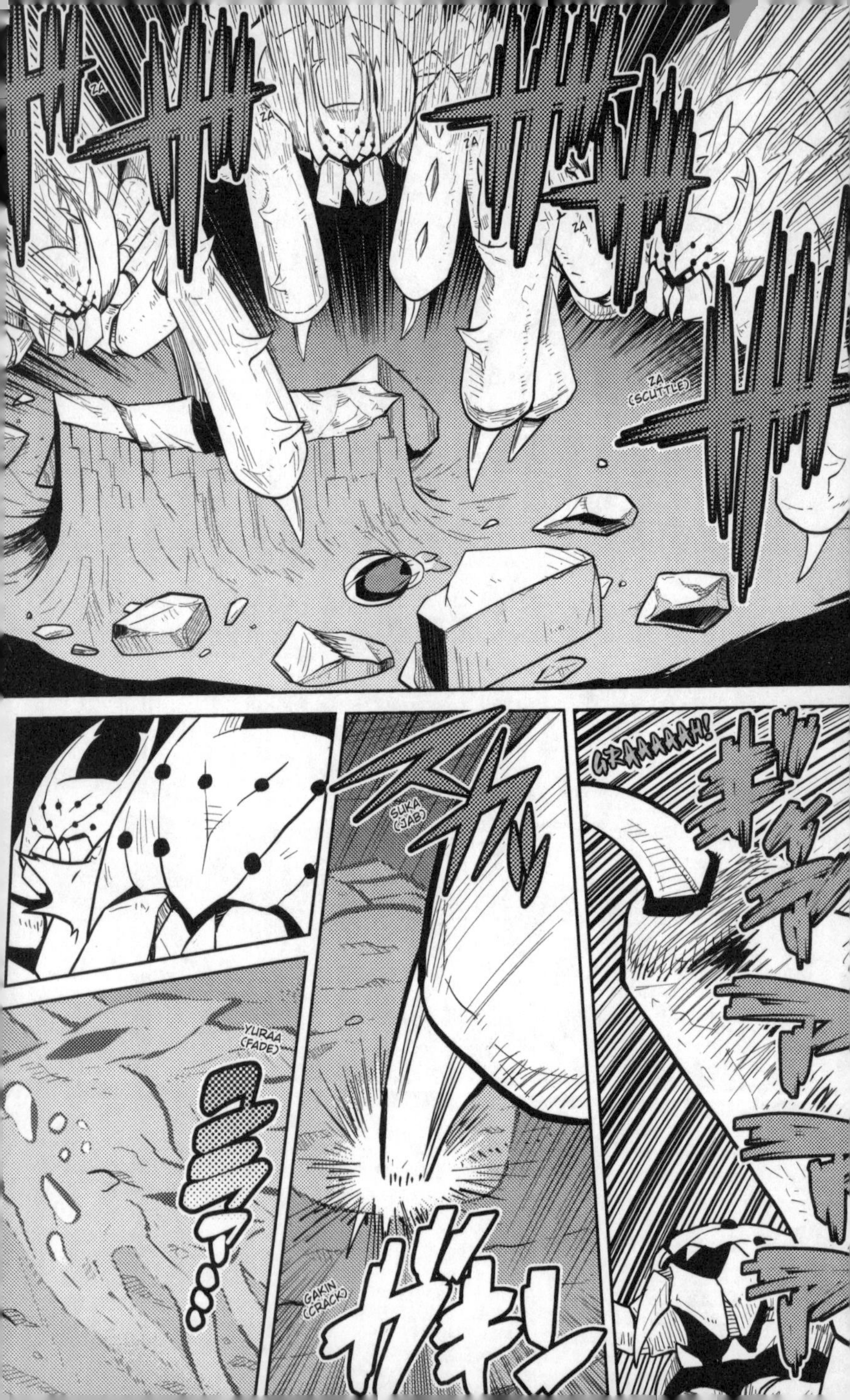
ZA (SCUTTLE)
ZA
ZA
ZA
ZA
GRAAAAAAH!
SUKA (JAB)
GAKIN (CRACK)
YURAA (FADE)

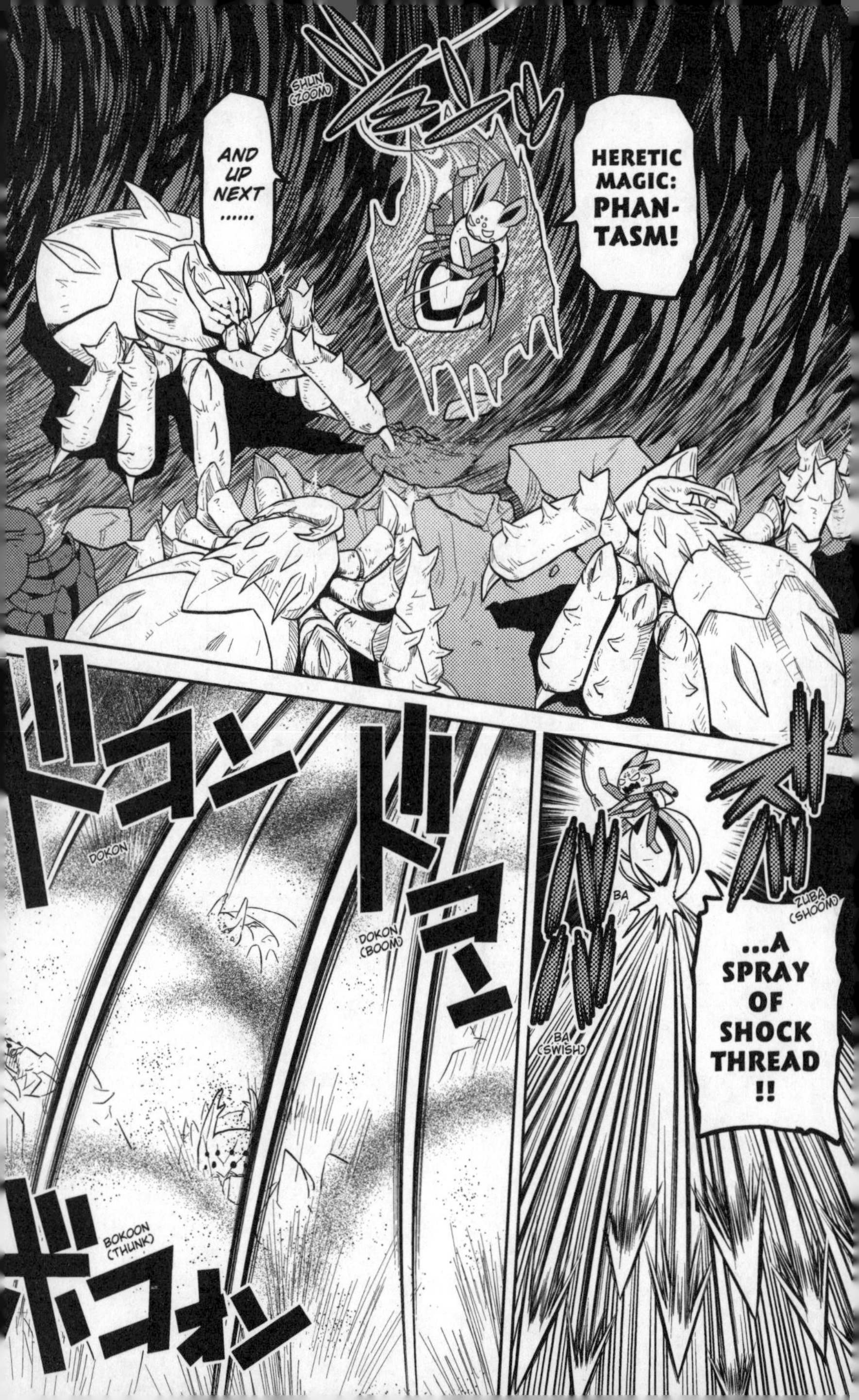
HERETIC MAGIC: PHANTASM!
SHUN (ZOOM)
AND UP NEXT......
ZUBA (SHOOM)
BA
BA (SWISH)
...A SPRAY OF SHOCK THREAD !!
DOKON (BOOM)
DOKON
BOKOON (THUNK)

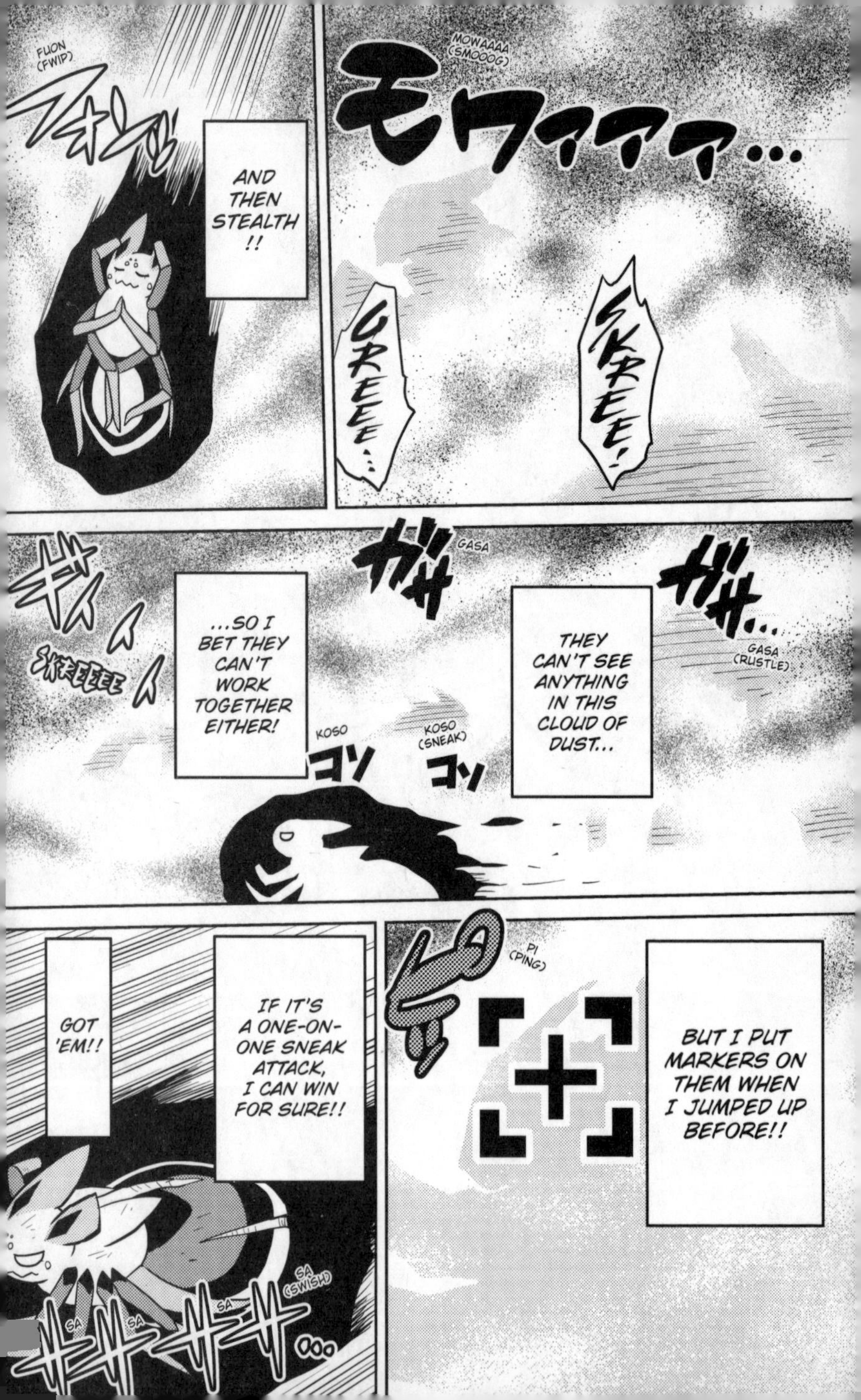
MOWAAAA (SMOOOG)
SKREEE!
GREEEE...
FUON (FWIP)
AND THEN STEALTH!!
GASA (RUSTLE)
THEY CAN'T SEE ANYTHING IN THIS CLOUD OF DUST...
GASA
KOSO (SNEAK)
KOSO
...SO I BET THEY CAN'T WORK TOGETHER EITHER!
SKREEEE
PI (PING)
BUT I PUT MARKERS ON THEM WHEN I JUMPED UP BEFORE!!
IF IT'S A ONE-ON-ONE SNEAK ATTACK, I CAN WIN FOR SURE!!
GOT 'EM!!
SA (SWISH)
SA
SA
SA

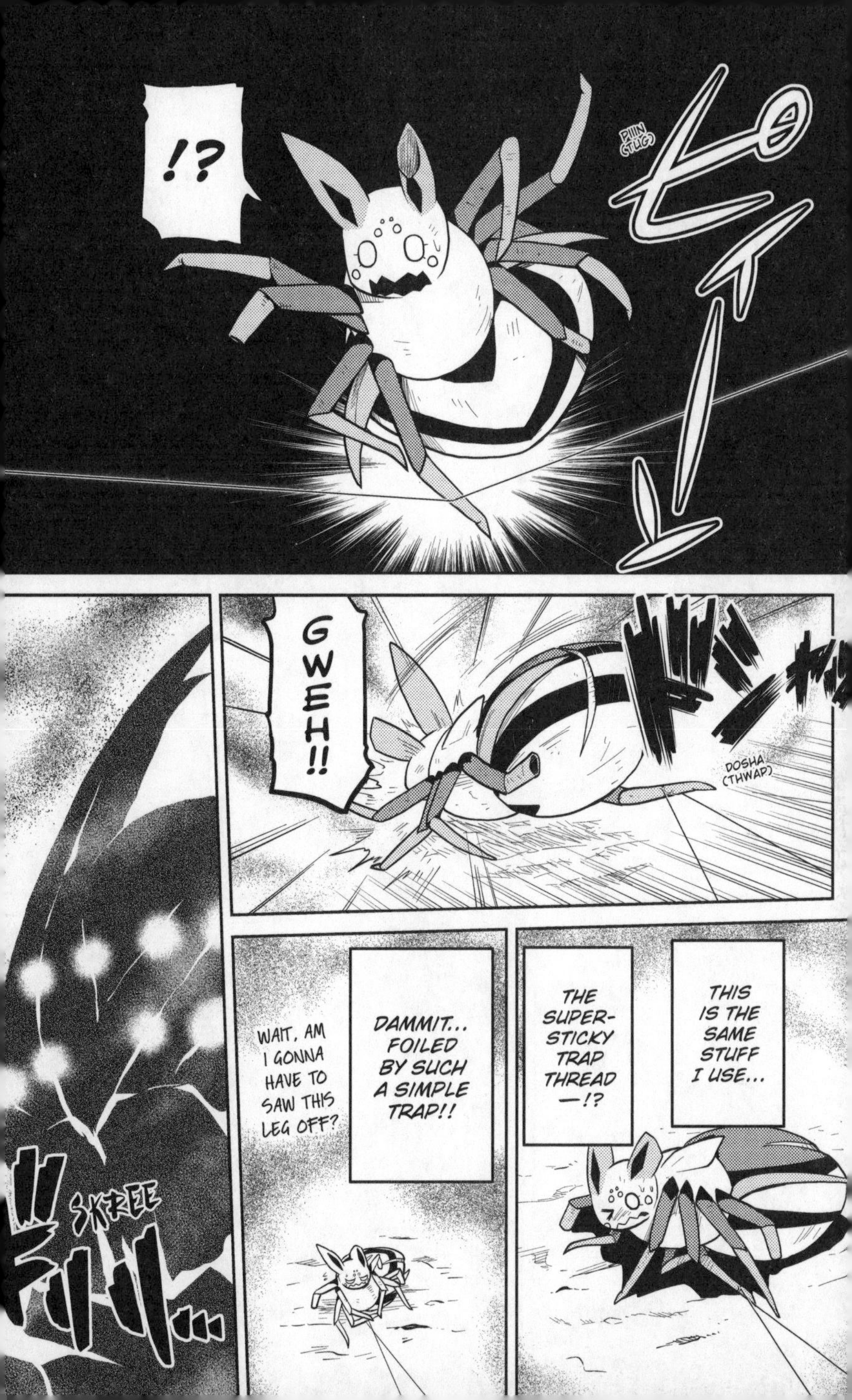
PIIN (TUG)
!?
DOSHA (THWAP)
GWEH!!
THIS IS THE SAME STUFF I USE...
THE SUPER-STICKY TRAP THREAD—!?
DAMMIT... FOILED BY SUCH A SIMPLE TRAP!!
WAIT, AM I GONNA HAVE TO SAW THIS LEG OFF?
SKREE

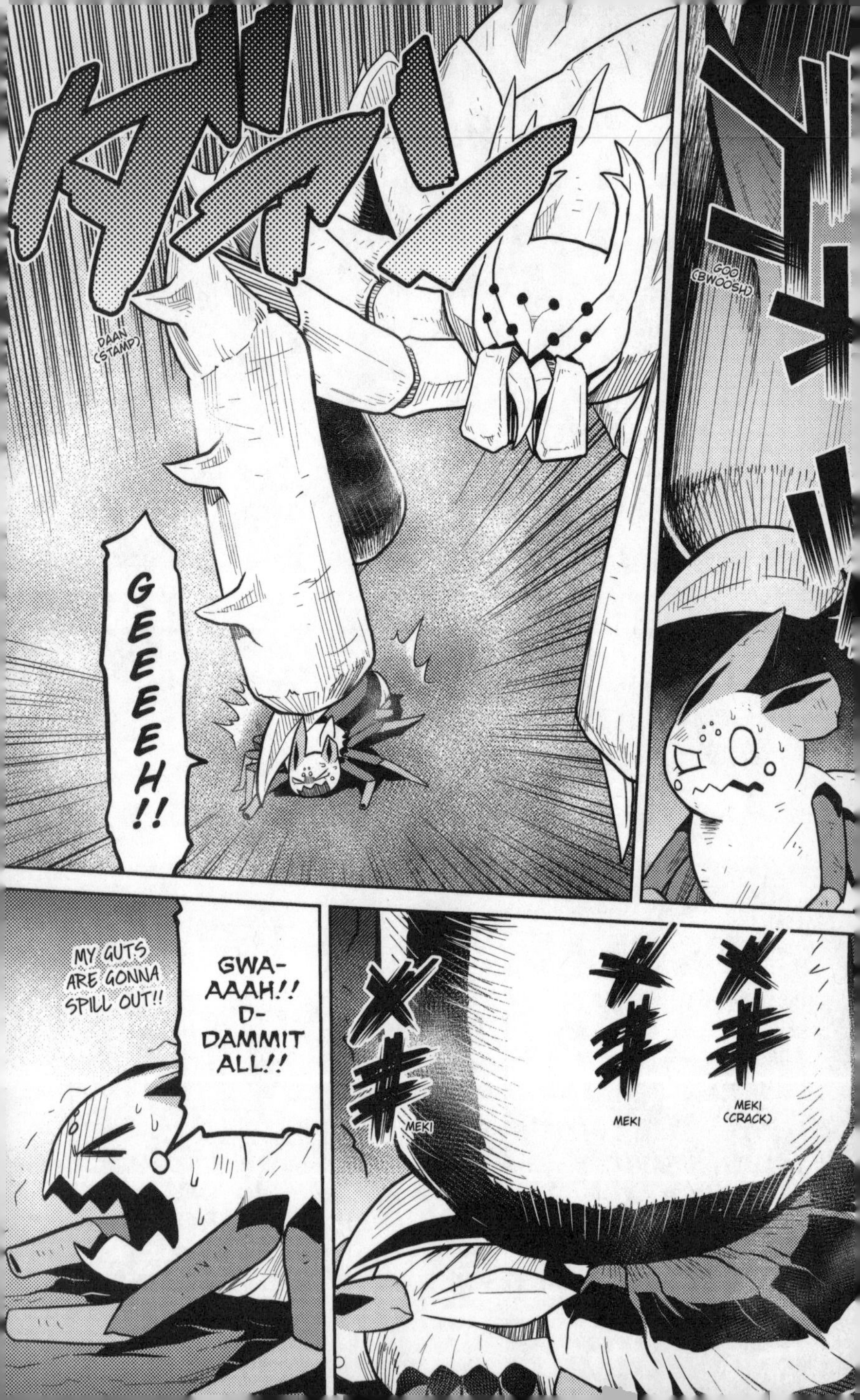
GOO (BWOOSH)
DAAN (STAMP)
GEEEEEH!!
MEKI (CRACK)
MEKI
MEKI
GWA-AAAH!! D-DAMMIT ALL!!
MY GUTS ARE GONNA SPILL OUT!!

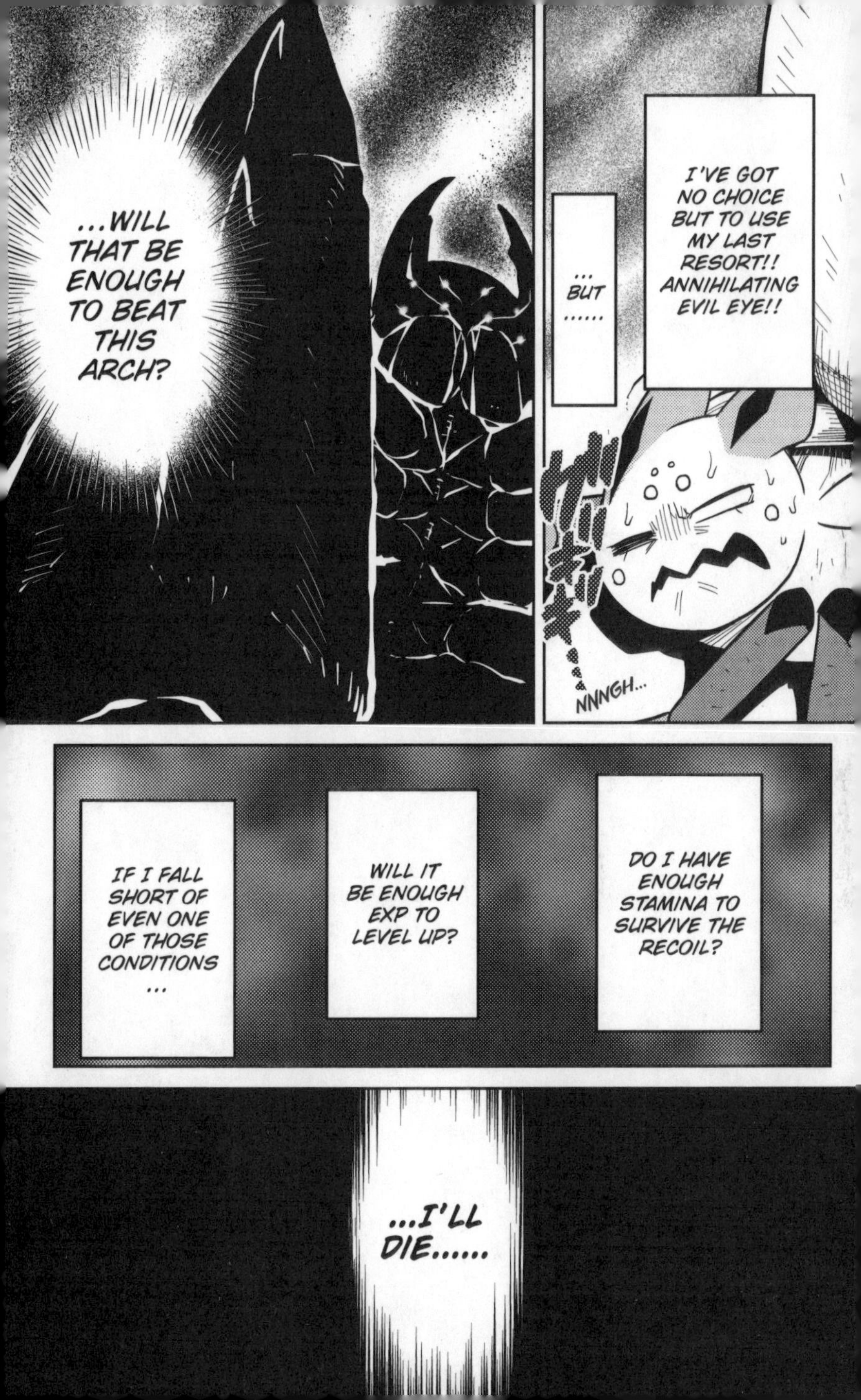
I'VE GOT NO CHOICE BUT TO USE MY LAST RESORT!! ANNIHILATING EVIL EYE!!
...BUT......
NNNGH...
...WILL THAT BE ENOUGH TO BEAT THIS ARCH?
DO I HAVE ENOUGH STAMINA TO SURVIVE THE RECOIL?
WILL IT BE ENOUGH EXP TO LEVEL UP?
IF I FALL SHORT OF EVEN ONE OF THOSE CONDITIONS...
...I'LL DIE......

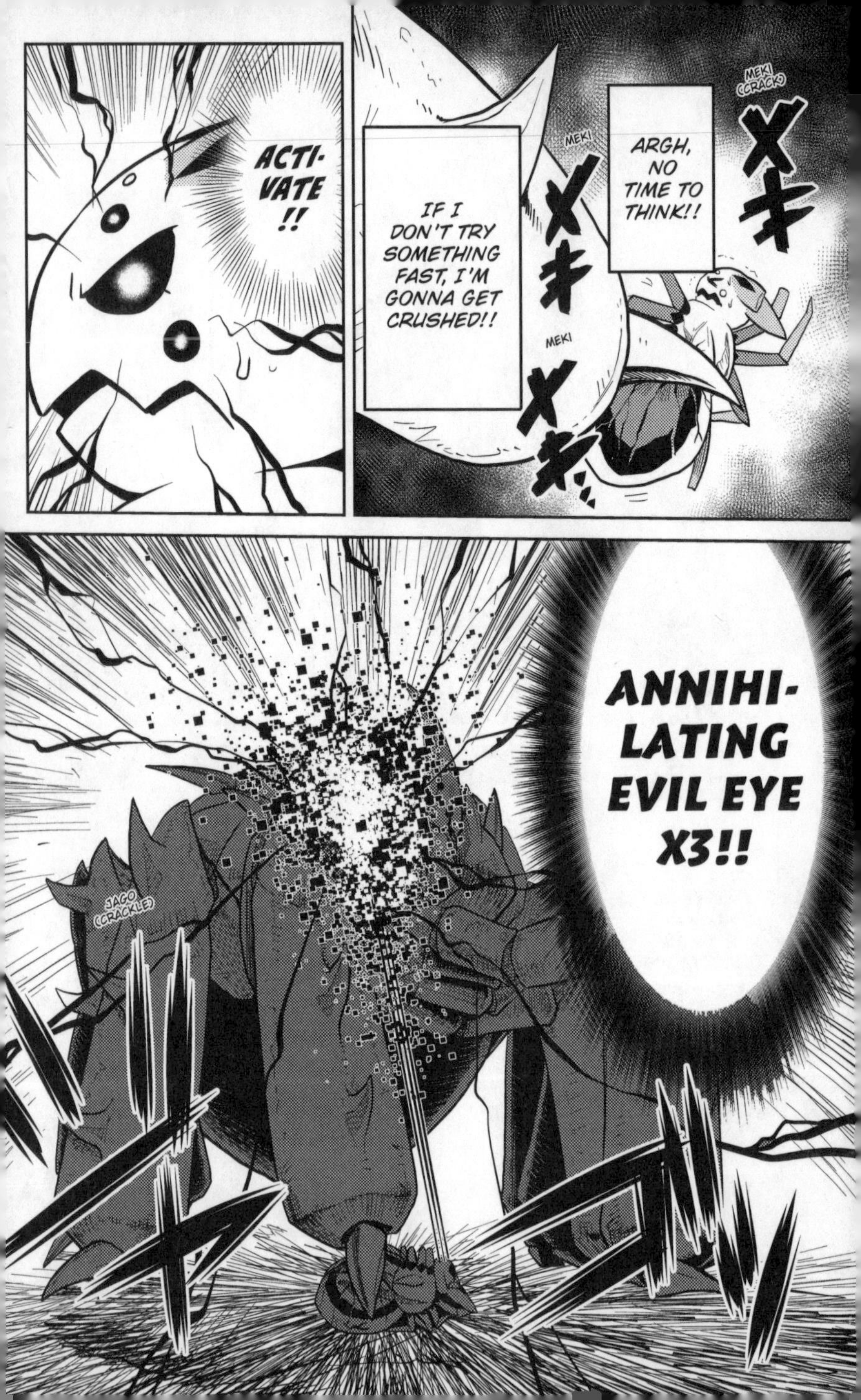
MEKI (CRACK)
ARGH, NO TIME TO THINK!!
MEKI
IF I DON'T TRY SOMETHING FAST, I'M GONNA GET CRUSHED!!
MEKI
ACTI-VATE!!
ANNIHI-LATING EVIL EYE X3!!
JAGO (CRACKLE)

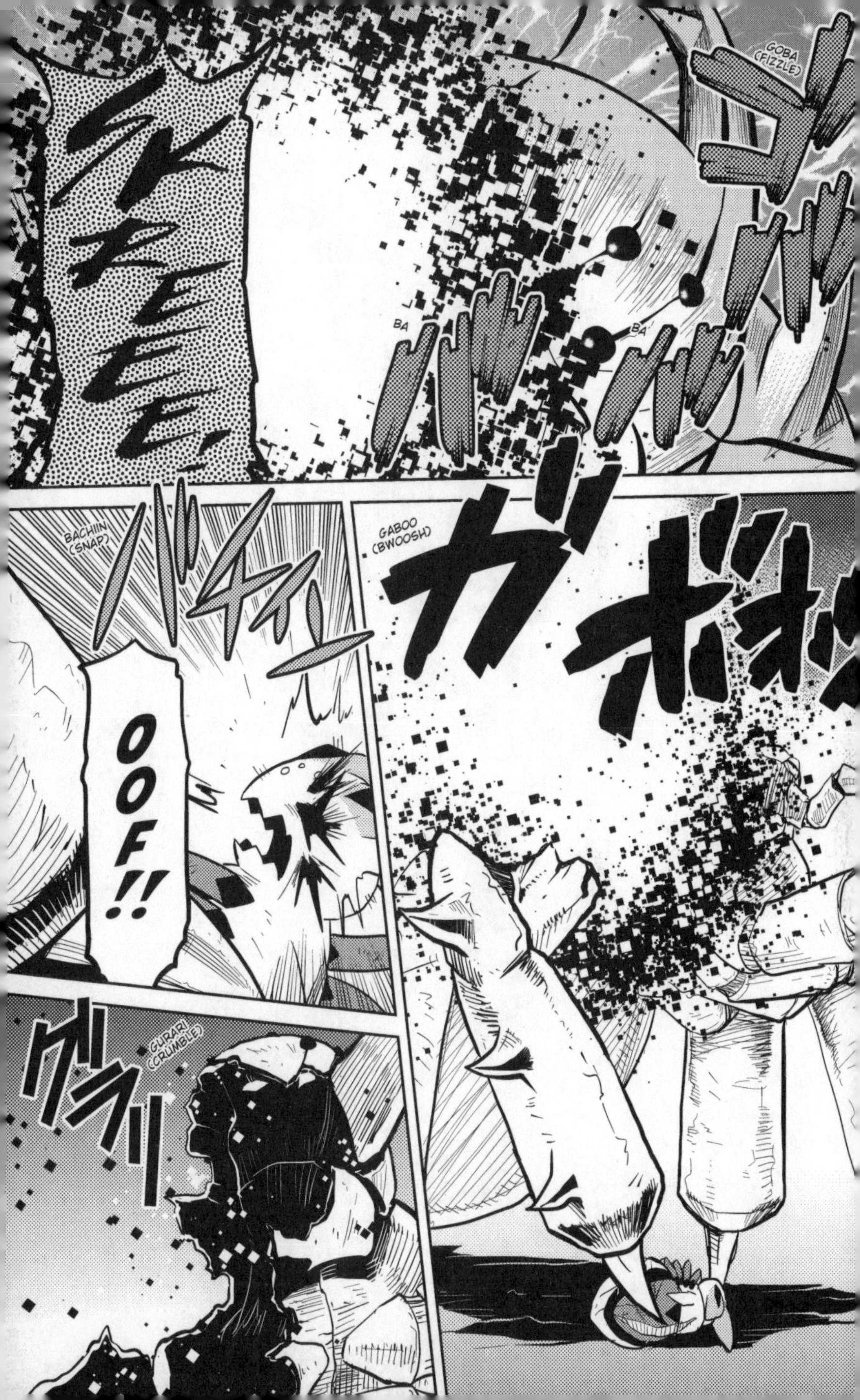
GOBA (FIZZLE)
BA
BA
GABOO (BWOOSH)
BACHIIN (SNAP)
OOF!!
GURARI (CRUMBLE)

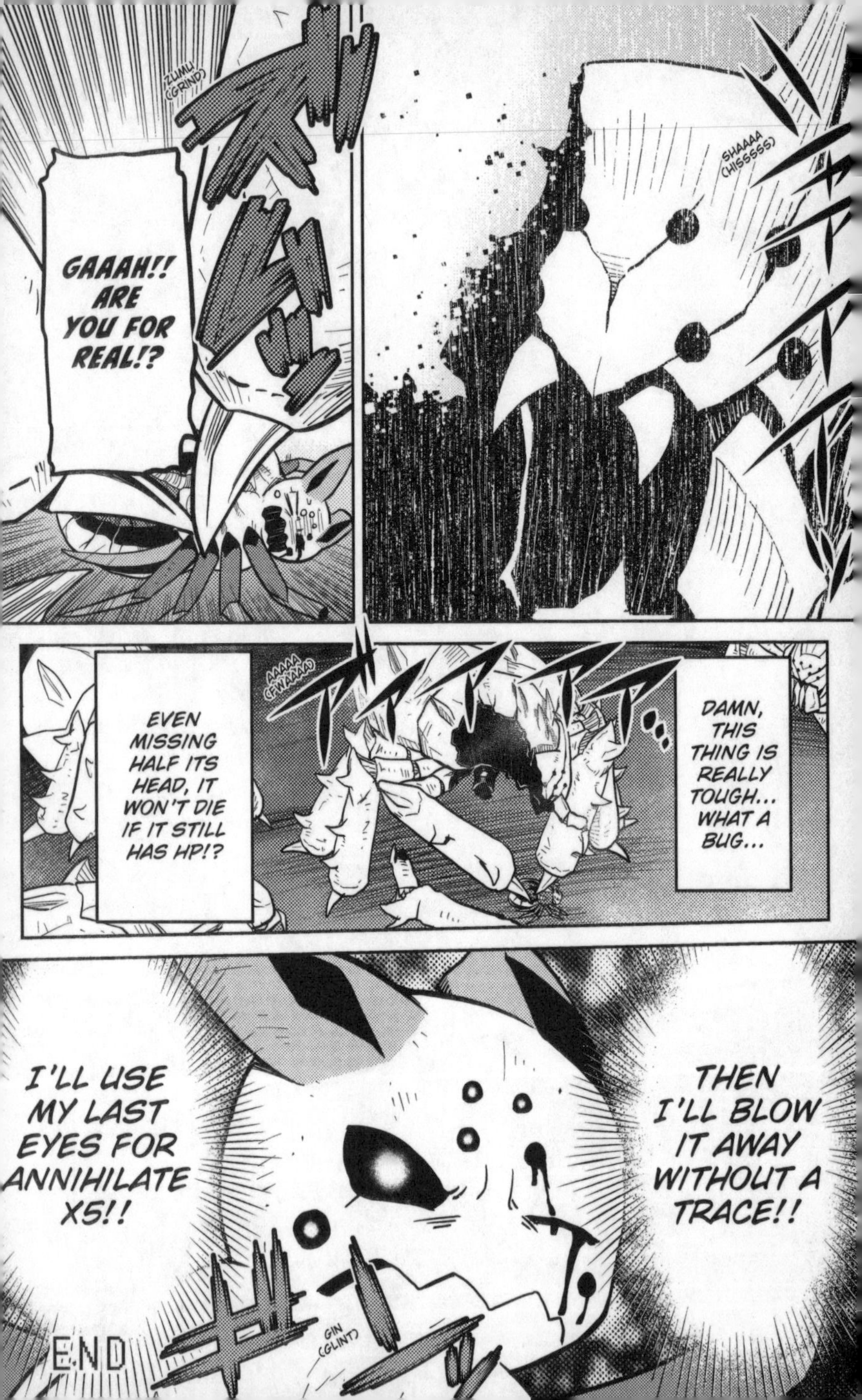
SHAAAA (HISSSSS)
ZUMU (GRIND)
GAAAH!! ARE YOU FOR REAL!?
DAMN, THIS THING IS REALLY TOUGH... WHAT A BUG...
AAAAA (FWAAAA)
EVEN MISSING HALF ITS HEAD, IT WON'T DIE IF IT STILL HAS HP!?
THEN I'LL BLOW IT AWAY WITHOUT A TRACE!!
I'LL USE MY LAST EYES FOR ANNIHILATE X5!!
GIN (GLINT)
END

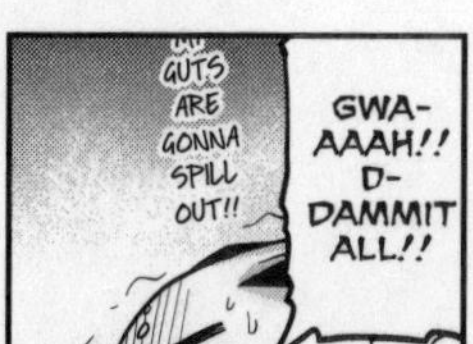
GWA-AAAH!! D-DAMMIT ALL!!
GUTS ARE GONNA SPILL OUT!!

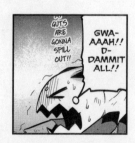

So I'm a Spider, So What?

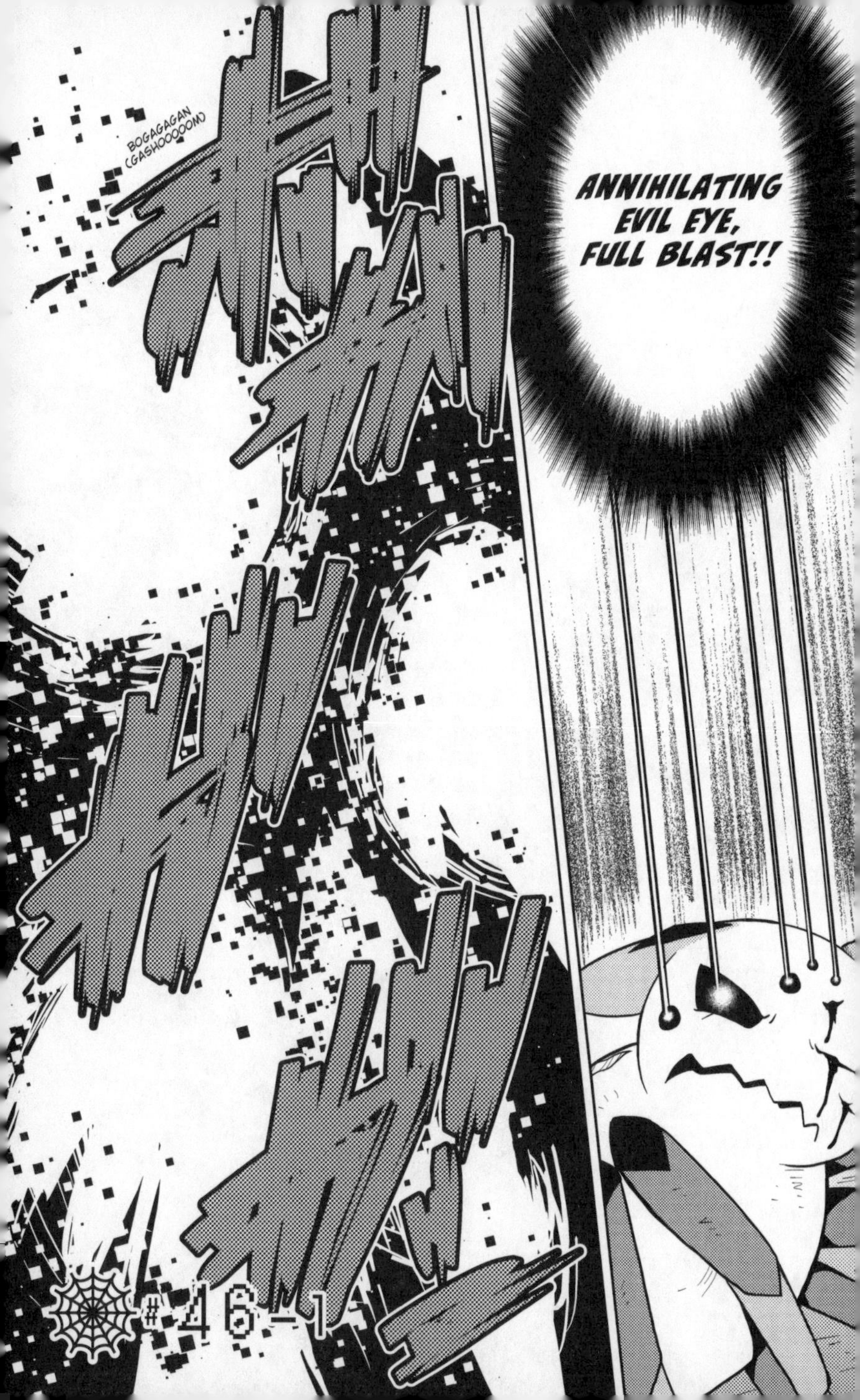
ANNIHILATING EVIL EYE, FULL BLAST!!
BOGAGAGAN (GASHOOOOOM)
#46-1

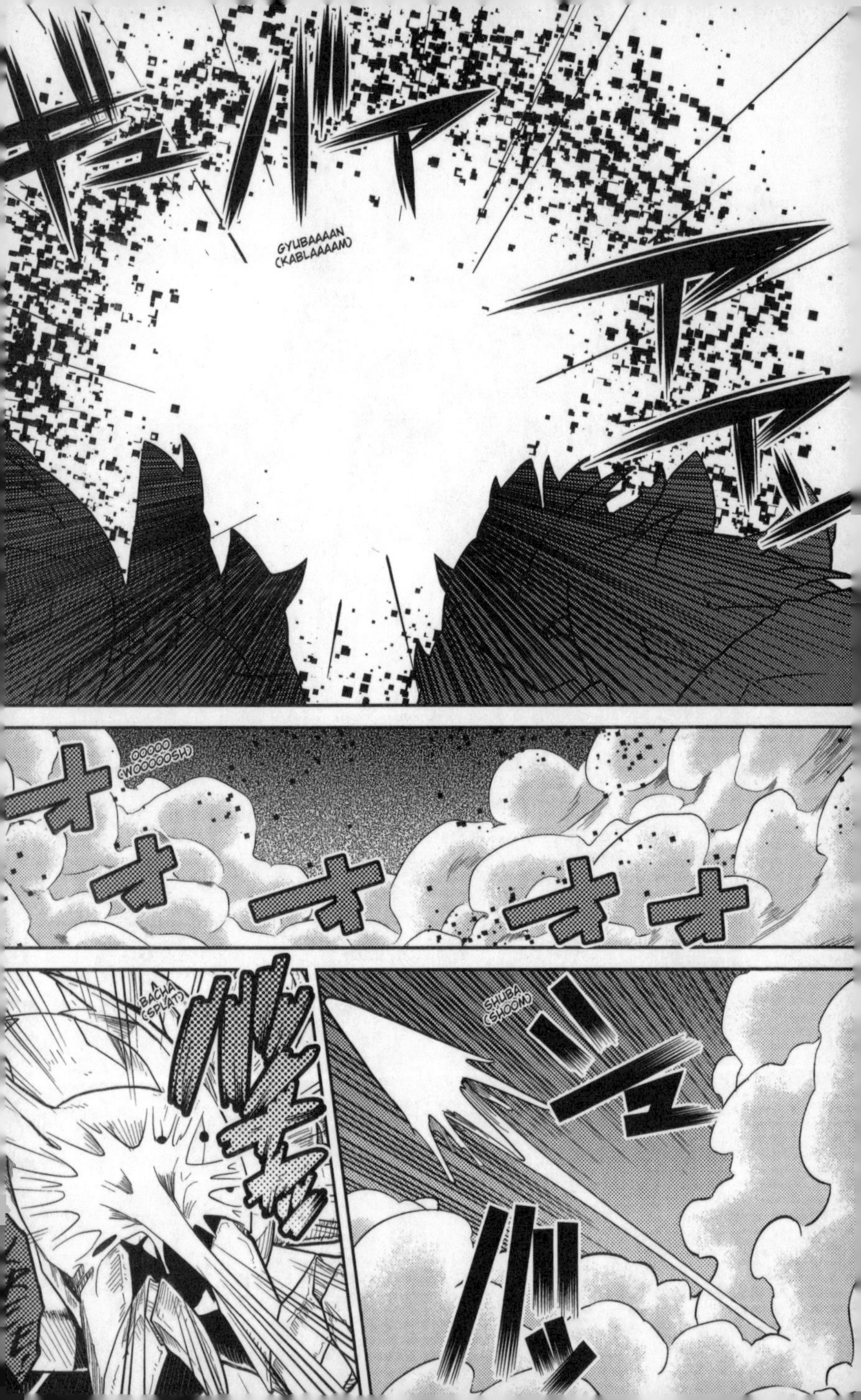
GYUBAAAAN (KABLAAAAM)
OOOOO (WOOOOOSH)
SHUBA (SHOOM)
BACHA (SPLAT)

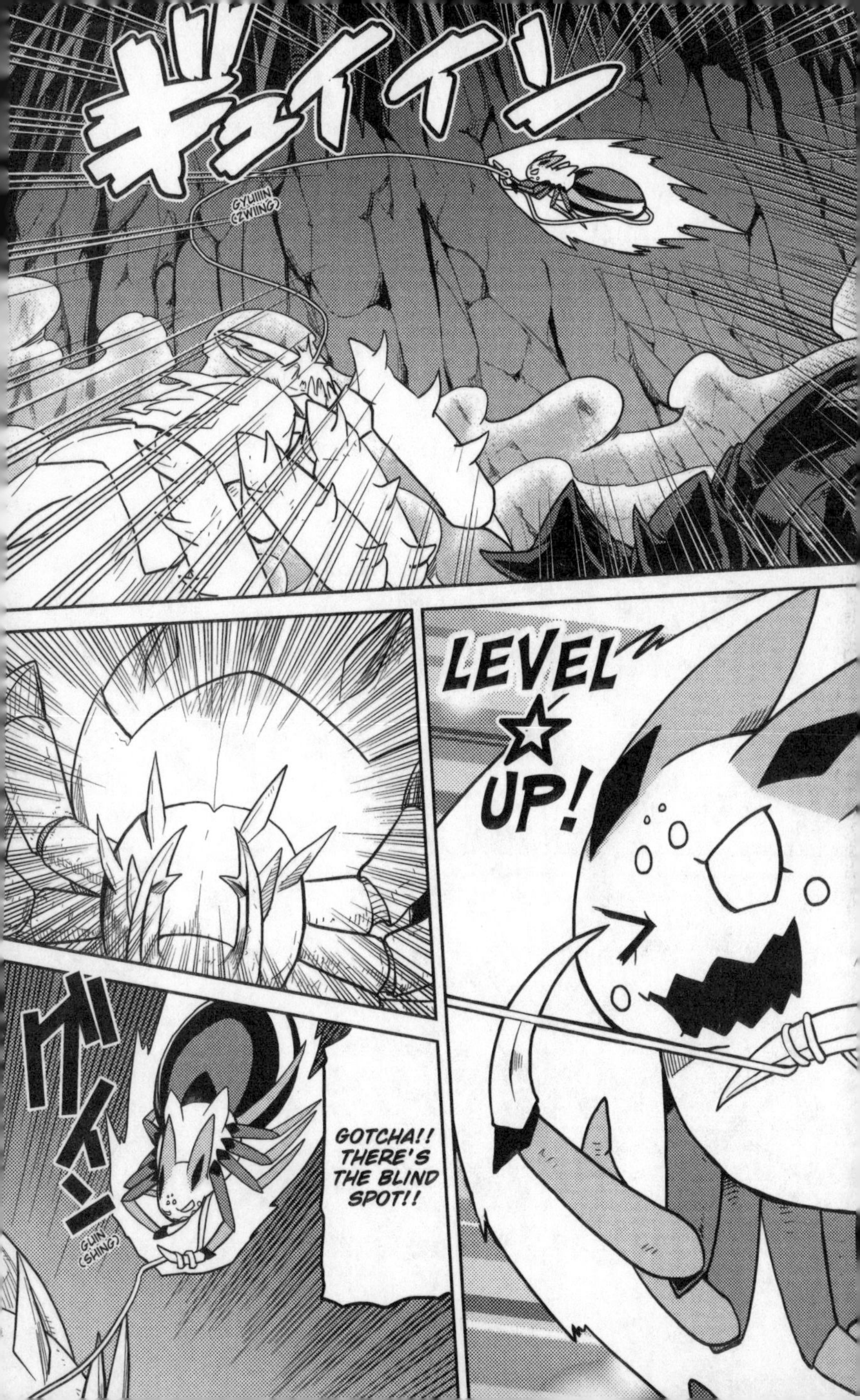
ギュイイン
GYUIIIN (ZWIING)
LEVEL ☆ UP!
GOTCHA!! THERE'S THE BLIND SPOT!!
GUIN (SHING)

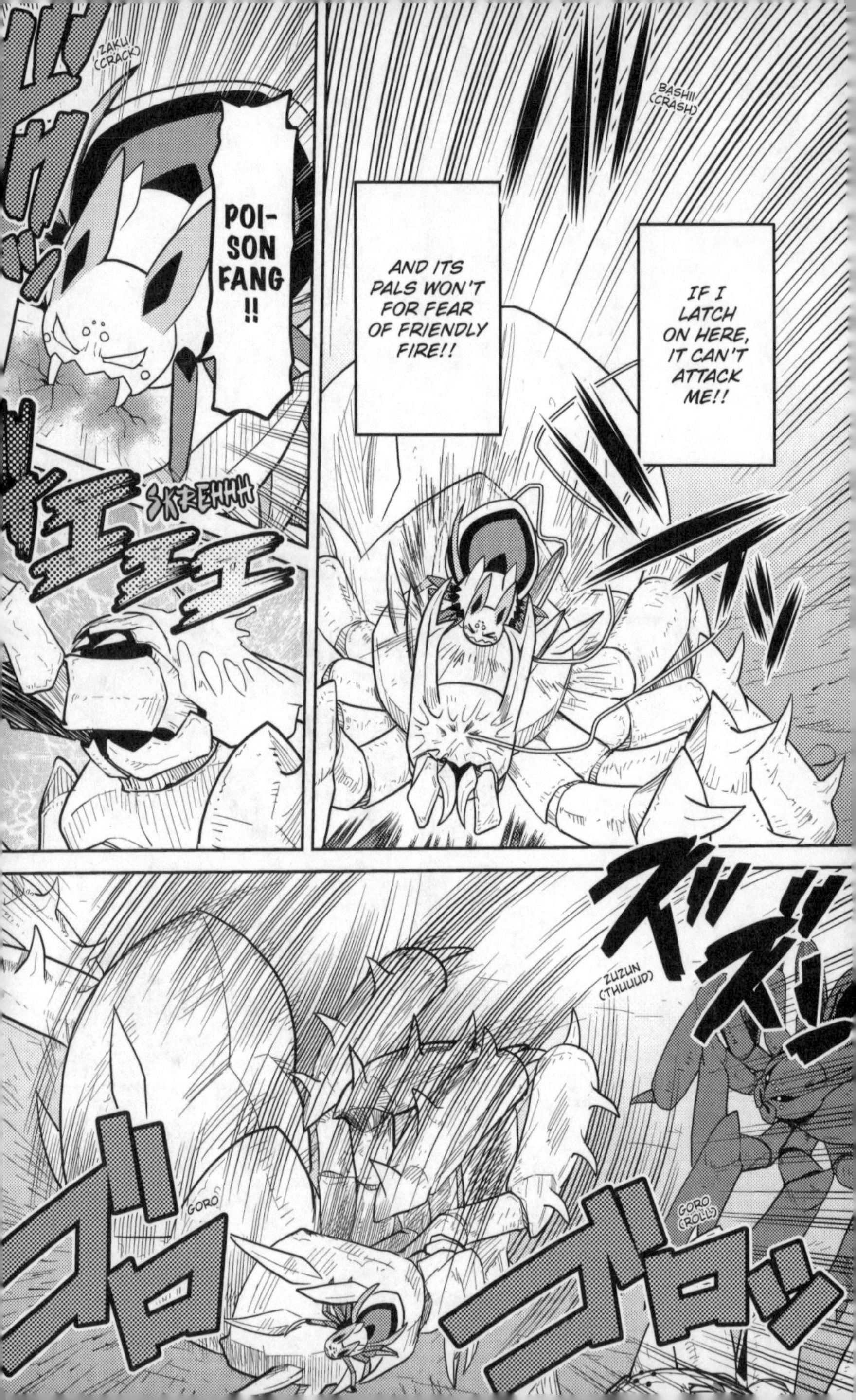
BASHII (CRASH)
IF I LATCH ON HERE, IT CAN'T ATTACK ME!!
AND ITS PALS WON'T FOR FEAR OF FRIENDLY FIRE!!
ZAKU (CRACK)
POI-SON FANG !!
SKREHHH
ZUZUN (THUUUD)
GORO (ROLL)
GORO

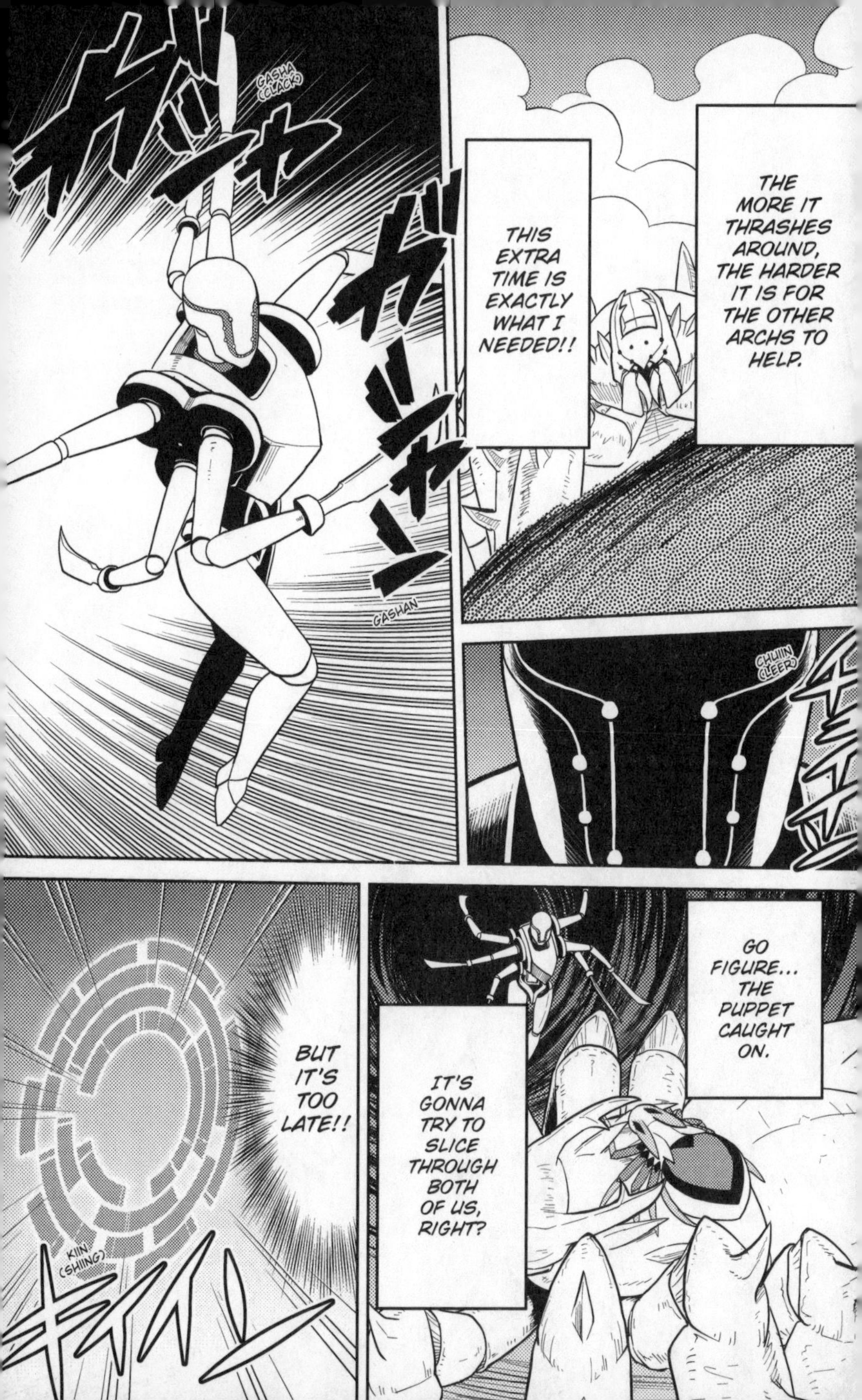
THE MORE IT THRASHES AROUND, THE HARDER IT IS FOR THE OTHER ARCHS TO HELP.
THIS EXTRA TIME IS EXACTLY WHAT I NEEDED!!
CHUIIN (LEER)
GASHA (CLACK)
GASHAN
GO FIGURE... THE PUPPET CAUGHT ON.
IT'S GONNA TRY TO SLICE THROUGH BOTH OF US, RIGHT?
BUT IT'S TOO LATE!!
KIIN (SHIING)

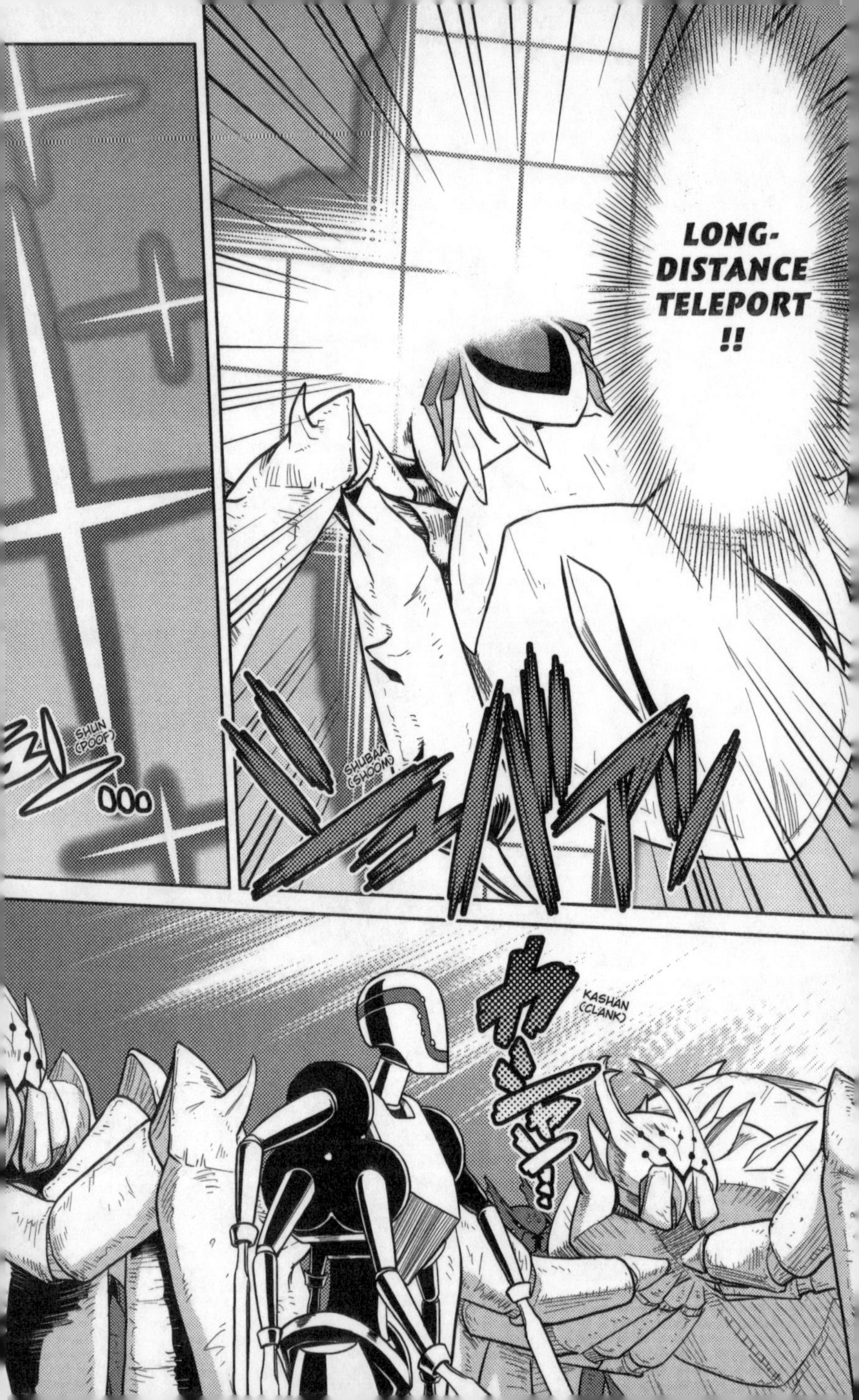
LONG-DISTANCE TELEPORT !!
SHUBAA (SHOOM)
SHUN (POOF)
KASHAN (CLANK)

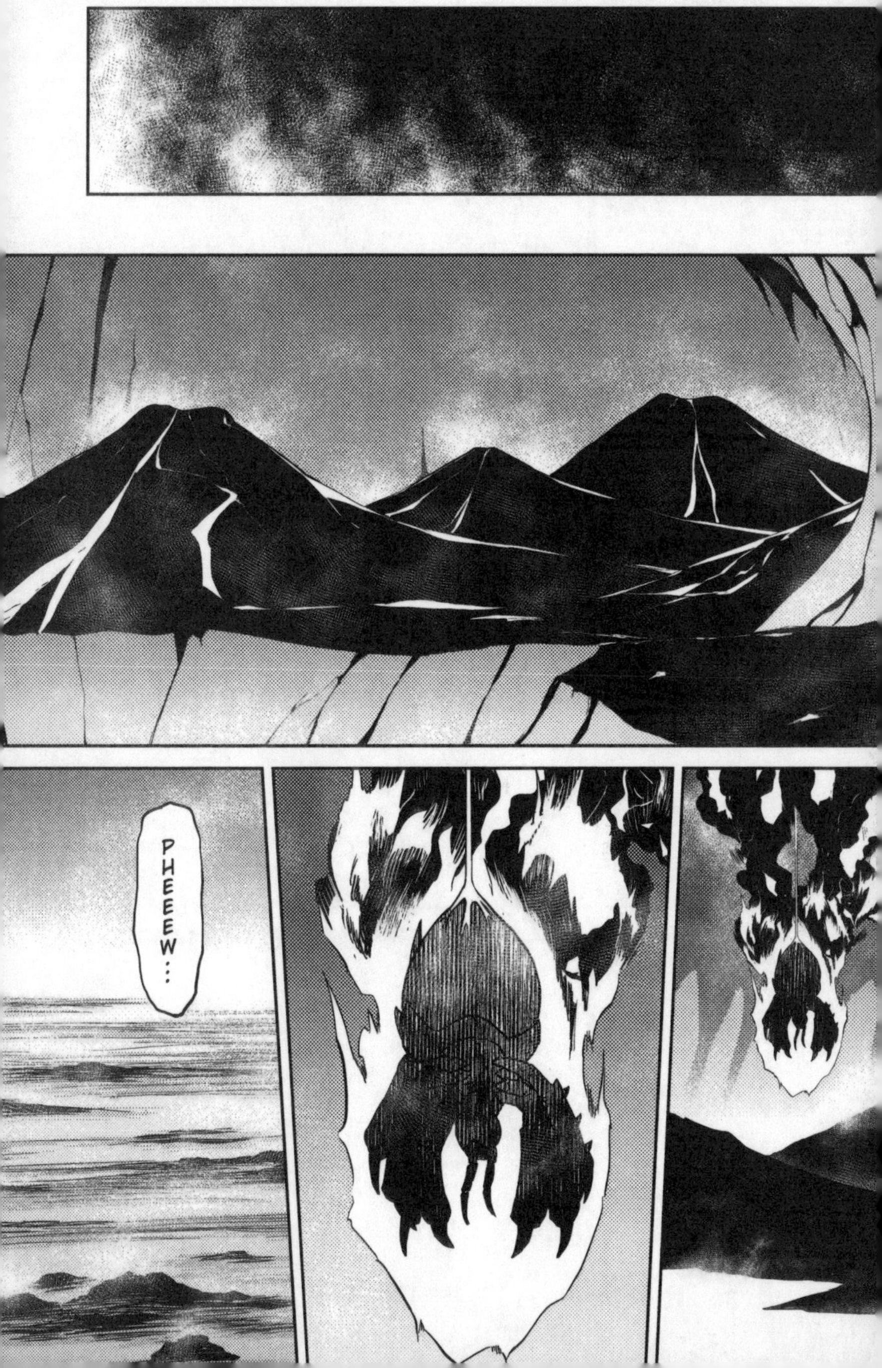
PHEEEW...

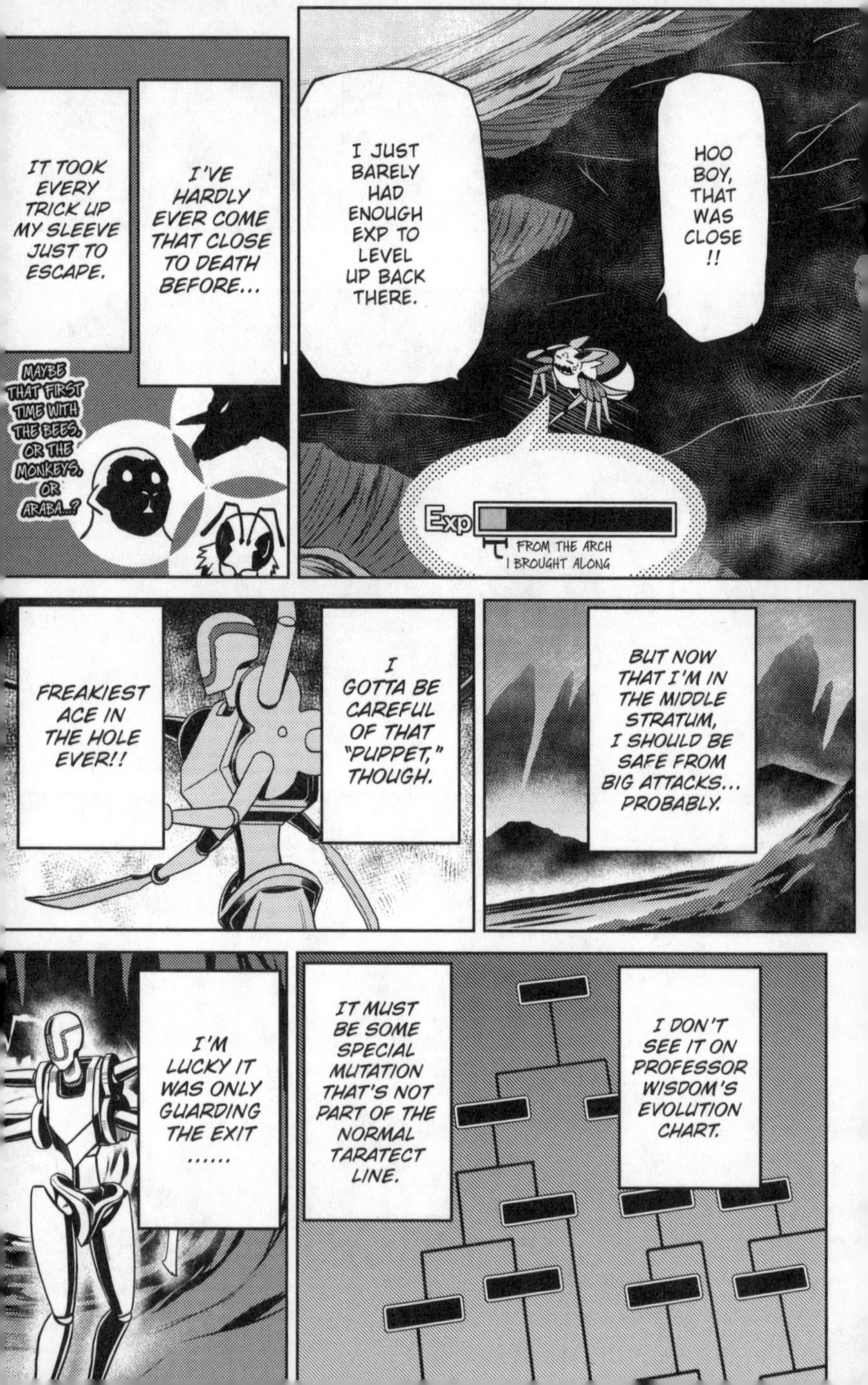
HOO BOY, THAT WAS CLOSE !!
I JUST BARELY HAD ENOUGH EXP TO LEVEL UP BACK THERE.
Exp
FROM THE ARCH I BROUGHT ALONG
I'VE HARDLY EVER COME THAT CLOSE TO DEATH BEFORE...
IT TOOK EVERY TRICK UP MY SLEEVE JUST TO ESCAPE.
MAYBE THAT FIRST TIME WITH THE BEES, OR THE MONKEYS, OR ARABA...?
BUT NOW THAT I'M IN THE MIDDLE STRATUM, I SHOULD BE SAFE FROM BIG ATTACKS... PROBABLY.
I GOTTA BE CAREFUL OF THAT "PUPPET," THOUGH.
FREAKIEST ACE IN THE HOLE EVER!!
I DON'T SEE IT ON PROFESSOR WISDOM'S EVOLUTION CHART.
IT MUST BE SOME SPECIAL MUTATION THAT'S NOT PART OF THE NORMAL TARATECT LINE.
I'M LUCKY IT WAS ONLY GUARDING THE EXIT ......

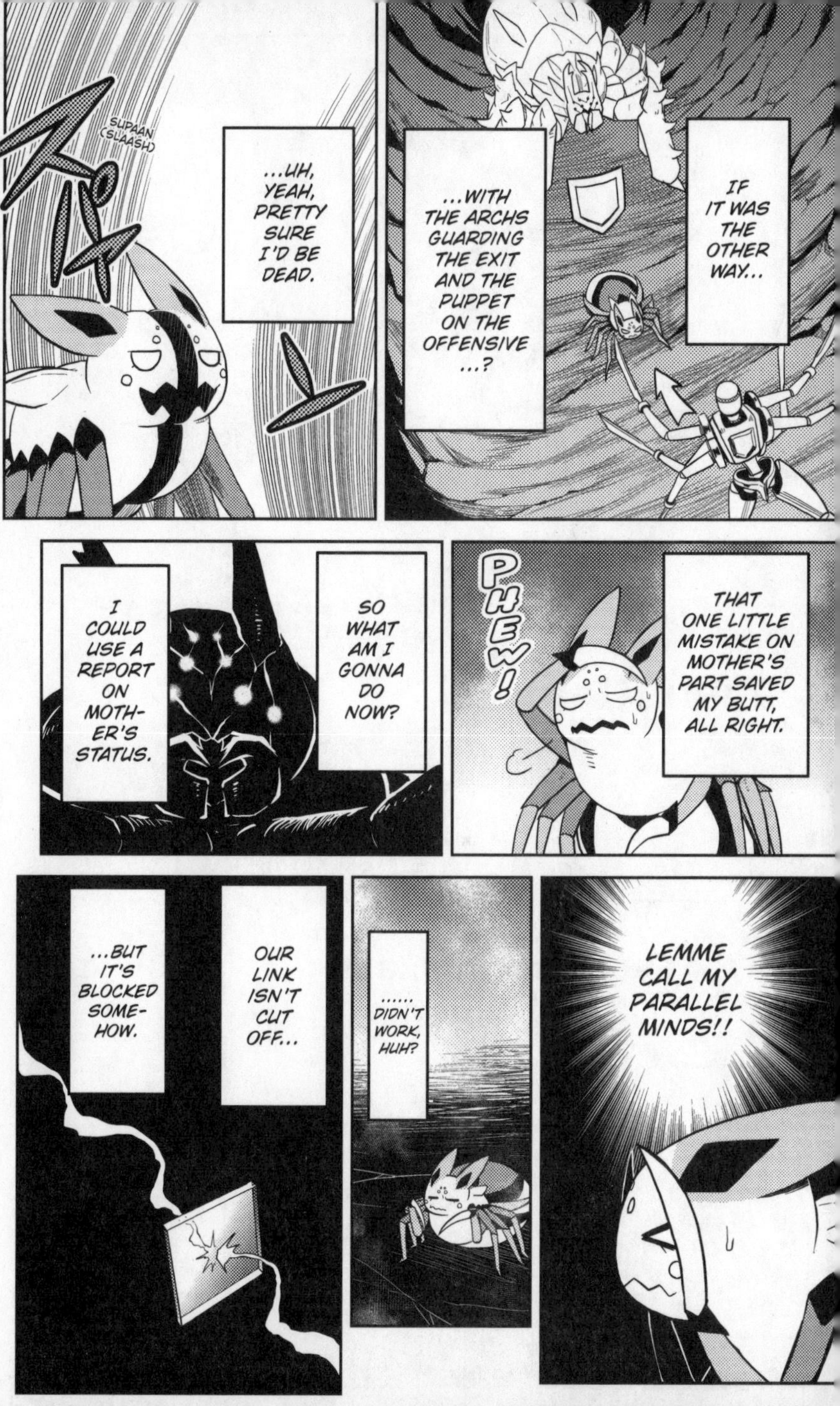
IF IT WAS THE OTHER WAY...
...WITH THE ARCHS GUARDING THE EXIT AND THE PUPPET ON THE OFFENSIVE ...?
...UH, YEAH, PRETTY SURE I'D BE DEAD.
SUPAAN (SLAASH)
THAT ONE LITTLE MISTAKE ON MOTHER'S PART SAVED MY BUTT, ALL RIGHT.
PHEW!
SO WHAT AM I GONNA DO NOW?
I COULD USE A REPORT ON MOTH-ER'S STATUS.
LEMME CALL MY PARALLEL MINDS!!
...... DIDN'T WORK, HUH?
OUR LINK ISN'T CUT OFF...
...BUT IT'S BLOCKED SOME-HOW.

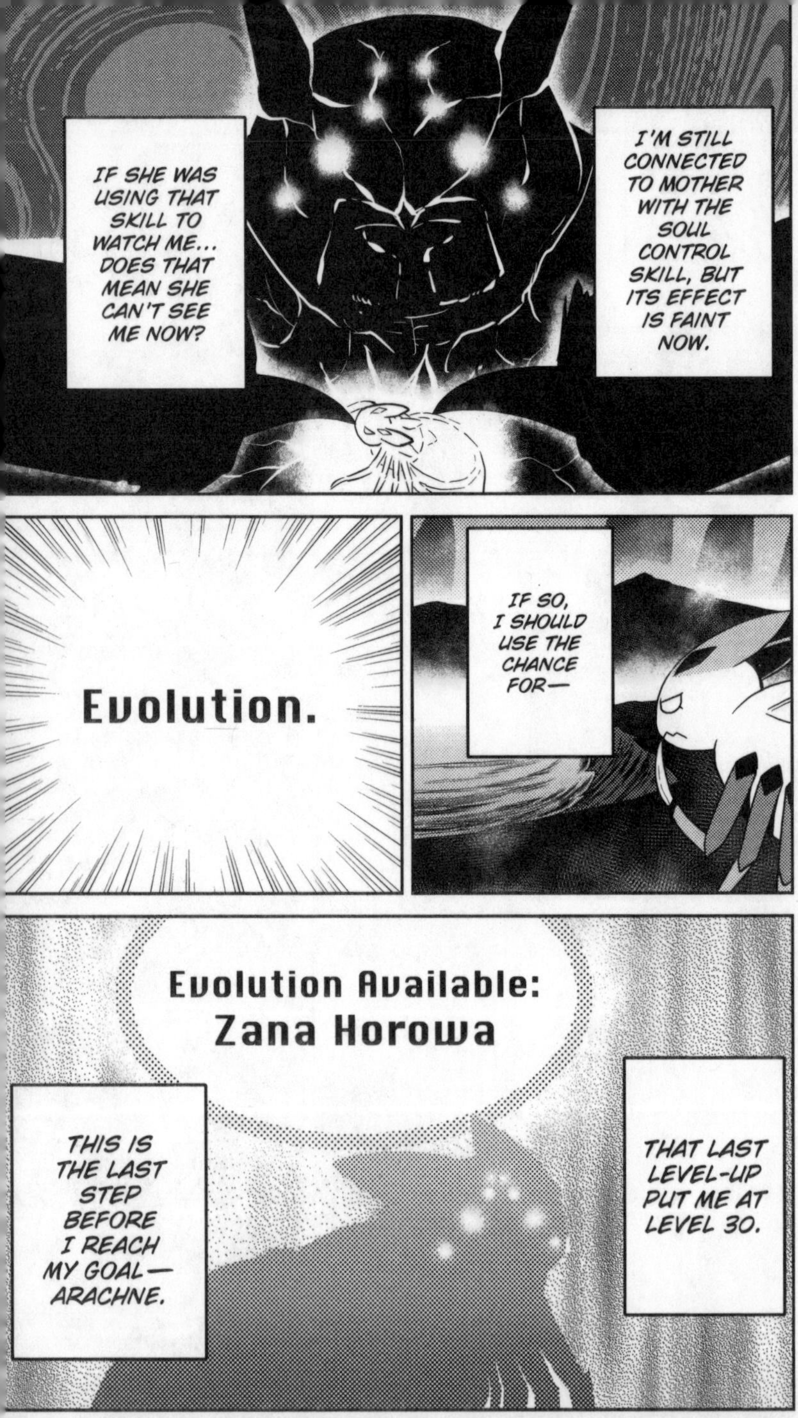
I'M STILL CONNECTED TO MOTHER WITH THE SOUL CONTROL SKILL, BUT ITS EFFECT IS FAINT NOW.
IF SHE WAS USING THAT SKILL TO WATCH ME... DOES THAT MEAN SHE CAN'T SEE ME NOW?
IF SO, I SHOULD USE THE CHANCE FOR—
Evolution.
Evolution Available: Zana Horowa
THAT LAST LEVEL-UP PUT ME AT LEVEL 30.
THIS IS THE LAST STEP BEFORE I REACH MY GOAL— ARACHNE.

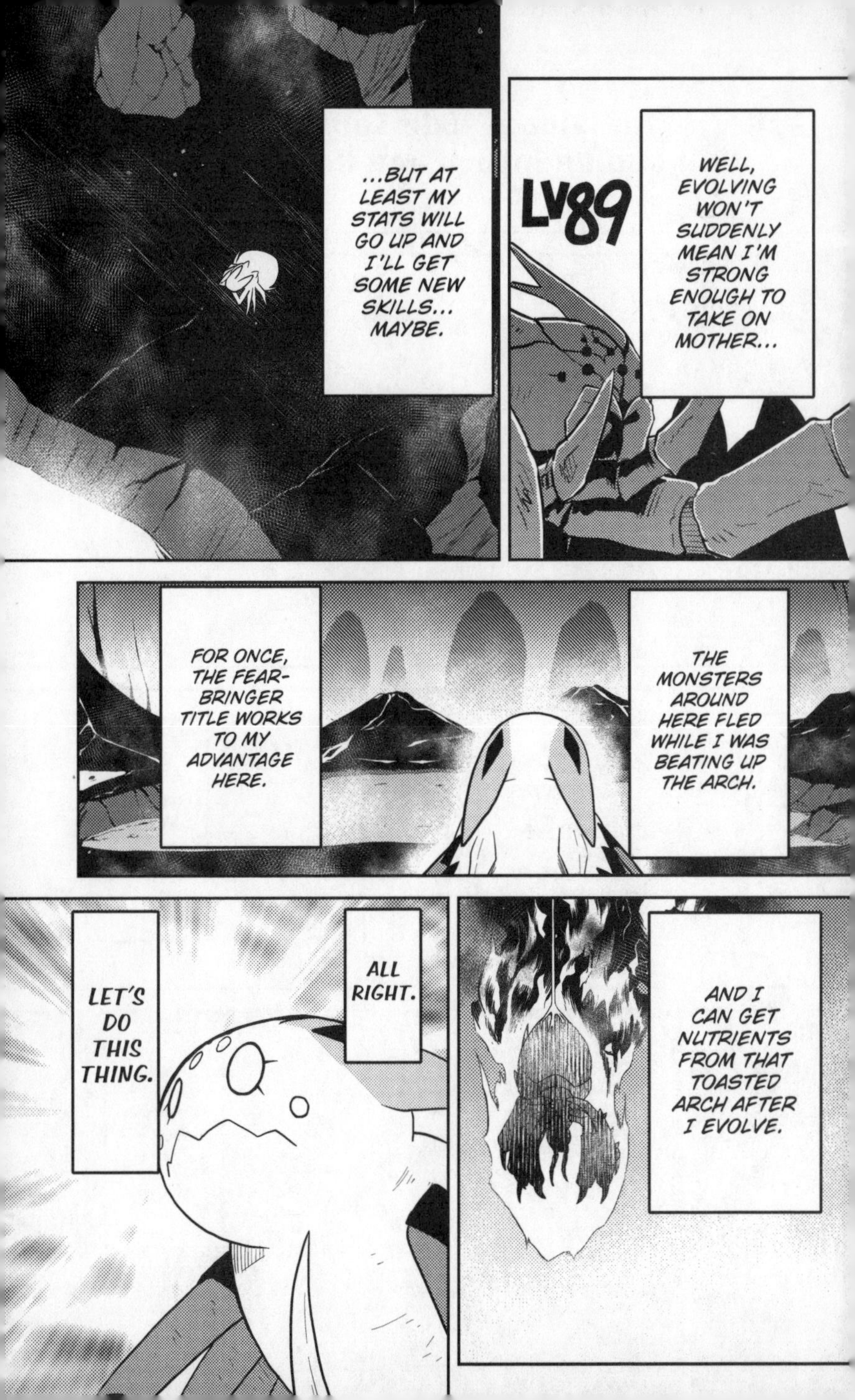
LV89
WELL, EVOLVING WON'T SUDDENLY MEAN I'M STRONG ENOUGH TO TAKE ON MOTHER...
...BUT AT LEAST MY STATS WILL GO UP AND I'LL GET SOME NEW SKILLS... MAYBE.
THE MONSTERS AROUND HERE FLED WHILE I WAS BEATING UP THE ARCH.
FOR ONCE, THE FEAR-BRINGER TITLE WORKS TO MY ADVANTAGE HERE.
AND I CAN GET NUTRIENTS FROM THAT TOASTED ARCH AFTER I EVOLVE.
ALL RIGHT.
LET'S DO THIS THING.

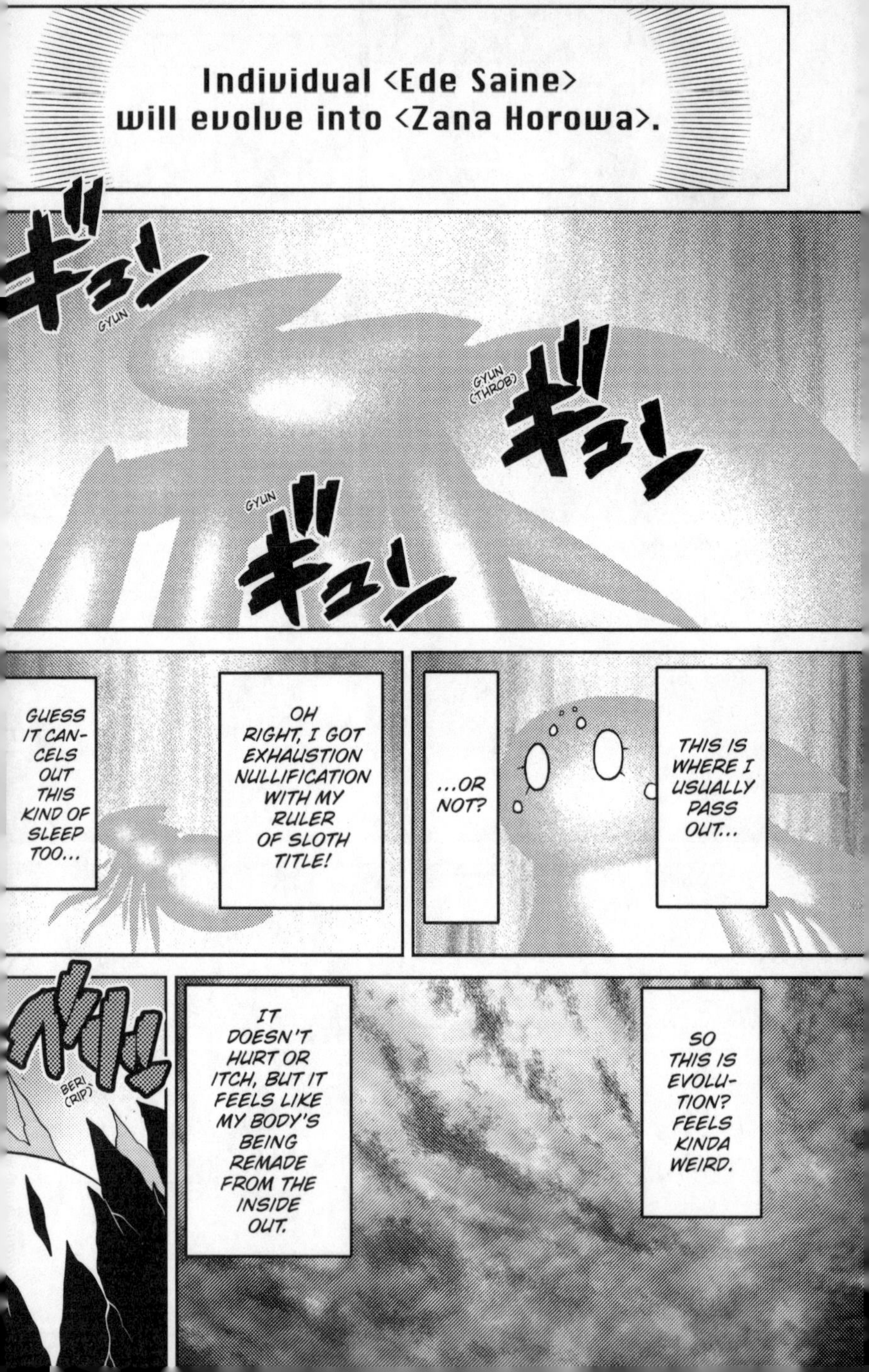
Individual <Ede Saine> will evolve into <Zana Horowa>.
GYUN (THROB)
GYUN
GYUN
THIS IS WHERE I USUALLY PASS OUT...
...OR NOT?
OH RIGHT, I GOT EXHAUSTION NULLIFICATION WITH MY RULER OF SLOTH TITLE!
GUESS IT CANCELS OUT THIS KIND OF SLEEP TOO...
SO THIS IS EVOLUTION? FEELS KINDA WEIRD.
IT DOESN'T HURT OR ITCH, BUT IT FEELS LIKE MY BODY'S BEING REMADE FROM THE INSIDE OUT.
BERI (RIP)

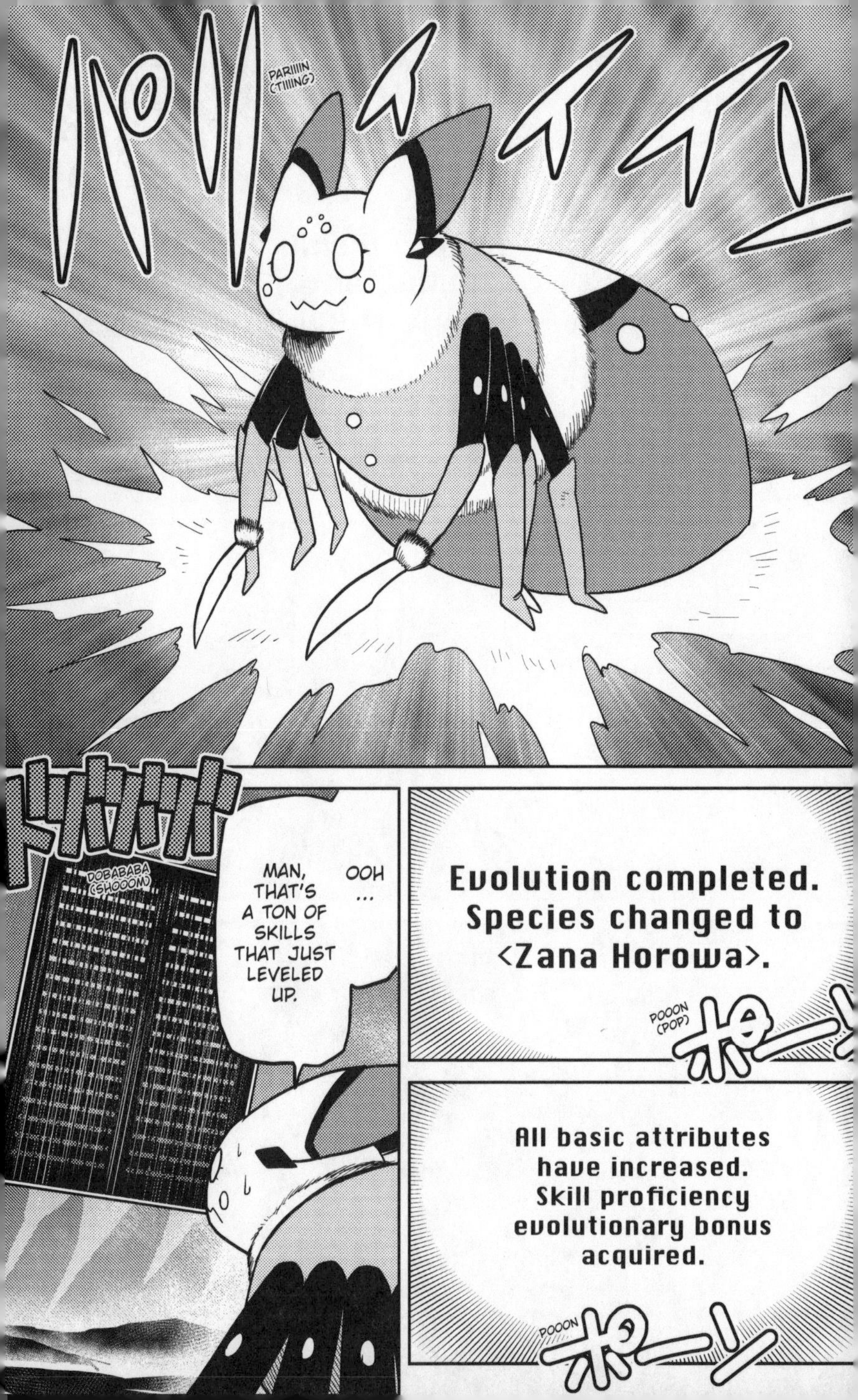
PARIIIIN (TIIIING)
Evolution completed. Species changed to <Zana Horowa>.
POOON (POP)
All basic attributes have increased. Skill proficiency evolutionary bonus acquired.
POOON
DOBABABA (SHOOOM)
OOH ...
MAN, THAT'S A TON OF SKILLS THAT JUST LEVELED UP.

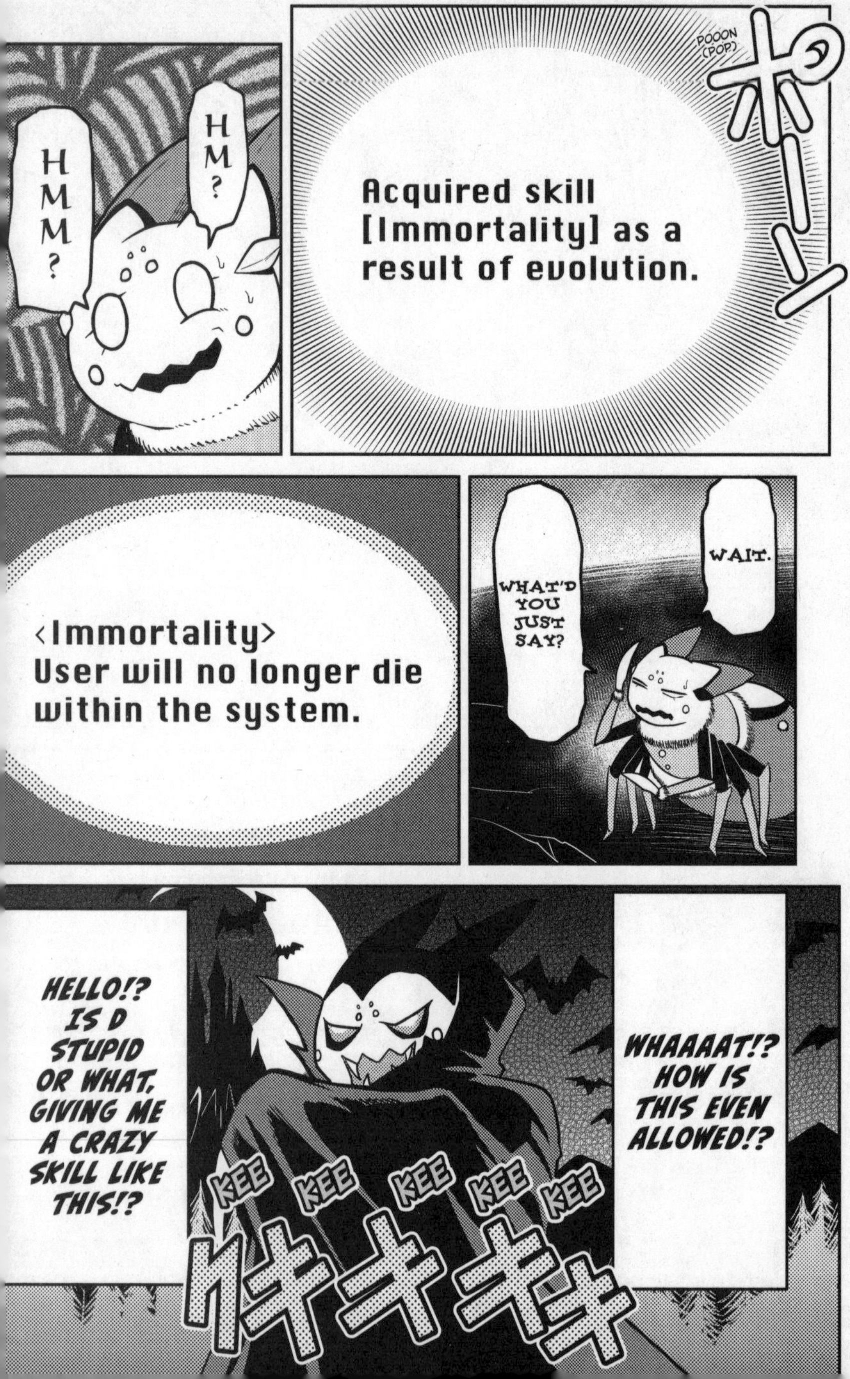
POOON (POP)
Acquired skill [Immortality] as a result of evolution.
HM?
HMM?
WAIT.
WHAT'D YOU JUST SAY?
<Immortality>
User will no longer die within the system.
WHAAAAT!? HOW IS THIS EVEN ALLOWED!?
HELLO!? IS D STUPID OR WHAT, GIVING ME A CRAZY SKILL LIKE THIS!?
KEE KEE KEE KEE KEE

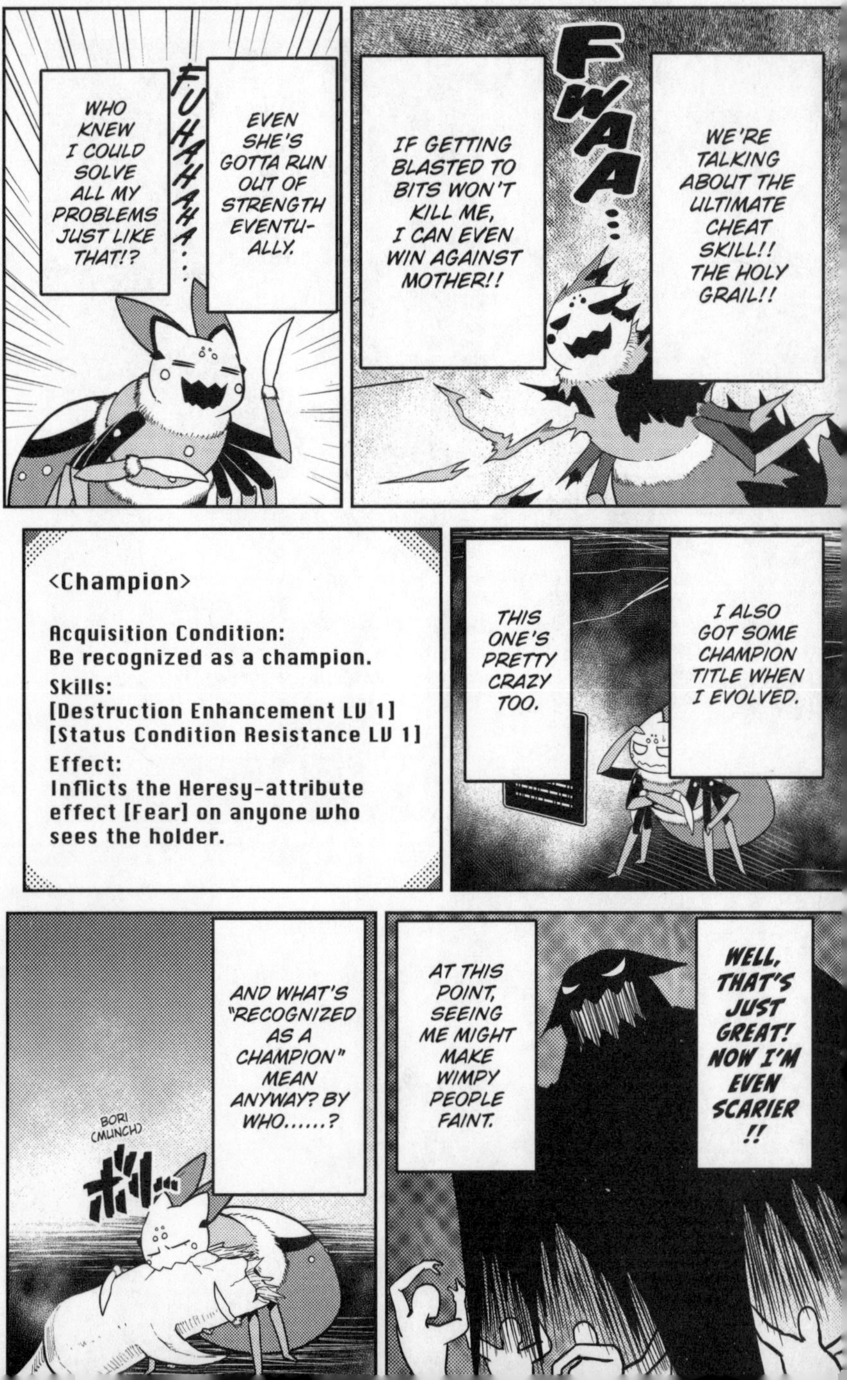
FWAA...
WE'RE TALKING ABOUT THE ULTIMATE CHEAT SKILL!! THE HOLY GRAIL!!
IF GETTING BLASTED TO BITS WON'T KILL ME, I CAN EVEN WIN AGAINST MOTHER!!
FUHAHAHAHA...
EVEN SHE'S GOTTA RUN OUT OF STRENGTH EVENTU-ALLY.
WHO KNEW I COULD SOLVE ALL MY PROBLEMS JUST LIKE THAT!?
I ALSO GOT SOME CHAMPION TITLE WHEN I EVOLVED.
THIS ONE'S PRETTY CRAZY TOO.
<Champion>
Acquisition Condition:
Be recognized as a champion.
Skills:
[Destruction Enhancement LV 1]
[Status Condition Resistance LV 1]
Effect:
Inflicts the Heresy-attribute effect [Fear] on anyone who sees the holder.
WELL, THAT'S JUST GREAT! NOW I'M EVEN SCARIER!!
AT THIS POINT, SEEING ME MIGHT MAKE WIMPY PEOPLE FAINT.
AND WHAT'S "RECOGNIZED AS A CHAMPION" MEAN ANYWAY? BY WHO......?
BORI (MUNCH)

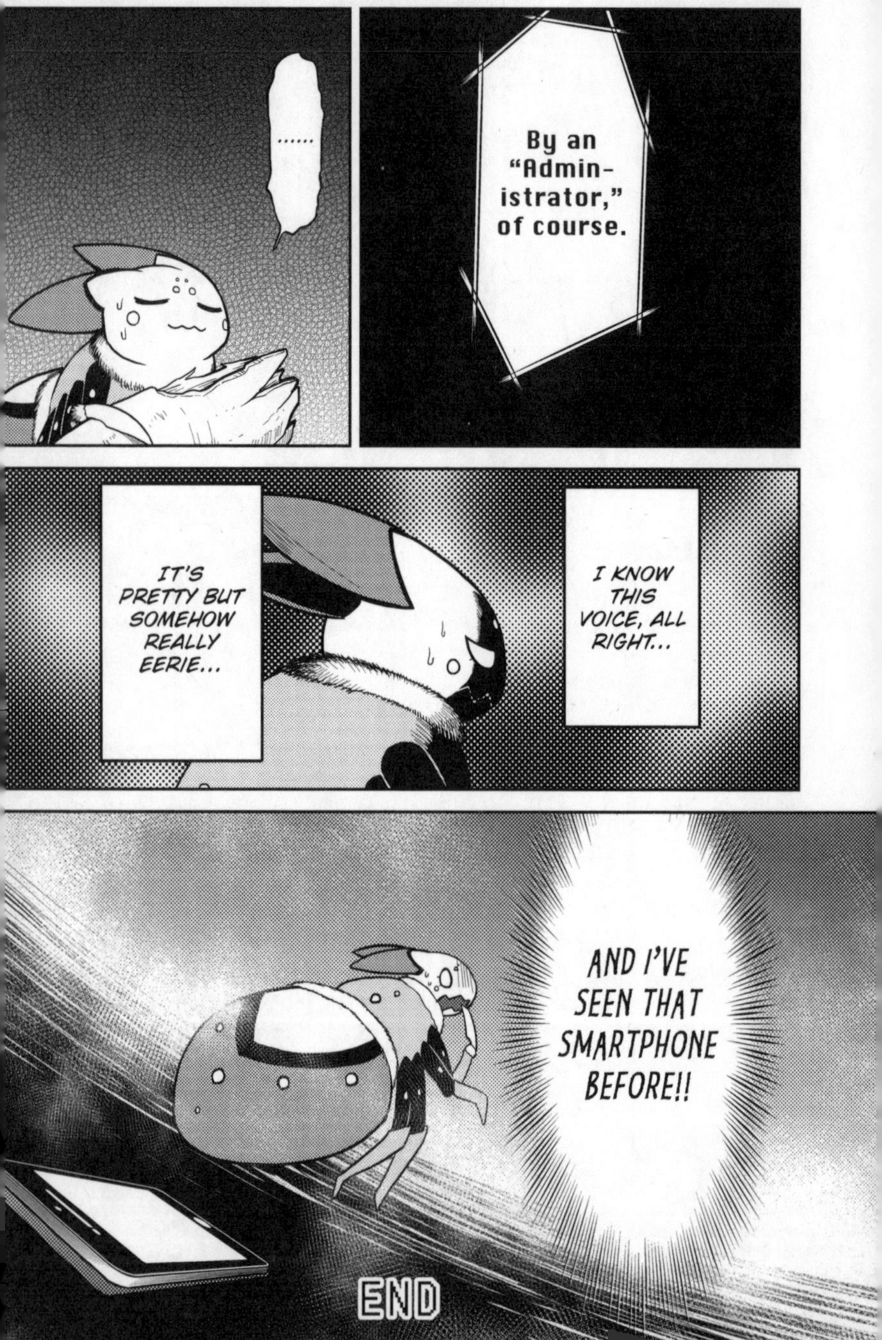
By an "Administrator," of course.
......
I KNOW THIS VOICE, ALL RIGHT...
IT'S PRETTY BUT SOMEHOW REALLY EERIE...
AND I'VE SEEN THAT SMARTPHONE BEFORE!!
END

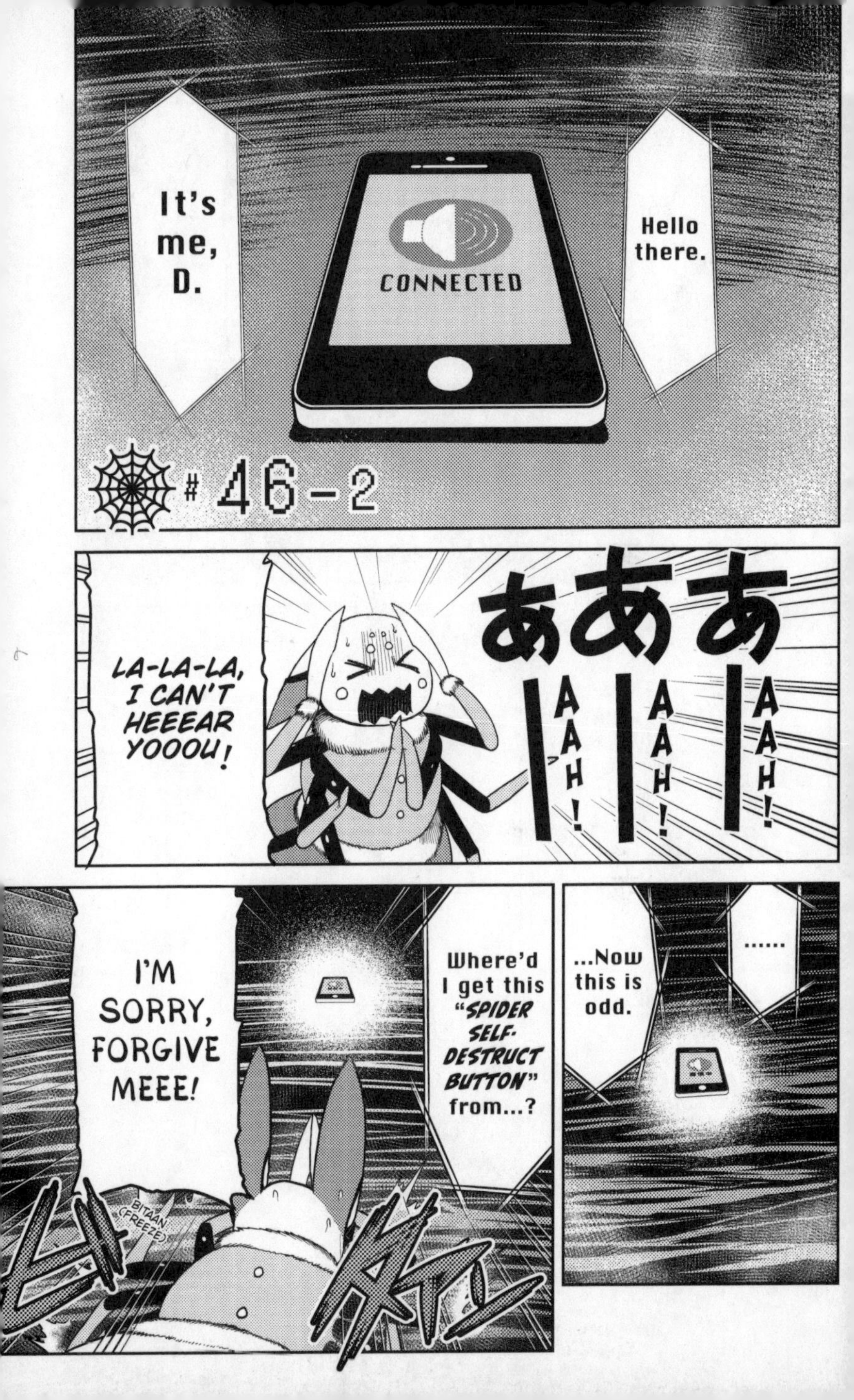
Hello there.
CONNECTED
It's me, D.
#46-2
あああ
AAAH!
AAAH!
AAAH!
LA-LA-LA, I CAN'T HEEEAR YOOOU!
......
...Now this is odd.
Where'd I get this "SPIDER SELF-DESTRUCT BUTTON" from...?
I'M SORRY, FORGIVE MEEE!
BITAAN (FREEZE)

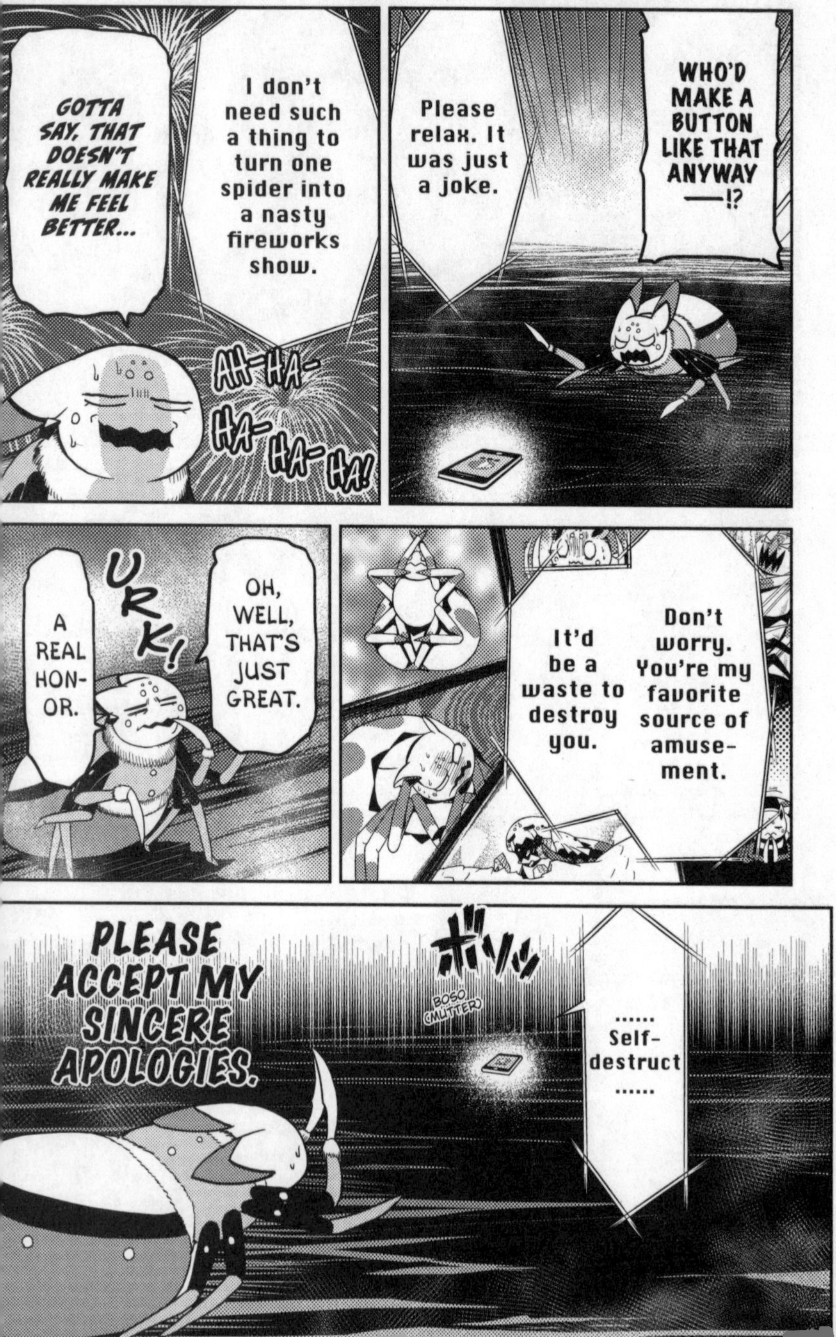
WHO'D MAKE A BUTTON LIKE THAT ANYWAY—!?
Please relax. It was just a joke.
I don't need such a thing to turn one spider into a nasty fireworks show.
GOTTA SAY, THAT DOESN'T REALLY MAKE ME FEEL BETTER...
AH-HA-HA-HA-HA!
Don't worry. You're my favorite source of amuse-ment.
It'd be a waste to destroy you.
OH, WELL, THAT'S JUST GREAT.
URK!
A REAL HON-OR.
......Self-destruct......
BOSO (MUTTER)
PLEASE ACCEPT MY SINCERE APOLOGIES.

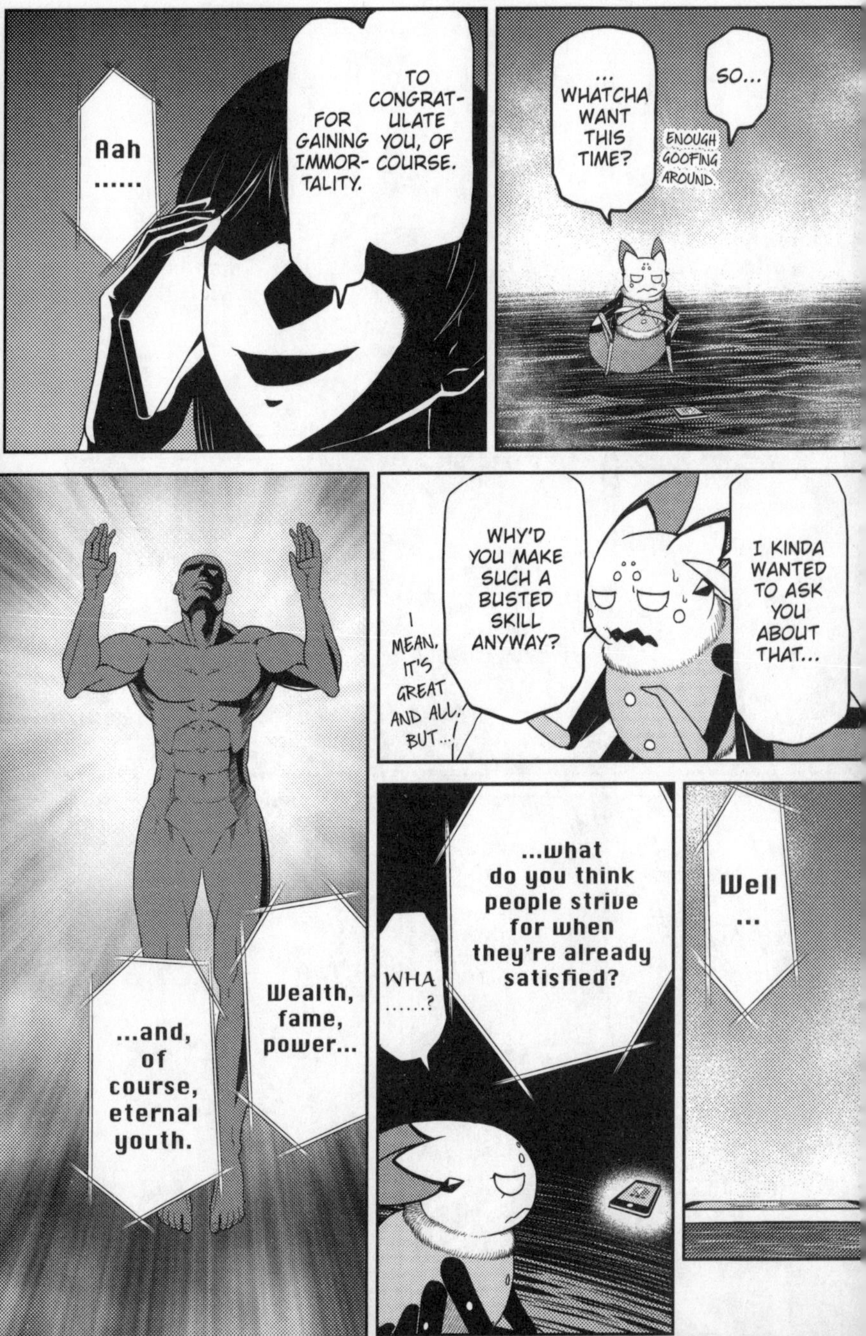
SO...
...WHATCHA WANT THIS TIME?
ENOUGH GOOFING AROUND.
TO CONGRATULATE YOU, OF COURSE.
FOR GAINING IMMORTALITY.
Aah ......
I KINDA WANTED TO ASK YOU ABOUT THAT...
WHY'D YOU MAKE SUCH A BUSTED SKILL ANYWAY?
I MEAN, IT'S GREAT AND ALL, BUT...!
Well ...
...what do you think people strive for when they're already satisfied?
WHA ......?
Wealth, fame, power...
...and, of course, eternal youth.

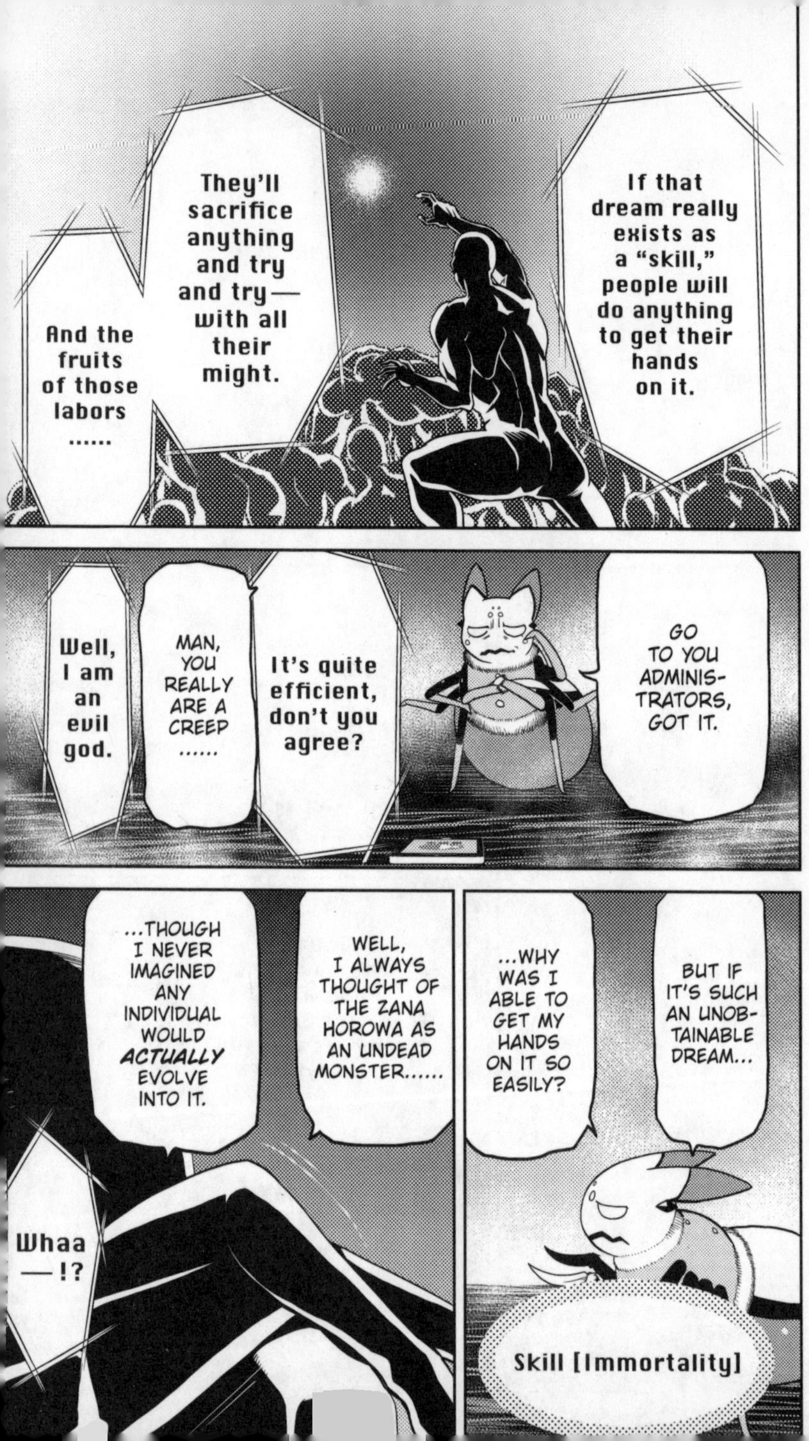
If that dream really exists as a "skill," people will do anything to get their hands on it.
They'll sacrifice anything and try and try—with all their might.
And the fruits of those labors......
GO TO YOU ADMINISTRATORS, GOT IT.
It's quite efficient, don't you agree?
MAN, YOU REALLY ARE A CREEP......
Well, I am an evil god.
BUT IF IT'S SUCH AN UNOBTAINABLE DREAM...
...WHY WAS I ABLE TO GET MY HANDS ON IT SO EASILY?
Skill [Immortality]
WELL, I ALWAYS THOUGHT OF THE ZANA HOROWA AS AN UNDEAD MONSTER......
...THOUGH I NEVER IMAGINED ANY INDIVIDUAL WOULD *ACTUALLY* EVOLVE INTO IT.
Whaa—!?

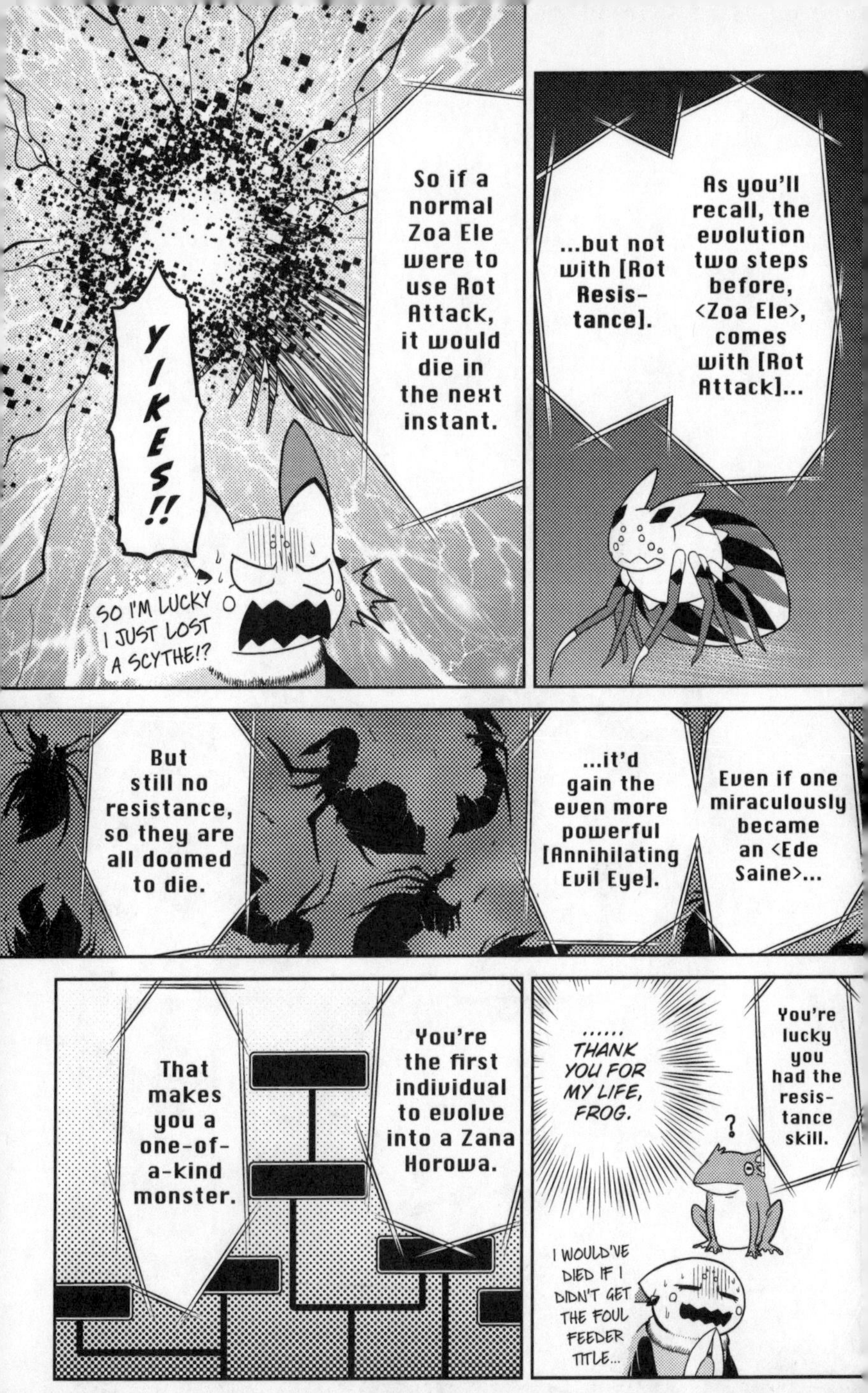
As you'll recall, the evolution two steps before, <Zoa Ele>, comes with [Rot Attack]...
...but not with [Rot Resistance].
So if a normal Zoa Ele were to use Rot Attack, it would die in the next instant.
YIKES!!
SO I'M LUCKY I JUST LOST A SCYTHE!?
Even if one miraculously became an <Ede Saine>...
...it'd gain the even more powerful [Annihilating Evil Eye].
But still no resistance, so they are all doomed to die.
You're lucky you had the resistance skill.
...... THANK YOU FOR MY LIFE, FROG.
?
I WOULD'VE DIED IF I DIDN'T GET THE FOUL FEEDER TITLE...
You're the first individual to evolve into a Zana Horowa.
That makes you a one-of-a-kind monster.

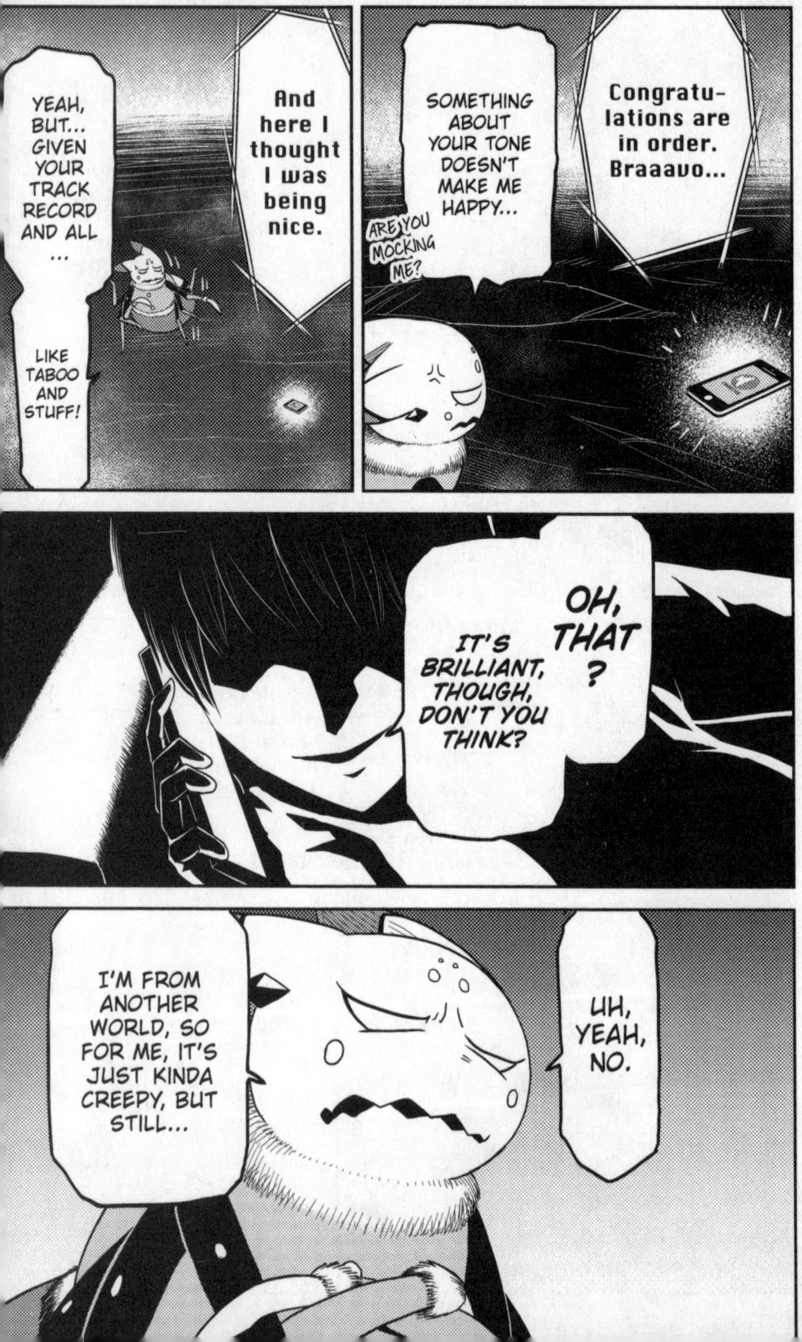
Congratulations are in order. Braaavo...
SOMETHING ABOUT YOUR TONE DOESN'T MAKE ME HAPPY...
ARE YOU MOCKING ME?
And here I thought I was being nice.
YEAH, BUT... GIVEN YOUR TRACK RECORD AND ALL...
LIKE TABOO AND STUFF!
OH, THAT?
IT'S BRILLIANT, THOUGH, DON'T YOU THINK?
UH, YEAH, NO.
I'M FROM ANOTHER WORLD, SO FOR ME, IT'S JUST KINDA CREEPY, BUT STILL...

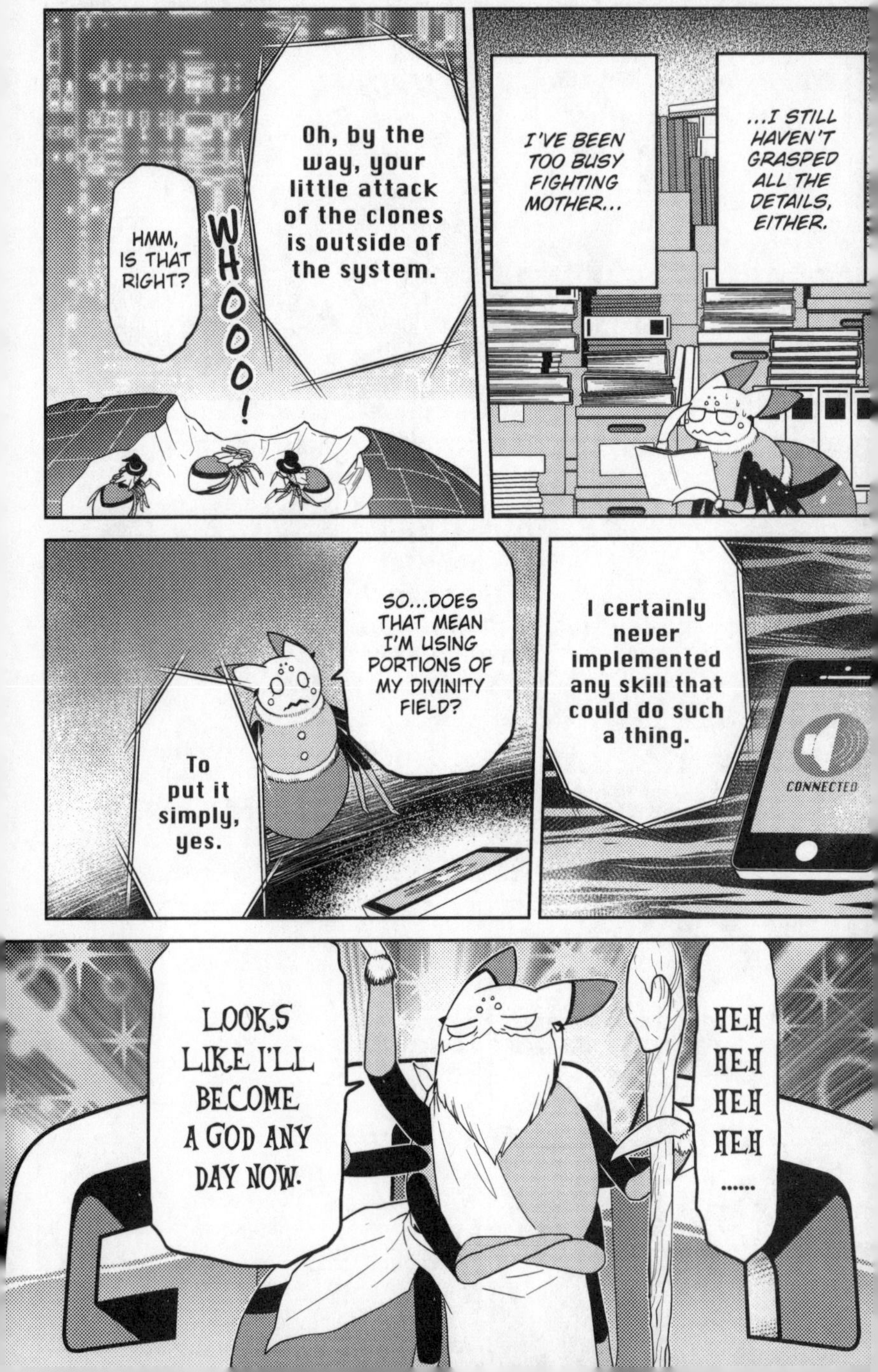
...I STILL HAVEN'T GRASPED ALL THE DETAILS, EITHER.
I'VE BEEN TOO BUSY FIGHTING MOTHER...
Oh, by the way, your little attack of the clones is outside of the system.
WHOOOO!
HMM, IS THAT RIGHT?
I certainly never implemented any skill that could do such a thing.
CONNECTED
SO...DOES THAT MEAN I'M USING PORTIONS OF MY DIVINITY FIELD?
To put it simply, yes.
HEH HEH HEH HEH ......
LOOKS LIKE I'LL BECOME A GOD ANY DAY NOW.

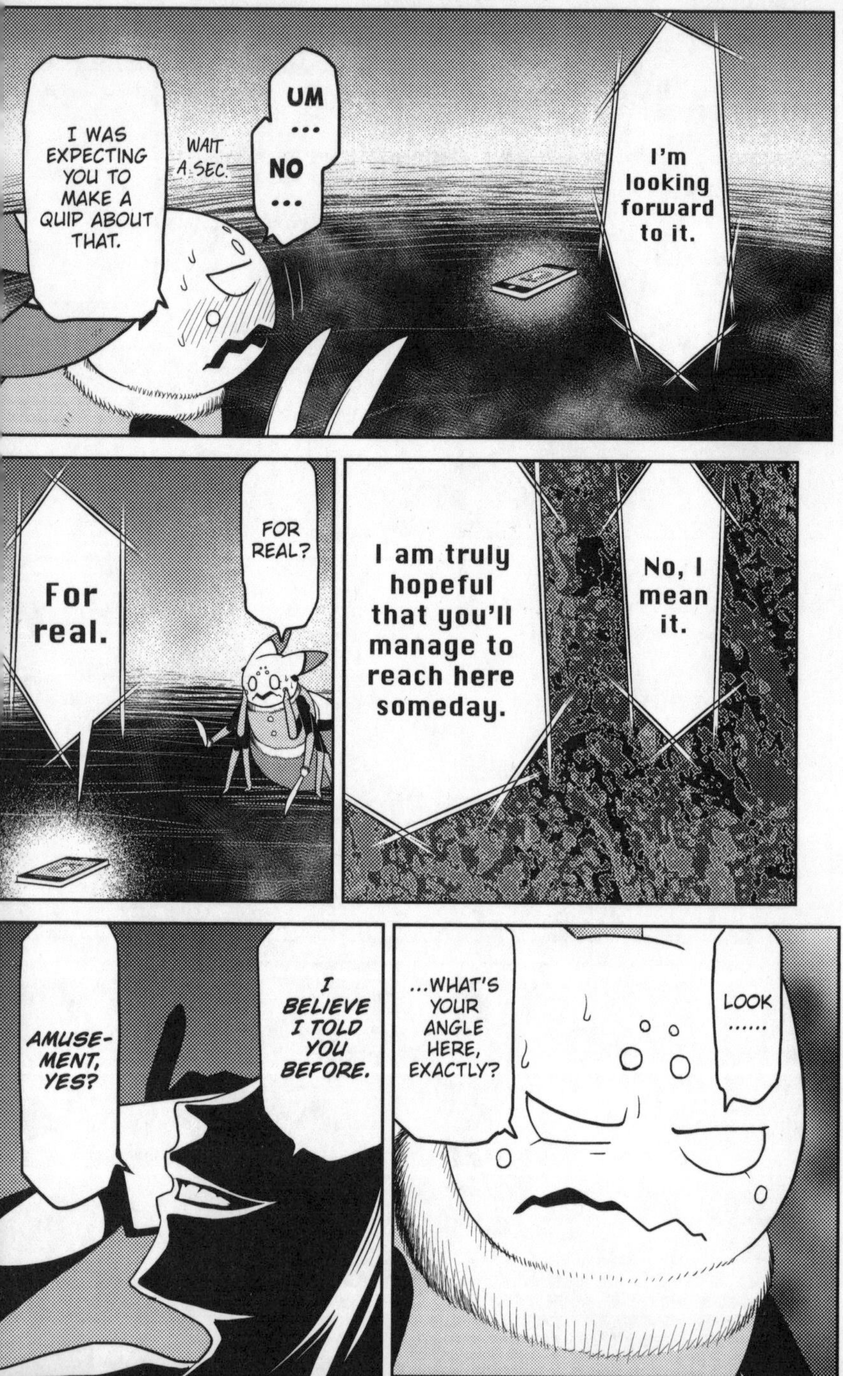
I'm looking forward to it.
UM... NO...
WAIT A SEC.
I WAS EXPECTING YOU TO MAKE A QUIP ABOUT THAT.
No, I mean it.
I am truly hopeful that you'll manage to reach here someday.
FOR REAL?
For real.
LOOK......
...WHAT'S YOUR ANGLE HERE, EXACTLY?
I BELIEVE I TOLD YOU BEFORE.
AMUSEMENT, YES?

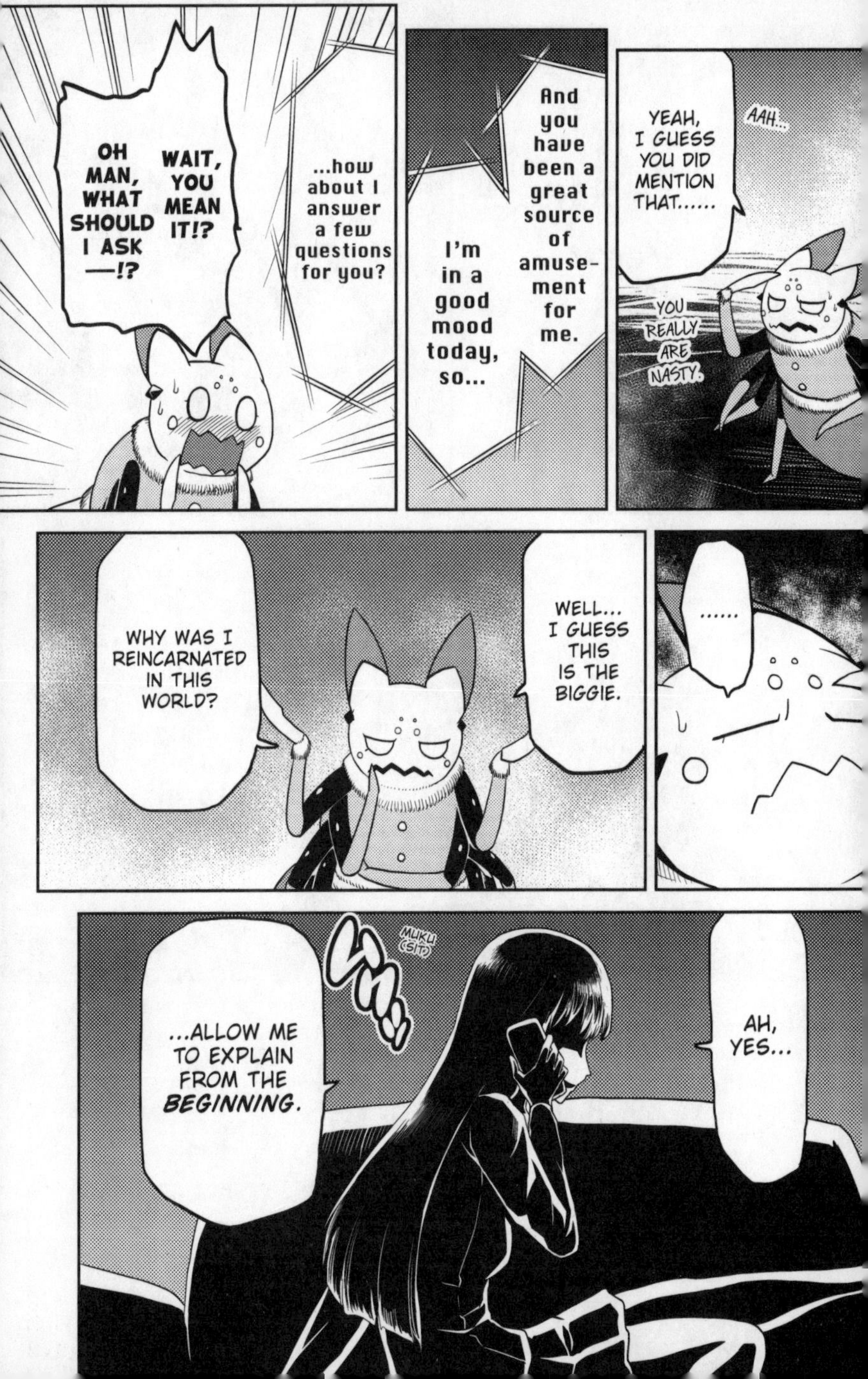
YEAH, I GUESS YOU DID MENTION THAT......
AAH...
YOU REALLY ARE NASTY.
And you have been a great source of amusement for me.
I'm in a good mood today, so...
...how about I answer a few questions for you?
WAIT, YOU MEAN IT!?
OH MAN, WHAT SHOULD I ASK—!?
......
WELL... I GUESS THIS IS THE BIGGIE.
WHY WAS I REINCARNATED IN THIS WORLD?
AH, YES...
MUKU (SIT)
...ALLOW ME TO EXPLAIN FROM THE *BEGINNING*.

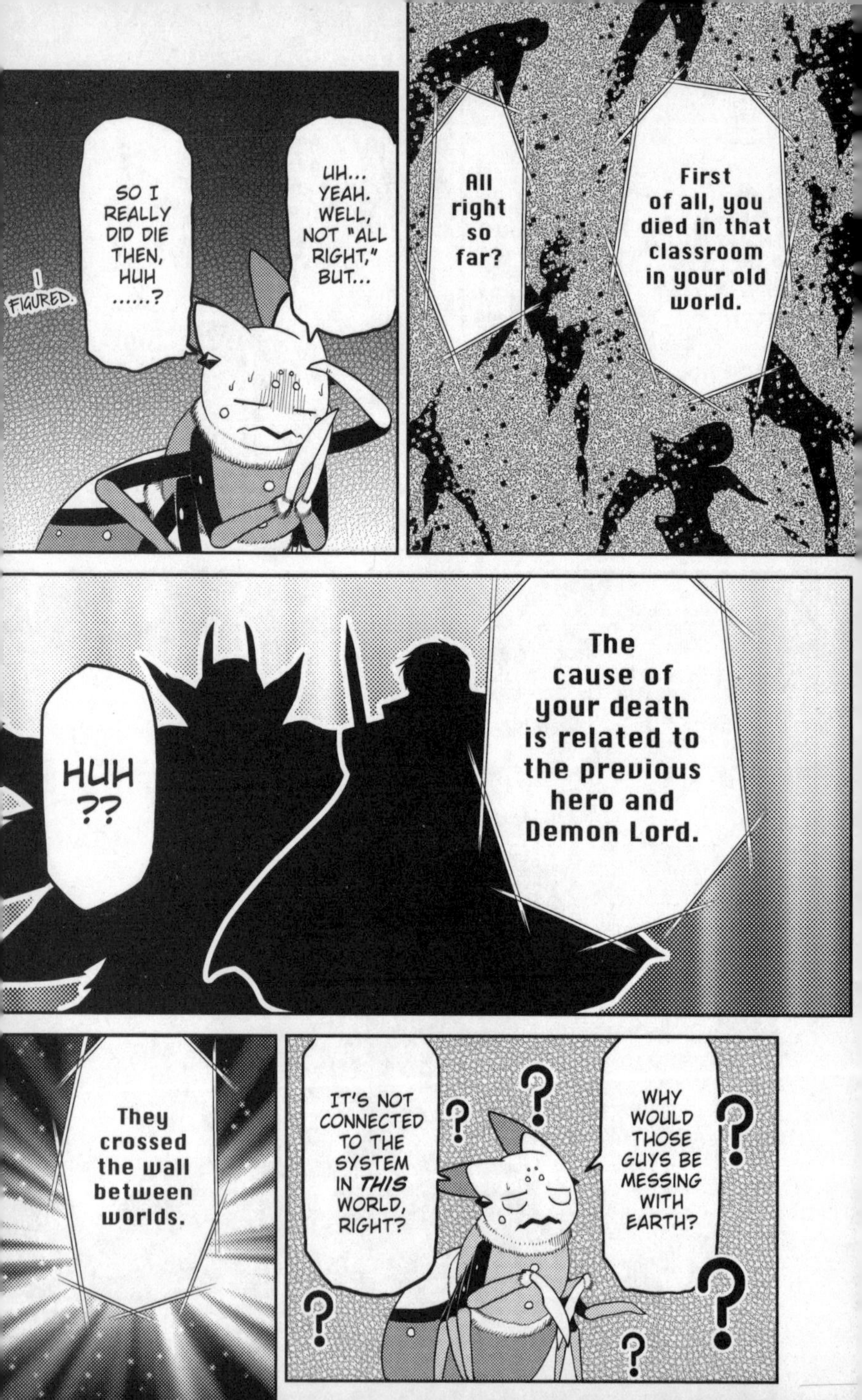
First of all, you died in that classroom in your old world.
All right so far?
UH... YEAH. WELL, NOT "ALL RIGHT," BUT...
SO I REALLY DID DIE THEN, HUH ......?
I FIGURED.
The cause of your death is related to the previous hero and Demon Lord.
HUH ??
WHY WOULD THOSE GUYS BE MESSING WITH EARTH?
IT'S NOT CONNECTED TO THE SYSTEM IN *THIS* WORLD, RIGHT?
They crossed the wall between worlds.

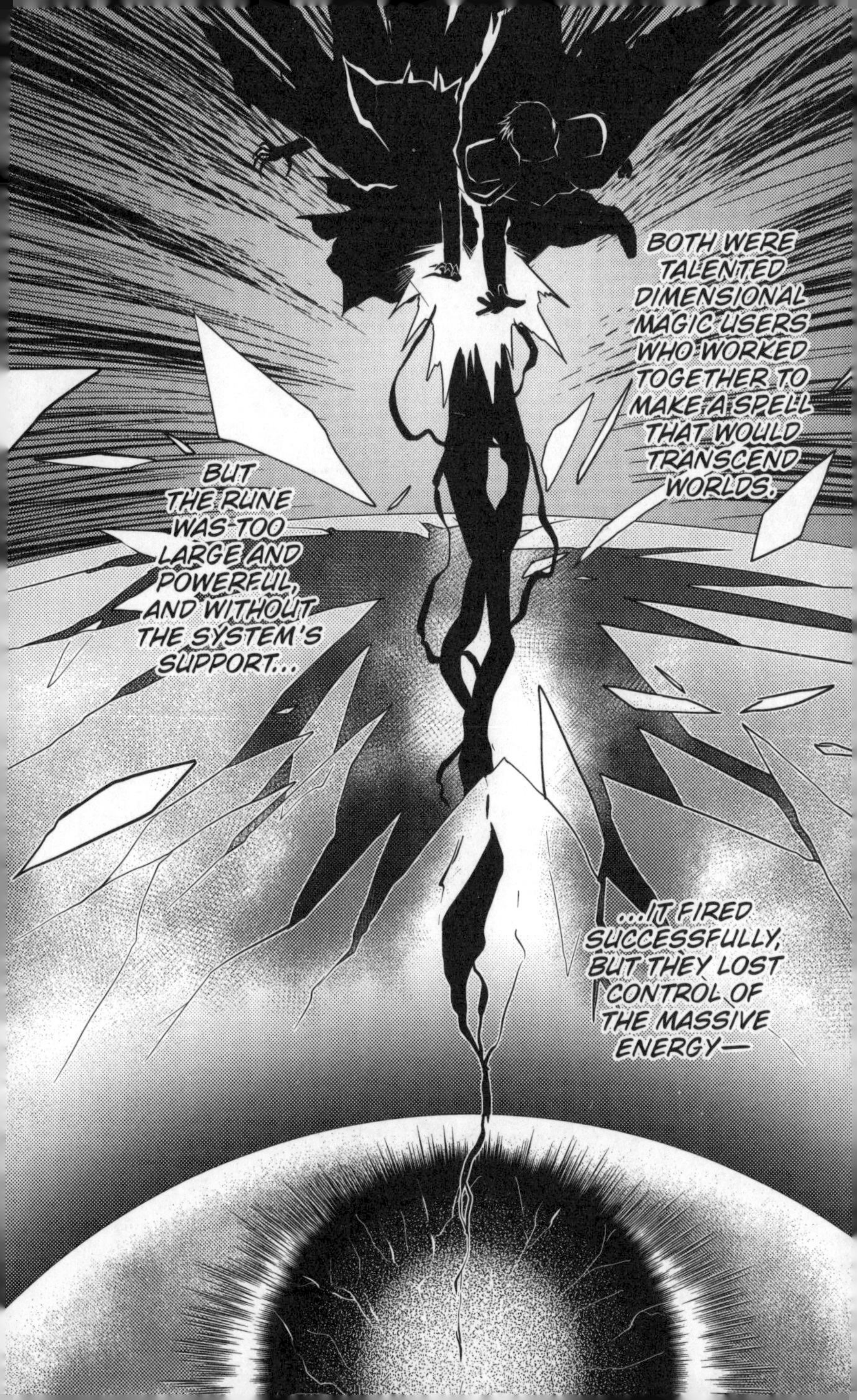
BOTH WERE TALENTED DIMENSIONAL MAGIC USERS WHO WORKED TOGETHER TO MAKE A SPELL THAT WOULD TRANSCEND WORLDS.
BUT THE RUNE WAS TOO LARGE AND POWERFUL, AND WITHOUT THE SYSTEM'S SUPPORT...
...IT FIRED SUCCESSFULLY, BUT THEY LOST CONTROL OF THE MASSIVE ENERGY—

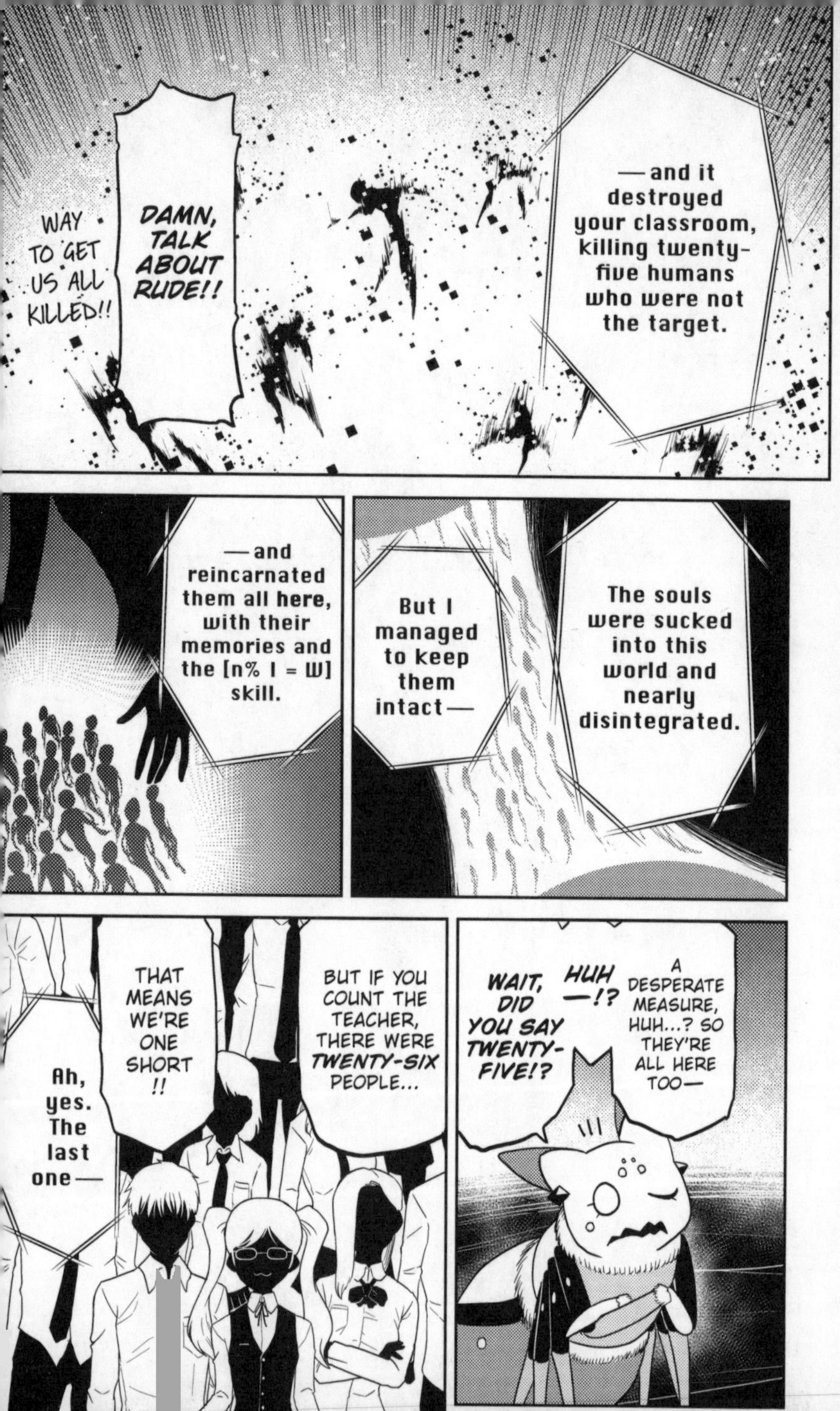
—and it destroyed your classroom, killing twenty-five humans who were not the target.
DAMN, TALK ABOUT RUDE!!
WAY TO GET US ALL KILLED!!
The souls were sucked into this world and nearly disintegrated.
But I managed to keep them intact—
—and reincarnated them all here, with their memories and the [n% I = W] skill.
A DESPERATE MEASURE, HUH...? SO THEY'RE ALL HERE TOO—
HUH—!?
WAIT, DID YOU SAY TWENTY-FIVE!?
BUT IF YOU COUNT THE TEACHER, THERE WERE TWENTY-SIX PEOPLE...
THAT MEANS WE'RE ONE SHORT!!
Ah, yes. The last one—

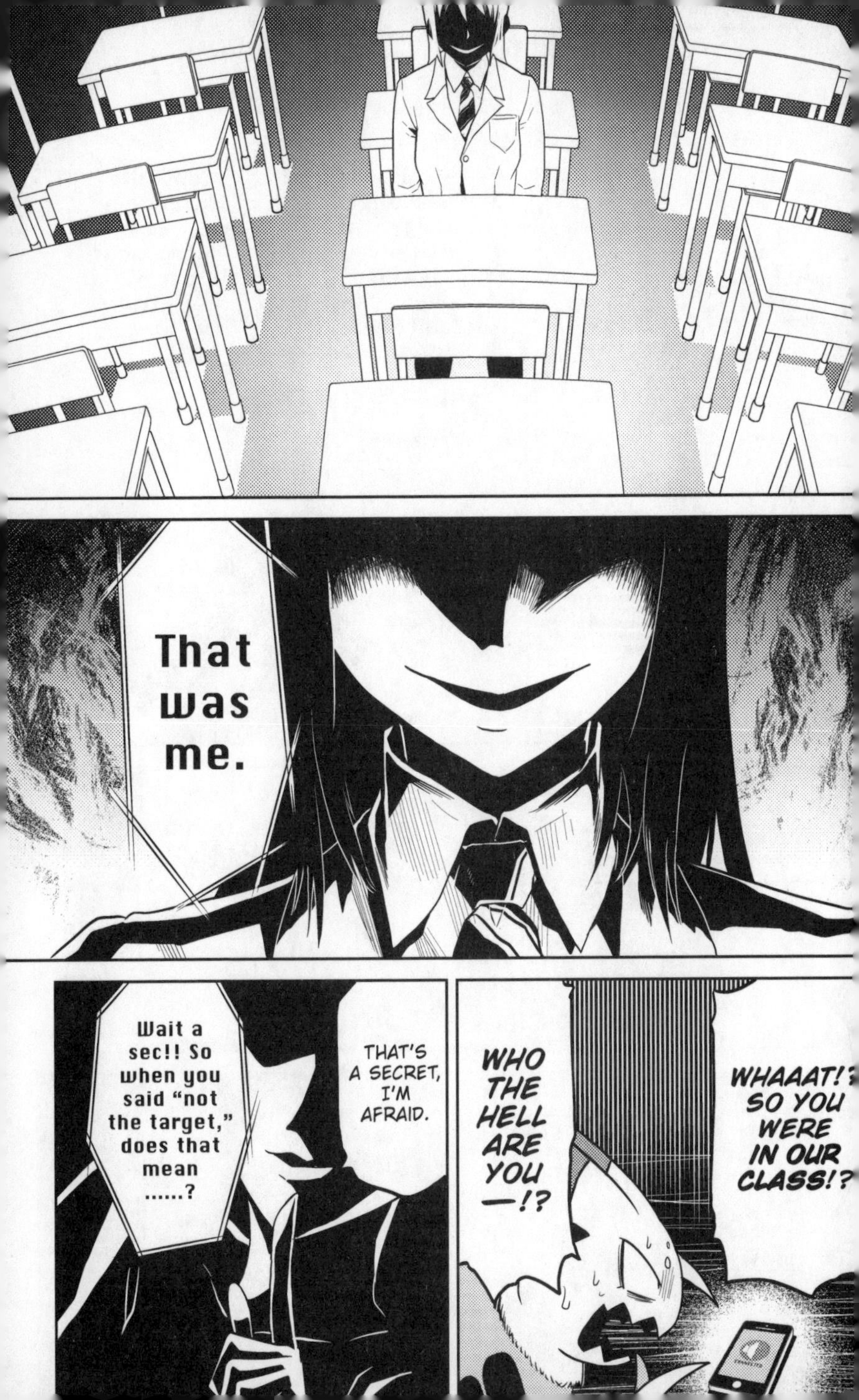
That was me.
WHAAAT!? SO YOU WERE IN OUR CLASS!?
WHO THE HELL ARE YOU—!?
THAT'S A SECRET, I'M AFRAID.
Wait a sec!! So when you said "not the target," does that mean ......?

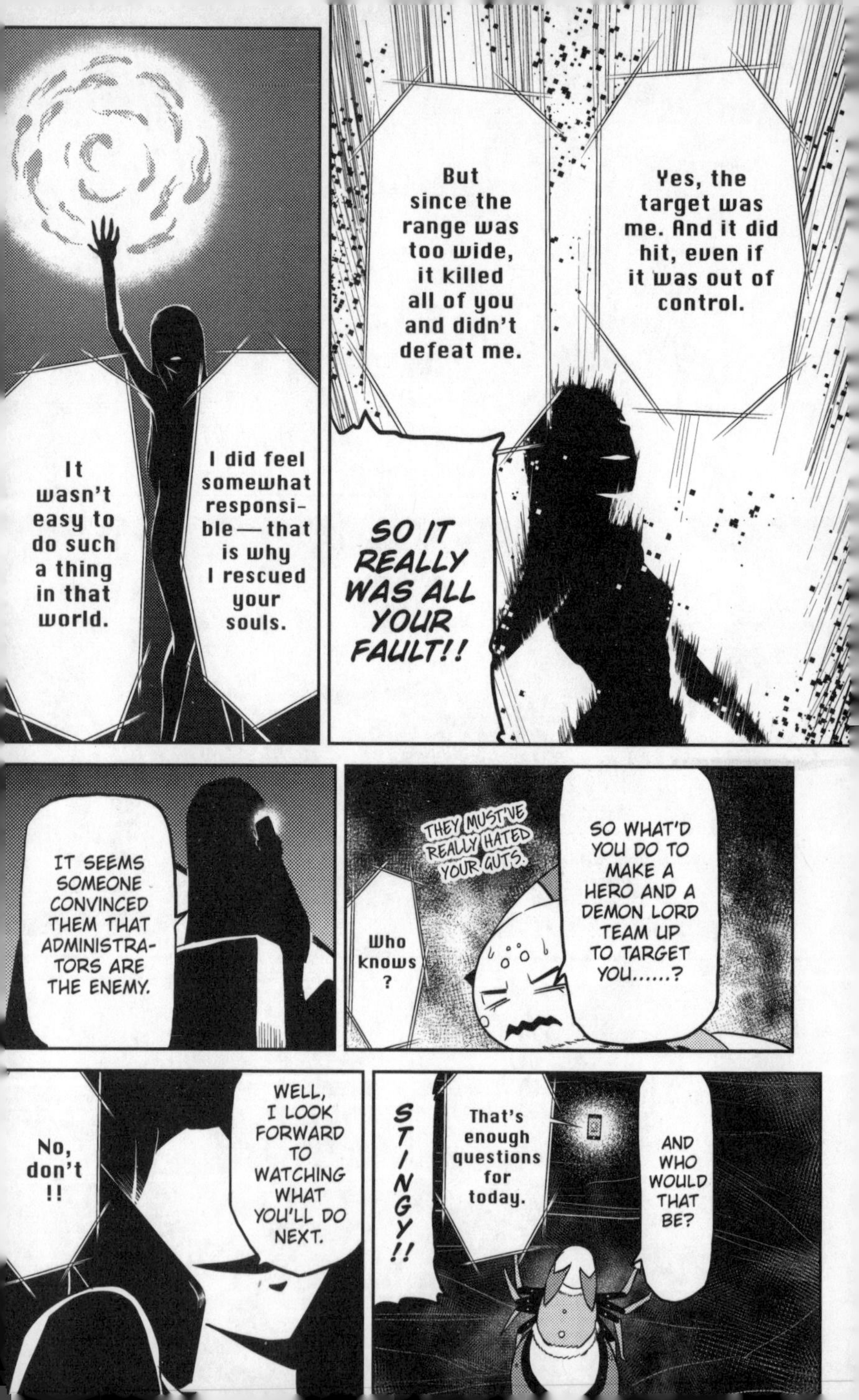
Yes, the target was me. And it did hit, even if it was out of control.
But since the range was too wide, it killed all of you and didn't defeat me.
SO IT REALLY WAS ALL YOUR FAULT!!
I did feel somewhat responsi-ble—that is why I rescued your souls.
It wasn't easy to do such a thing in that world.
SO WHAT'D YOU DO TO MAKE A HERO AND A DEMON LORD TEAM UP TO TARGET YOU......?
THEY MUST'VE REALLY HATED YOUR GUTS.
Who knows?
IT SEEMS SOMEONE CONVINCED THEM THAT ADMINISTRA-TORS ARE THE ENEMY.
AND WHO WOULD THAT BE?
That's enough questions for today.
STINGY!!
WELL, I LOOK FORWARD TO WATCHING WHAT YOU'LL DO NEXT.
No, don't!!

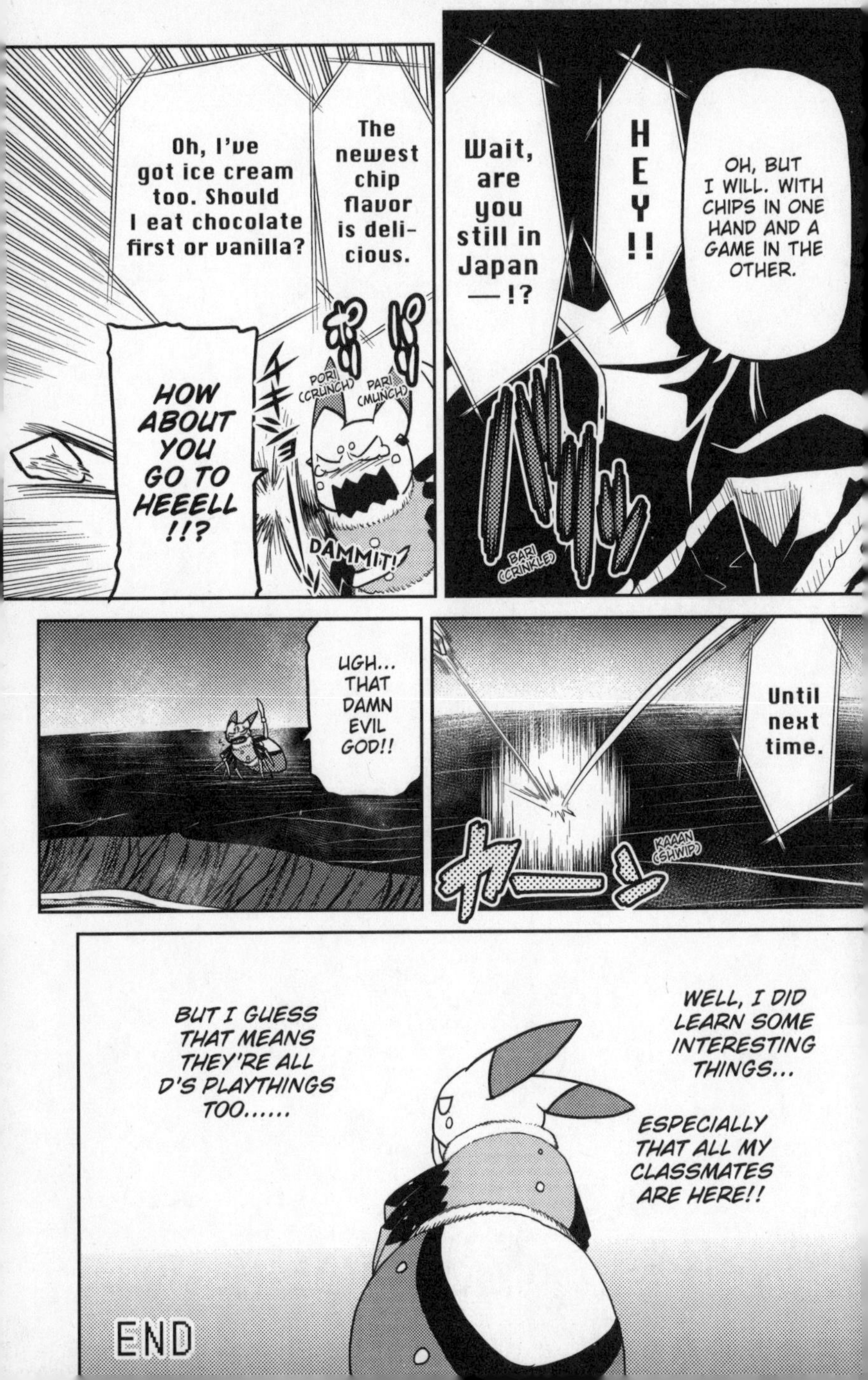
OH, BUT I WILL. WITH CHIPS IN ONE HAND AND A GAME IN THE OTHER.
HEY!!
Wait, are you still in Japan—!?
BARI (CRINKLE)
The newest chip flavor is deli-cious.
Oh, I've got ice cream too. Should I eat chocolate first or vanilla?
PORI (CRUNCH)
PARI (MUNCH)
HOW ABOUT YOU GO TO HEEELL!!?
DAMMIT!
Until next time.
KAAAN (SHWIP)
UGH... THAT DAMN EVIL GOD!!
WELL, I DID LEARN SOME INTERESTING THINGS...
ESPECIALLY THAT ALL MY CLASSMATES ARE HERE!!
BUT I GUESS THAT MEANS THEY'RE ALL D'S PLAYTHINGS TOO......
END

so **I'm** a **Spider**, so **What?**

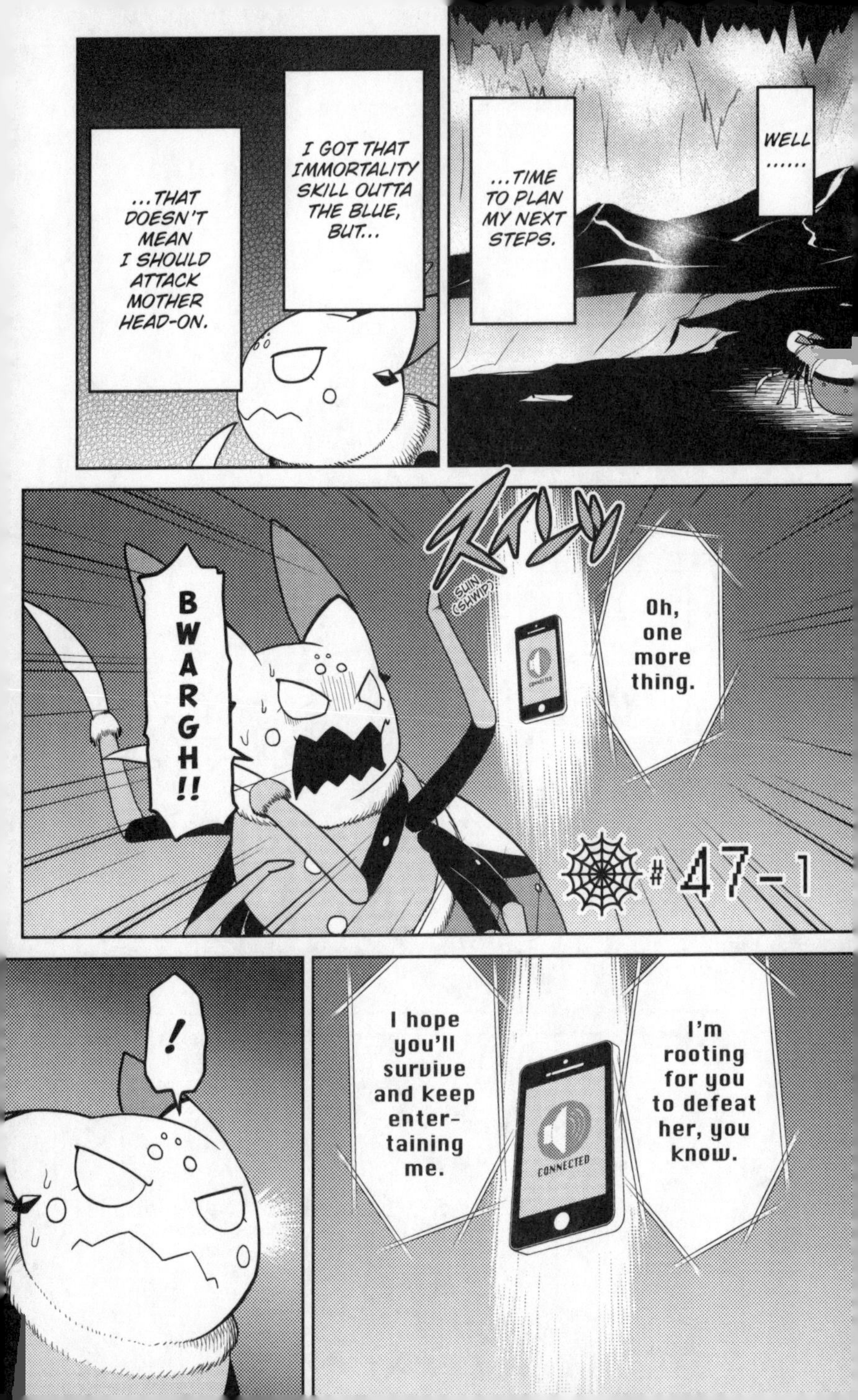
WELL ......
...TIME TO PLAN MY NEXT STEPS.
I GOT THAT IMMORTALITY SKILL OUTTA THE BLUE, BUT...
...THAT DOESN'T MEAN I SHOULD ATTACK MOTHER HEAD-ON.
SUIN (SHWIP)
Oh, one more thing.
BWARGH!!
#47-1
I'm rooting for you to defeat her, you know.
CONNECTED
I hope you'll survive and keep entertaining me.
!

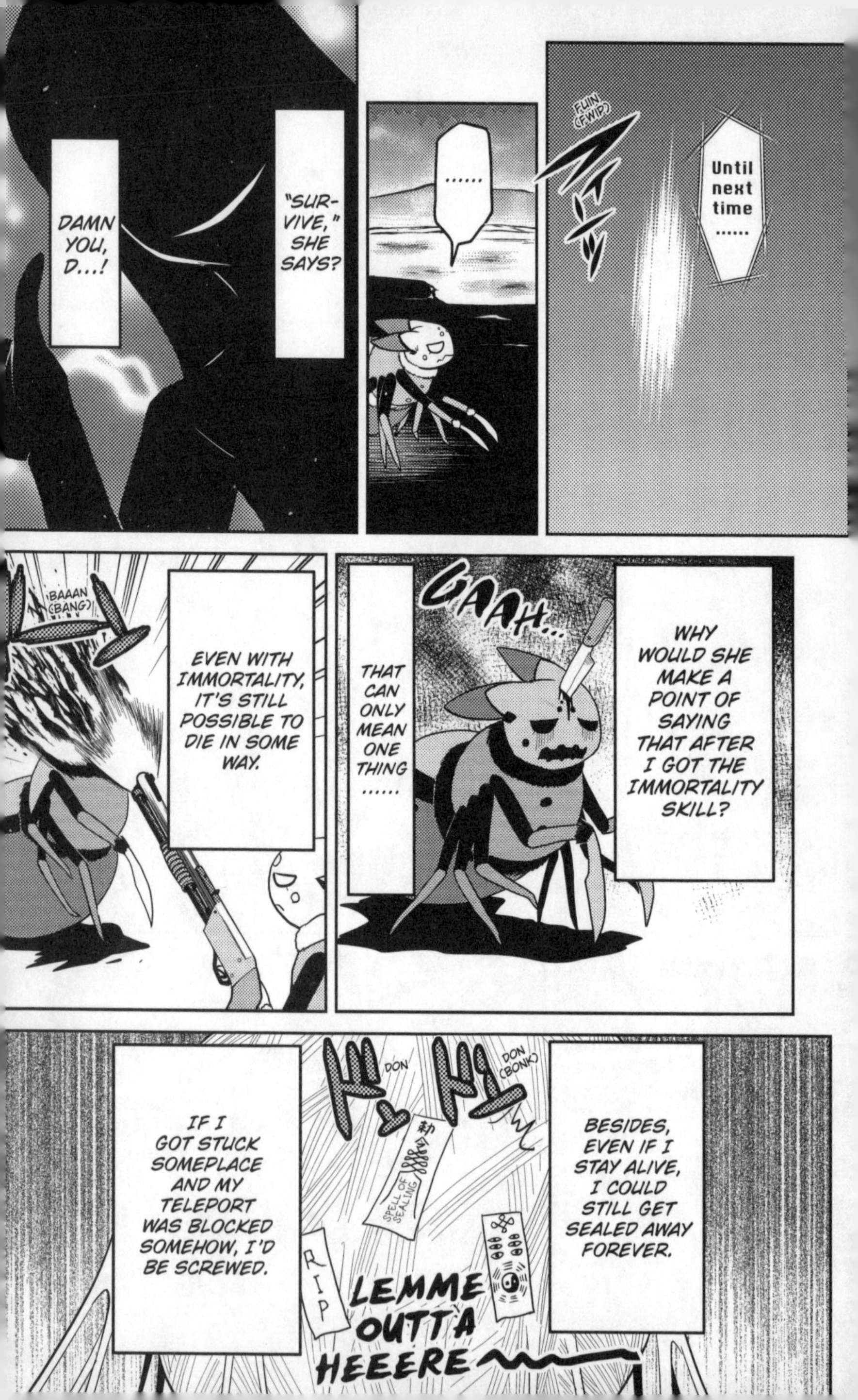
FUIN (FWIP)
Until next time ......
......
"SUR-VIVE," SHE SAYS?
DAMN YOU, D...!
WHY WOULD SHE MAKE A POINT OF SAYING THAT AFTER I GOT THE IMMORTALITY SKILL?
GAAH...
THAT CAN ONLY MEAN ONE THING ......
BAAAN (BANG)
EVEN WITH IMMORTALITY, IT'S STILL POSSIBLE TO DIE IN SOME WAY.
BESIDES, EVEN IF I STAY ALIVE, I COULD STILL GET SEALED AWAY FOREVER.
DON (BONK)
DON
IF I GOT STUCK SOMEPLACE AND MY TELEPORT WAS BLOCKED SOMEHOW, I'D BE SCREWED.
SPELL OF SEALING
RIP
LEMME OUTTA HEEERE

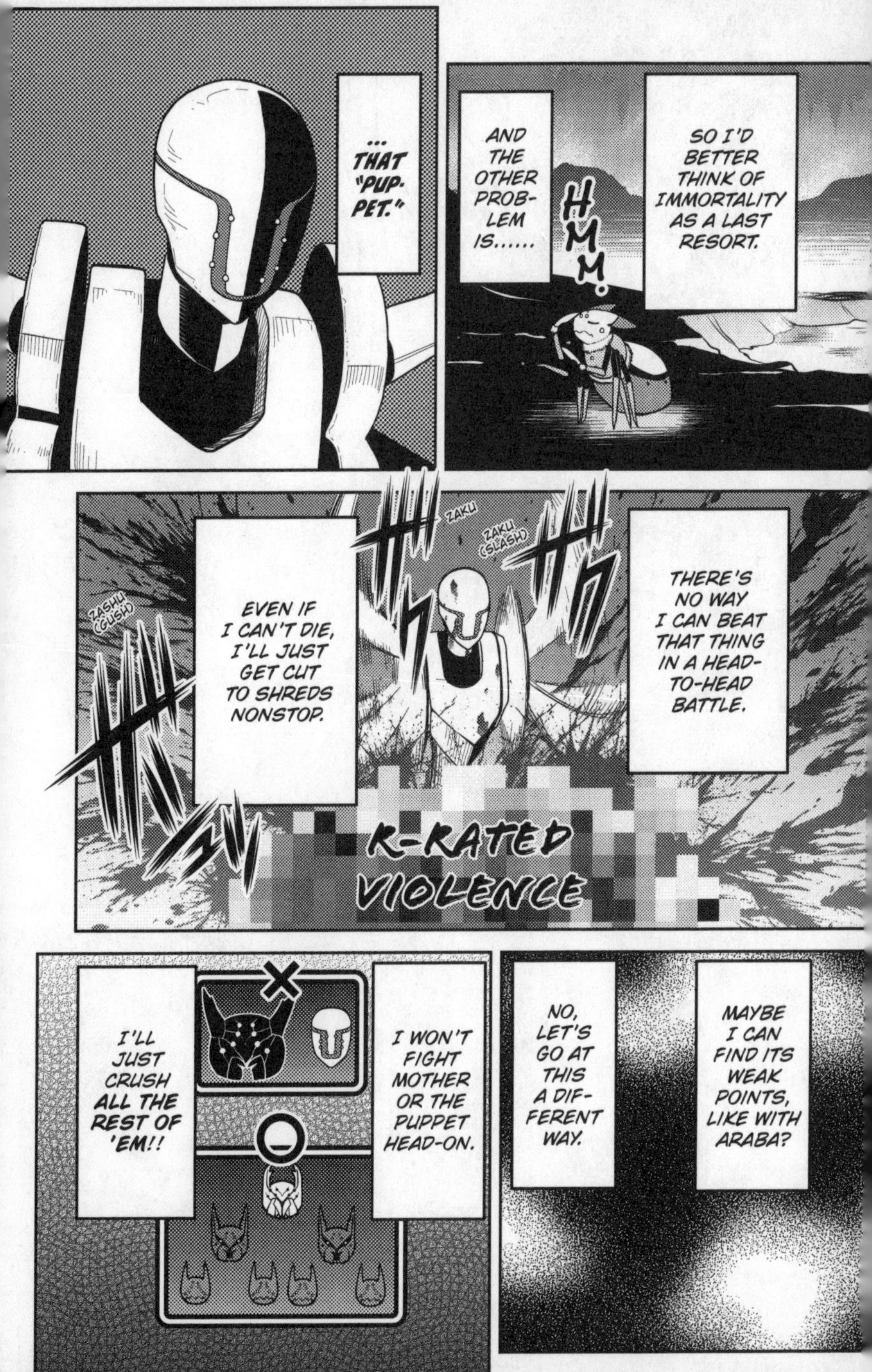

SO I'D BETTER THINK OF IMMORTALITY AS A LAST RESORT.
AND THE OTHER PROBLEM IS......
HMM!
...THAT "PUPPET."
THERE'S NO WAY I CAN BEAT THAT THING IN A HEAD-TO-HEAD BATTLE.
ZAKU
ZAKU (SLASH)
EVEN IF I CAN'T DIE, I'LL JUST GET CUT TO SHREDS NONSTOP.
ZASHU (GUSH)
R-RATED VIOLENCE
MAYBE I CAN FIND ITS WEAK POINTS, LIKE WITH ARABA?
NO, LET'S GO AT THIS A DIFFERENT WAY.
I WON'T FIGHT MOTHER OR THE PUPPET HEAD-ON.
I'LL JUST CRUSH ALL THE REST OF 'EM!!

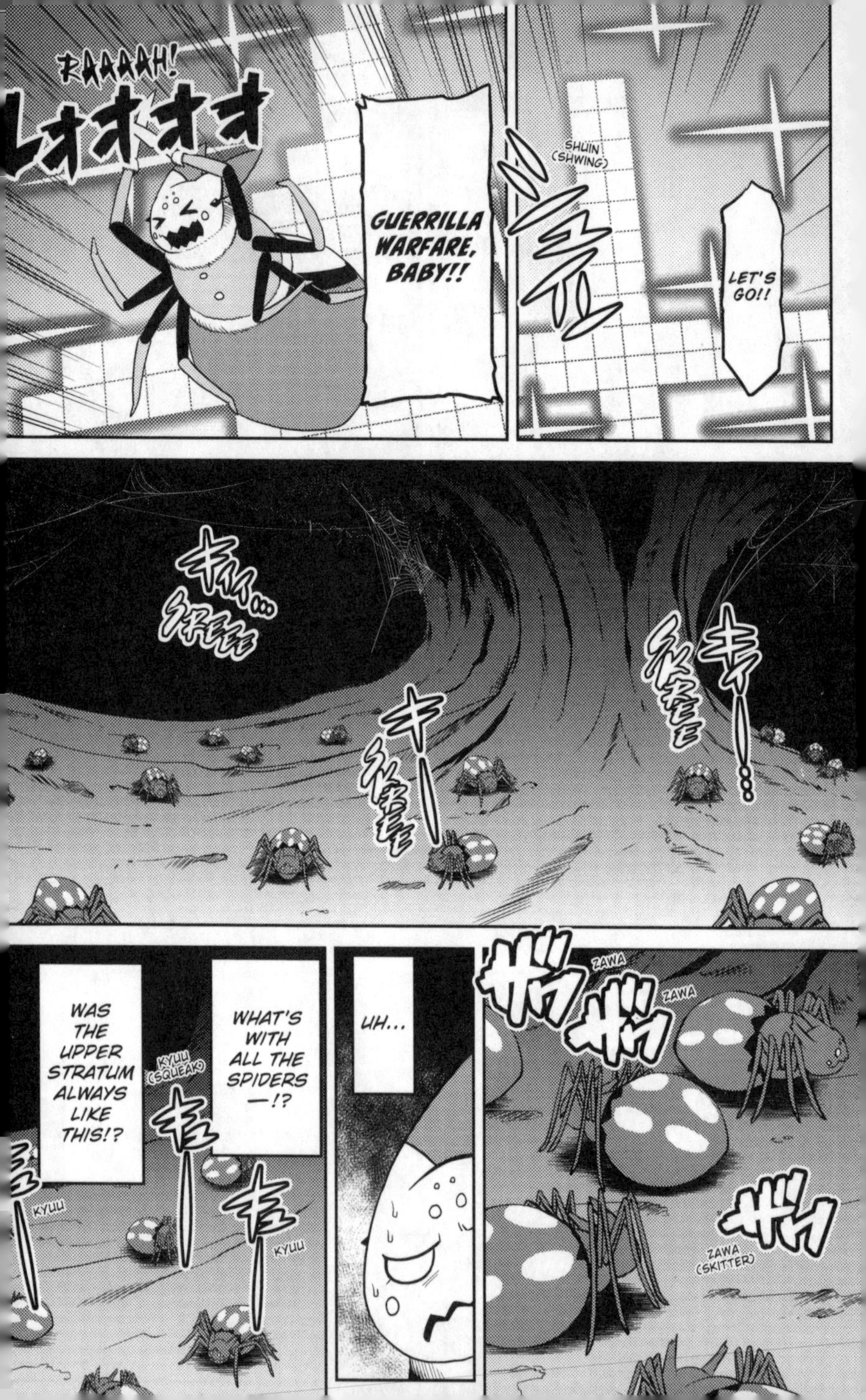
SHUIN (SHWING)
LET'S GO!!
RAAAAH!
GUERRILLA WARFARE, BABY!!
SKREEE
SKREEE
SKREEE
ZAWA
ZAWA
ZAWA (SKITTER)
UH...
WHAT'S WITH ALL THE SPIDERS—!?
KYUU (SQUEAK)
KYUU
WAS THE UPPER STRATUM ALWAYS LIKE THIS!?
KYUU

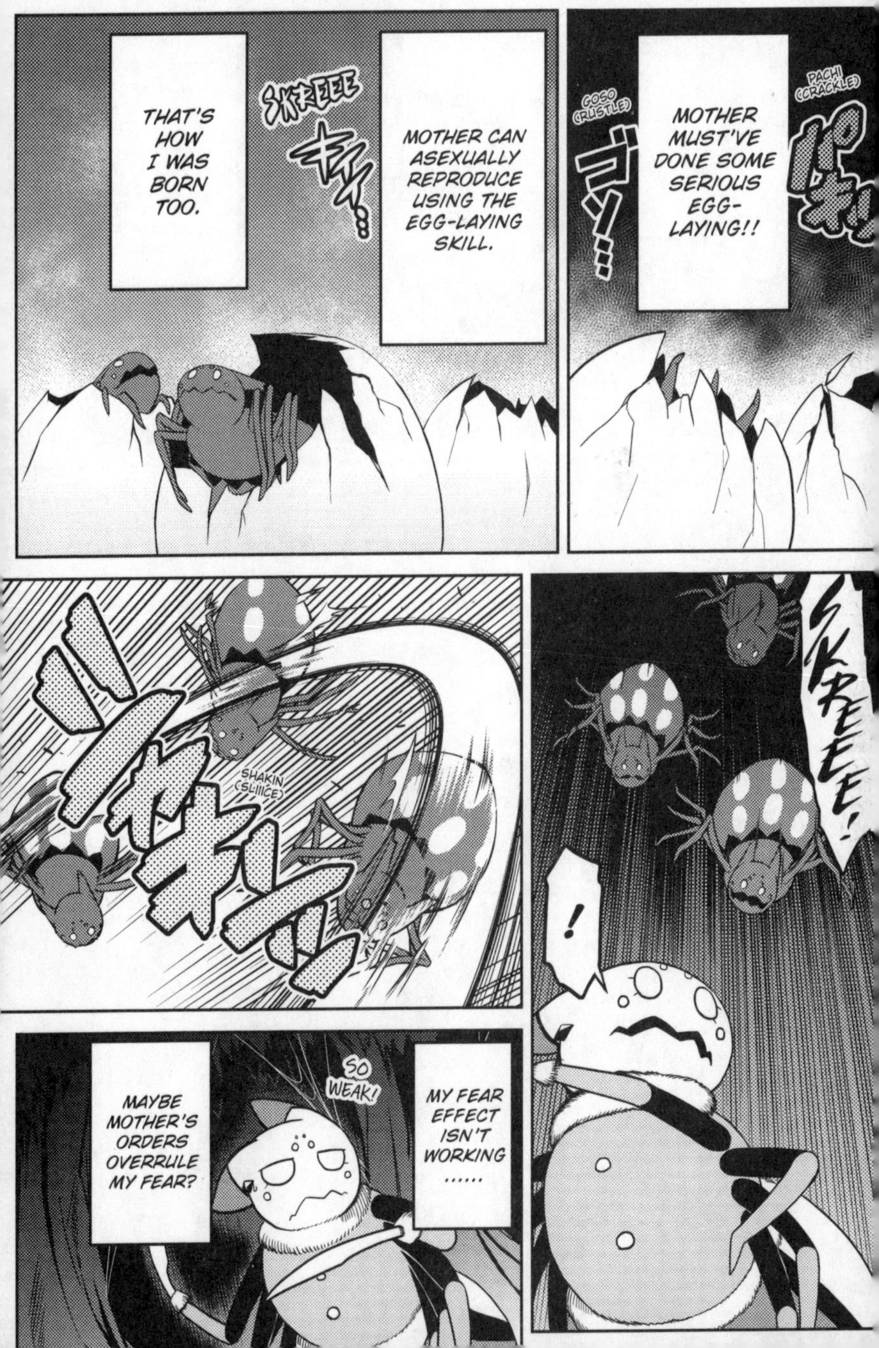
PACHI (CRACKLE)
MOTHER MUST'VE DONE SOME SERIOUS EGG-LAYING!!
GOSO (RUSTLE)
MOTHER CAN ASEXUALLY REPRODUCE USING THE EGG-LAYING SKILL.
SKREEE
THAT'S HOW I WAS BORN TOO.
SKREEE!
!
SHAKIN (SLIIICE)
MY FEAR EFFECT ISN'T WORKING ......
SO WEAK!
MAYBE MOTHER'S ORDERS OVERRULE MY FEAR?

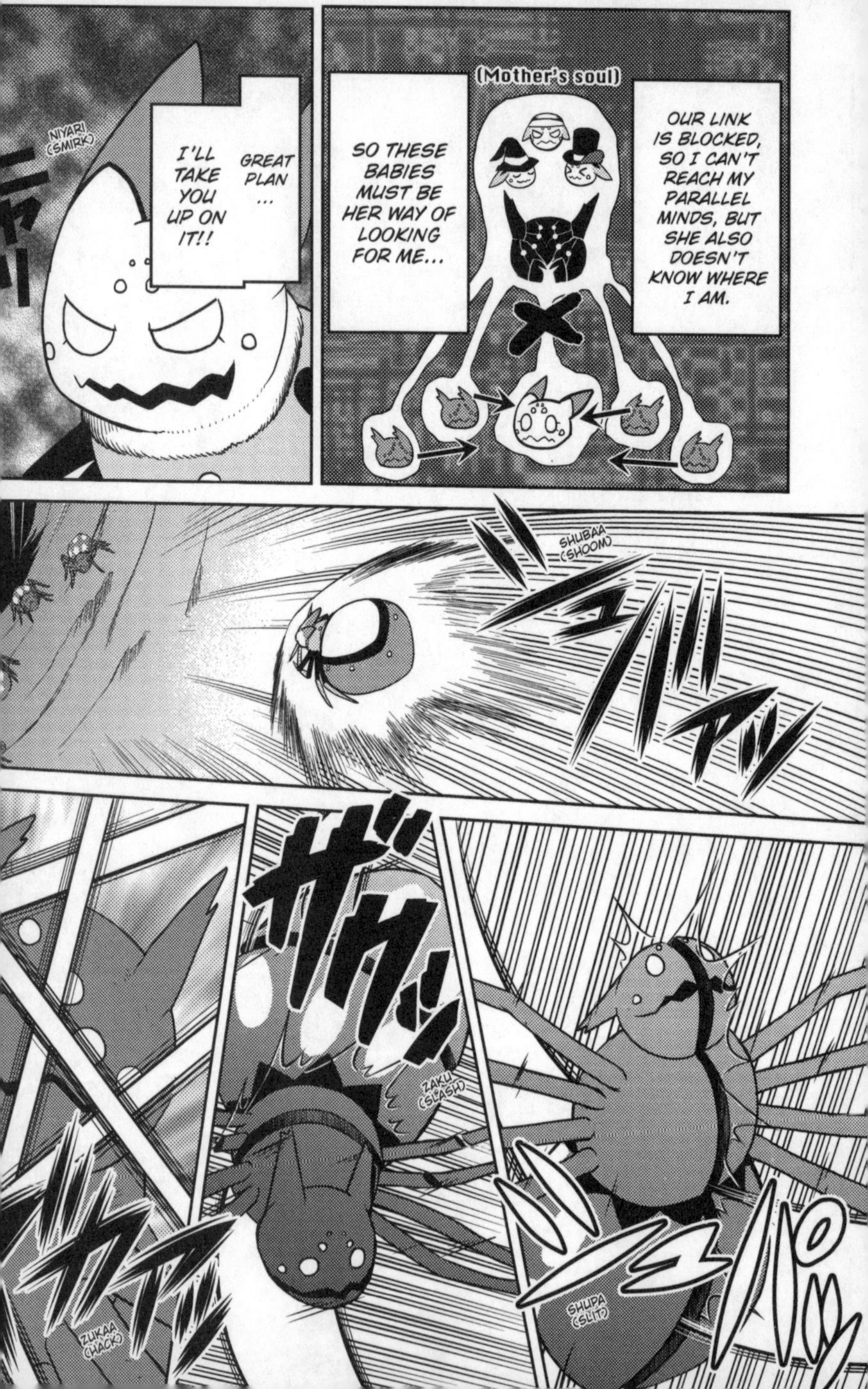
(Mother's soul)
OUR LINK IS BLOCKED, SO I CAN'T REACH MY PARALLEL MINDS, BUT SHE ALSO DOESN'T KNOW WHERE I AM.
SO THESE BABIES MUST BE HER WAY OF LOOKING FOR ME...
GREAT PLAN ...
I'LL TAKE YOU UP ON IT!!
NIYARI (SMIRK)
SHUBAA (SHOOM)
SHUPA (SLIT)
ZAKU (SLASH)
ZUKAA (HACK)

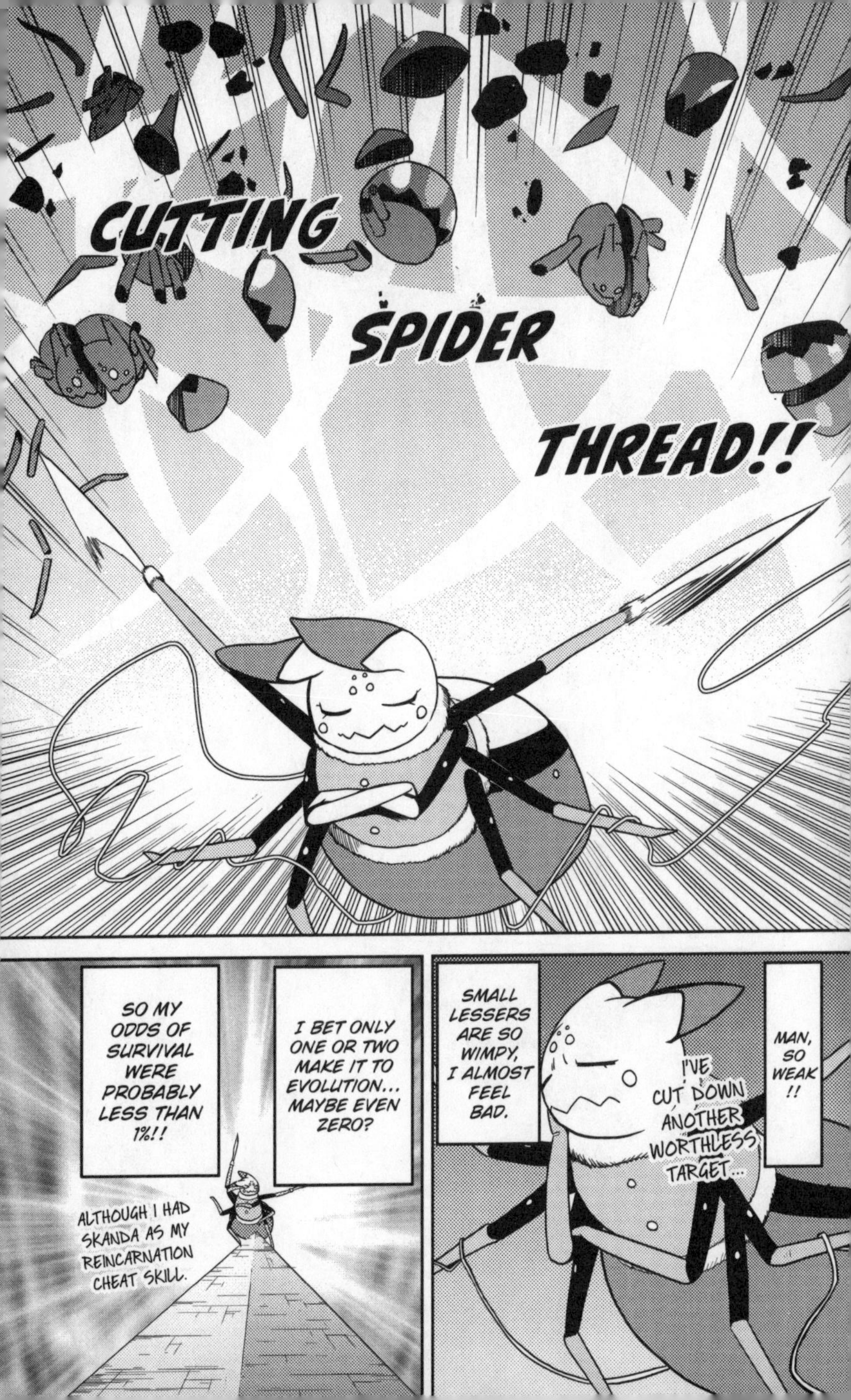
CUTTING SPIDER THREAD!!
MAN, SO WEAK!!
I'VE CUT DOWN ANOTHER WORTHLESS TARGET...
SMALL LESSERS ARE SO WIMPY, I ALMOST FEEL BAD.
I BET ONLY ONE OR TWO MAKE IT TO EVOLUTION... MAYBE EVEN ZERO?
SO MY ODDS OF SURVIVAL WERE PROBABLY LESS THAN 1%!!
ALTHOUGH I HAD SKANDA AS MY REINCARNATION CHEAT SKILL.

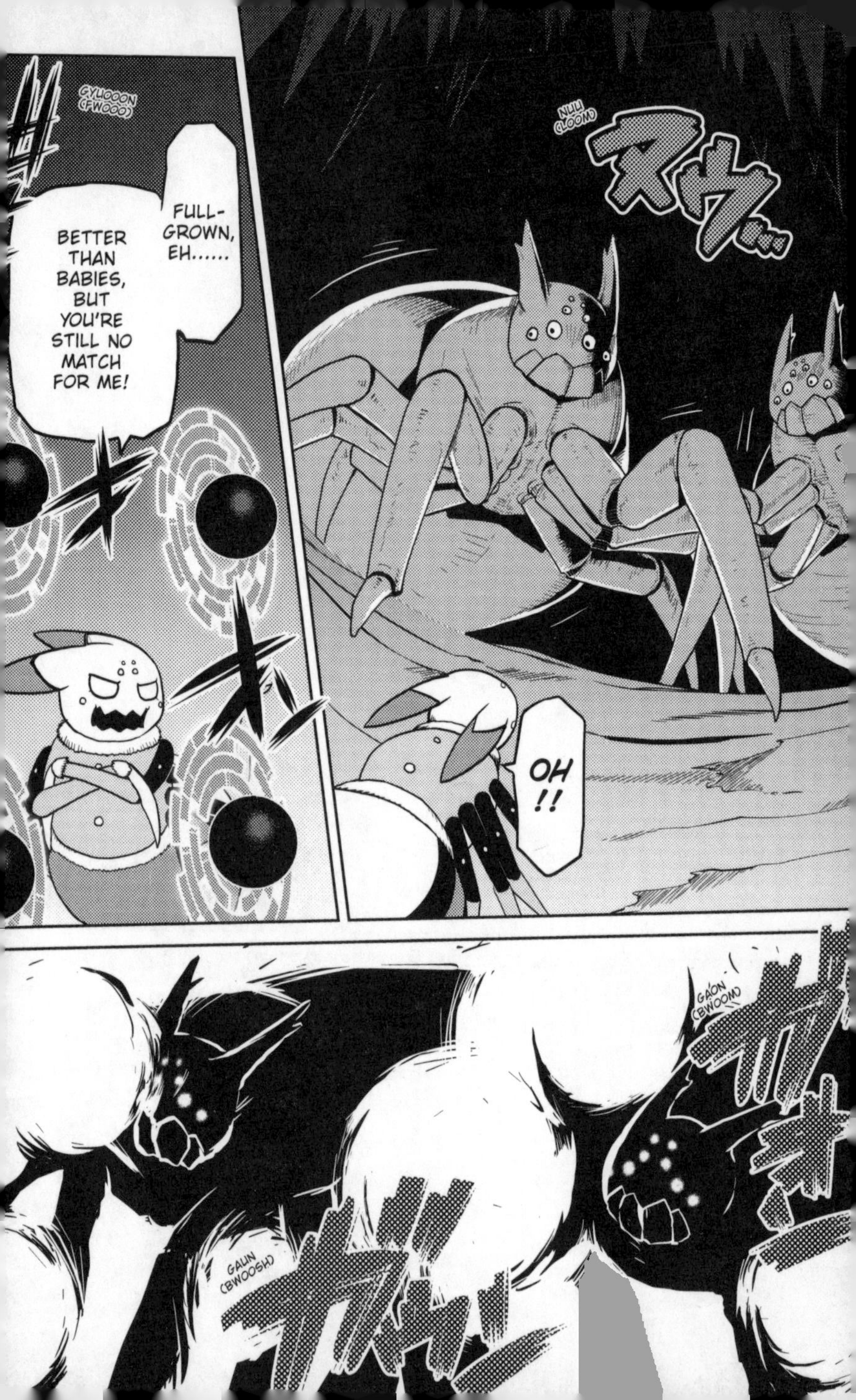
NUU
(LOOM)
ヌウ…
OH!!
GYUOOON
(FWOOO)
FULL-GROWN, EH......
BETTER THAN BABIES, BUT YOU'RE STILL NO MATCH FOR ME!
GAON
(BWOOM)
GAUN
(BWOOSH)

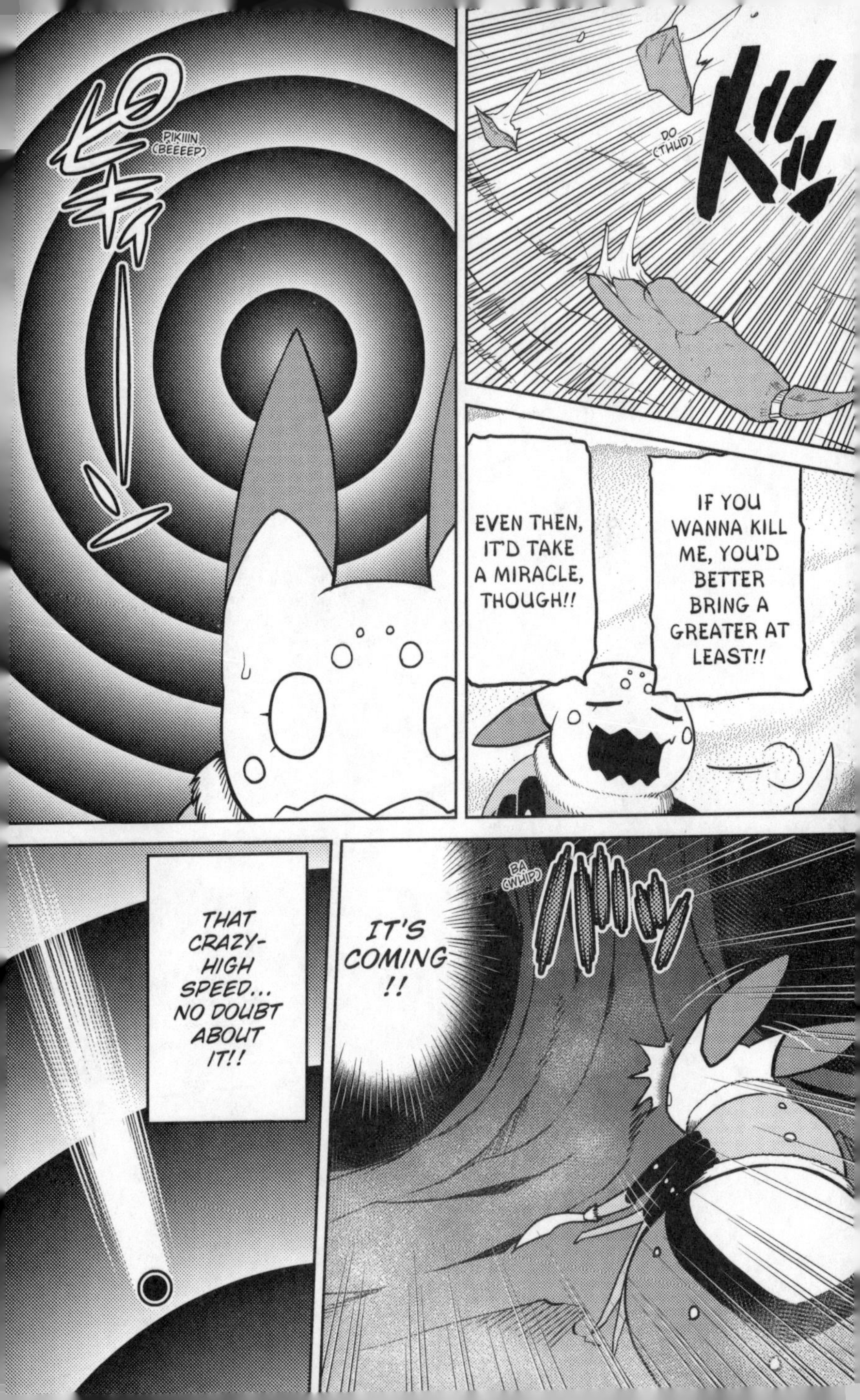
DO
(THUD)
IF YOU WANNA KILL ME, YOU'D BETTER BRING A GREATER AT LEAST!!
EVEN THEN, IT'D TAKE A MIRACLE, THOUGH!!
PIKIIIN
(BEEEEP)
BA
(WHIP)
IT'S COMING!!
THAT CRAZY-HIGH SPEED... NO DOUBT ABOUT IT!!

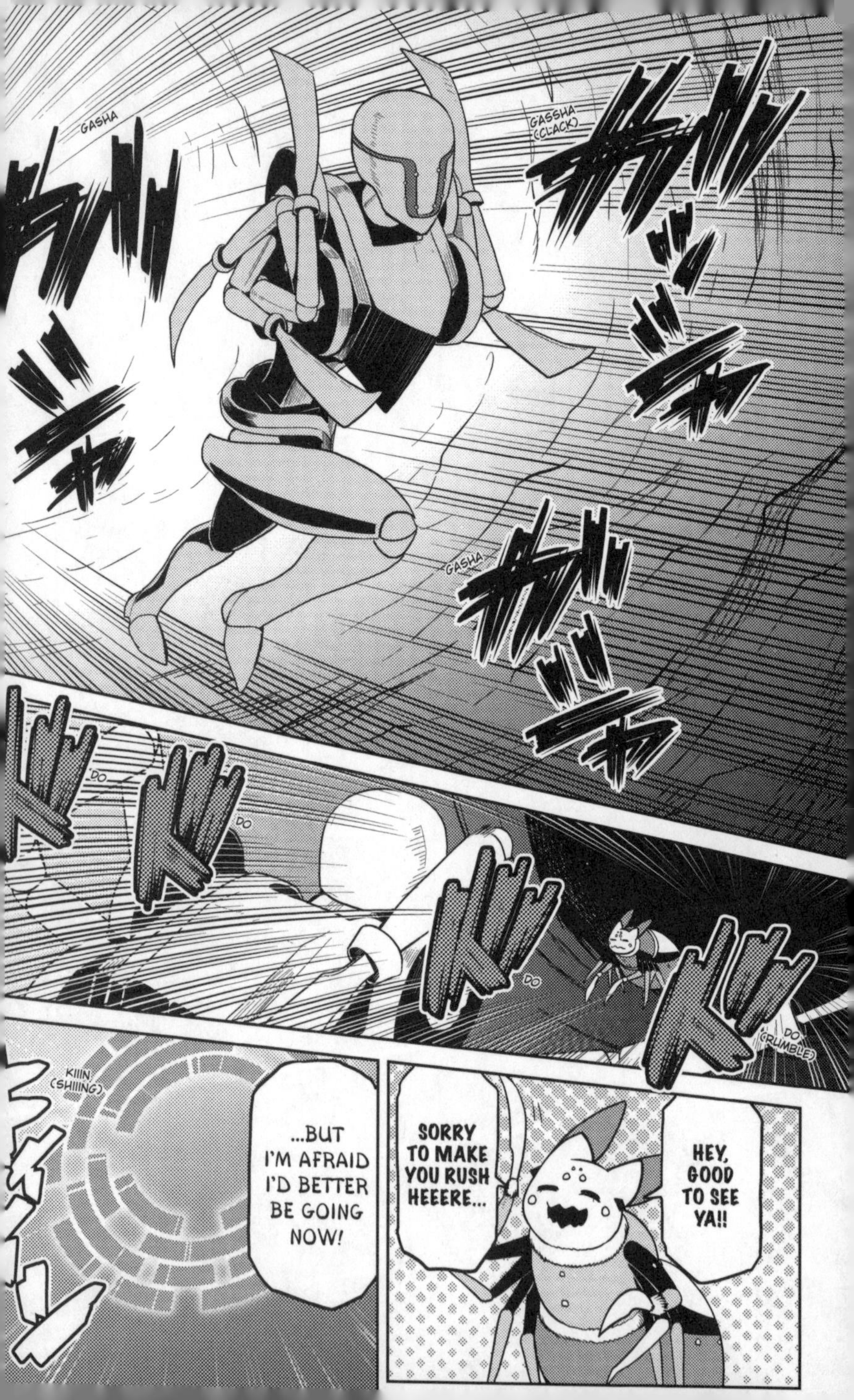
GASSHA (CLACK)
GASHA
GASHA
DO (CRUMBLE)
DO
DO
DO
HEY, GOOD TO SEE YA!!
SORRY TO MAKE YOU RUSH HEEERE...
...BUT I'M AFRAID I'D BETTER BE GOING NOW!
KIIIN (SHIIING)

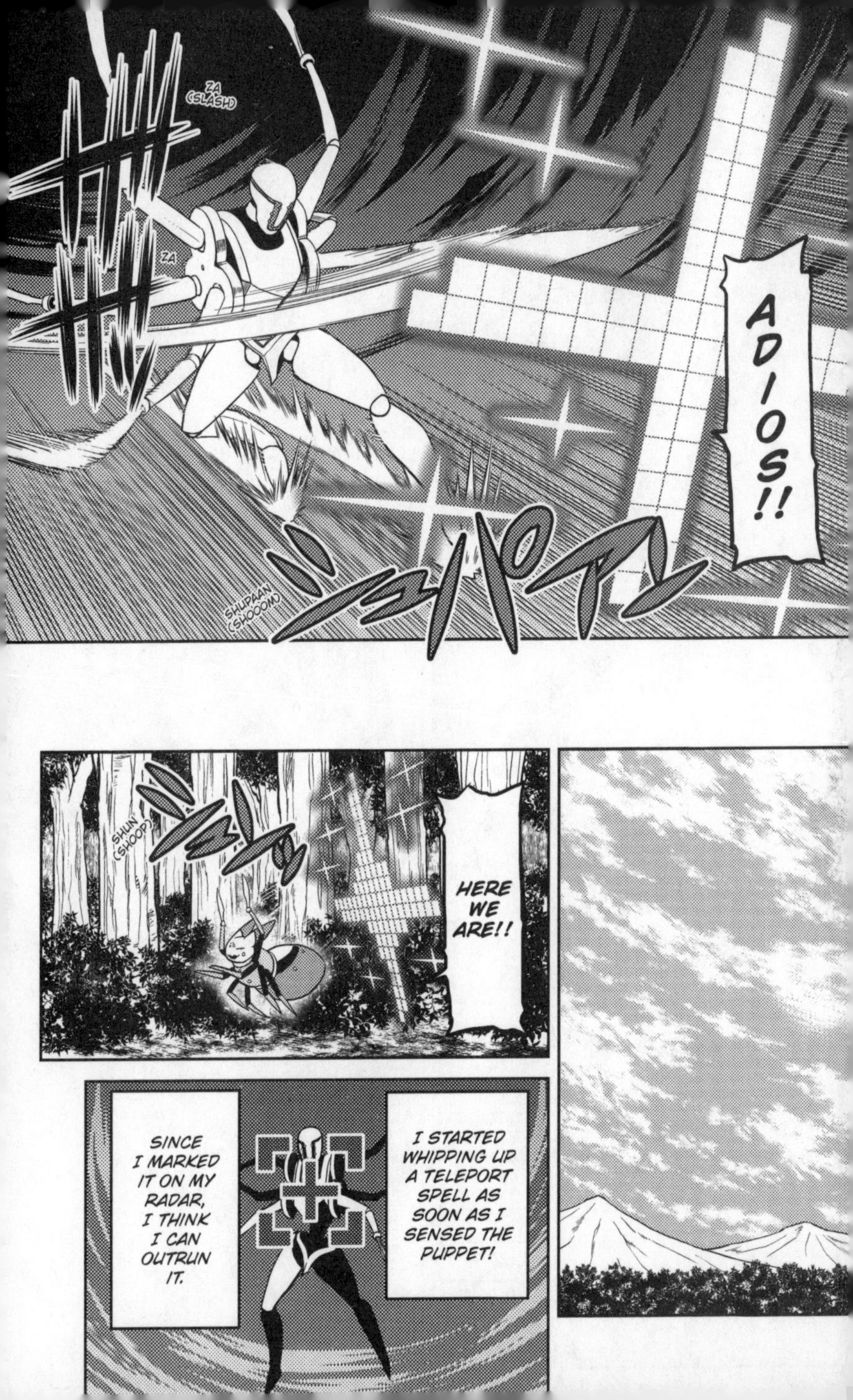
ADIOS!!
ZA (SLASH)
ZA
SHUPAAN (SHOOOM)
HERE WE ARE!!
SHUN (SHOOP)
I STARTED WHIPPING UP A TELEPORT SPELL AS SOON AS I SENSED THE PUPPET!
SINCE I MARKED IT ON MY RADAR, I THINK I CAN OUTRUN IT.

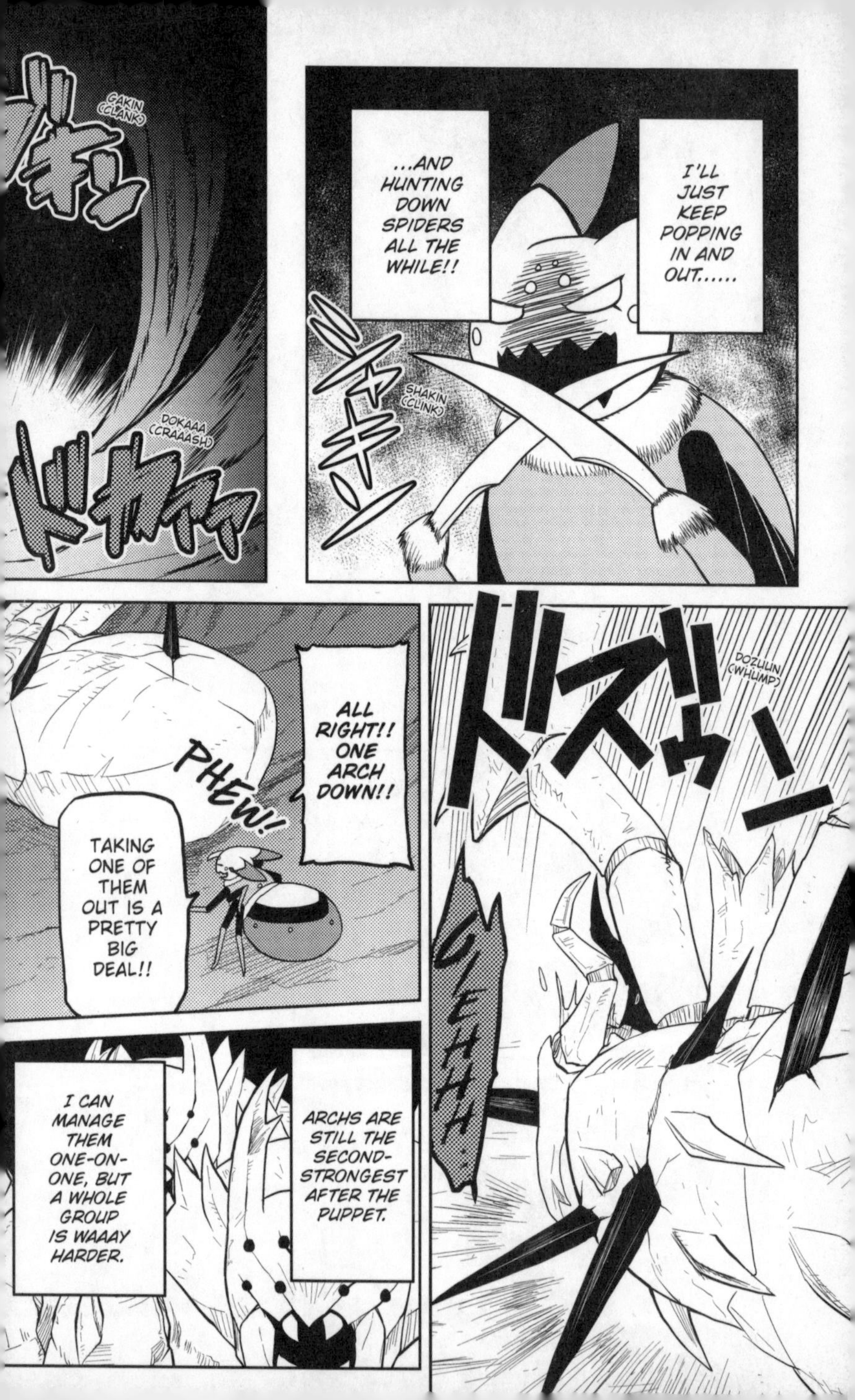
I'LL JUST KEEP POPPING IN AND OUT......
...AND HUNTING DOWN SPIDERS ALL THE WHILE!!
SHAKIN (CLINK)
GAKIN (CLANK)
DOKAAA (CRAAASH)
DOZULUN (WHUMP)
ALL RIGHT!! ONE ARCH DOWN!!
PHEW!
TAKING ONE OF THEM OUT IS A PRETTY BIG DEAL!!
ARCHS ARE STILL THE SECOND-STRONGEST AFTER THE PUPPET.
I CAN MANAGE THEM ONE-ON-ONE, BUT A WHOLE GROUP IS WAAAY HARDER.

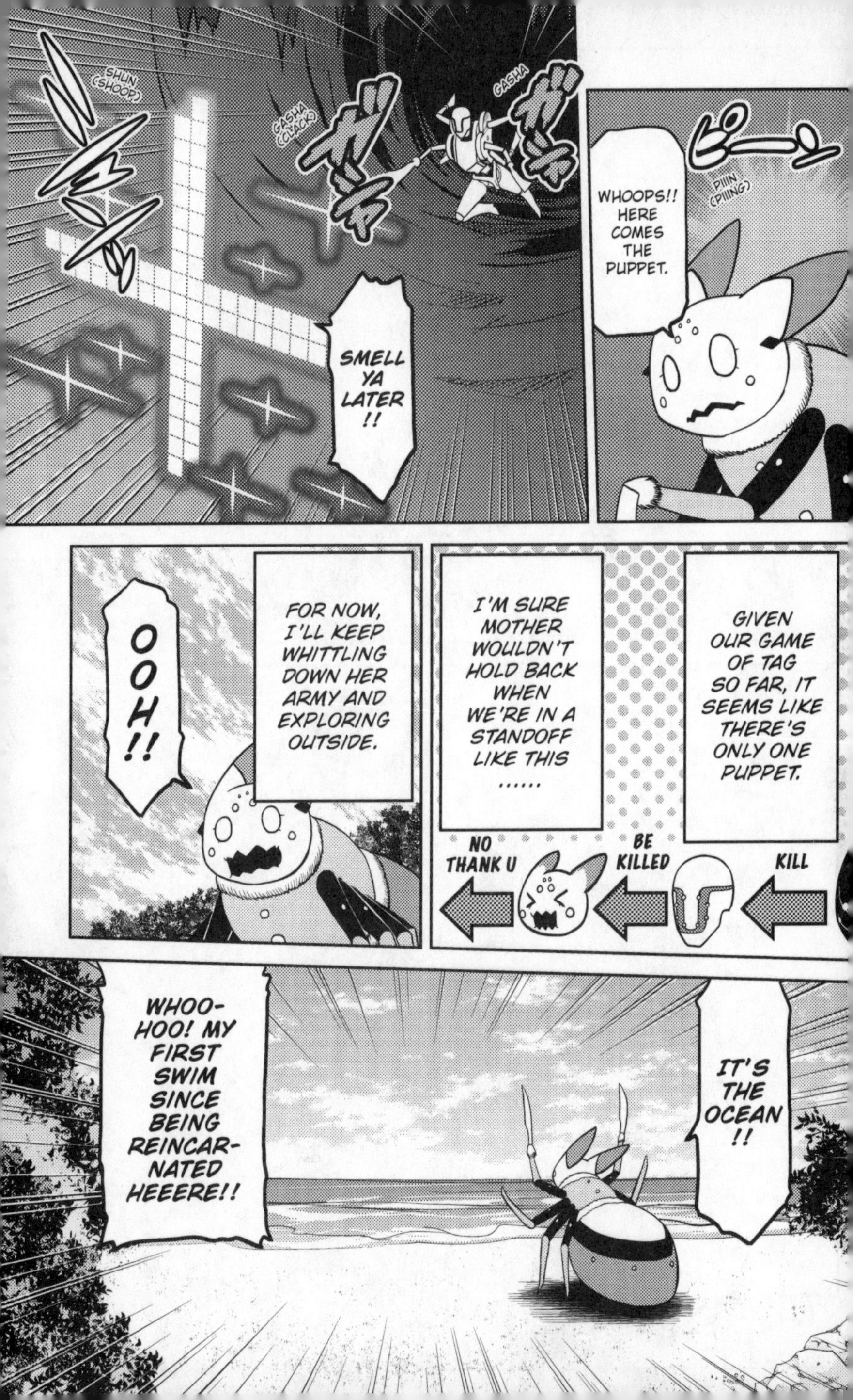
PIIIN (PIIING)
WHOOPS!! HERE COMES THE PUPPET.
GASHA
GASHA (CLACK)
SHUN (SHOOP)
SMELL YA LATER!!
GIVEN OUR GAME OF TAG SO FAR, IT SEEMS LIKE THERE'S ONLY ONE PUPPET.
I'M SURE MOTHER WOULDN'T HOLD BACK WHEN WE'RE IN A STANDOFF LIKE THIS ......
KILL
BE KILLED
NO THANK U
FOR NOW, I'LL KEEP WHITTLING DOWN HER ARMY AND EXPLORING OUTSIDE.
OOH!!
IT'S THE OCEAN!!
WHOO-HOO! MY FIRST SWIM SINCE BEING REINCAR-NATED HEEERE!!

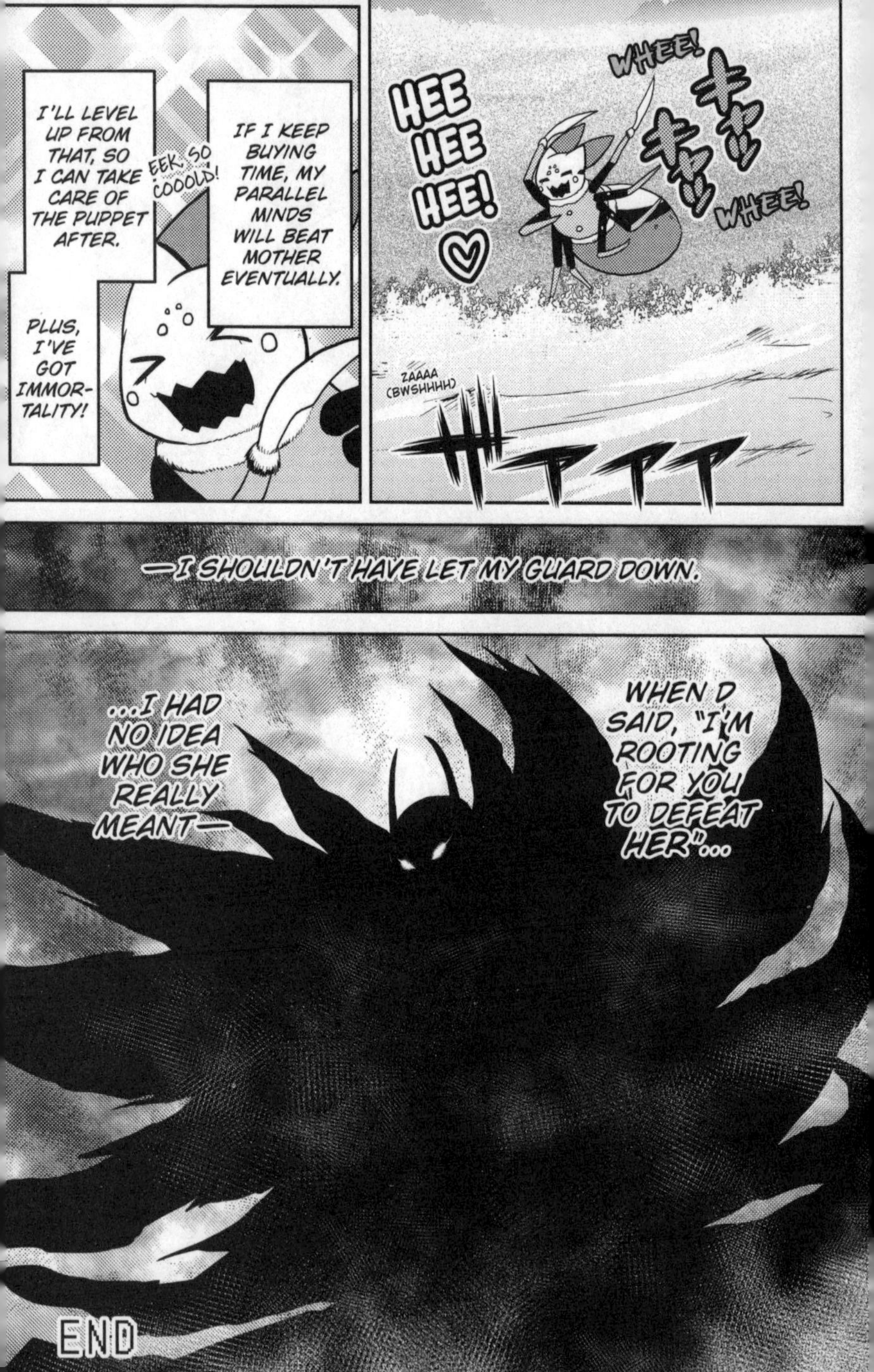
HEE HEE HEE! ♡
WHEE!
キャッ キャッ
WHEE!
ZAAAA (BWSHHHH)
ザァァァ
IF I KEEP BUYING TIME, MY PARALLEL MINDS WILL BEAT MOTHER EVENTUALLY.
EEK, SO COOOLD!
I'LL LEVEL UP FROM THAT, SO I CAN TAKE CARE OF THE PUPPET AFTER.
PLUS, I'VE GOT IMMORTALITY!
—I SHOULDN'T HAVE LET MY GUARD DOWN.
WHEN D SAID, "I'M ROOTING FOR YOU TO DEFEAT HER"...
...I HAD NO IDEA WHO SHE REALLY MEANT—
END

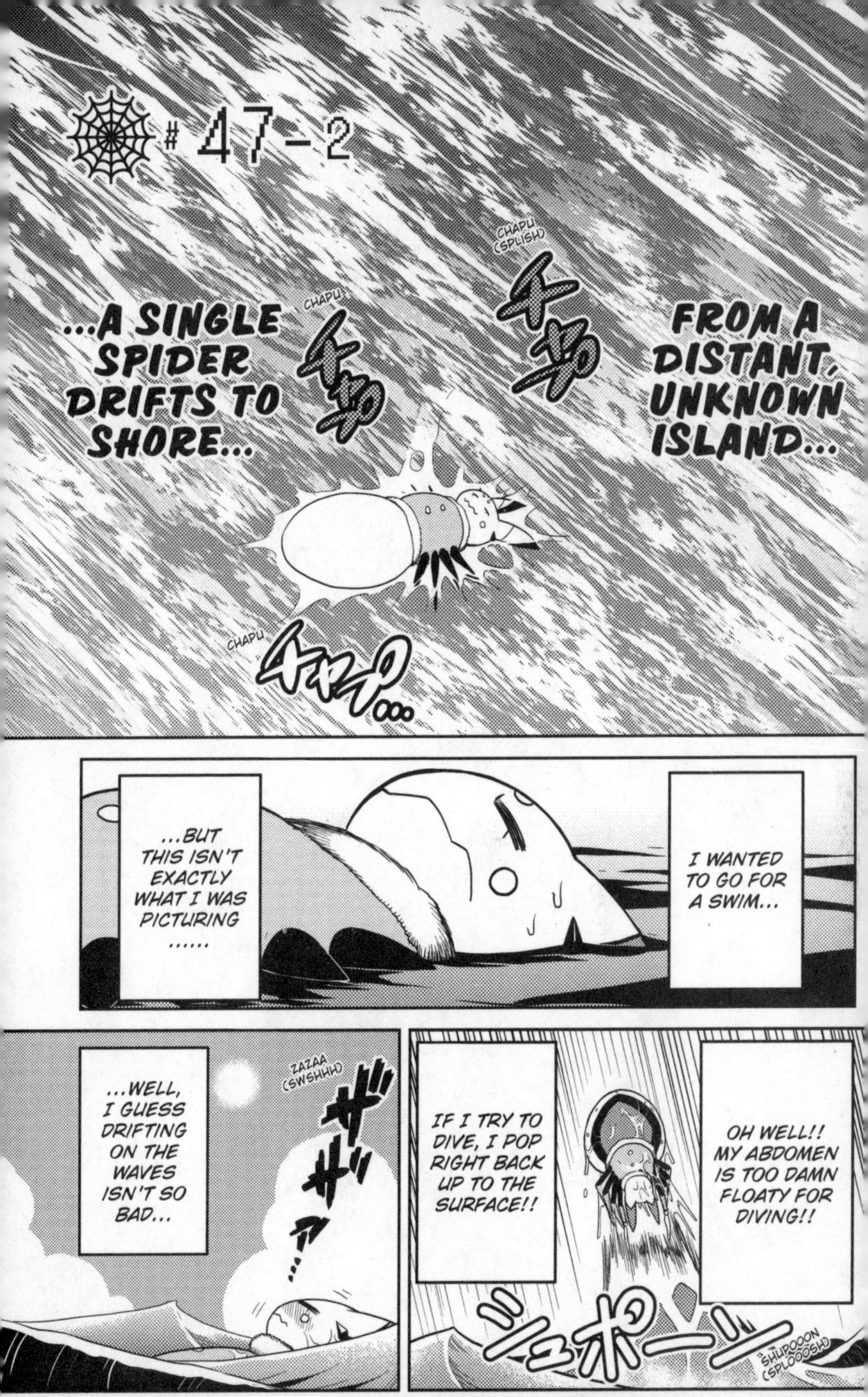
#47-2
FROM A DISTANT, UNKNOWN ISLAND...
CHAPU (SPLISH)
CHAPU
...A SINGLE SPIDER DRIFTS TO SHORE...
CHAPU
I WANTED TO GO FOR A SWIM...
...BUT THIS ISN'T EXACTLY WHAT I WAS PICTURING ......
OH WELL!! MY ABDOMEN IS TOO DAMN FLOATY FOR DIVING!!
IF I TRY TO DIVE, I POP RIGHT BACK UP TO THE SURFACE!!
SHUPOOON (SPLOOOSH)
ZAZAA (SWSHHH)
...WELL, I GUESS DRIFTING ON THE WAVES ISN'T SO BAD...

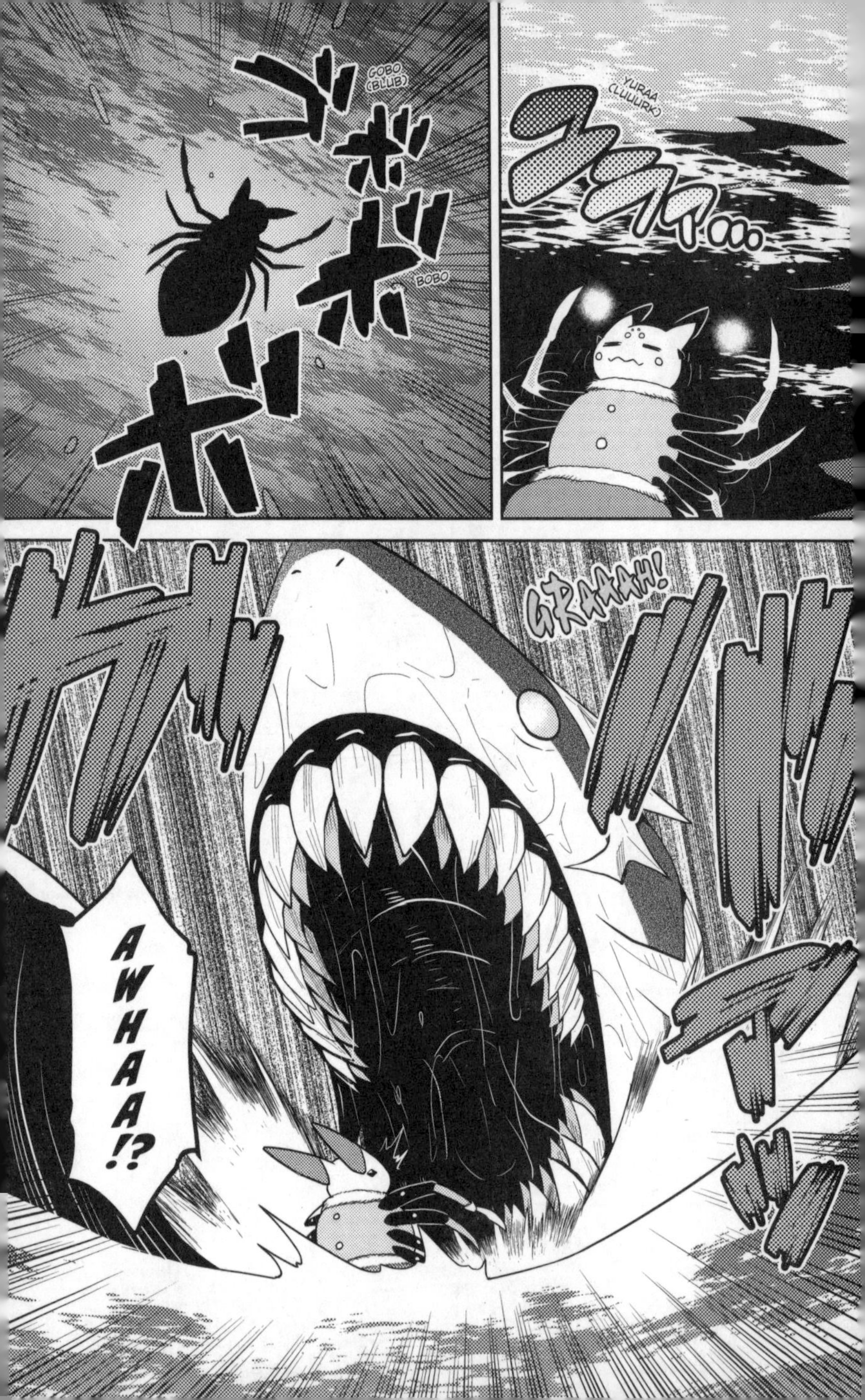
YURAA (LUUURK)
GOBO (BLUB)
BOBO
GRAAAH!
AWHAAA!?

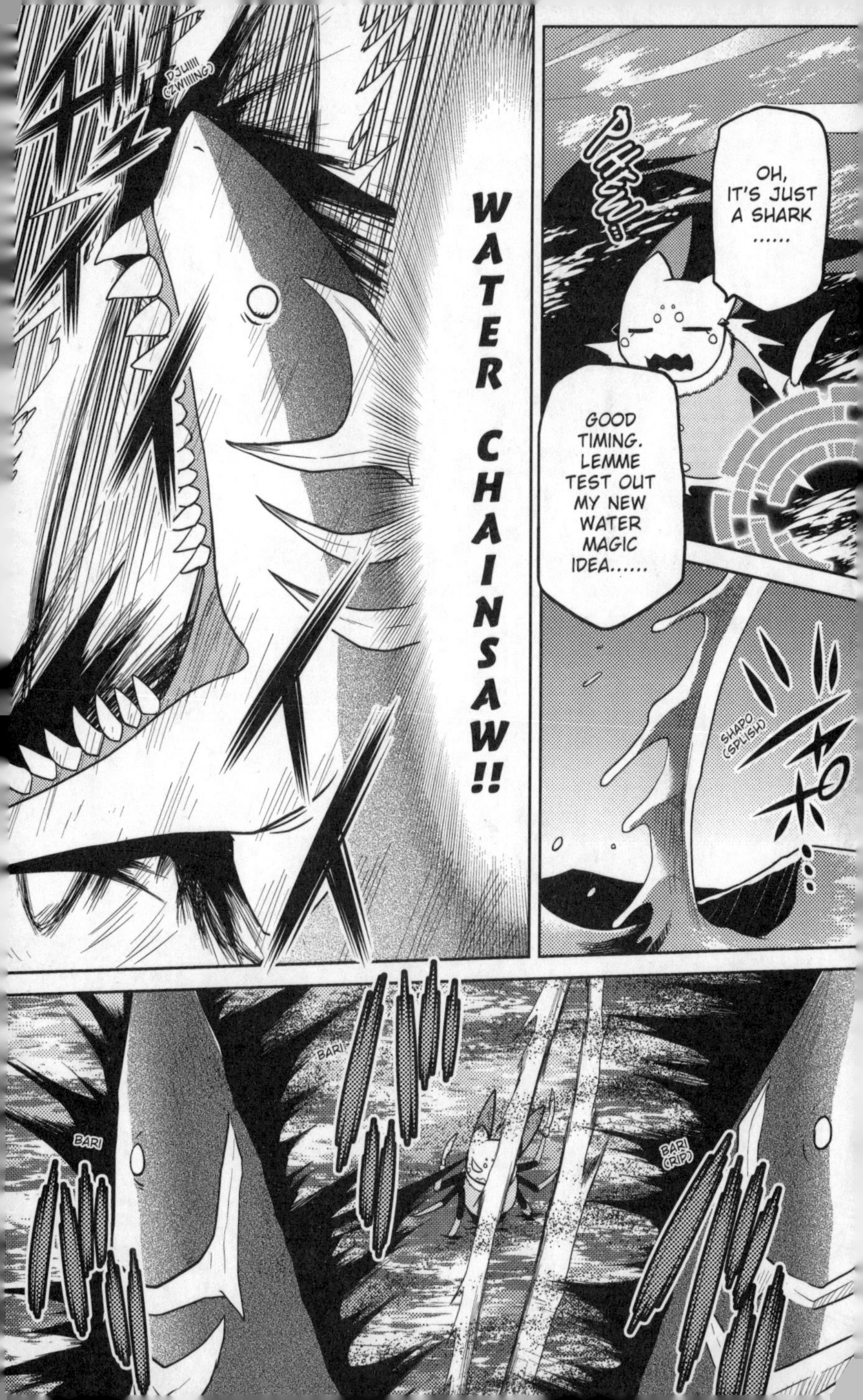
PHEW!..
OH, IT'S JUST A SHARK ......
GOOD TIMING. LEMME TEST OUT MY NEW WATER MAGIC IDEA......
SHAPO (SPLISH)
DJUIIII (ZWIIIING)
WATER CHAINSAW!!
BARI (RIP)
BARI
BARI

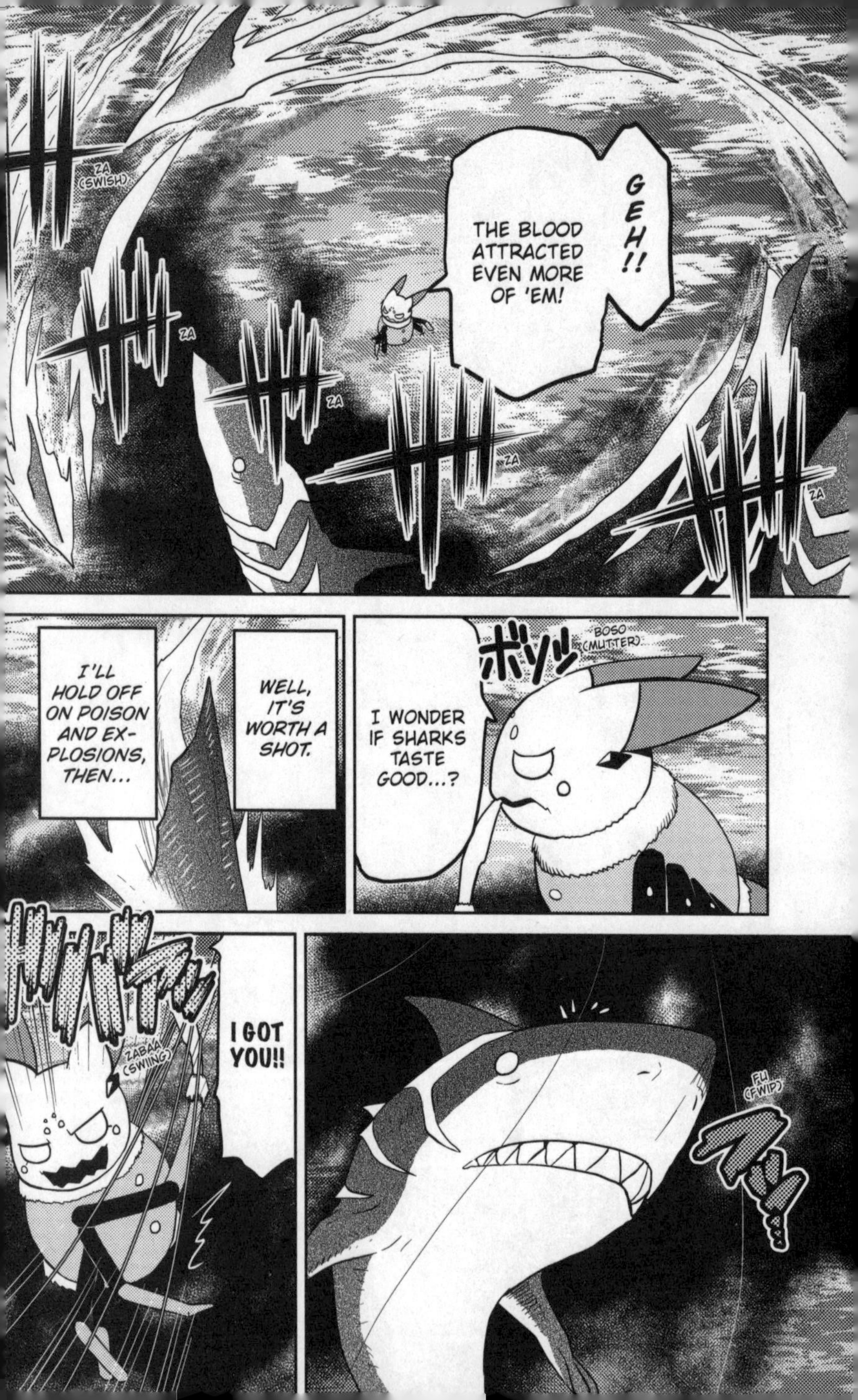
GEH!!
THE BLOOD ATTRACTED EVEN MORE OF 'EM!
ZA
ZA
ZA
ZA
ZA (SWISH)
ボソッ
BOSO (MUTTER)
I WONDER IF SHARKS TASTE GOOD...?
WELL, IT'S WORTH A SHOT.
I'LL HOLD OFF ON POISON AND EX-PLOSIONS, THEN...
FU (FWIP)
I GOT YOU!!
ZABAA (SWIING)

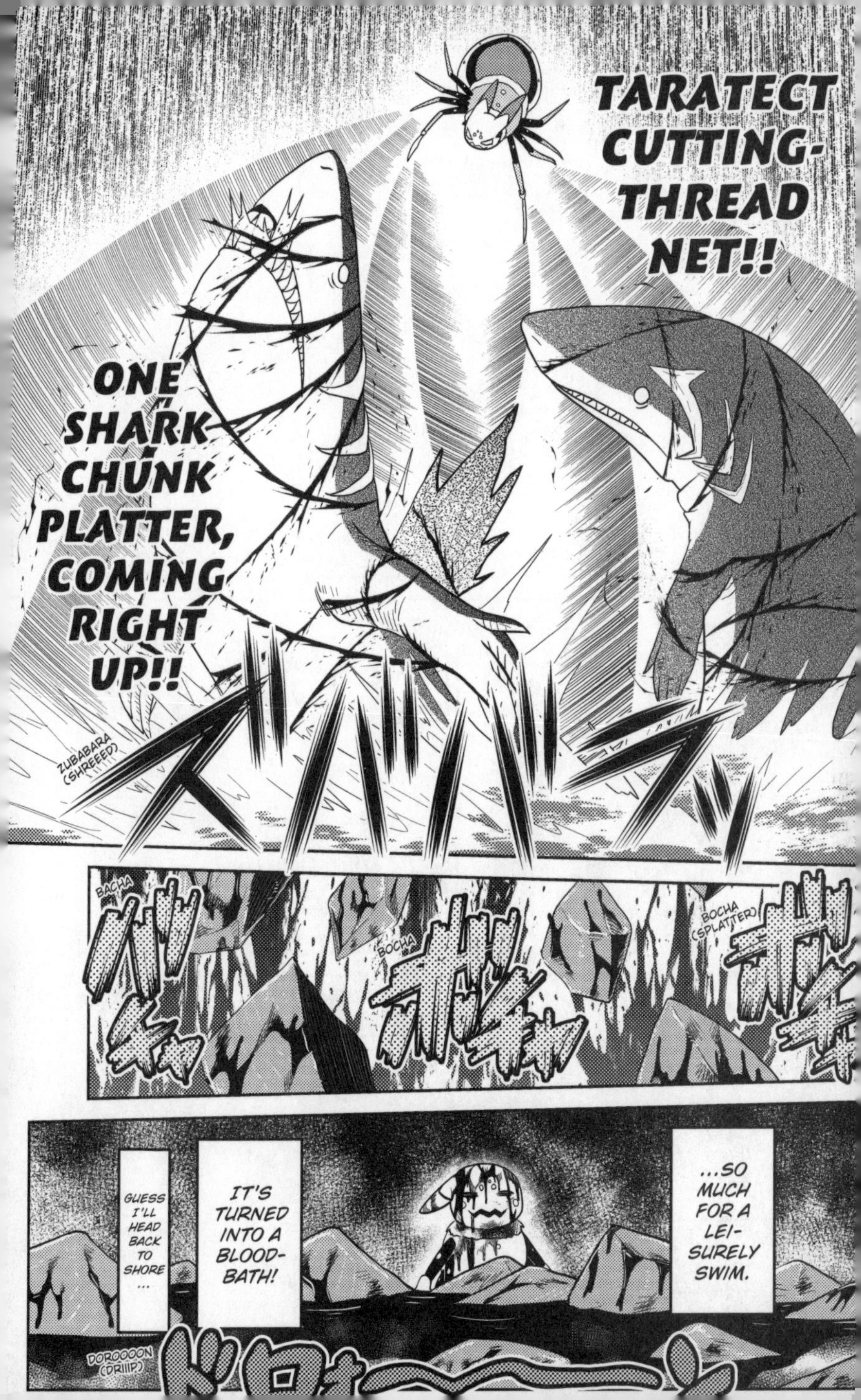
TARATECT CUTTING-THREAD NET!!
ONE SHARK CHUNK PLATTER, COMING RIGHT UP!!
ZUBABARA (SHREEED)
BOCHA (SPLATTER)
BOCHA
BACHA
...SO MUCH FOR A LEI-SURELY SWIM.
IT'S TURNED INTO A BLOOD-BATH!
GUESS I'LL HEAD BACK TO SHORE...
DOROOOON (DRIIIP)

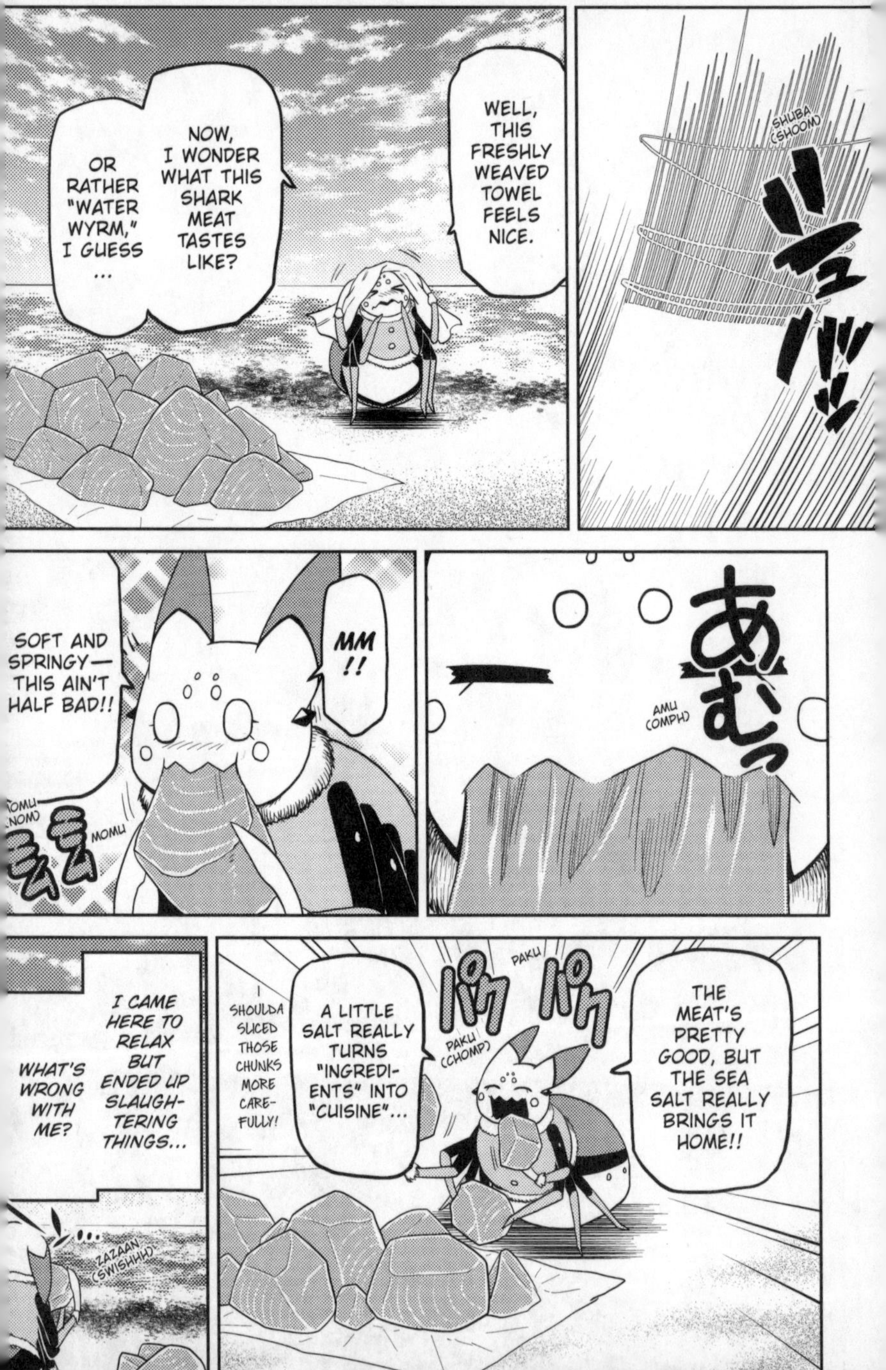
SHUBA (SHOOM)
WELL, THIS FRESHLY WEAVED TOWEL FEELS NICE.
NOW, I WONDER WHAT THIS SHARK MEAT TASTES LIKE?
OR RATHER "WATER WYRM," I GUESS ...
あむっ
AMU (COMPH)
MM!!
SOFT AND SPRINGY— THIS AIN'T HALF BAD!!
MOMU
MOMU (NOM)
THE MEAT'S PRETTY GOOD, BUT THE SEA SALT REALLY BRINGS IT HOME!!
PAKU
パクパク
PAKU (CHOMP)
A LITTLE SALT REALLY TURNS "INGREDI-ENTS" INTO "CUISINE"...
I SHOULDA SLICED THOSE CHUNKS MORE CARE-FULLY!
I CAME HERE TO RELAX BUT ENDED UP SLAUGH-TERING THINGS...
WHAT'S WRONG WITH ME?
...
ZAZAAN (SWISHHH)

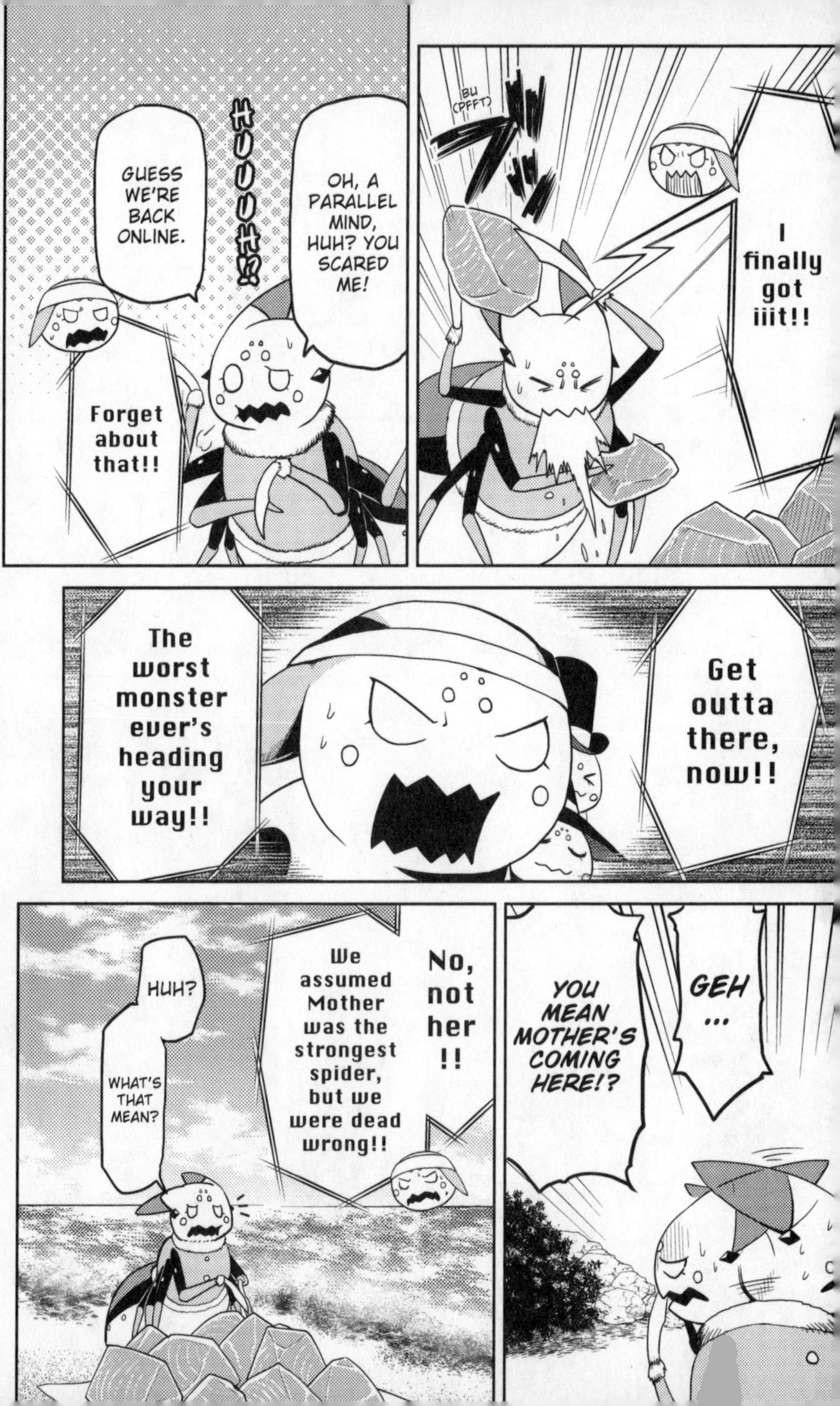
BU (PFFT)
I finally got iiit!!
OH, A PARALLEL MIND, HUH? YOU SCARED ME!
HUUUH!?
GUESS WE'RE BACK ONLINE.
Forget about that!!
Get outta there, now!!
The worst monster ever's heading your way!!
GEH...
YOU MEAN MOTHER'S COMING HERE!?
No, not her!!
We assumed Mother was the strongest spider, but we were dead wrong!!
HUH?
WHAT'S THAT MEAN?

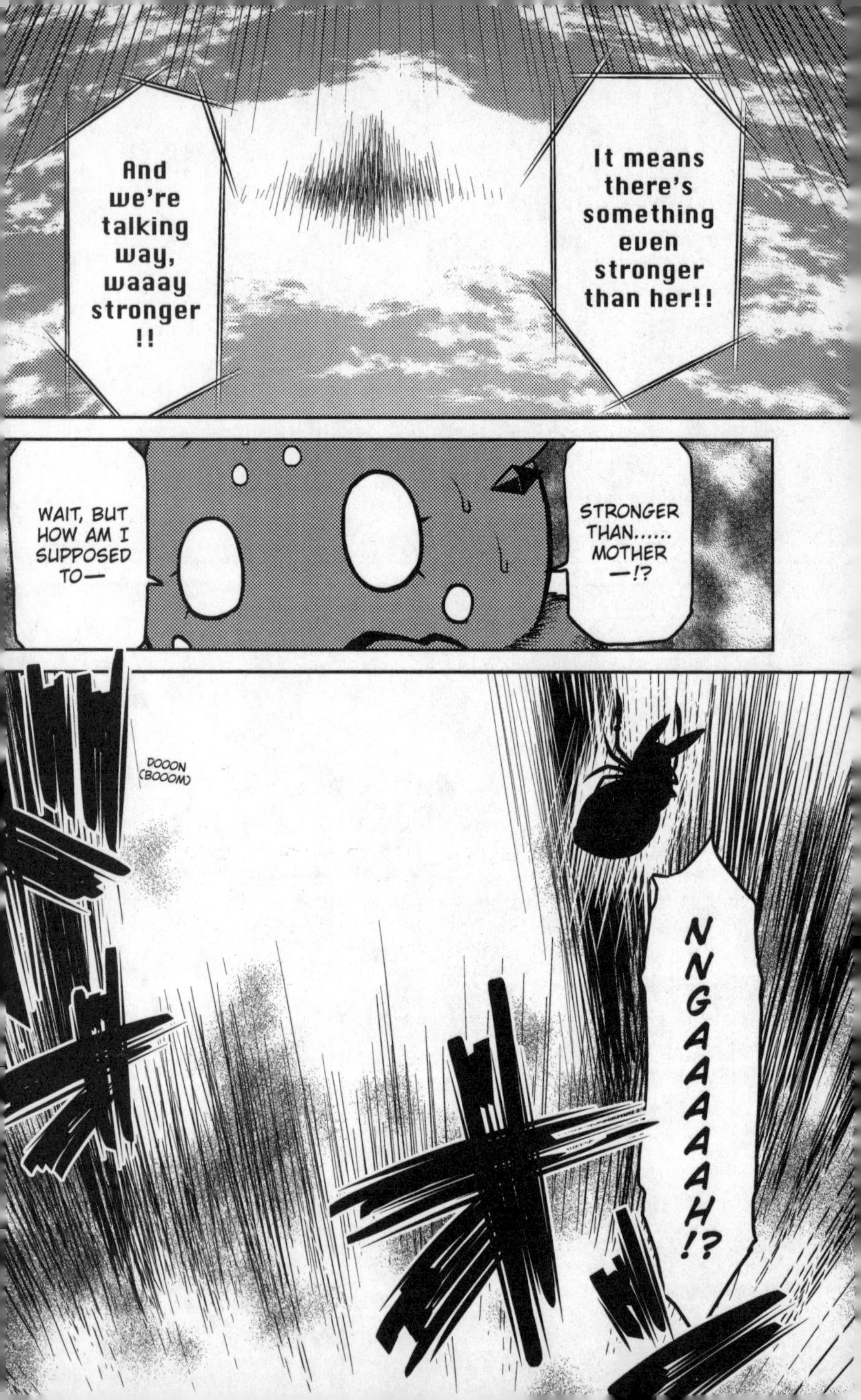
It means there's something even stronger than her!!
And we're talking way, waaay stronger!!
STRONGER THAN...... MOTHER—!?
WAIT, BUT HOW AM I SUPPOSED TO—
NNGAAAAAAAH!?
DOOON (BOOOM)

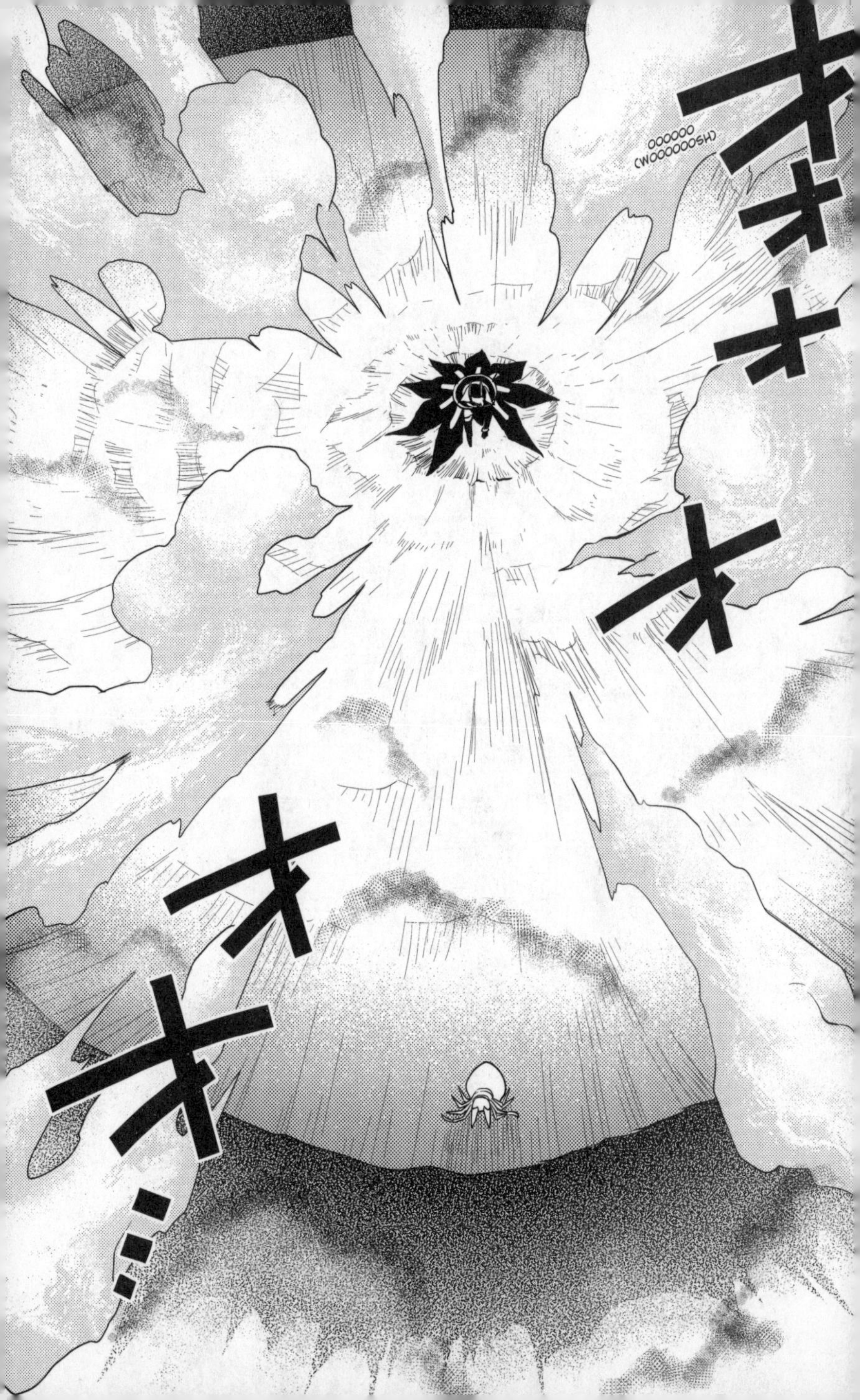
オォォォオオオ…
(WOOOOOOOSH
OOOOOO)

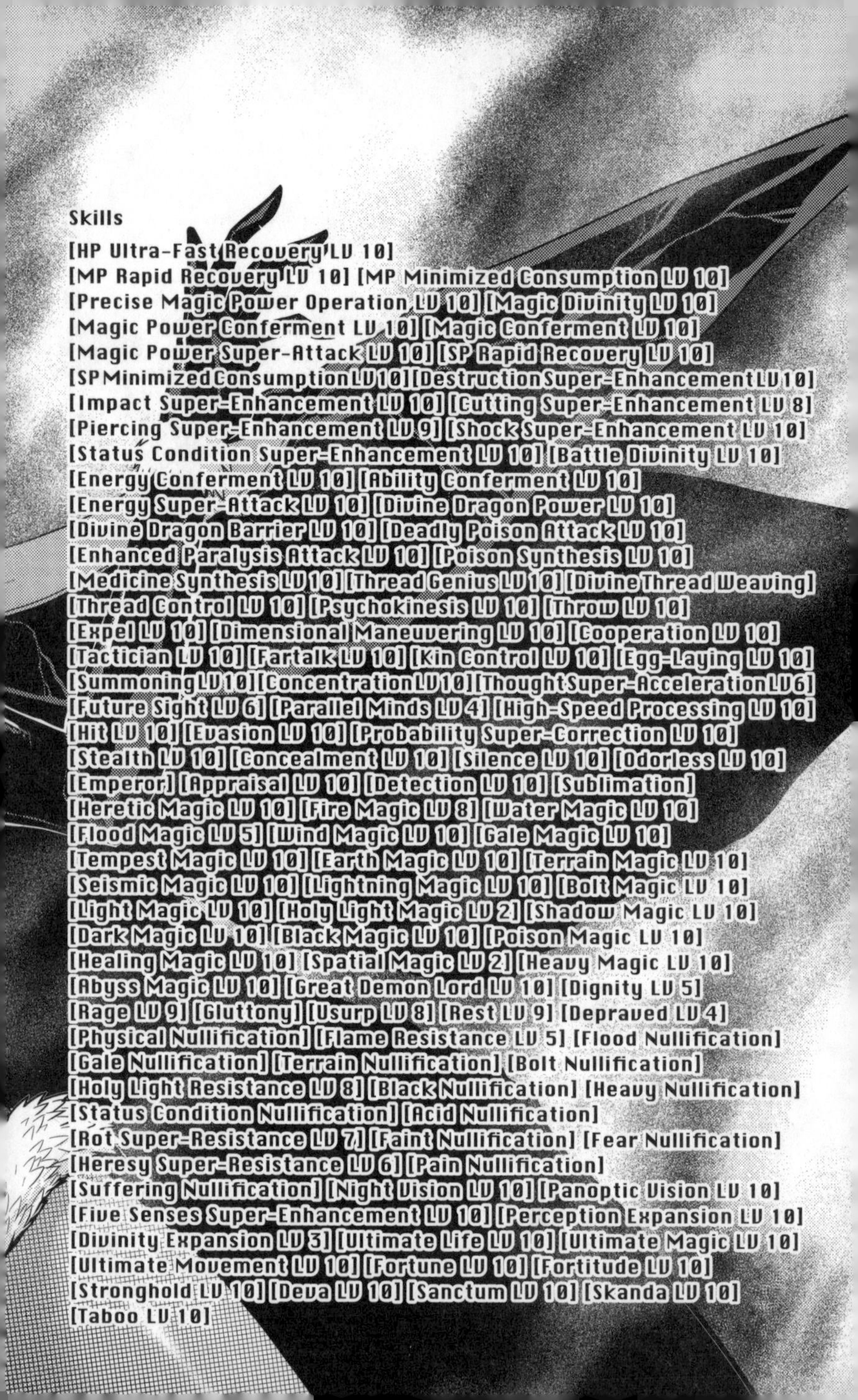

Skills

[HP Ultra-Fast Recovery LV 10]
[MP Rapid Recovery LV 10] [MP Minimized Consumption LV 10]
[Precise Magic Power Operation LV 10] [Magic Divinity LV 10]
[Magic Power Conferment LV 10] [Magic Conferment LV 10]
[Magic Power Super-Attack LV 10] [SP Rapid Recovery LV 10]
[SP Minimized Consumption LV 10] [Destruction Super-Enhancement LV 10]
[Impact Super-Enhancement LV 10] [Cutting Super-Enhancement LV 8]
[Piercing Super-Enhancement LV 9] [Shock Super-Enhancement LV 10]
[Status Condition Super-Enhancement LV 10] [Battle Divinity LV 10]
[Energy Conferment LV 10] [Ability Conferment LV 10]
[Energy Super-Attack LV 10] [Divine Dragon Power LV 10]
[Divine Dragon Barrier LV 10] [Deadly Poison Attack LV 10]
[Enhanced Paralysis Attack LV 10] [Poison Synthesis LV 10]
[Medicine Synthesis LV 10] [Thread Genius LV 10] [Divine Thread Weaving]
[Thread Control LV 10] [Psychokinesis LV 10] [Throw LV 10]
[Expel LV 10] [Dimensional Maneuvering LV 10] [Cooperation LV 10]
[Tactician LV 10] [Fartalk LV 10] [Kin Control LV 10] [Egg-Laying LV 10]
[Summoning LV 10] [Concentration LV 10] [Thought Super-Acceleration LV 6]
[Future Sight LV 6] [Parallel Minds LV 4] [High-Speed Processing LV 10]
[Hit LV 10] [Evasion LV 10] [Probability Super-Correction LV 10]
[Stealth LV 10] [Concealment LV 10] [Silence LV 10] [Odorless LV 10]
[Emperor] [Appraisal LV 10] [Detection LV 10] [Sublimation]
[Heretic Magic LV 10] [Fire Magic LV 8] [Water Magic LV 10]
[Flood Magic LV 5] [Wind Magic LV 10] [Gale Magic LV 10]
[Tempest Magic LV 10] [Earth Magic LV 10] [Terrain Magic LV 10]
[Seismic Magic LV 10] [Lightning Magic LV 10] [Bolt Magic LV 10]
[Light Magic LV 10] [Holy Light Magic LV 2] [Shadow Magic LV 10]
[Dark Magic LV 10] [Black Magic LV 10] [Poison Magic LV 10]
[Healing Magic LV 10] [Spatial Magic LV 2] [Heavy Magic LV 10]
[Abyss Magic LV 10] [Great Demon Lord LV 10] [Dignity LV 5]
[Rage LV 9] [Gluttony] [Usurp LV 8] [Rest LV 9] [Depraved LV 4]
[Physical Nullification] [Flame Resistance LV 5] [Flood Nullification]
[Gale Nullification] [Terrain Nullification] [Bolt Nullification]
[Holy Light Resistance LV 8] [Black Nullification] [Heavy Nullification]
[Status Condition Nullification] [Acid Nullification]
[Rot Super-Resistance LV 7] [Faint Nullification] [Fear Nullification]
[Heresy Super-Resistance LV 6] [Pain Nullification]
[Suffering Nullification] [Night Vision LV 10] [Panoptic Vision LV 10]
[Five Senses Super-Enhancement LV 10] [Perception Expansion LV 10]
[Divinity Expansion LV 3] [Ultimate Life LV 10] [Ultimate Magic LV 10]
[Ultimate Movement LV 10] [Fortune LV 10] [Fortitude LV 10]
[Stronghold LV 10] [Deva LV 10] [Sanctum LV 10] [Skanda LV 10]
[Taboo LV 10]

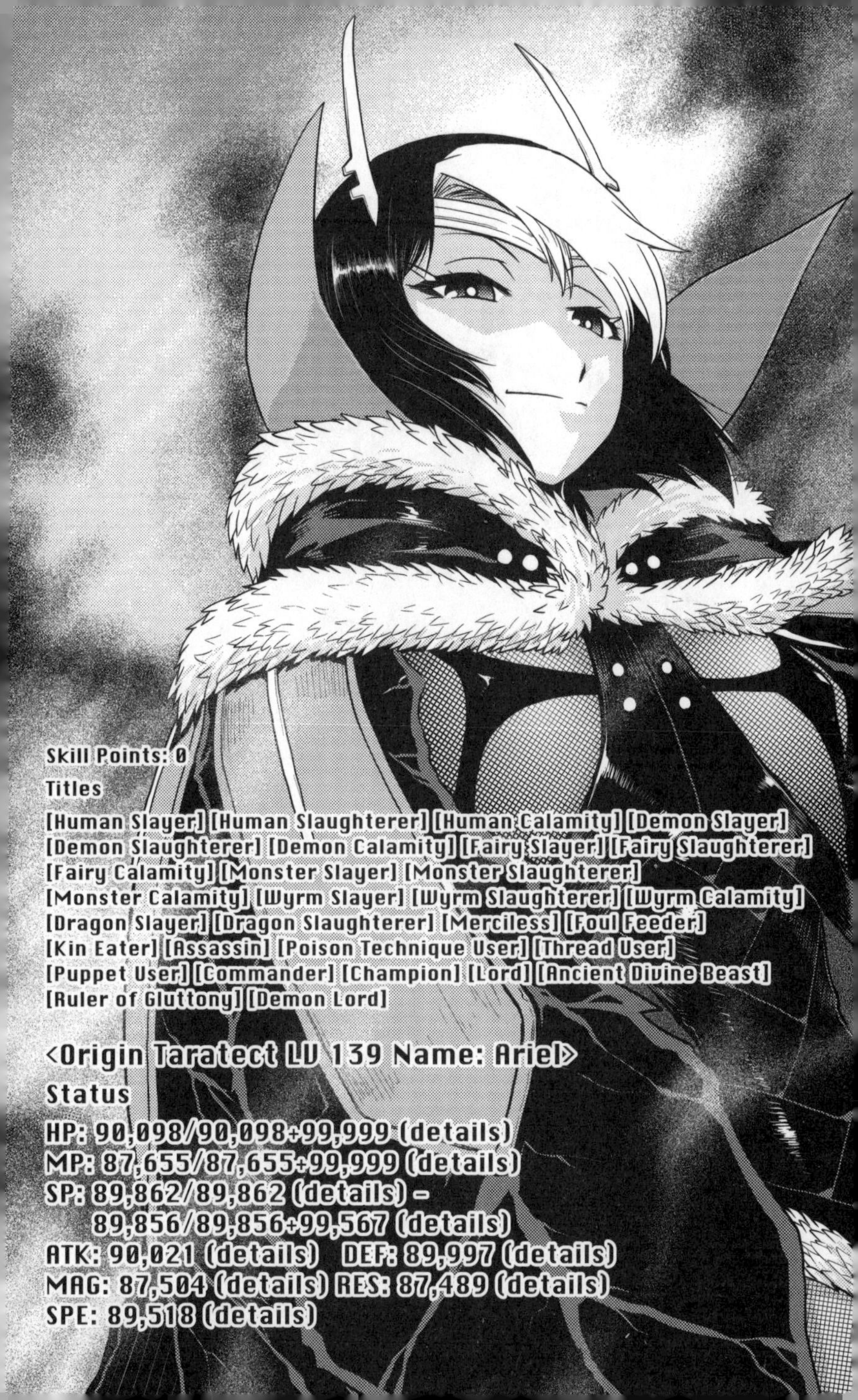
Skill Points: 0
Titles
[Human Slayer] [Human Slaughterer] [Human Calamity] [Demon Slayer] [Demon Slaughterer] [Demon Calamity] [Fairy Slayer] [Fairy Slaughterer] [Fairy Calamity] [Monster Slayer] [Monster Slaughterer] [Monster Calamity] [Wyrm Slayer] [Wyrm Slaughterer] [Wyrm Calamity] [Dragon Slayer] [Dragon Slaughterer] [Merciless] [Foul Feeder] [Kin Eater] [Assassin] [Poison Technique User] [Thread User] [Puppet User] [Commander] [Champion] [Lord] [Ancient Divine Beast] [Ruler of Gluttony] [Demon Lord]
<Origin Taratect LV 139 Name: Ariel>
Status
HP: 90,098/90,098+99,999 (details)
MP: 87,655/87,655+99,999 (details)
SP: 89,862/89,862 (details) – 89,856/89,856+99,567 (details)
ATK: 90,021 (details) DEF: 89,997 (details)
MAG: 87,504 (details) RES: 87,489 (details)
SPE: 89,518 (details)

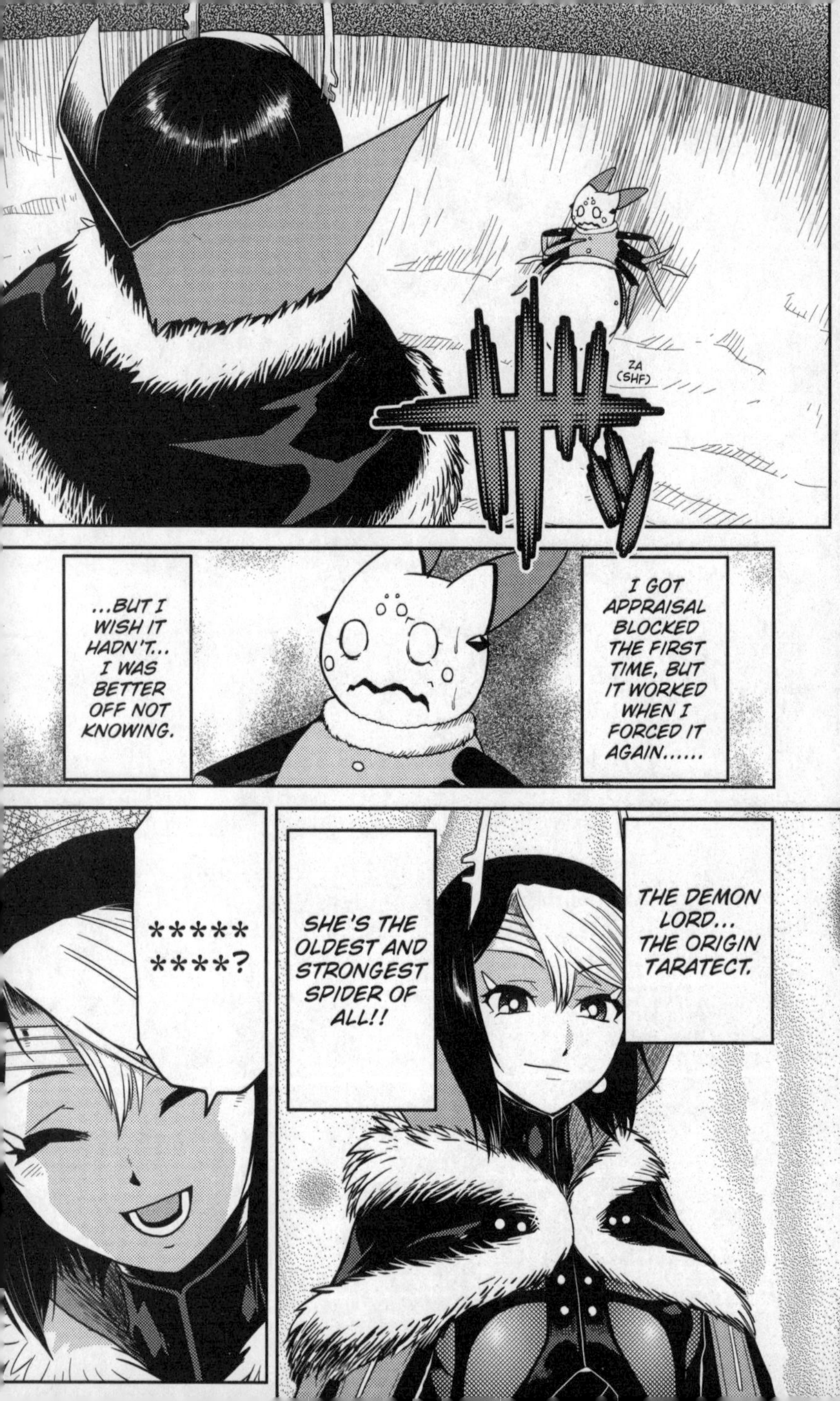
ZA (SHF)
I GOT APPRAISAL BLOCKED THE FIRST TIME, BUT IT WORKED WHEN I FORCED IT AGAIN......
...BUT I WISH IT HADN'T... I WAS BETTER OFF NOT KNOWING.
THE DEMON LORD... THE ORIGIN TARATECT.
SHE'S THE OLDEST AND STRONGEST SPIDER OF ALL!!
*****
****?

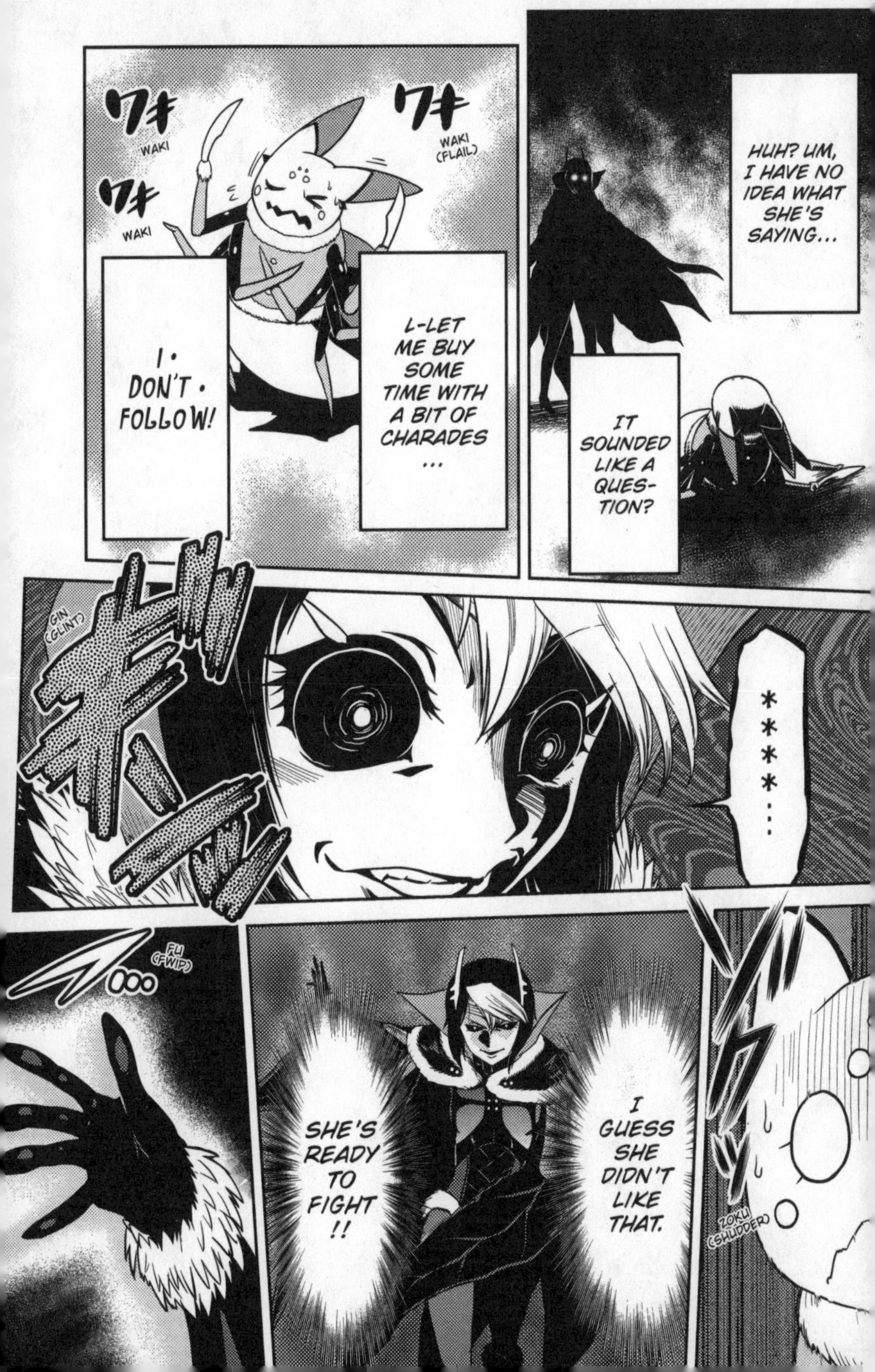
HUH? UM, I HAVE NO IDEA WHAT SHE'S SAYING...
IT SOUNDED LIKE A QUES-TION?
ワキ
WAKI (FLAIL)
L-LET ME BUY SOME TIME WITH A BIT OF CHARADES...
ワキ
WAKI
ワキ
WAKI
I · DON'T · FOLLOW!
****...
GIN (GLINT)
ZOKU (SHUDDER)
I GUESS SHE DIDN'T LIKE THAT.
SHE'S READY TO FIGHT!!
FU (FWIP)

GO
(SMASH)

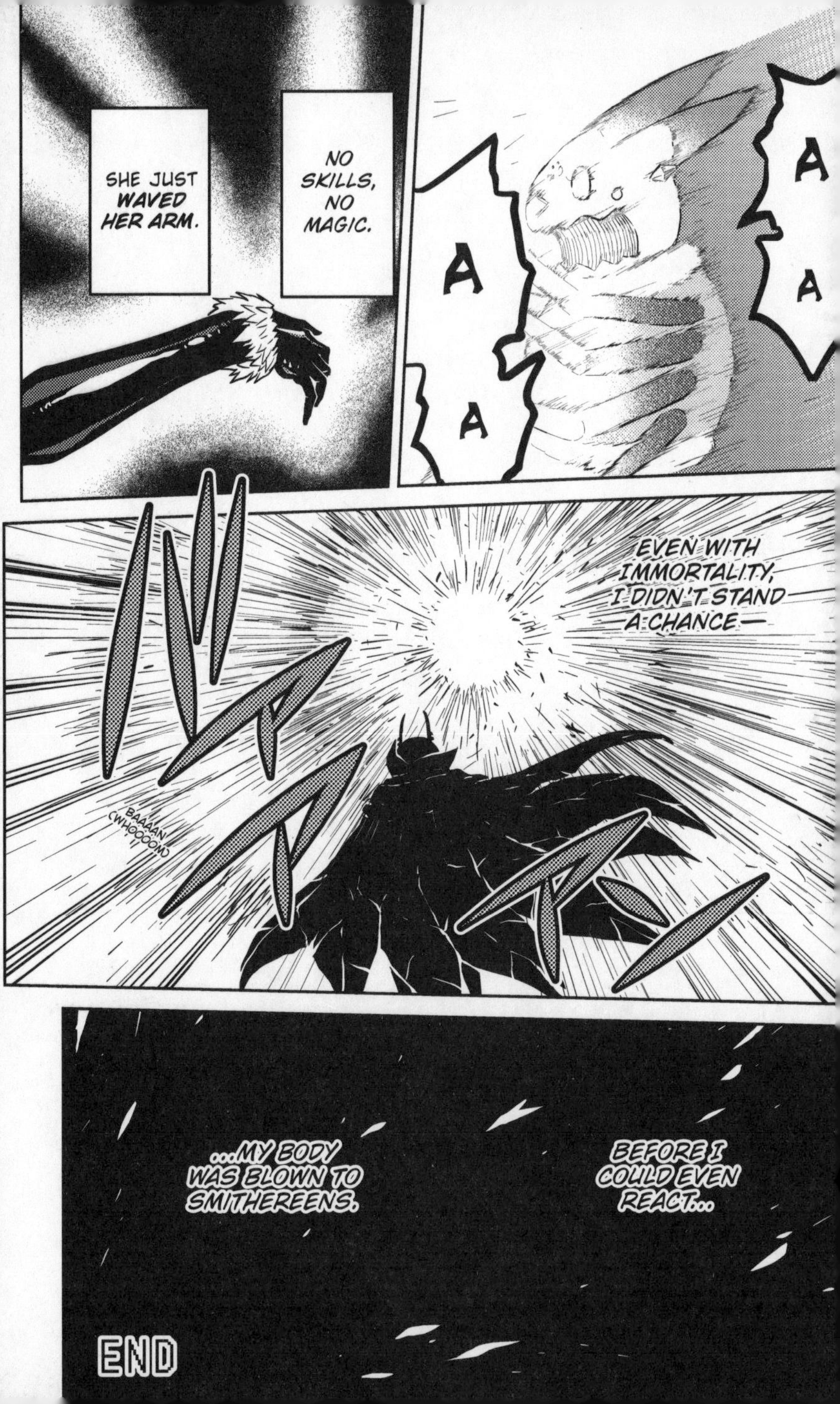
A
A
A
A
NO SKILLS, NO MAGIC.
SHE JUST WAVED HER ARM.
EVEN WITH IMMORTALITY, I DIDN'T STAND A CHANCE—
BAAAAN (WHOOOOM)
BEFORE I COULD EVEN REACT...
...MY BODY WAS BLOWN TO SMITHEREENS.
END

So I'm a Spider, So What?

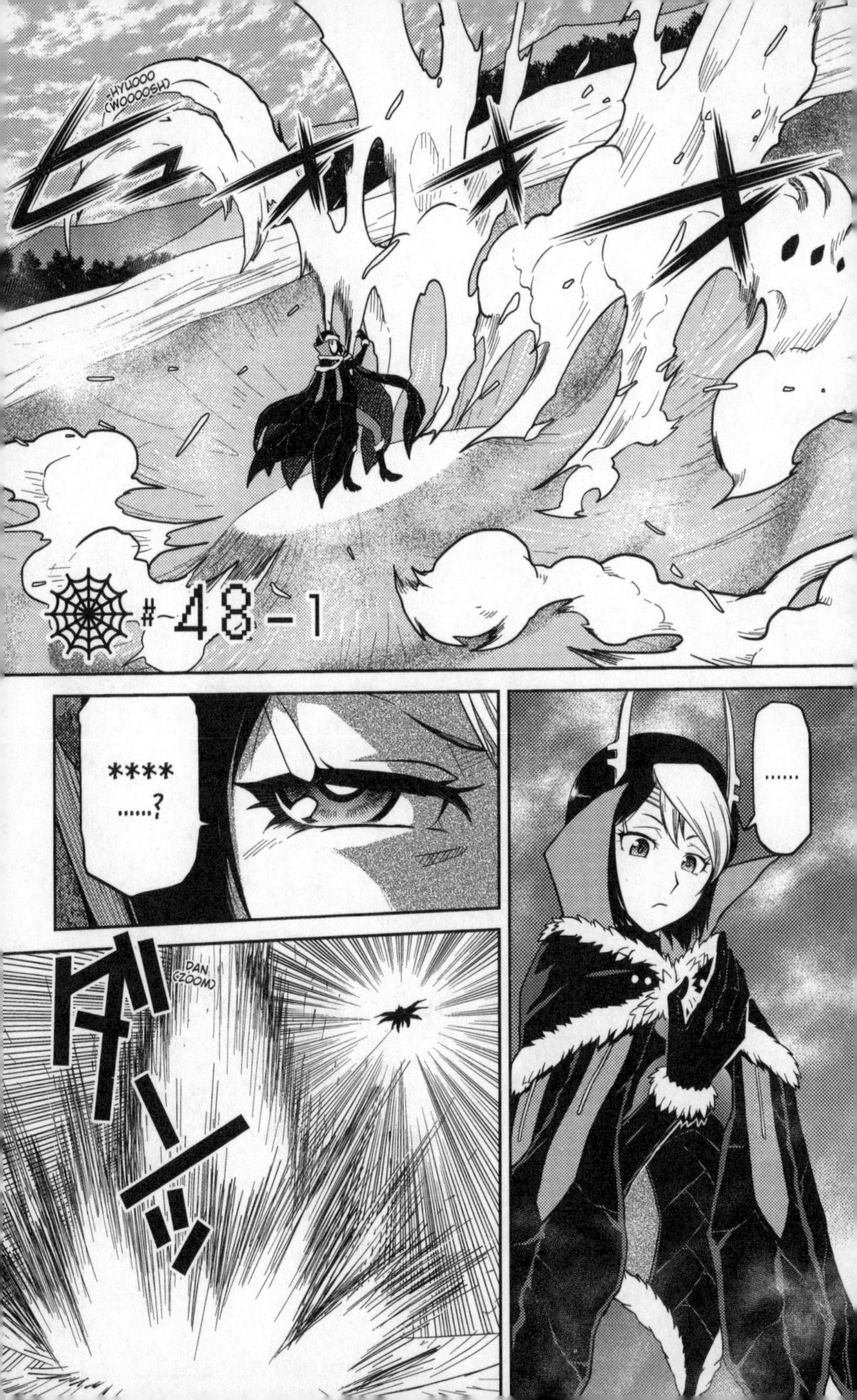
HYUOOO (WOOOOSH)
#48-1
......
****......?
DAN (ZOOM)

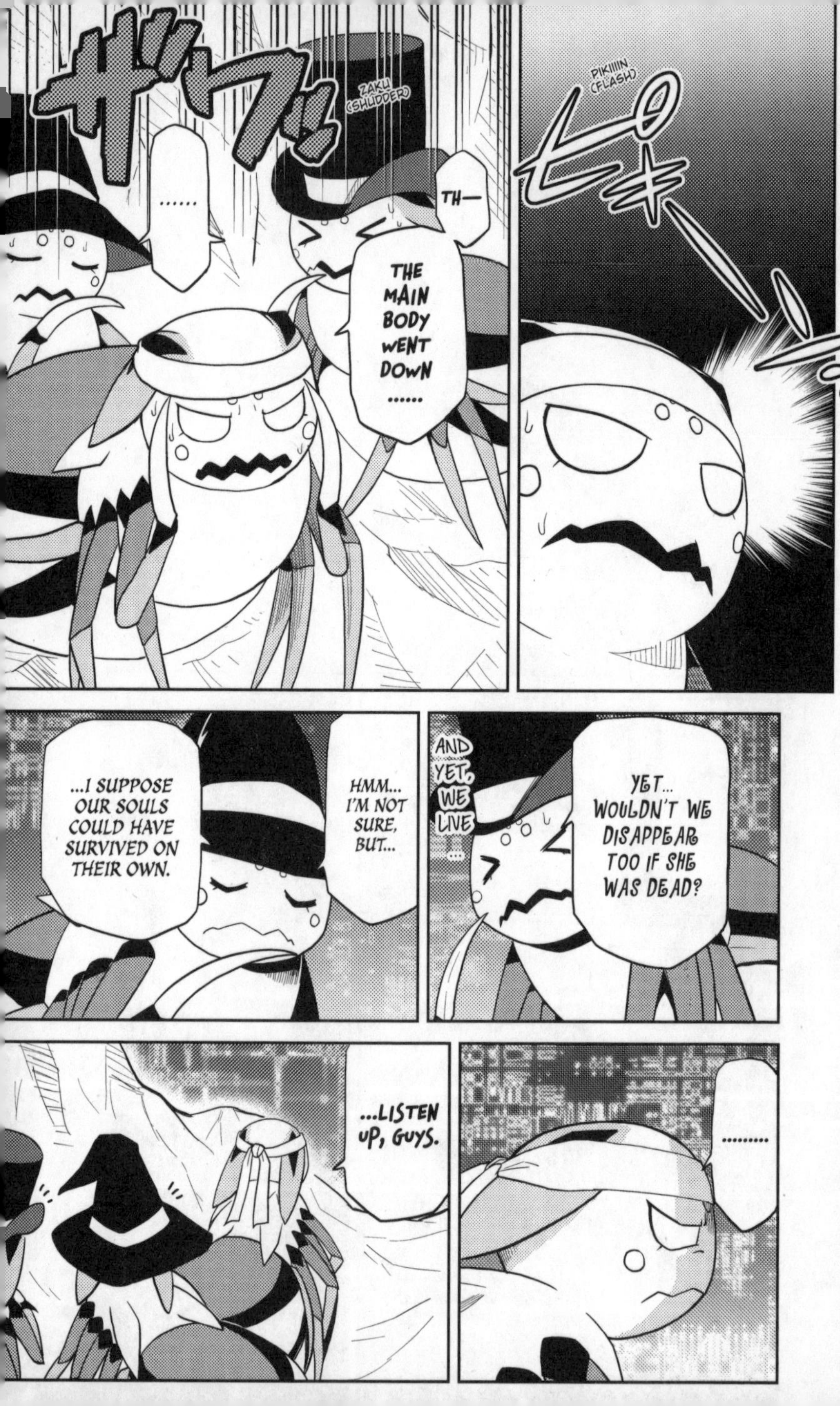
PIKIIIN (FLASH)
ZAKU (SHUDDER)
TH—
THE MAIN BODY WENT DOWN ......
......
YET... WOULDN'T WE DISAPPEAR TOO IF SHE WAS DEAD?
AND YET, WE LIVE ......
HMM... I'M NOT SURE, BUT...
...I SUPPOSE OUR SOULS COULD HAVE SURVIVED ON THEIR OWN.
....
...LISTEN UP, GUYS.

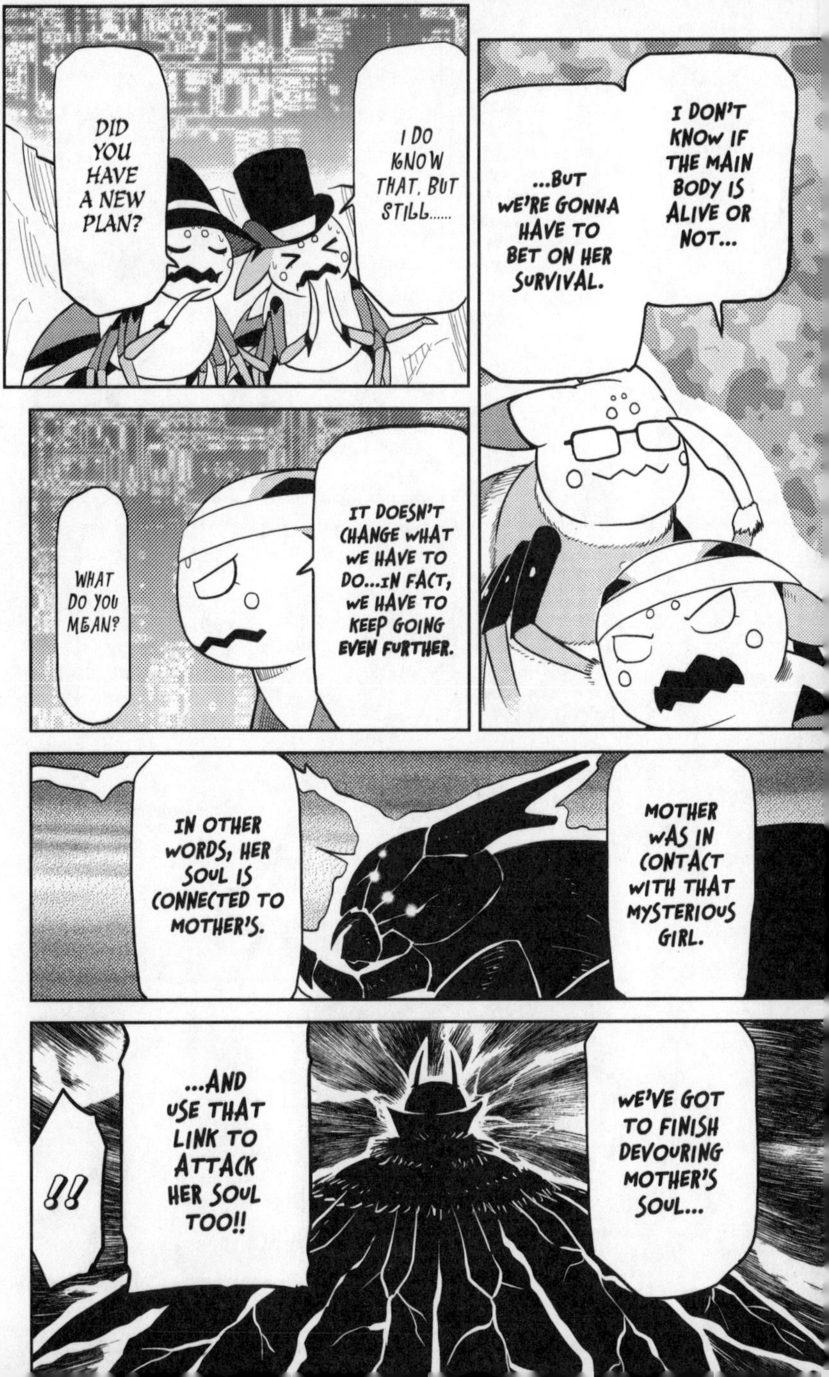
I DON'T KNOW IF THE MAIN BODY IS ALIVE OR NOT...
...BUT WE'RE GONNA HAVE TO BET ON HER SURVIVAL.
I DO KNOW THAT, BUT STILL......
DID YOU HAVE A NEW PLAN?
IT DOESN'T CHANGE WHAT WE HAVE TO DO...IN FACT, WE HAVE TO KEEP GOING EVEN FURTHER.
WHAT DO YOU MEAN?
MOTHER WAS IN CONTACT WITH THAT MYSTERIOUS GIRL.
IN OTHER WORDS, HER SOUL IS CONNECTED TO MOTHER'S.
WE'VE GOT TO FINISH DEVOURING MOTHER'S SOUL...
...AND USE THAT LINK TO ATTACK HER SOUL TOO!!
!!

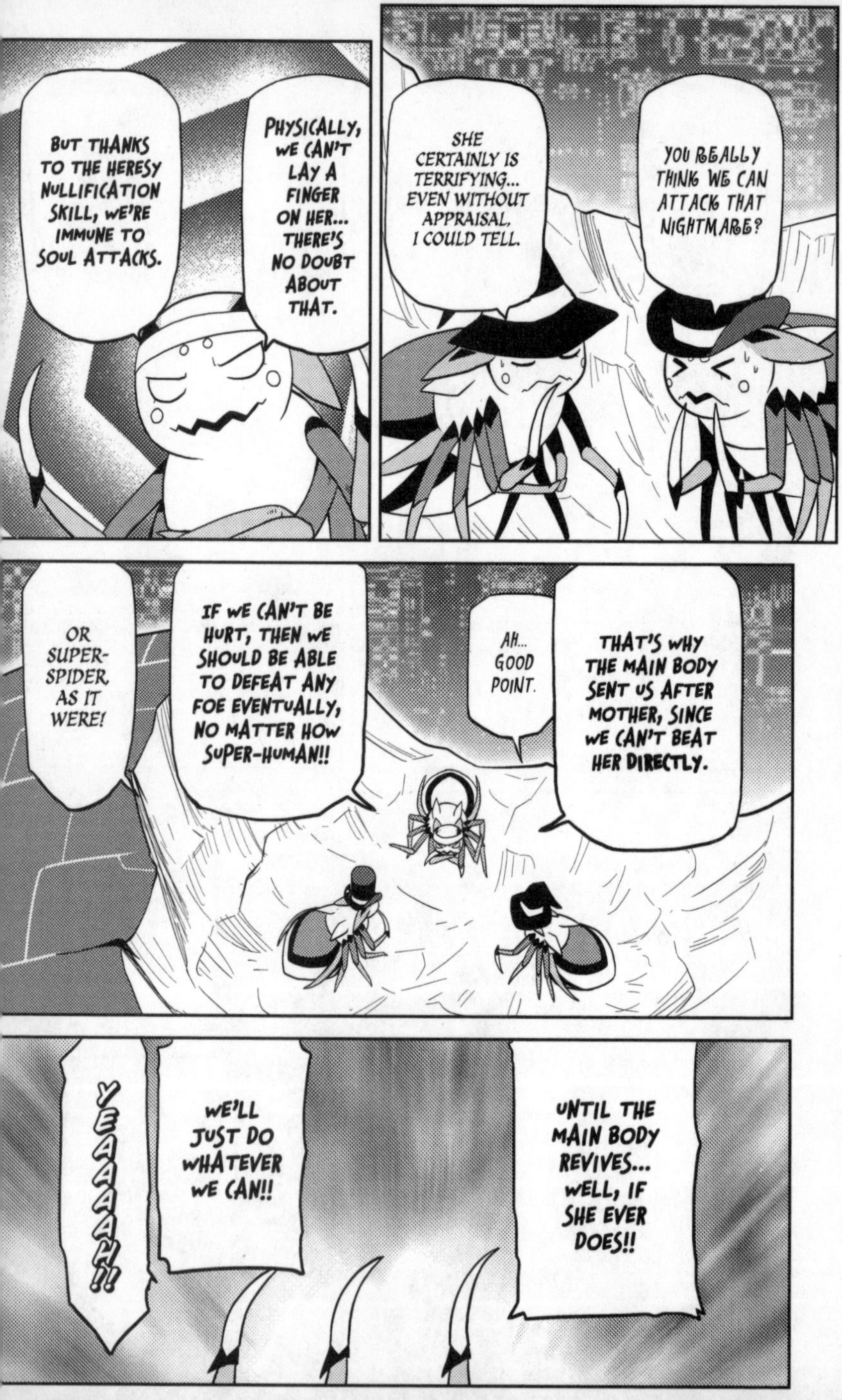
YOU REALLY THINK WE CAN ATTACK THAT NIGHTMARE?
SHE CERTAINLY IS TERRIFYING... EVEN WITHOUT APPRAISAL, I COULD TELL.
PHYSICALLY, WE CAN'T LAY A FINGER ON HER... THERE'S NO DOUBT ABOUT THAT.
BUT THANKS TO THE HERESY NULLIFICATION SKILL, WE'RE IMMUNE TO SOUL ATTACKS.
THAT'S WHY THE MAIN BODY SENT US AFTER MOTHER, SINCE WE CAN'T BEAT HER DIRECTLY.
AH... GOOD POINT.
IF WE CAN'T BE HURT, THEN WE SHOULD BE ABLE TO DEFEAT ANY FOE EVENTUALLY, NO MATTER HOW SUPER-HUMAN!!
OR SUPER-SPIDER, AS IT WERE!
UNTIL THE MAIN BODY REVIVES... WELL, IF SHE EVER DOES!!
WE'LL JUST DO WHATEVER WE CAN!!
YEAAAAAH!!

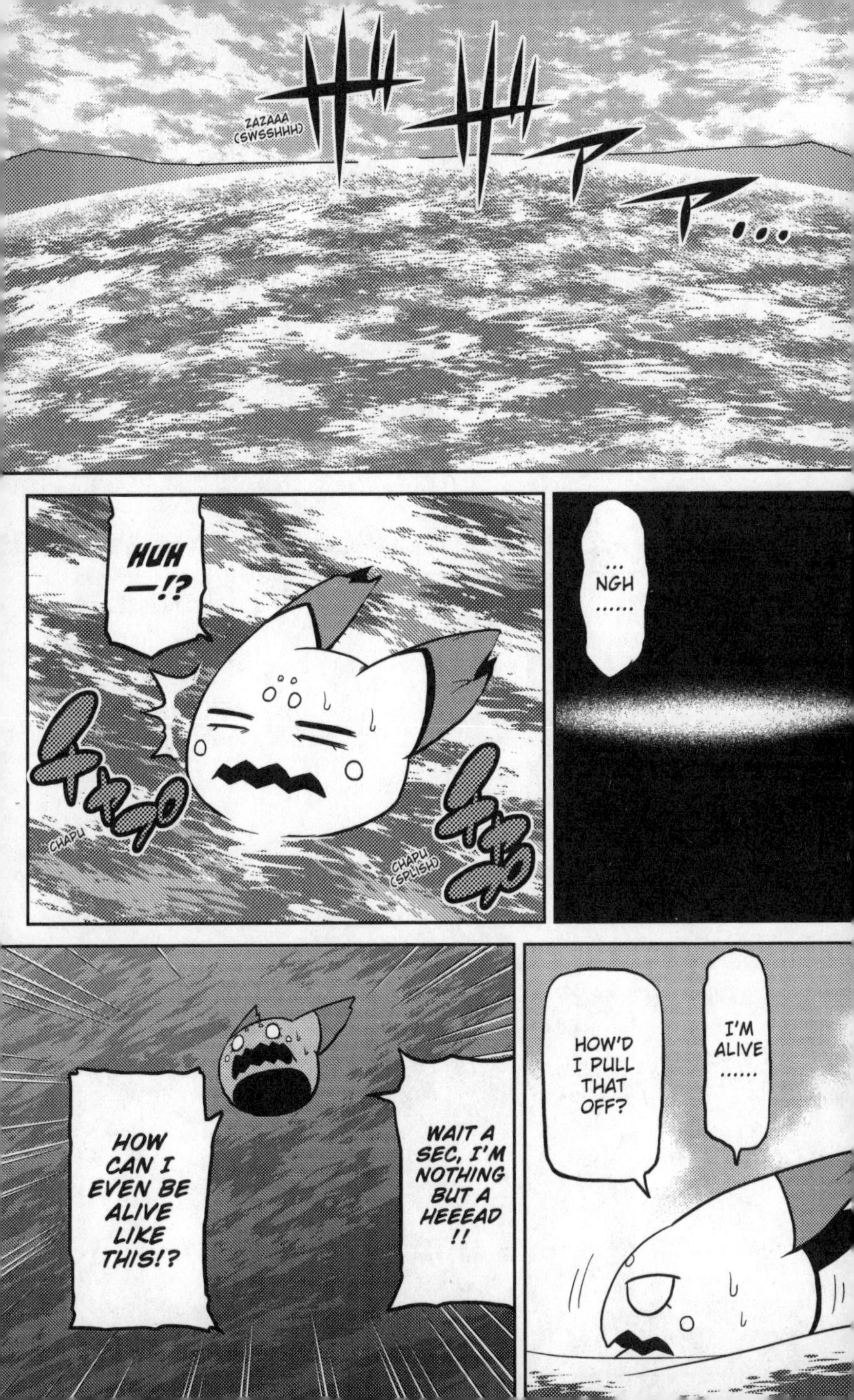

ZAZAAA (SWSSHHH)
... NGH ......
HUH —!?
CHAPU (SPLISH)
CHAPU
I'M ALIVE ......
HOW'D I PULL THAT OFF?
WAIT A SEC, I'M NOTHING BUT A HEEEAD !!
HOW CAN I EVEN BE ALIVE LIKE THIS!?

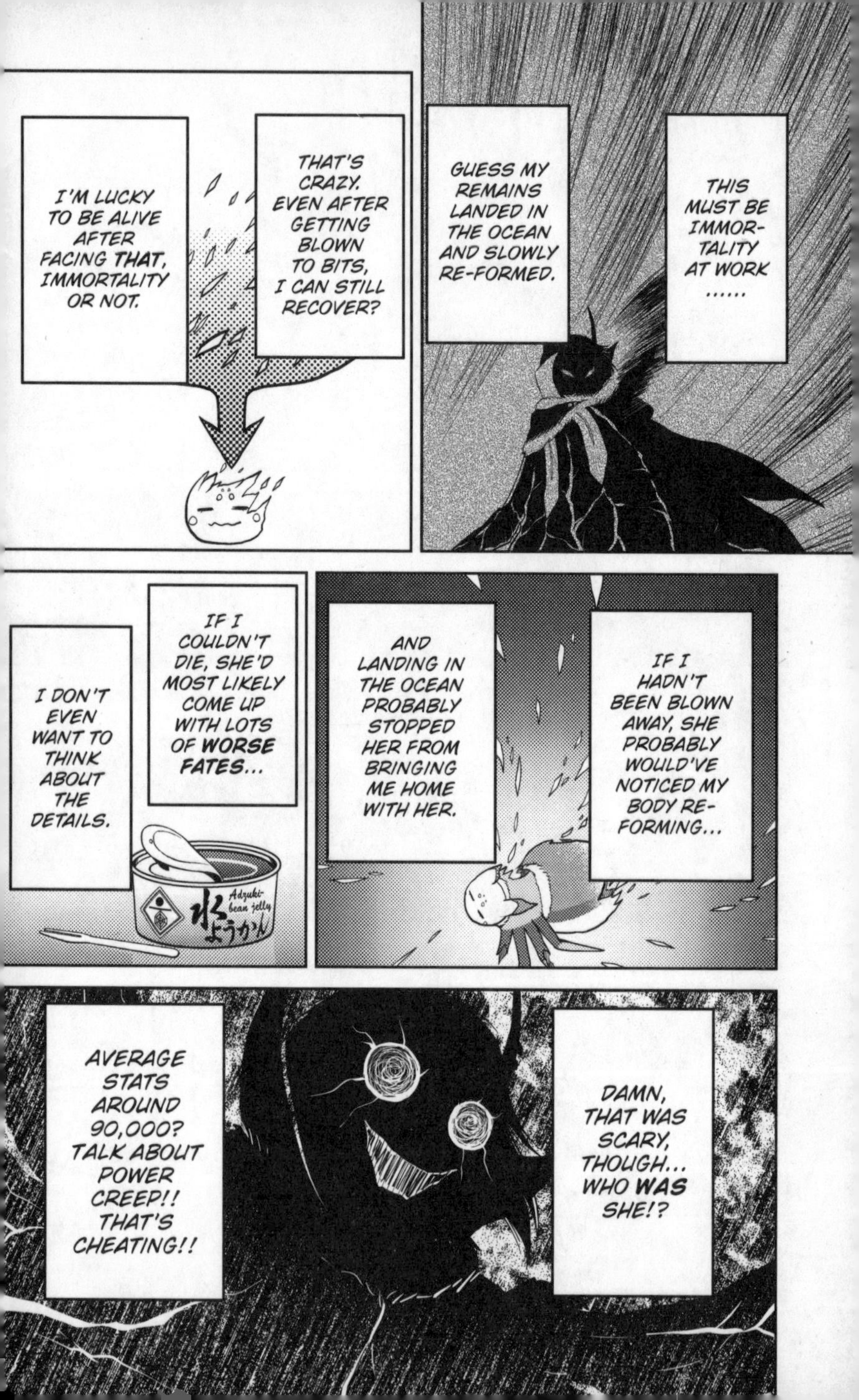
THIS MUST BE IMMORTALITY AT WORK......
GUESS MY REMAINS LANDED IN THE OCEAN AND SLOWLY RE-FORMED.
THAT'S CRAZY. EVEN AFTER GETTING BLOWN TO BITS, I CAN STILL RECOVER?
I'M LUCKY TO BE ALIVE AFTER FACING **THAT**, IMMORTALITY OR NOT.
IF I HADN'T BEEN BLOWN AWAY, SHE PROBABLY WOULD'VE NOTICED MY BODY RE-FORMING...
AND LANDING IN THE OCEAN PROBABLY STOPPED HER FROM BRINGING ME HOME WITH HER.
IF I COULDN'T DIE, SHE'D MOST LIKELY COME UP WITH LOTS OF **WORSE FATES**...
I DON'T EVEN WANT TO THINK ABOUT THE DETAILS.
Adzuki-bean jelly
水ようかん
DAMN, THAT WAS SCARY, THOUGH... WHO **WAS** SHE!?
AVERAGE STATS AROUND 90,000? TALK ABOUT POWER CREEP!! THAT'S CHEATING!!

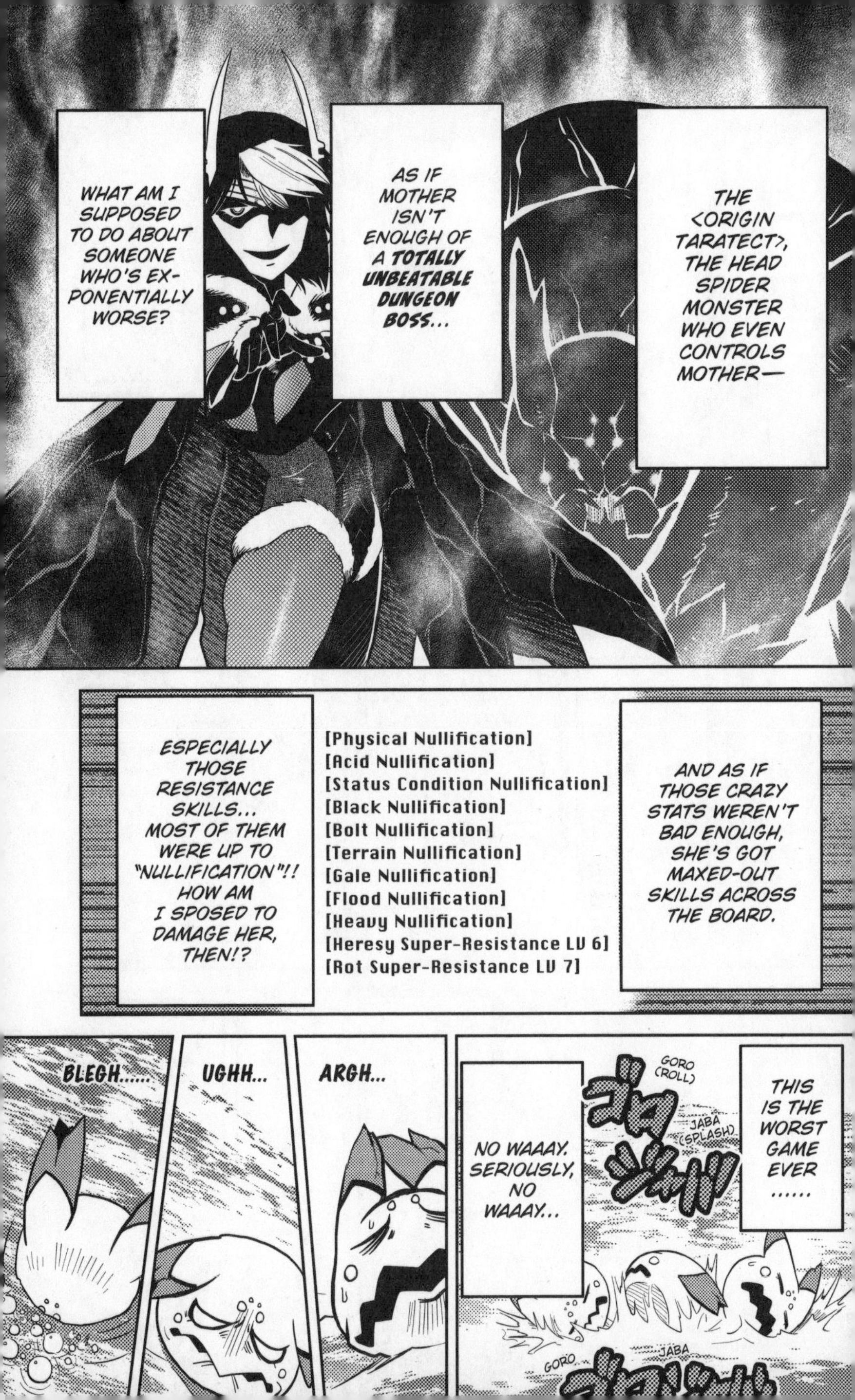
THE <ORIGIN TARATECT>, THE HEAD SPIDER MONSTER WHO EVEN CONTROLS MOTHER—
AS IF MOTHER ISN'T ENOUGH OF A **TOTALLY UNBEATABLE DUNGEON BOSS...**
WHAT AM I SUPPOSED TO DO ABOUT SOMEONE WHO'S EX-PONENTIALLY WORSE?
AND AS IF THOSE CRAZY STATS WEREN'T BAD ENOUGH, SHE'S GOT MAXED-OUT SKILLS ACROSS THE BOARD.
[Physical Nullification]
[Acid Nullification]
[Status Condition Nullification]
[Black Nullification]
[Bolt Nullification]
[Terrain Nullification]
[Gale Nullification]
[Flood Nullification]
[Heavy Nullification]
[Heresy Super-Resistance LV 6]
[Rot Super-Resistance LV 7]
ESPECIALLY THOSE RESISTANCE SKILLS... MOST OF THEM WERE UP TO "NULLIFICATION"!! HOW AM I SPOSED TO DAMAGE HER, THEN!?
THIS IS THE WORST GAME EVER ......
GORO (ROLL)
JABA (SPLASH)
NO WAAAY. SERIOUSLY, NO WAAAY...
GORO
JABA
ARGH...
UGHH...
BLEGH......

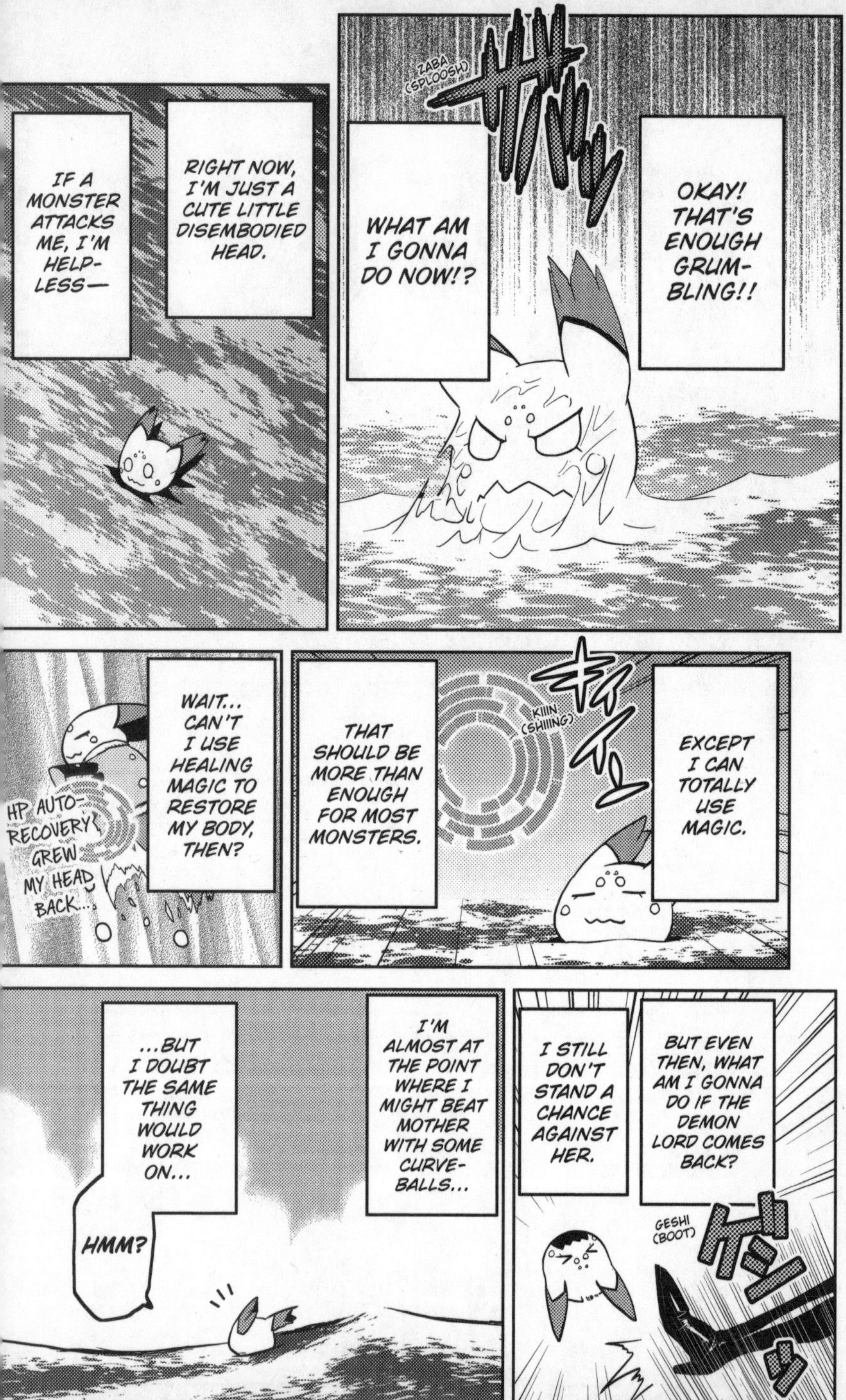
OKAY! THAT'S ENOUGH GRUMBLING!!
ZABA (SPLOOSH)
WHAT AM I GONNA DO NOW!?
RIGHT NOW, I'M JUST A CUTE LITTLE DISEMBODIED HEAD.
IF A MONSTER ATTACKS ME, I'M HELPLESS—
EXCEPT I CAN TOTALLY USE MAGIC.
KIIIN (SHIIING)
THAT SHOULD BE MORE THAN ENOUGH FOR MOST MONSTERS.
WAIT... CAN'T I USE HEALING MAGIC TO RESTORE MY BODY, THEN?
HP AUTO-RECOVERY GREW MY HEAD BACK...
BUT EVEN THEN, WHAT AM I GONNA DO IF THE DEMON LORD COMES BACK?
I STILL DON'T STAND A CHANCE AGAINST HER.
GESHI (BOOT)
I'M ALMOST AT THE POINT WHERE I MIGHT BEAT MOTHER WITH SOME CURVE-BALLS...
...BUT I DOUBT THE SAME THING WOULD WORK ON...
HMM?

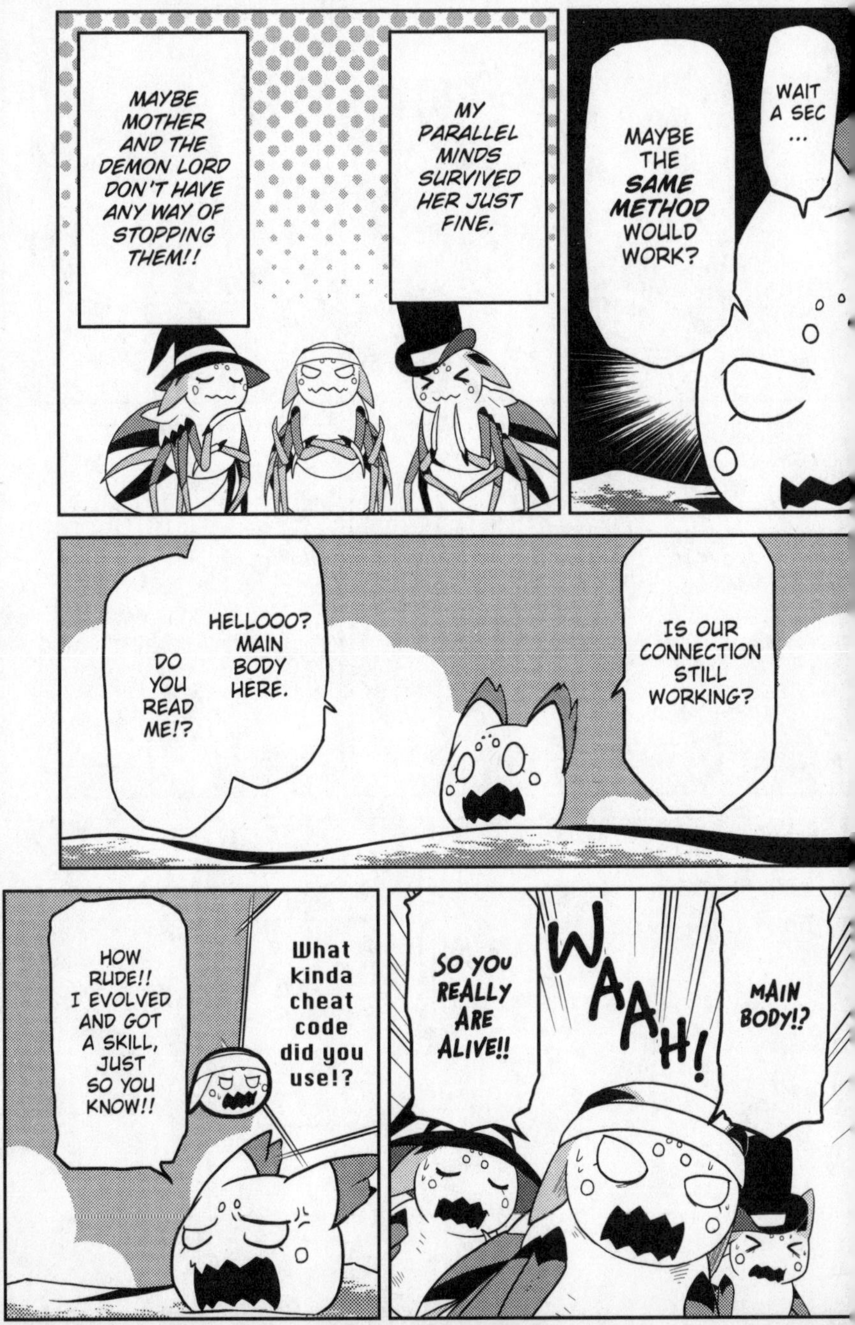
WAIT A SEC...
MAYBE THE SAME METHOD WOULD WORK?
MY PARALLEL MINDS SURVIVED HER JUST FINE.
MAYBE MOTHER AND THE DEMON LORD DON'T HAVE ANY WAY OF STOPPING THEM!!
IS OUR CONNECTION STILL WORKING?
HELLOOO? MAIN BODY HERE.
DO YOU READ ME!?
MAIN BODY!?
WAAAH!
SO YOU REALLY ARE ALIVE!!
What kinda cheat code did you use!?
HOW RUDE!! I EVOLVED AND GOT A SKILL, JUST SO YOU KNOW!!

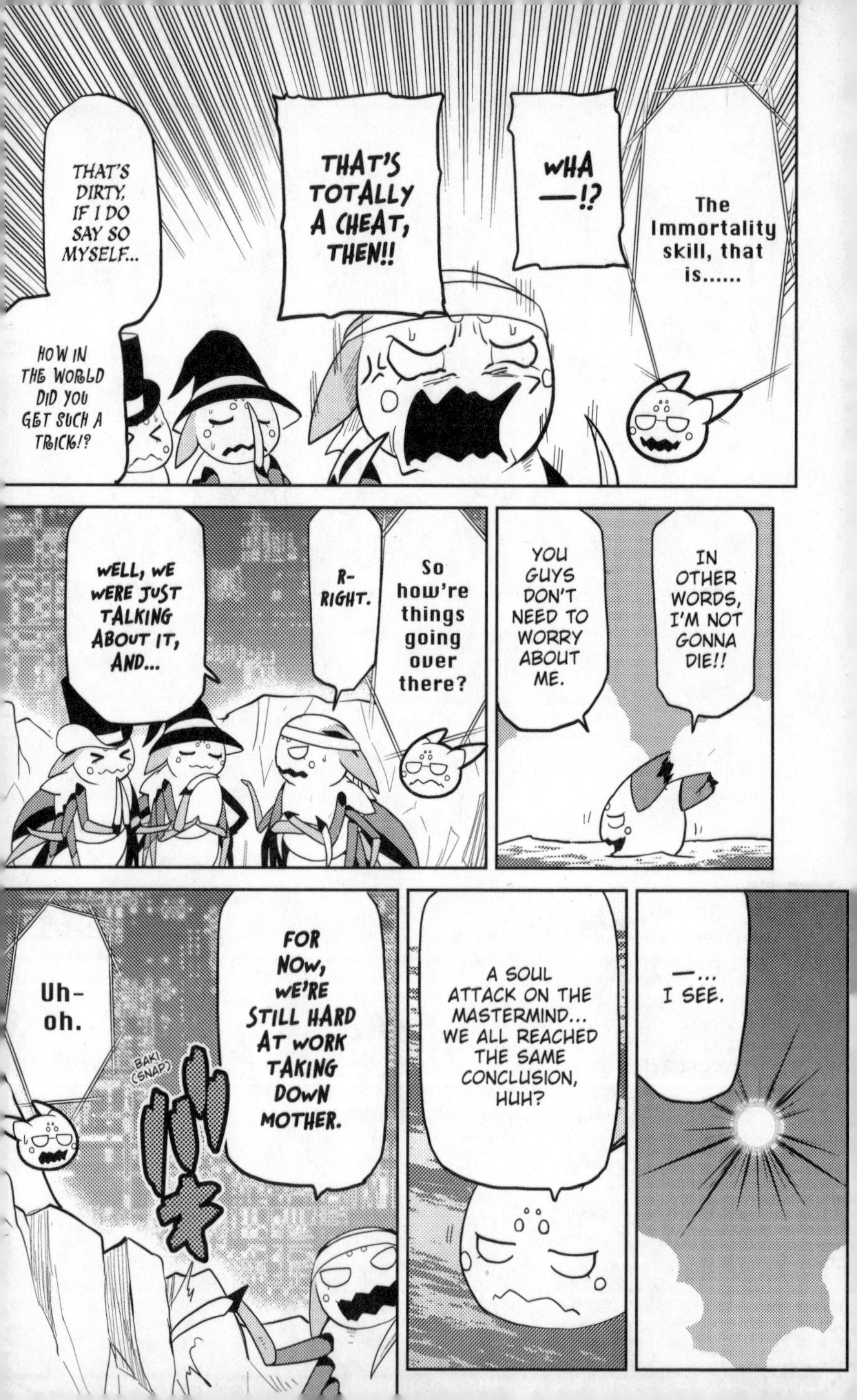
The Immortality skill, that is......
WHA—!?
THAT'S TOTALLY A CHEAT, THEN!!
THAT'S DIRTY, IF I DO SAY SO MYSELF...
HOW IN THE WORLD DID YOU GET SUCH A TRICK!?
IN OTHER WORDS, I'M NOT GONNA DIE!!
YOU GUYS DON'T NEED TO WORRY ABOUT ME.
So how're things going over there?
R-RIGHT.
WELL, WE WERE JUST TALKING ABOUT IT, AND...
—... I SEE.
A SOUL ATTACK ON THE MASTERMIND... WE ALL REACHED THE SAME CONCLUSION, HUH?
FOR NOW, WE'RE STILL HARD AT WORK TAKING DOWN MOTHER.
BAKI (SNAP)
Uh-oh.

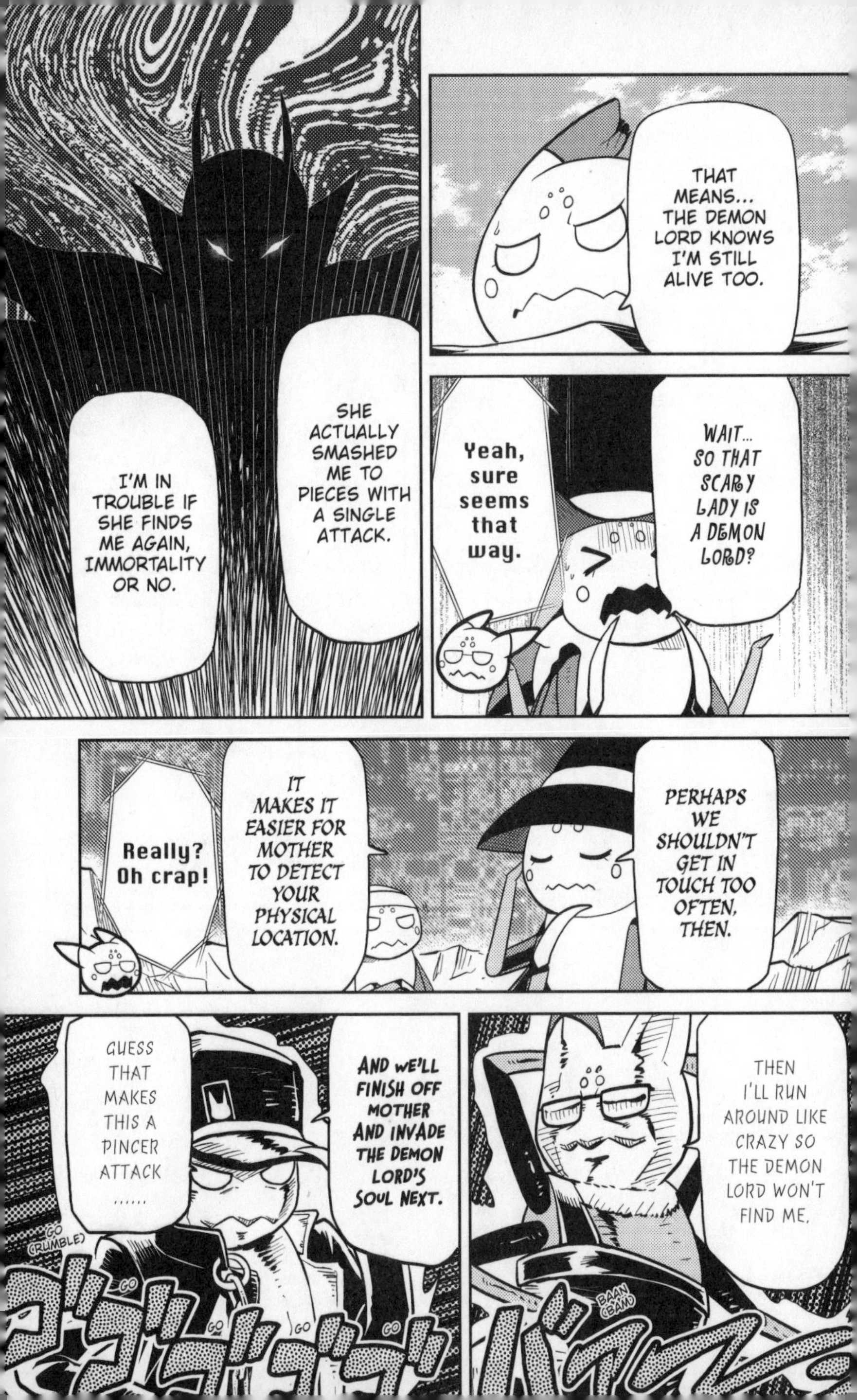
THAT MEANS... THE DEMON LORD KNOWS I'M STILL ALIVE TOO.
WAIT... SO THAT SCARY LADY IS A DEMON LORD?
Yeah, sure seems that way.
SHE ACTUALLY SMASHED ME TO PIECES WITH A SINGLE ATTACK.
I'M IN TROUBLE IF SHE FINDS ME AGAIN, IMMORTALITY OR NO.
PERHAPS WE SHOULDN'T GET IN TOUCH TOO OFTEN, THEN.
IT MAKES IT EASIER FOR MOTHER TO DETECT YOUR PHYSICAL LOCATION.
Really? Oh crap!
THEN I'LL RUN AROUND LIKE CRAZY SO THE DEMON LORD WON'T FIND ME.
BAAN (BAM)
AND WE'LL FINISH OFF MOTHER AND INVADE THE DEMON LORD'S SOUL NEXT.
GUESS THAT MAKES THIS A PINCER ATTACK ......
GO (RUMBLE)
GO
GO
GO

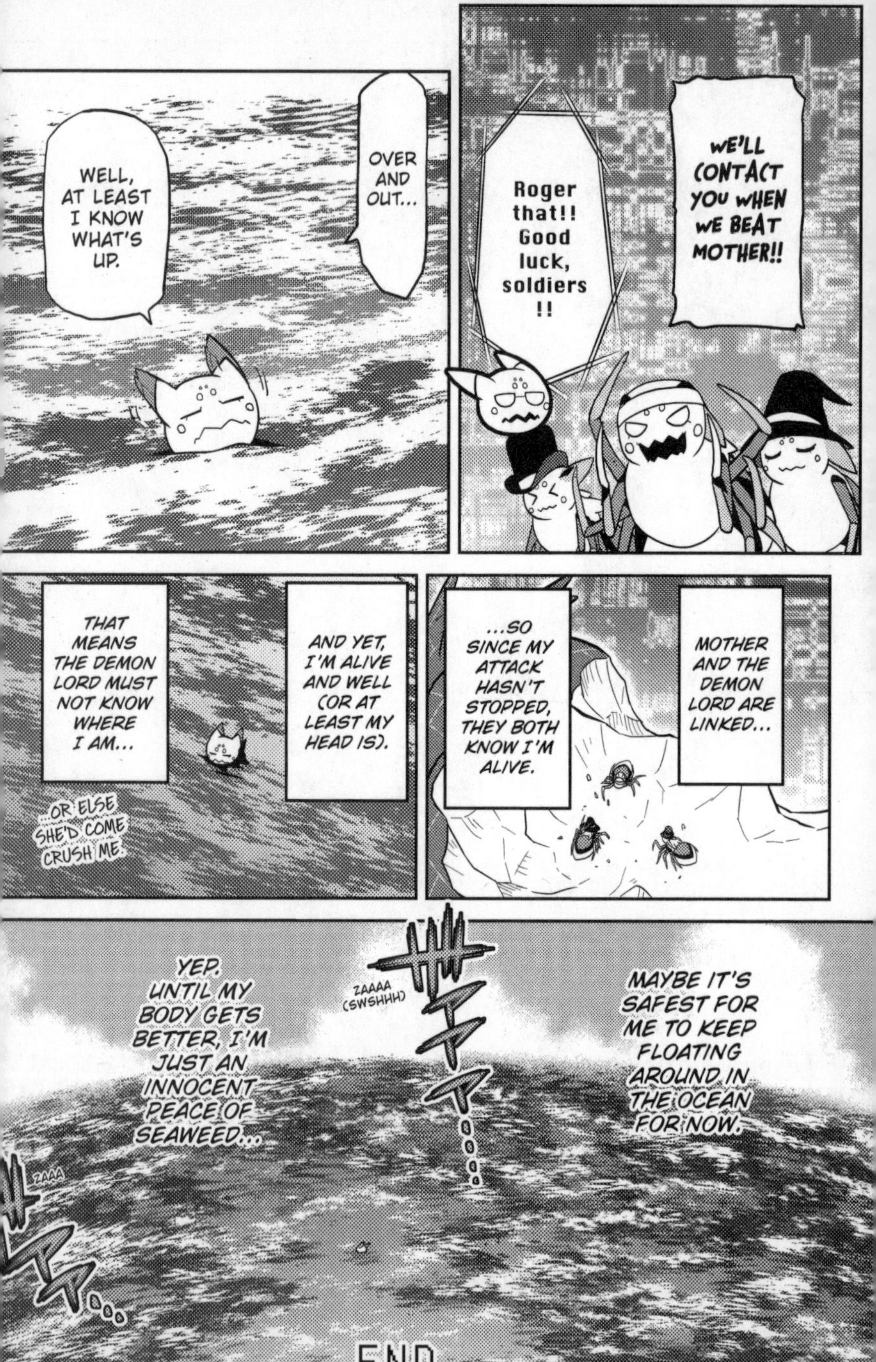
WE'LL CONTACT YOU WHEN WE BEAT MOTHER!!
Roger that!! Good luck, soldiers!!
OVER AND OUT...
WELL, AT LEAST I KNOW WHAT'S UP.
MOTHER AND THE DEMON LORD ARE LINKED...
...SO SINCE MY ATTACK HASN'T STOPPED, THEY BOTH KNOW I'M ALIVE.
AND YET, I'M ALIVE AND WELL (OR AT LEAST MY HEAD IS).
THAT MEANS THE DEMON LORD MUST NOT KNOW WHERE I AM...
...OR ELSE SHE'D COME CRUSH ME.
MAYBE IT'S SAFEST FOR ME TO KEEP FLOATING AROUND IN THE OCEAN FOR NOW.
ZAAAA (SWSHHH)
YEP. UNTIL MY BODY GETS BETTER, I'M JUST AN INNOCENT PEACE OF SEAWEED...
ZAAA

END

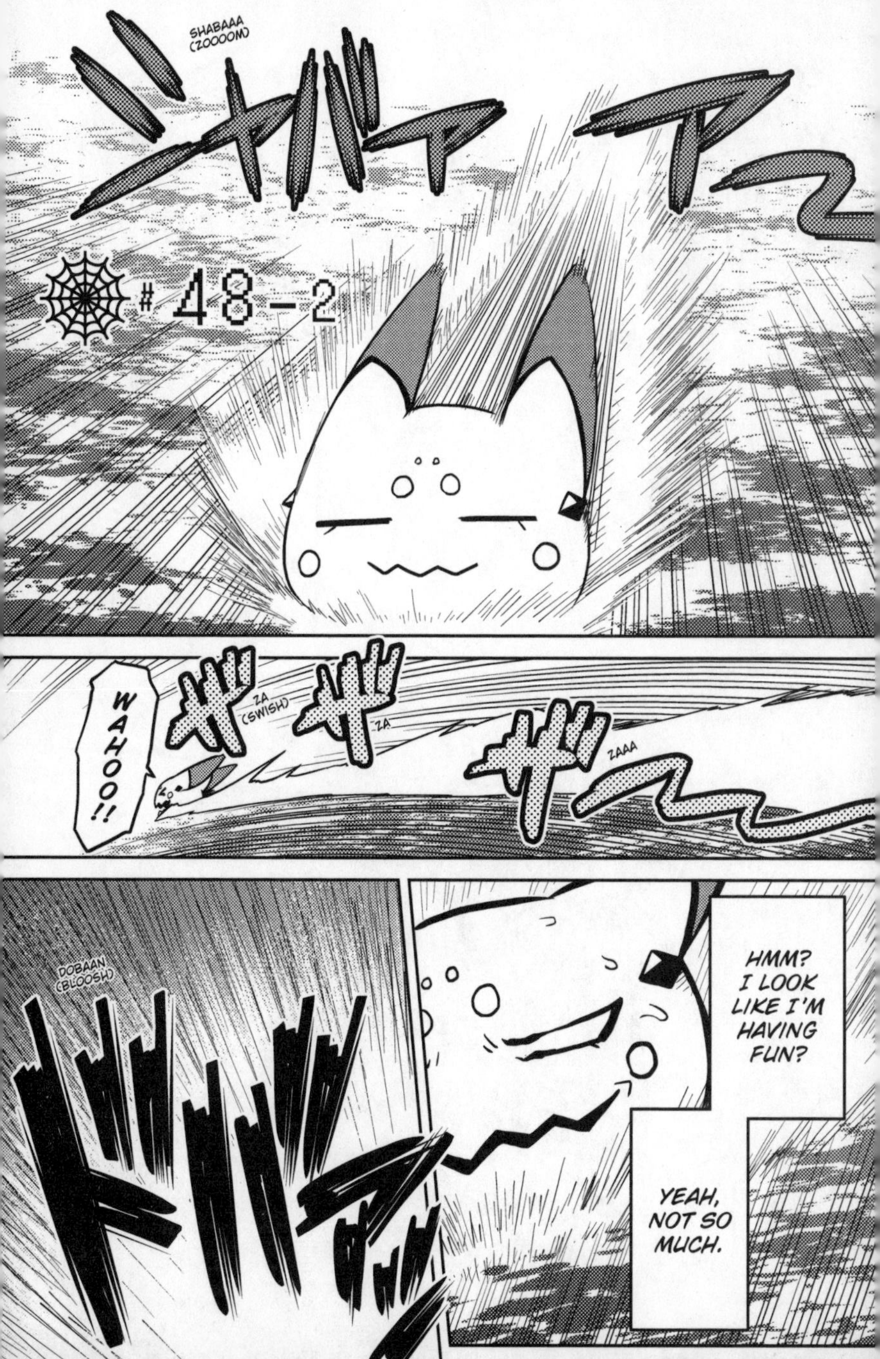
SHABAAA (ZOOOOM)
#48-2
ZAAA
ZA
ZA (SWISH)
WAHOOO!!
HMM? I LOOK LIKE I'M HAVING FUN?
YEAH, NOT SO MUCH.
DOBAAN (BLOOSH)

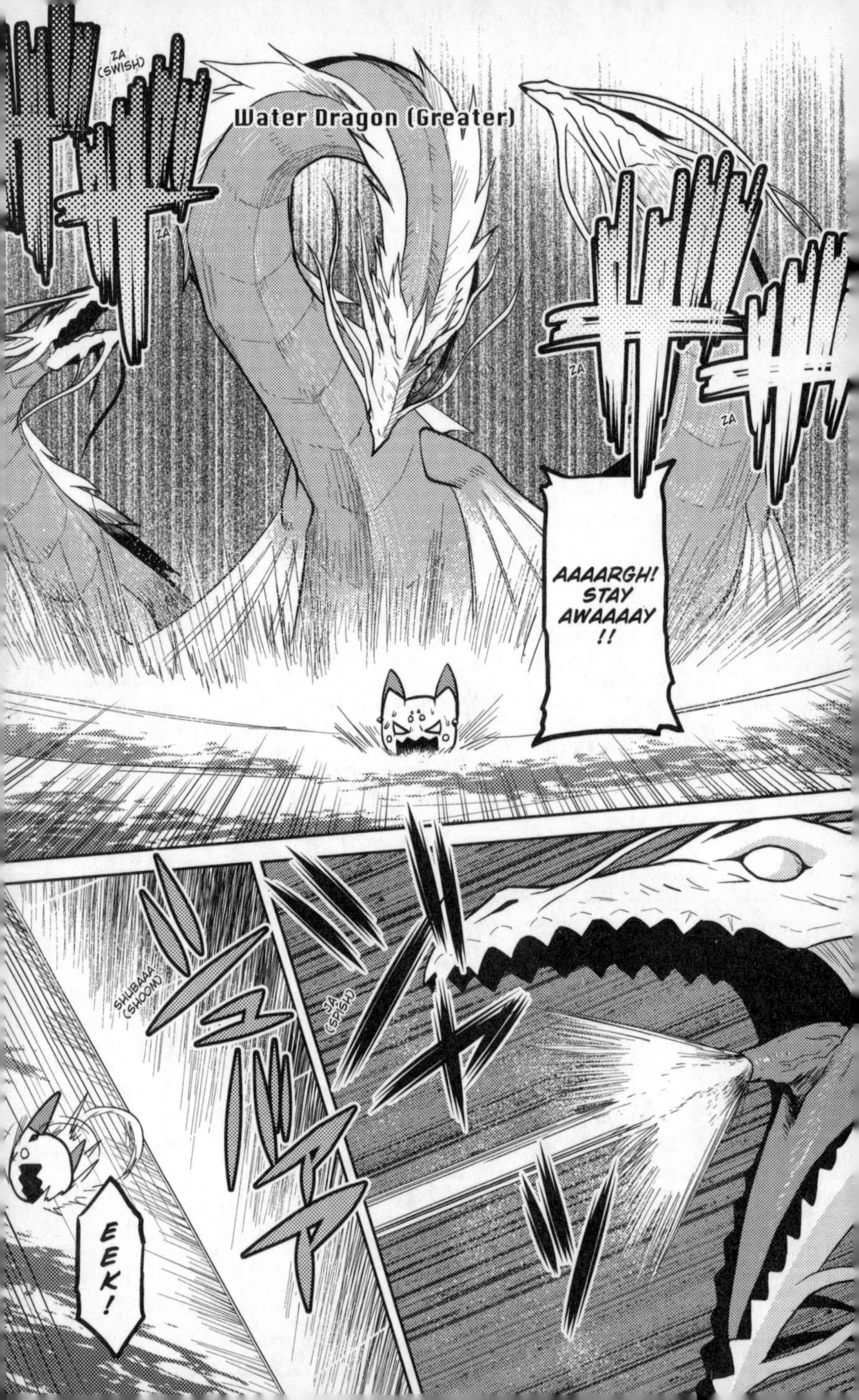
ZA (SWISH)
Water Dragon (Greater)
ZA
ZA
ZA
AAAARGH! STAY AWAAAAY !!
JA (SPISH)
SHUBAAA (SHOOM)
EEK!

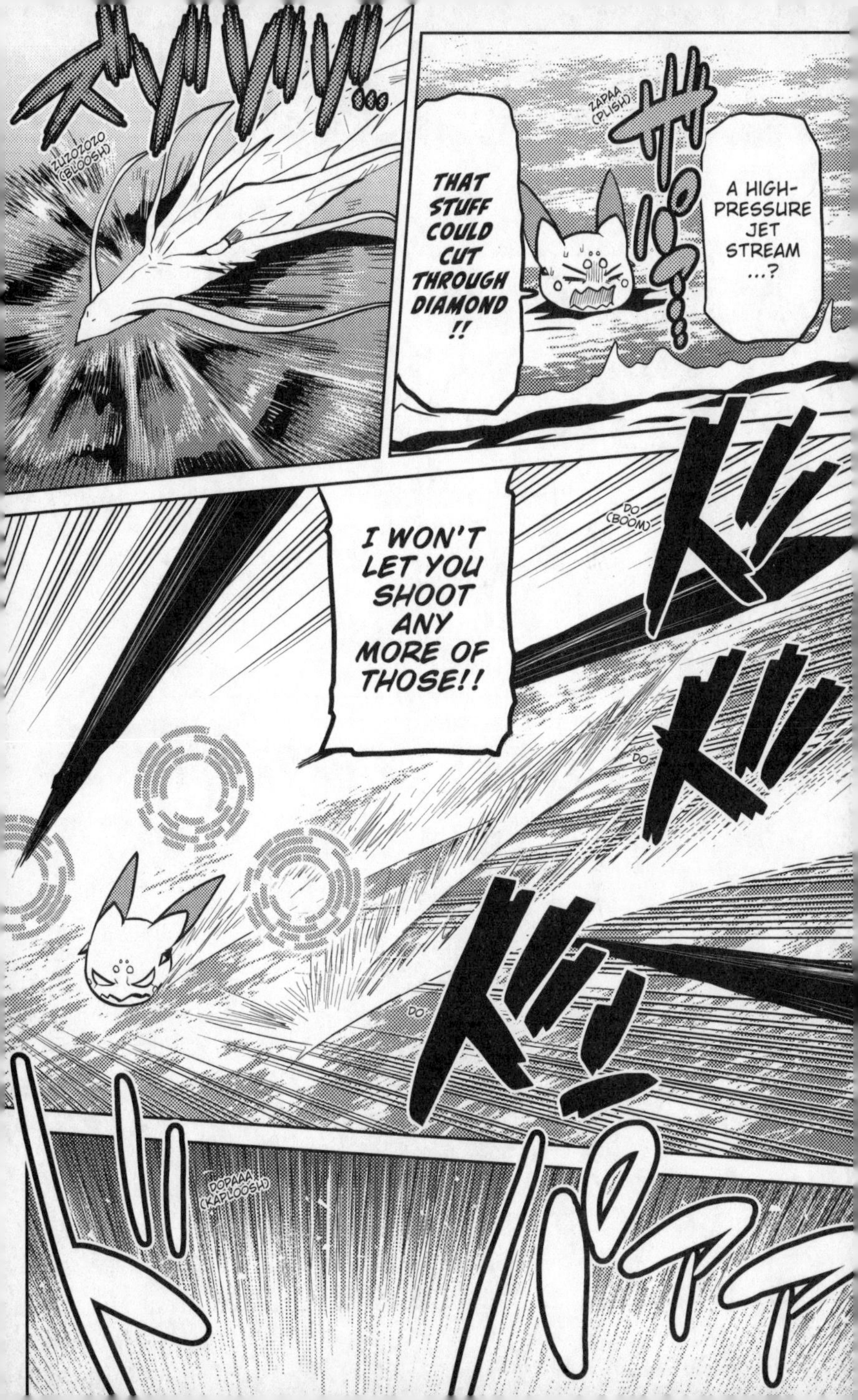
A HIGH-PRESSURE JET STREAM ...?
ZAPAA (PLISH)
THAT STUFF COULD CUT THROUGH DIAMOND !!
ZUZOZOZO (BLOOSH)
DO (BOOM)
I WON'T LET YOU SHOOT ANY MORE OF THOSE!!
DO
DO
DOPAAA (KAPLOOSH)

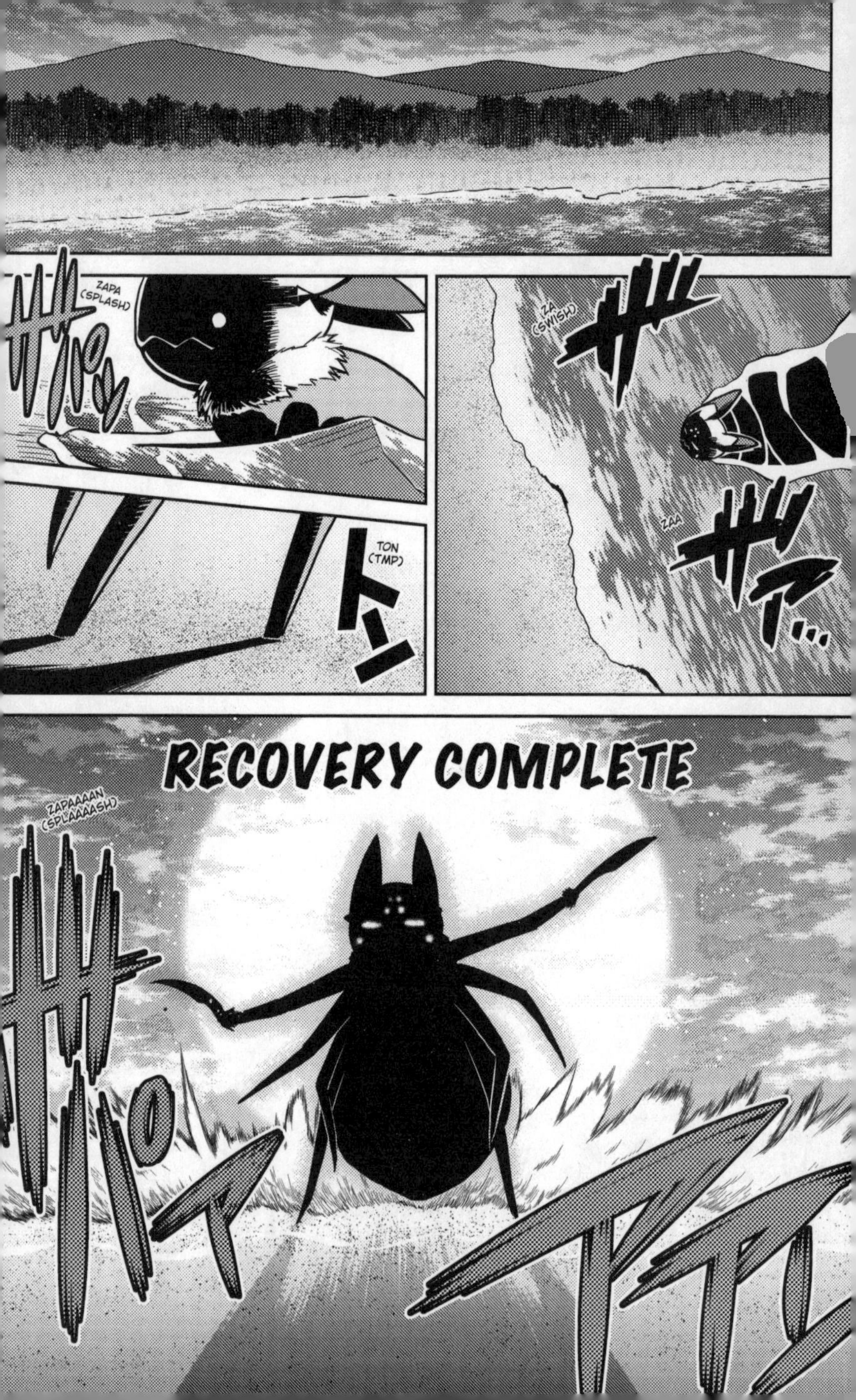
ZA (SWISH)
ZAA
ZAPA (SPLASH)
TON (TMP)
RECOVERY COMPLETE
ZAPAAAAN (SPLAAAASH)

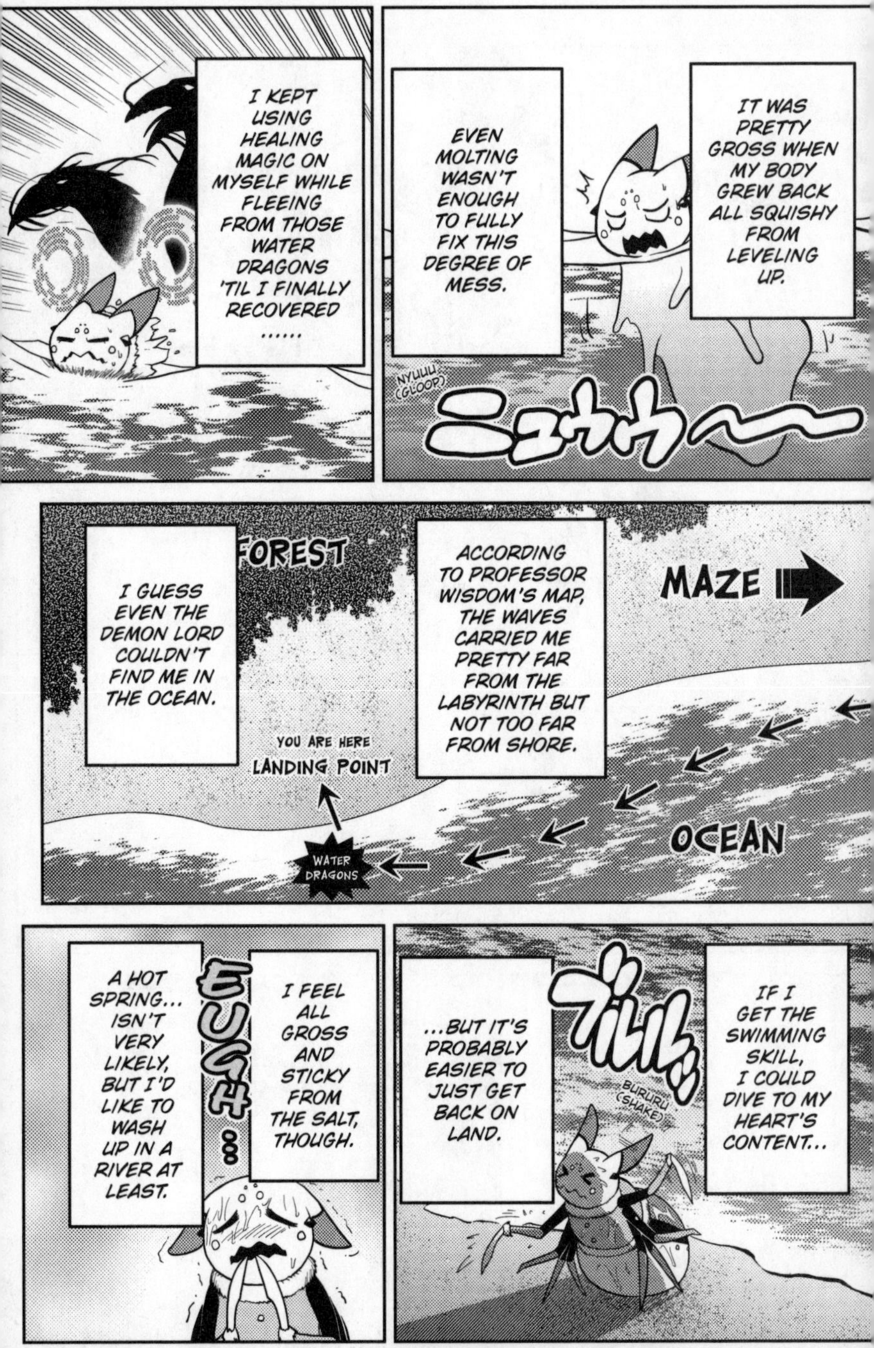
IT WAS PRETTY GROSS WHEN MY BODY GREW BACK ALL SQUISHY FROM LEVELING UP.
EVEN MOLTING WASN'T ENOUGH TO FULLY FIX THIS DEGREE OF MESS.
NYUUU (GLOOP)
I KEPT USING HEALING MAGIC ON MYSELF WHILE FLEEING FROM THOSE WATER DRAGONS 'TIL I FINALLY RECOVERED ......
MAZE
ACCORDING TO PROFESSOR WISDOM'S MAP, THE WAVES CARRIED ME PRETTY FAR FROM THE LABYRINTH BUT NOT TOO FAR FROM SHORE.
FOREST
I GUESS EVEN THE DEMON LORD COULDN'T FIND ME IN THE OCEAN.
YOU ARE HERE
LANDING POINT
OCEAN
WATER DRAGONS
IF I GET THE SWIMMING SKILL, I COULD DIVE TO MY HEART'S CONTENT...
BURURU (SHAKE)
...BUT IT'S PROBABLY EASIER TO JUST GET BACK ON LAND.
I FEEL ALL GROSS AND STICKY FROM THE SALT, THOUGH.
EUGH...
A HOT SPRING... ISN'T VERY LIKELY, BUT I'D LIKE TO WASH UP IN A RIVER AT LEAST.

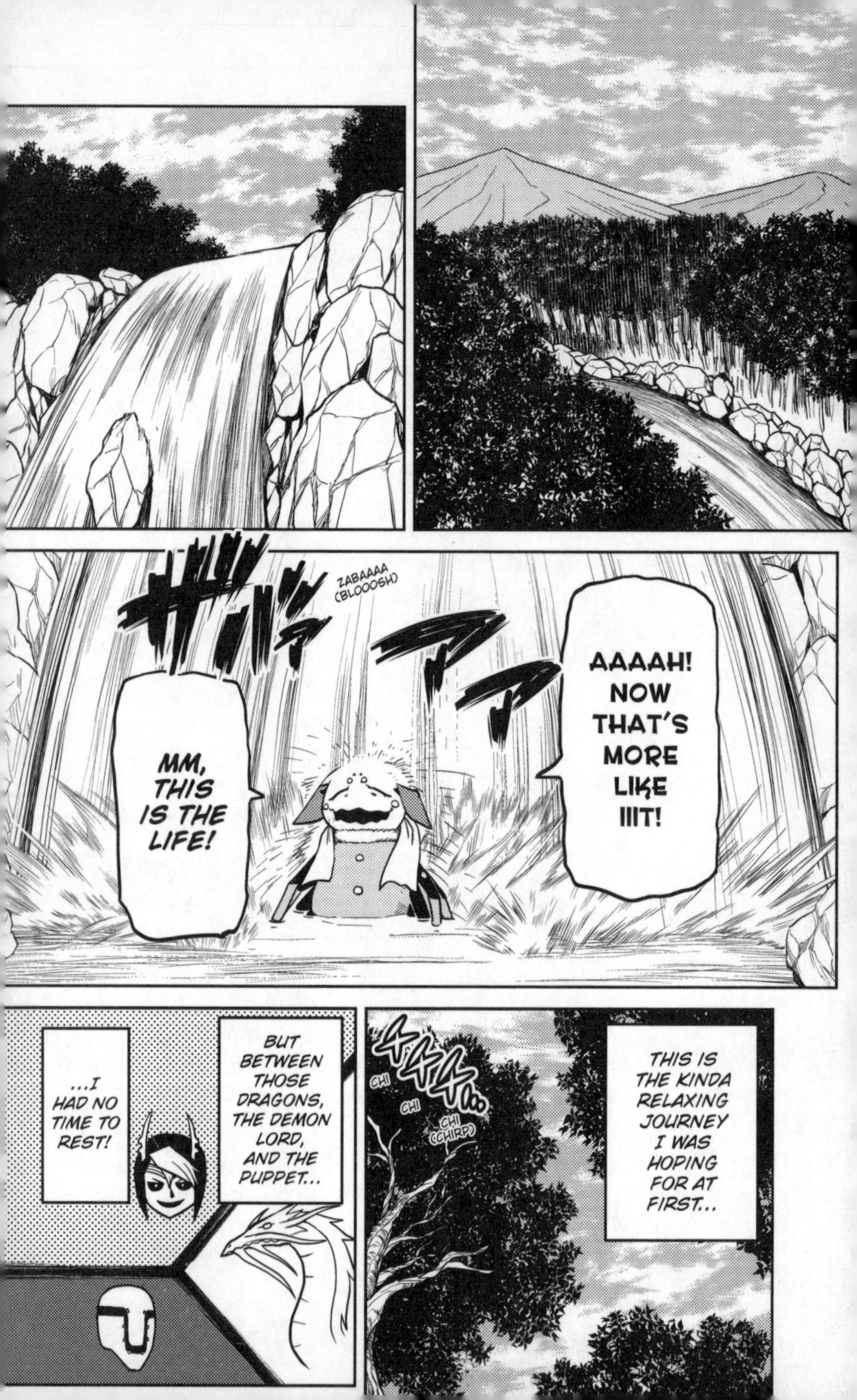
AAAAH! NOW THAT'S MORE LIKE IIIT!
ZABAAAA (BLOOOSH)
MM, THIS IS THE LIFE!
THIS IS THE KINDA RELAXING JOURNEY I WAS HOPING FOR AT FIRST...
CHI CHI CHI (CHIRP)
BUT BETWEEN THOSE DRAGONS, THE DEMON LORD, AND THE PUPPET...
...I HAD NO TIME TO REST!

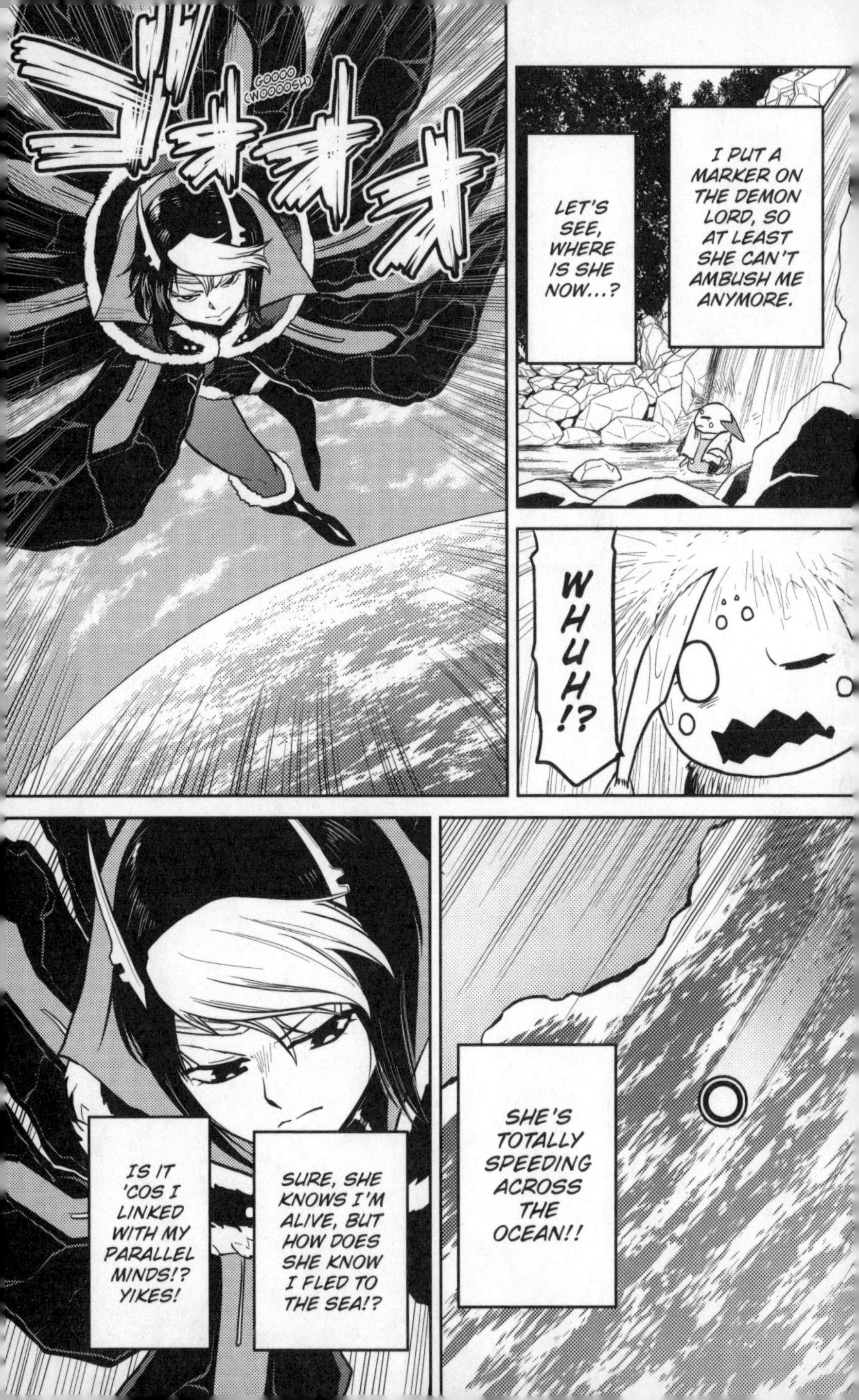
I PUT A MARKER ON THE DEMON LORD, SO AT LEAST SHE CAN'T AMBUSH ME ANYMORE.
LET'S SEE, WHERE IS SHE NOW...?
WHUH!?
GOOOO (WOOOOSH)
SHE'S TOTALLY SPEEDING ACROSS THE OCEAN!!
SURE, SHE KNOWS I'M ALIVE, BUT HOW DOES SHE KNOW I FLED TO THE SEA!?
IS IT 'COS I LINKED WITH MY PARALLEL MINDS!? YIKES!

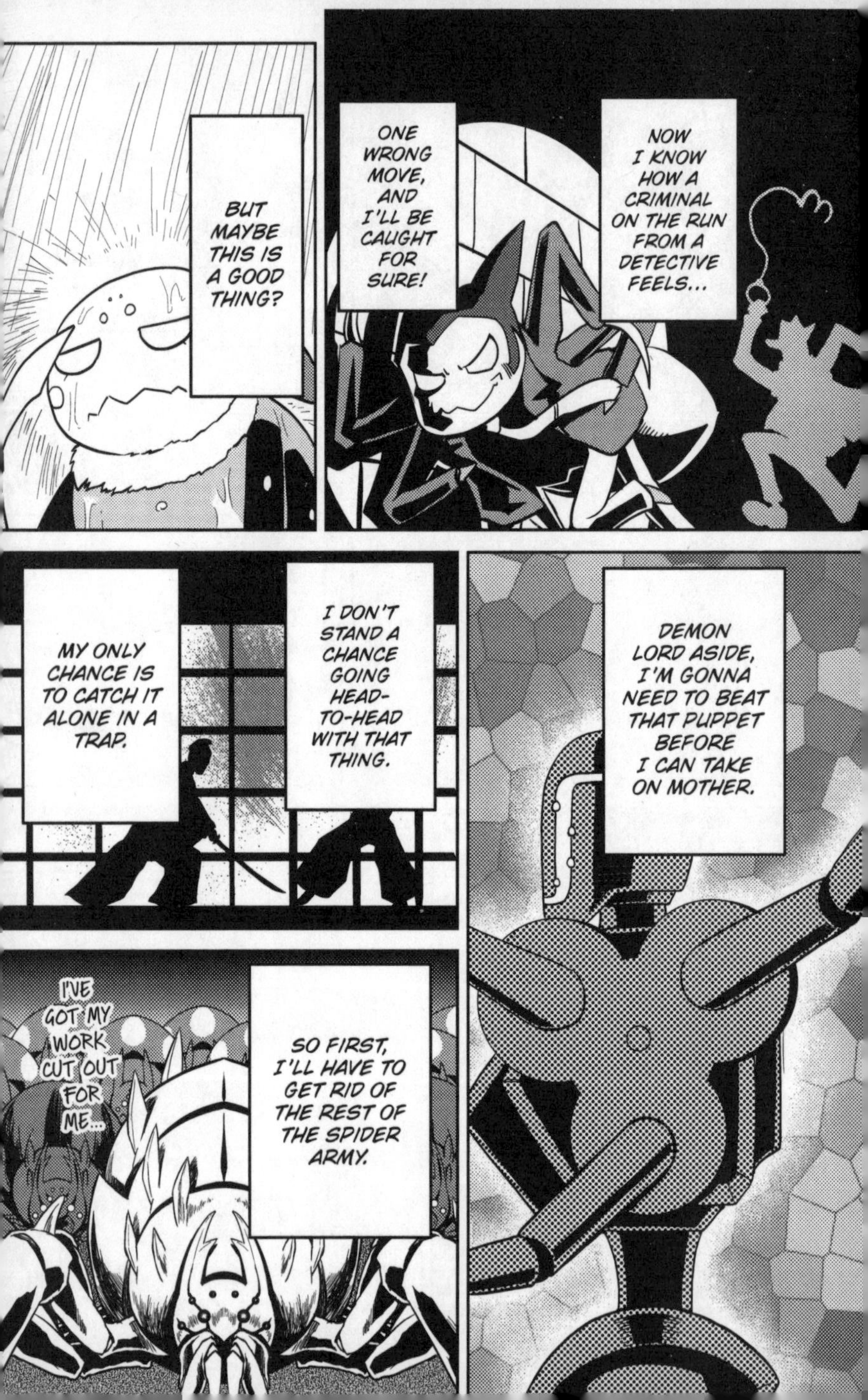
NOW I KNOW HOW A CRIMINAL ON THE RUN FROM A DETECTIVE FEELS...
ONE WRONG MOVE, AND I'LL BE CAUGHT FOR SURE!
BUT MAYBE THIS IS A GOOD THING?
DEMON LORD ASIDE, I'M GONNA NEED TO BEAT THAT PUPPET BEFORE I CAN TAKE ON MOTHER.
I DON'T STAND A CHANCE GOING HEAD-TO-HEAD WITH THAT THING.
MY ONLY CHANCE IS TO CATCH IT ALONE IN A TRAP.
SO FIRST, I'LL HAVE TO GET RID OF THE REST OF THE SPIDER ARMY.
I'VE GOT MY WORK CUT OUT FOR ME...

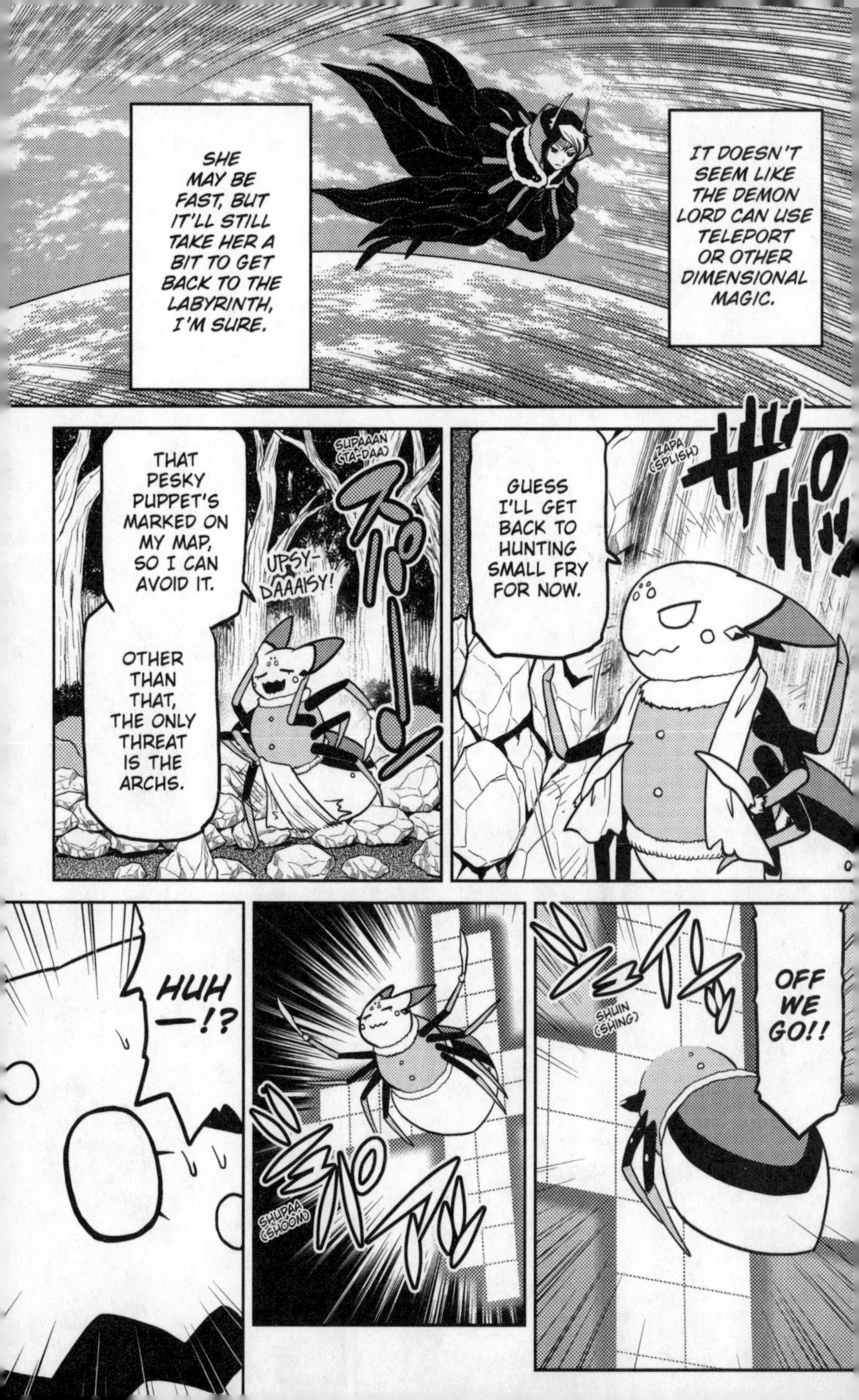
IT DOESN'T SEEM LIKE THE DEMON LORD CAN USE TELEPORT OR OTHER DIMENSIONAL MAGIC.
SHE MAY BE FAST, BUT IT'LL STILL TAKE HER A BIT TO GET BACK TO THE LABYRINTH, I'M SURE.
ZAPA (SPLISH)
GUESS I'LL GET BACK TO HUNTING SMALL FRY FOR NOW.
SUPAAAN (TA-DAA)
THAT PESKY PUPPET'S MARKED ON MY MAP, SO I CAN AVOID IT.
UPSY-DAAAISY!
OTHER THAN THAT, THE ONLY THREAT IS THE ARCHS.
OFF WE GO!!
SHUIN (SHING)
SHUPAA (SHOOM)
HUH—!?

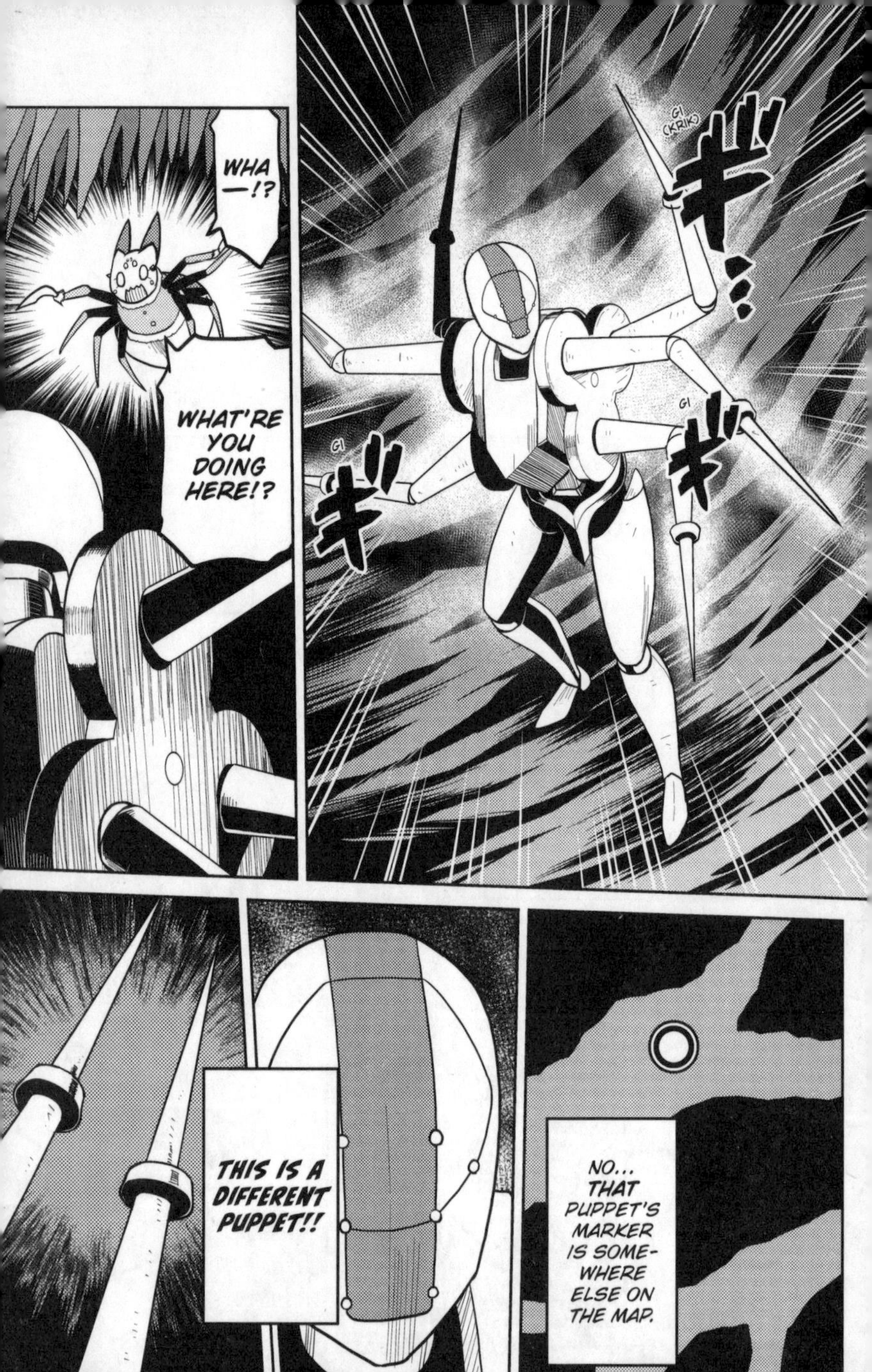
GI (KRIK)
GI
GI
WHA—!?
WHAT'RE YOU DOING HERE!?
NO... THAT PUPPET'S MARKER IS SOMEWHERE ELSE ON THE MAP.
THIS IS A DIFFERENT PUPPET!!

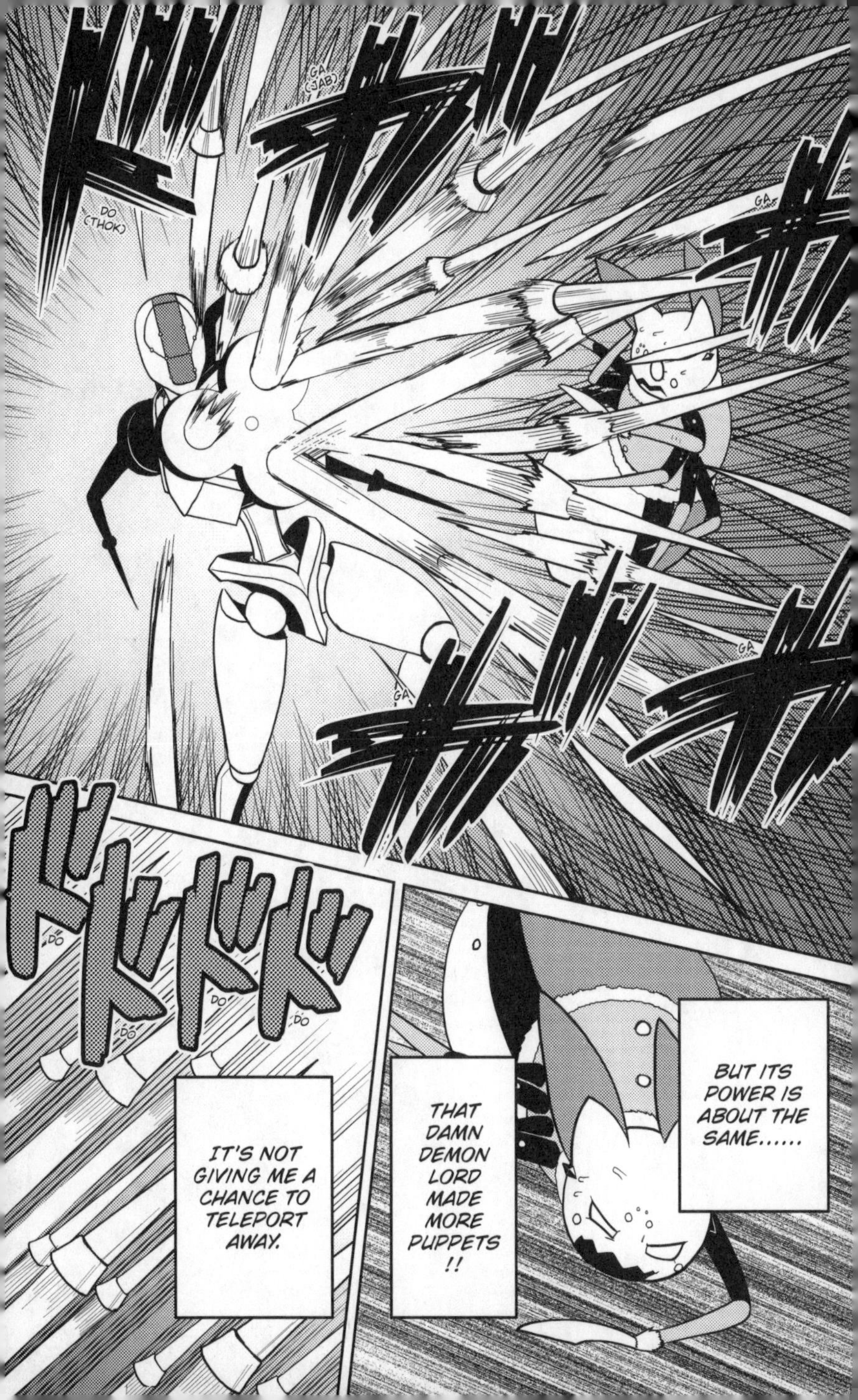
GA (JAB)
GA
DO (THOK)
GA
GA
BUT ITS POWER IS ABOUT THE SAME......
THAT DAMN DEMON LORD MADE MORE PUPPETS!!
DO
DO
DO
DO
IT'S NOT GIVING ME A CHANCE TO TELEPORT AWAY.

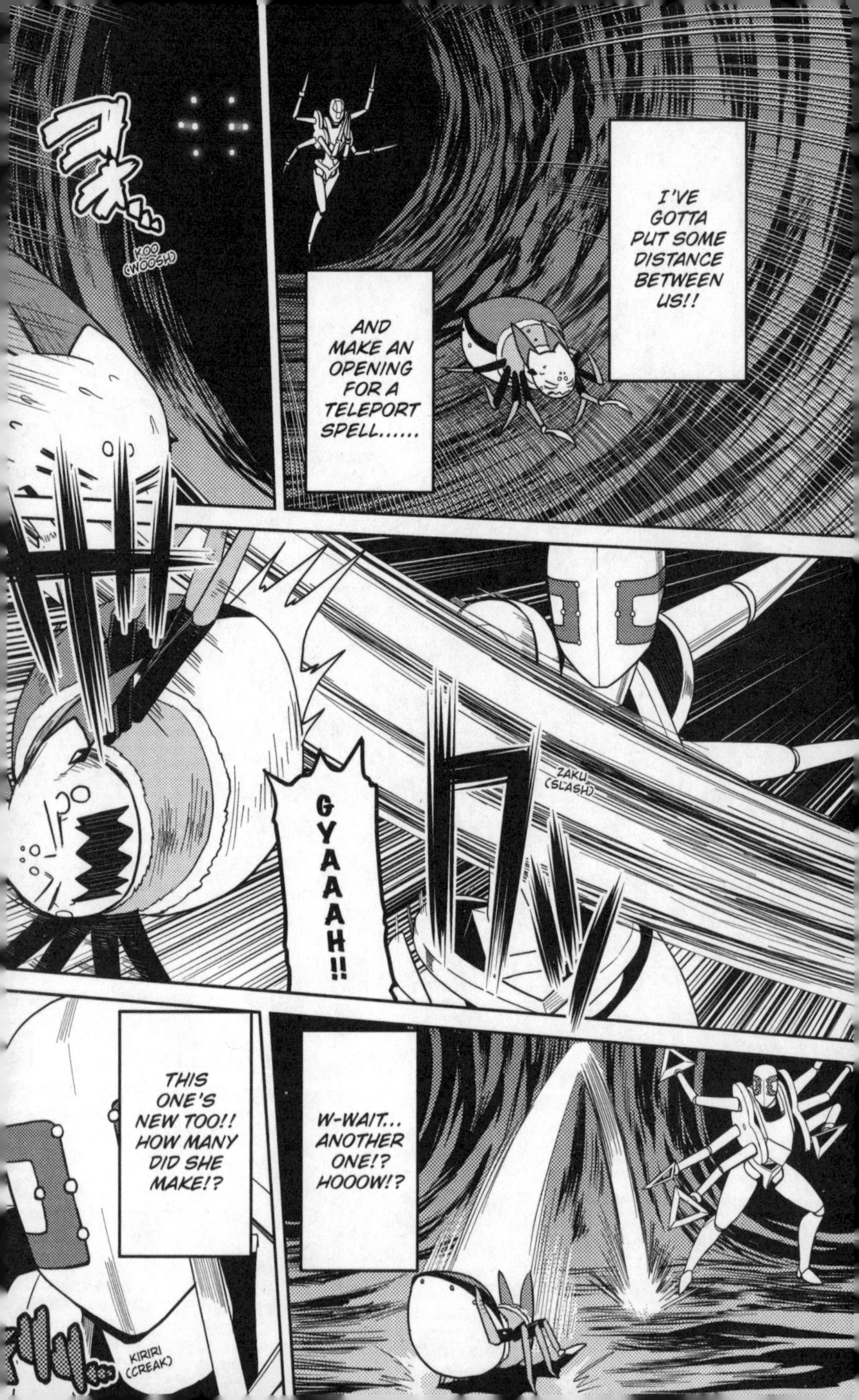
I'VE GOTTA PUT SOME DISTANCE BETWEEN US!!
AND MAKE AN OPENING FOR A TELEPORT SPELL......
KOO (WOOSH)
ZAKU (SLASH)
GYAAAH!!
W-WAIT... ANOTHER ONE!? HOOOW!?
THIS ONE'S NEW TOO!! HOW MANY DID SHE MAKE!?
KIRIRI (CREAK)

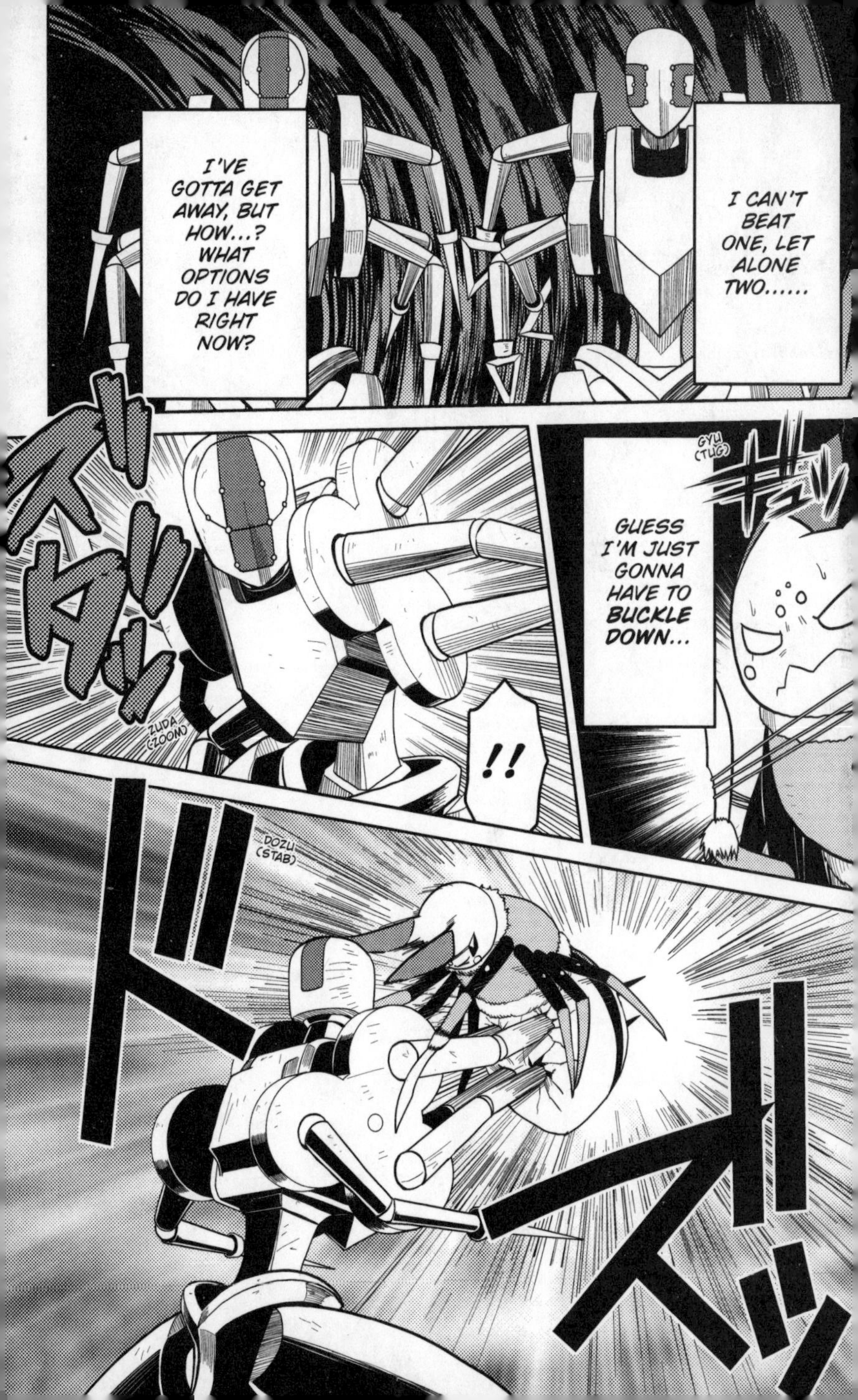
I CAN'T BEAT ONE, LET ALONE TWO......
I'VE GOTTA GET AWAY, BUT HOW...? WHAT OPTIONS DO I HAVE RIGHT NOW?
GYU (TUG)
GUESS I'M JUST GONNA HAVE TO BUCKLE DOWN...
!!
ZUDA (ZOOM)
DOZU (STAB)

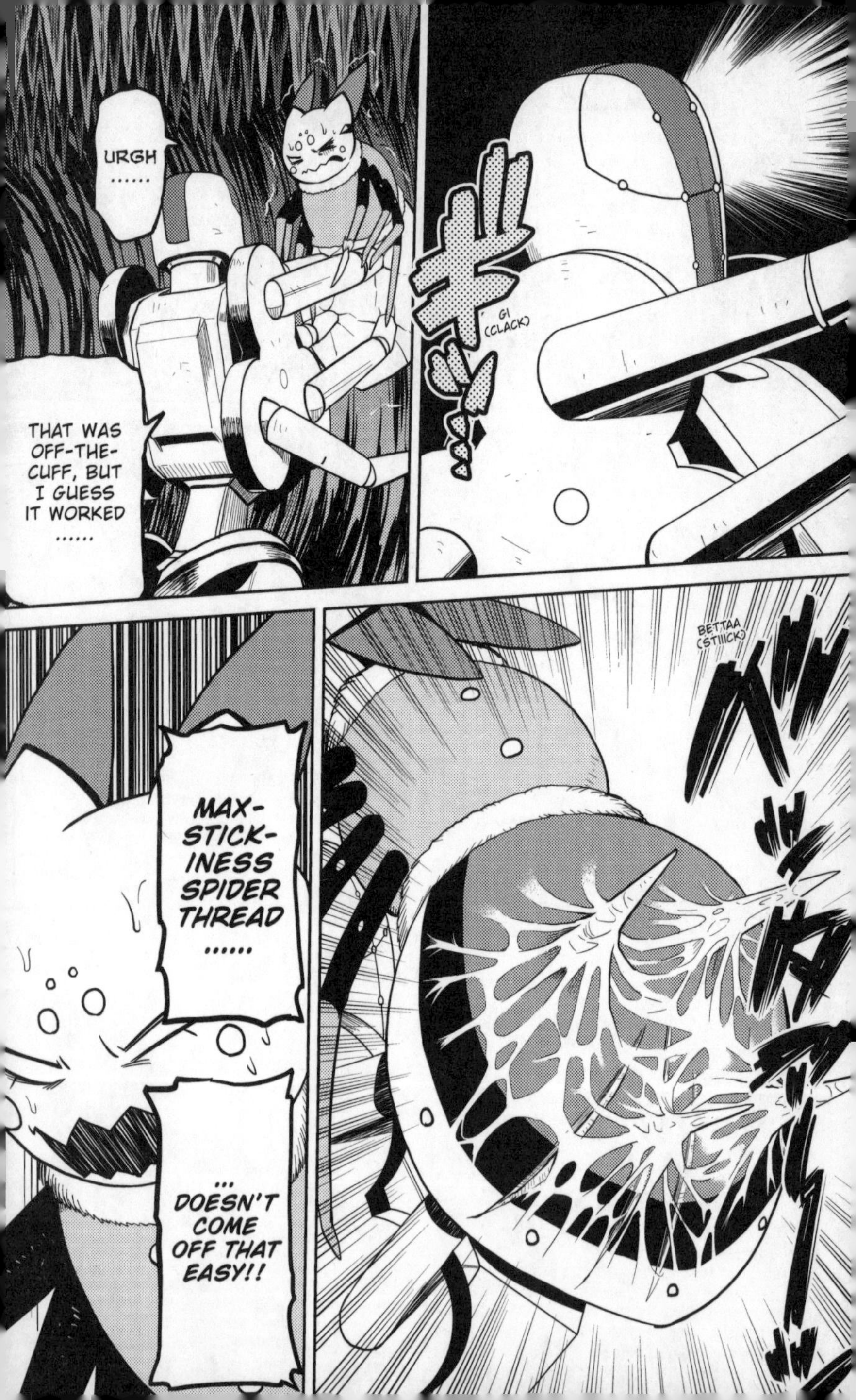
GI (CLACK)
URGH ......
THAT WAS OFF-THE-CUFF, BUT I GUESS IT WORKED ......
BETTAA (STIIICK)
MAX-STICKINESS SPIDER THREAD ......
... DOESN'T COME OFF THAT EASY!!

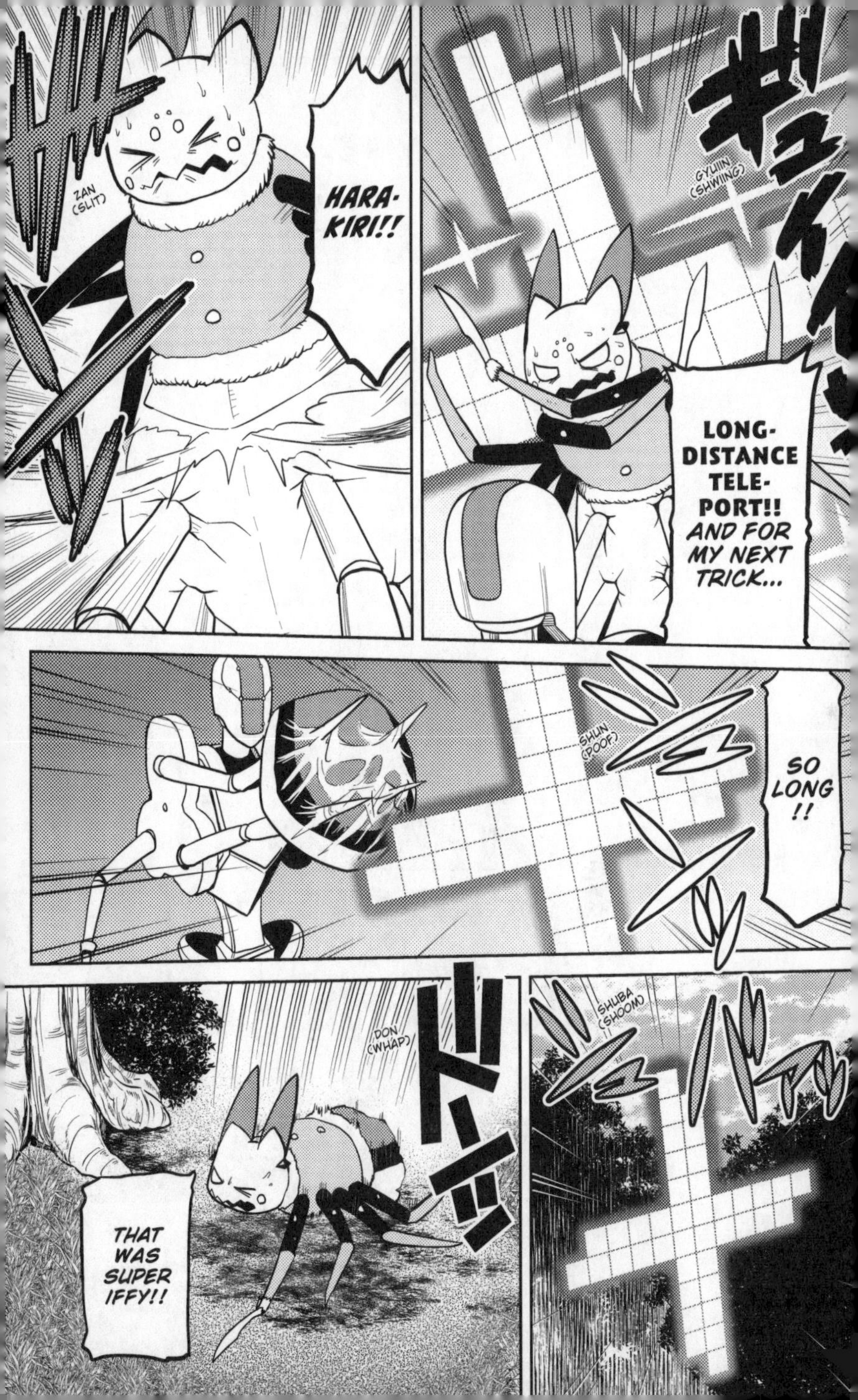
GYUIIN (SHWIING)
LONG-DISTANCE TELE-PORT!! AND FOR MY NEXT TRICK...
HARA-KIRI!!
ZAN (SLIT)
SO LONG!!
SHUN (POOF)
SHUBA (SHOON)
DON (WHAP)
THAT WAS SUPER IFFY!!

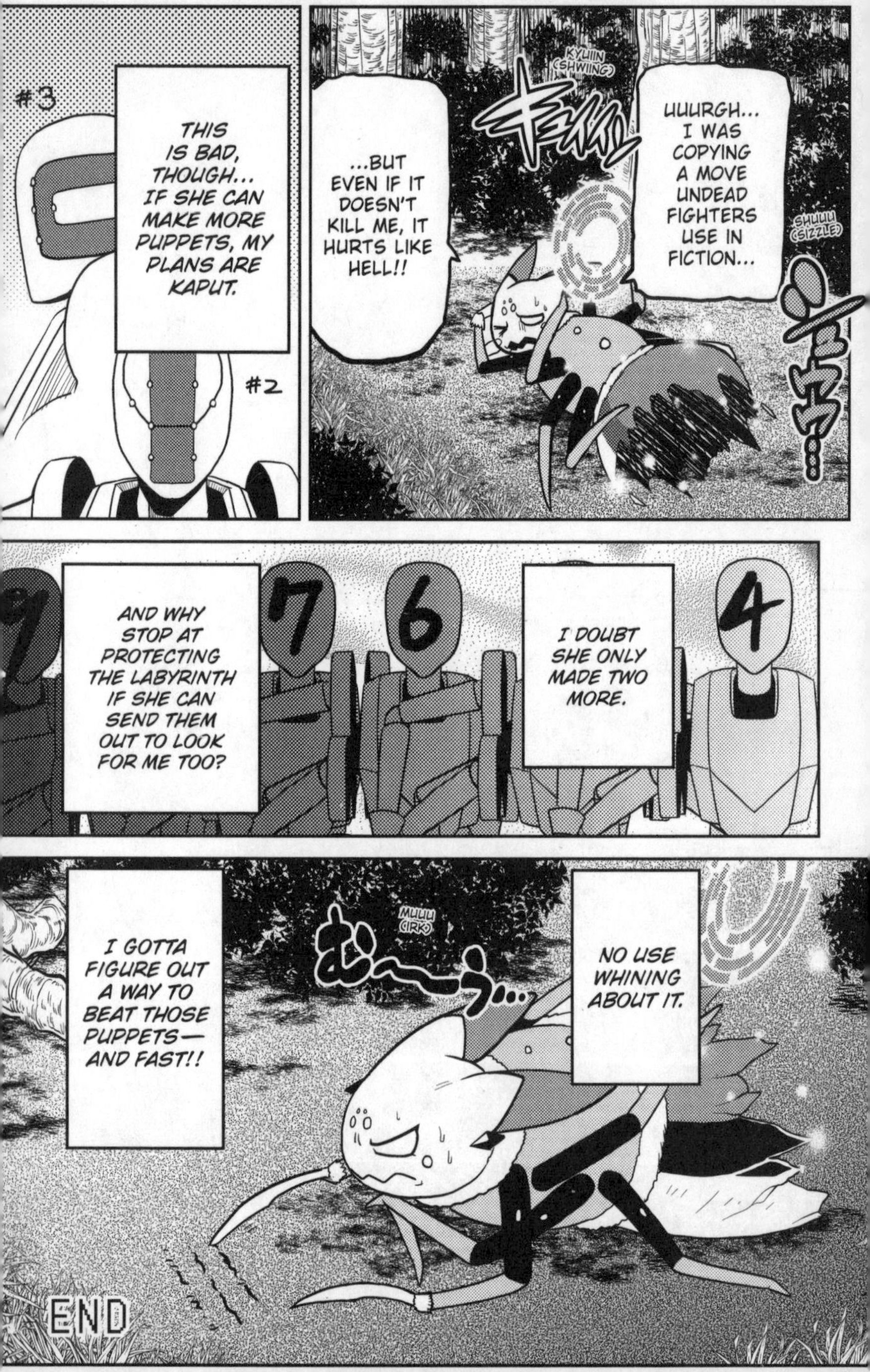
KYUIIN (SHWIING)
UUURGH... I WAS COPYING A MOVE UNDEAD FIGHTERS USE IN FICTION...
SHUUU (SIZZLE)
...BUT EVEN IF IT DOESN'T KILL ME, IT HURTS LIKE HELL!!
#3
THIS IS BAD, THOUGH... IF SHE CAN MAKE MORE PUPPETS, MY PLANS ARE KAPUT.
#2
I DOUBT SHE ONLY MADE TWO MORE.
AND WHY STOP AT PROTECTING THE LABYRINTH IF SHE CAN SEND THEM OUT TO LOOK FOR ME TOO?
NO USE WHINING ABOUT IT.
MUUU (IRK)
I GOTTA FIGURE OUT A WAY TO BEAT THOSE PUPPETS—AND FAST!!
END

So I'm a Spider, So What?

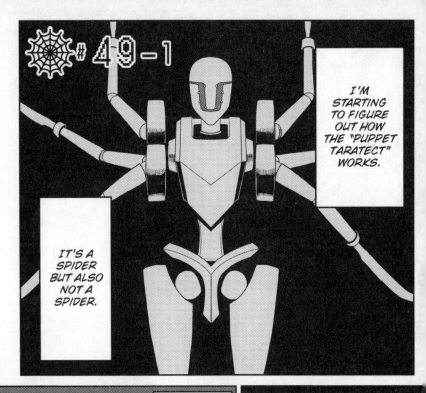

#49-1
I'M STARTING TO FIGURE OUT HOW THE "PUPPET TARATECT" WORKS.
IT'S A SPIDER BUT ALSO NOT A SPIDER.
AT THE DOLL'S HEART IS A "CORE" WITH TOUGH PHYSICAL AND MAGICAL COATING.
AND INSIDE IS A PALM-SIZED SPIDER.
THE SPIDER USES THREAD CONTROL TO MANIPULATE THE THREADS THROUGHOUT THE BODY AND MOVE IT.
ITS SKILLS AND MOVEMENTS ARE MORE SIMILAR TO A HUMAN'S THAN A SPIDER'S—
—BUT IT ALSO MOVES IN WAYS A HUMAN NEVER COULD, SO IT'S SUPER HARD TO READ!!

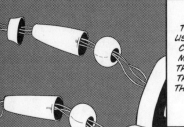

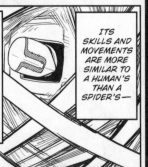

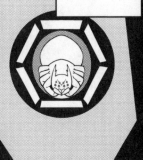

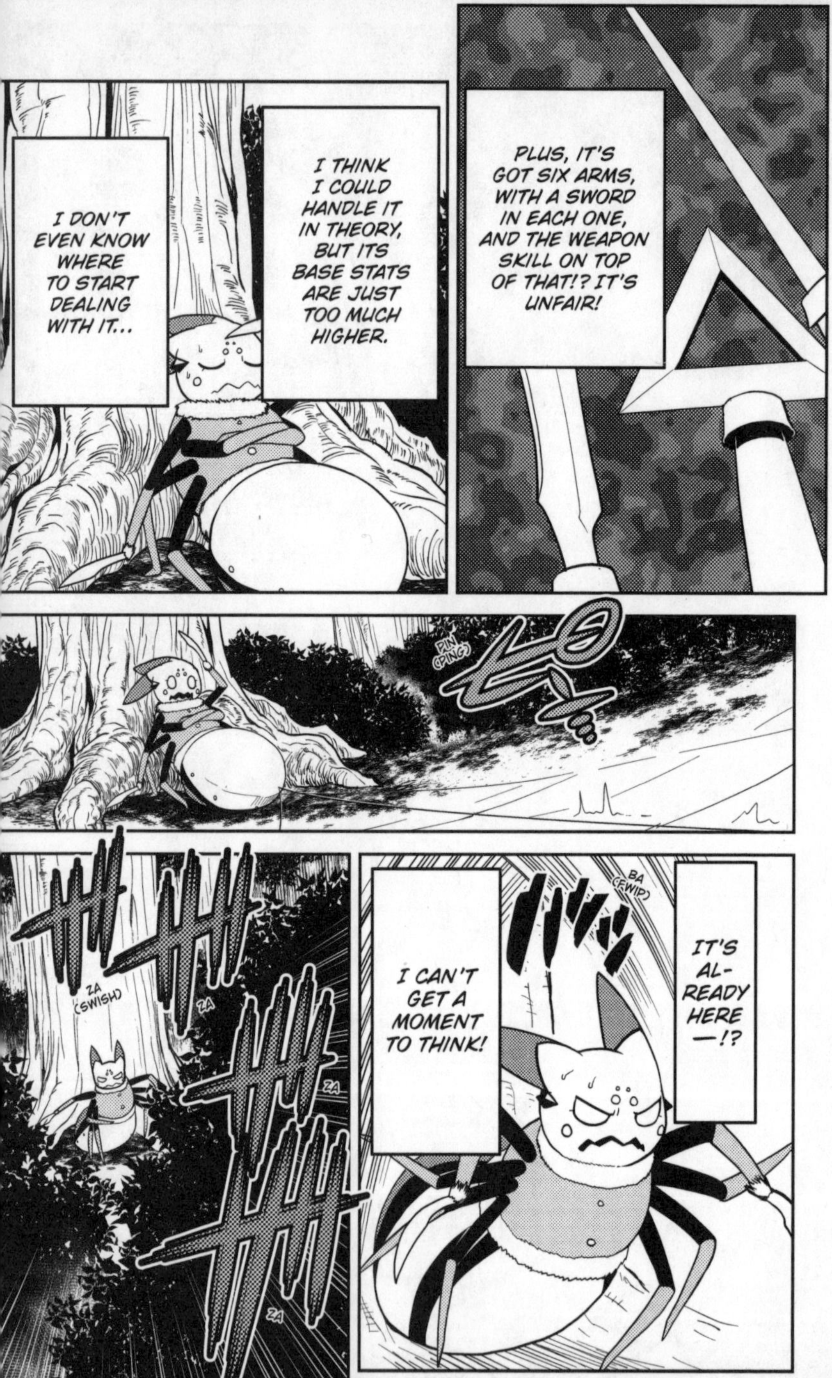
PLUS, IT'S GOT SIX ARMS, WITH A SWORD IN EACH ONE, AND THE WEAPON SKILL ON TOP OF THAT!? IT'S UNFAIR!
I THINK I COULD HANDLE IT IN THEORY, BUT ITS BASE STATS ARE JUST TOO MUCH HIGHER.
I DON'T EVEN KNOW WHERE TO START DEALING WITH IT...
PIN (PING)
BA (FWIP)
IT'S AL-READY HERE—!?
I CAN'T GET A MOMENT TO THINK!
ZA
ZA (SWISH)
ZA
ZA

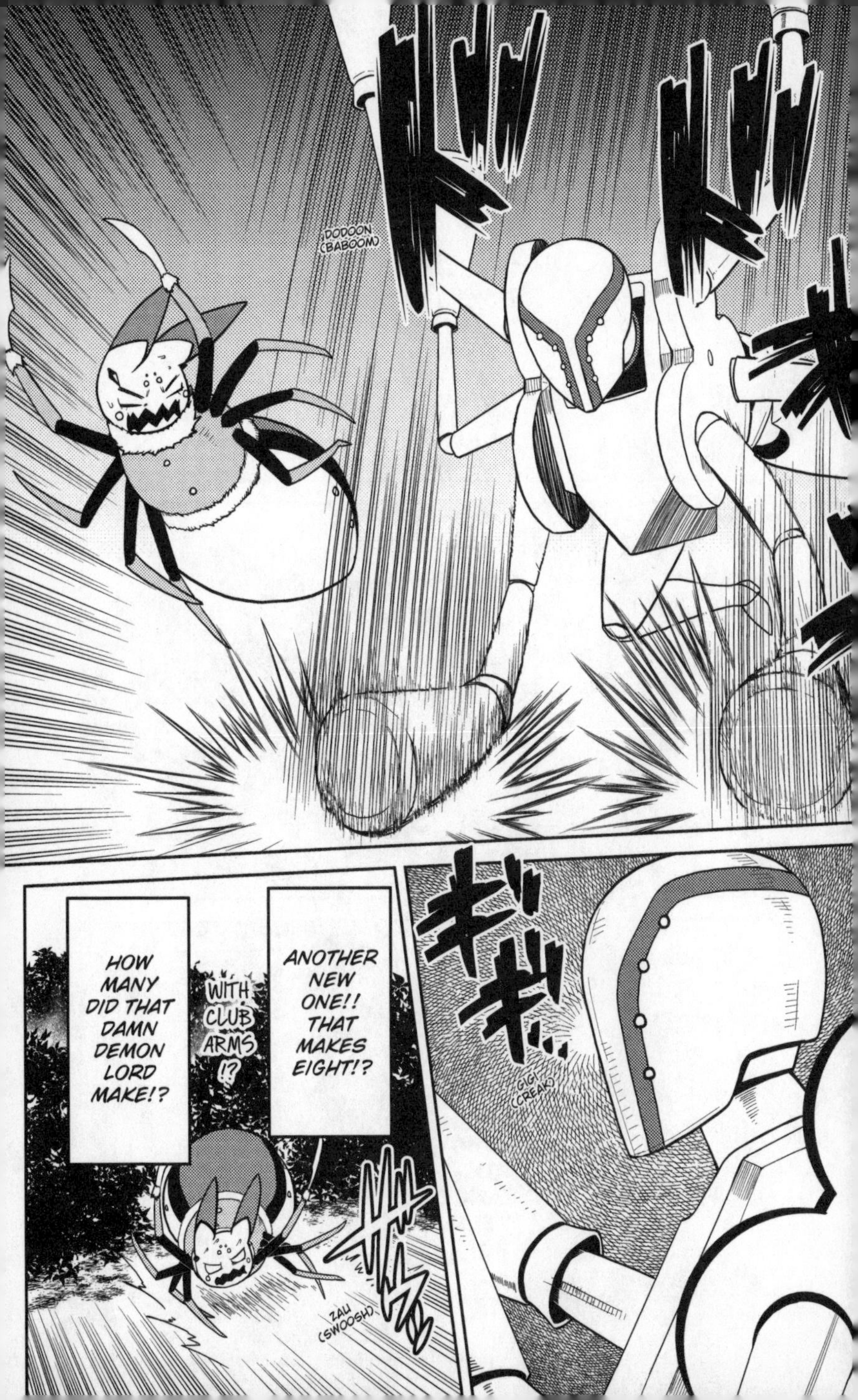
DODOON (BABOOM)
GIGI (CREAK)
ANOTHER NEW ONE!! THAT MAKES EIGHT!?
WITH CLUB ARMS!?
HOW MANY DID THAT DAMN DEMON LORD MAKE!?
ZAU (SWOOSH)

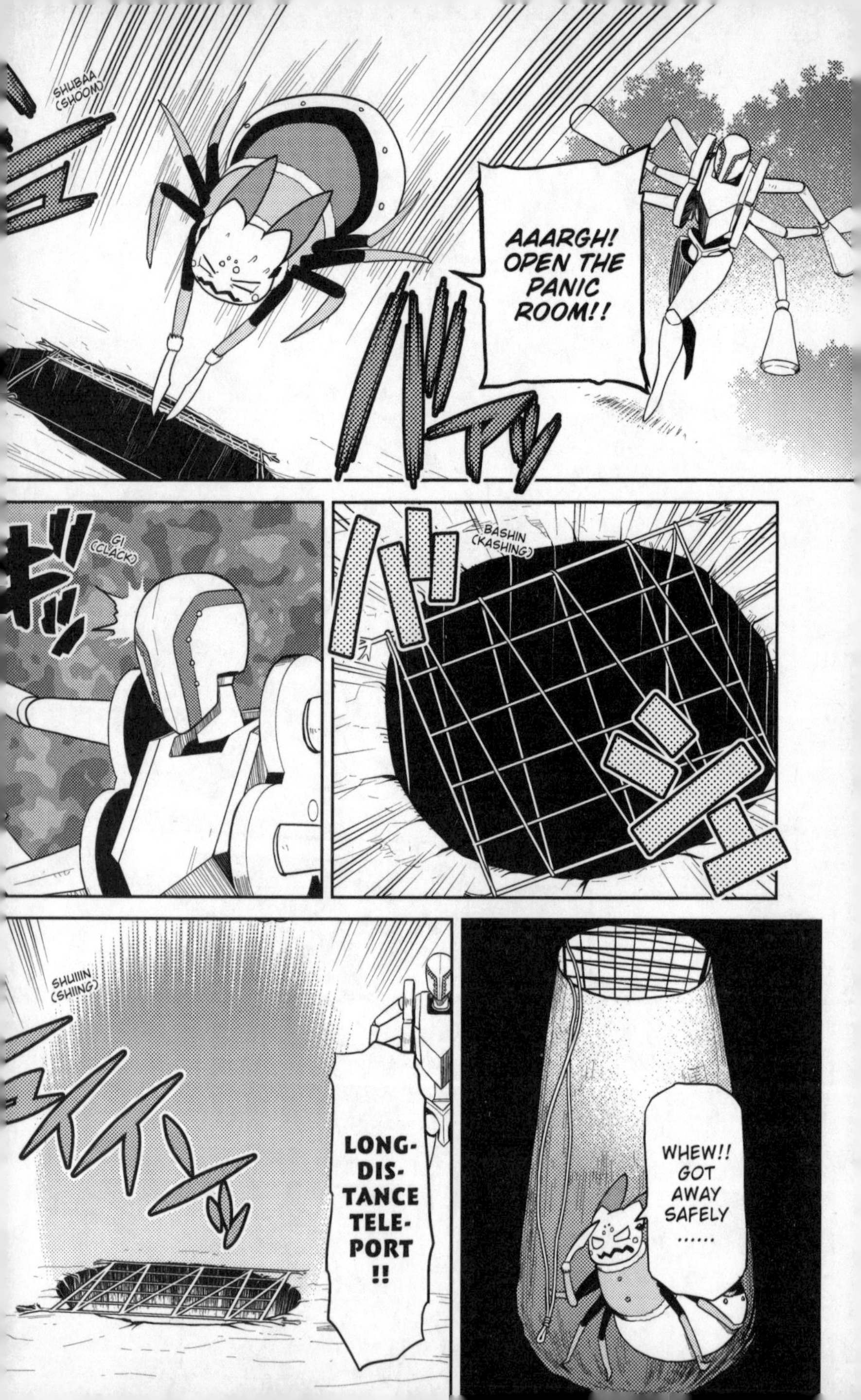
AAARGH! OPEN THE PANIC ROOM!!
SHUBAA (SHOOM)
BASHIN (KASHING)
GI (CLACK)
WHEW!! GOT AWAY SAFELY ......
LONG-DISTANCE TELEPORT!!
SHUIIIN (SHIING)

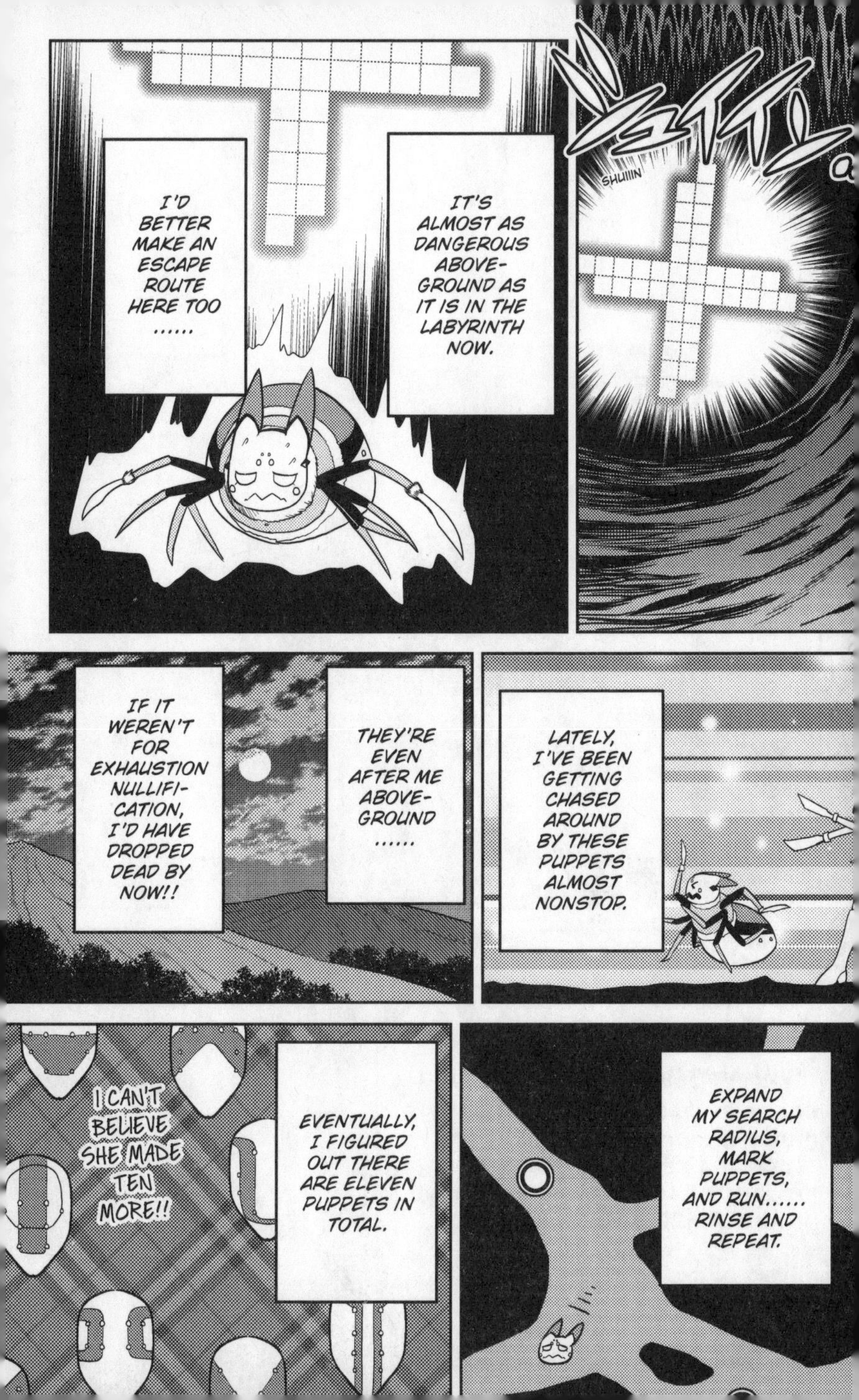
SHUIIIN
IT'S ALMOST AS DANGEROUS ABOVE-GROUND AS IT IS IN THE LABYRINTH NOW.
I'D BETTER MAKE AN ESCAPE ROUTE HERE TOO......
LATELY, I'VE BEEN GETTING CHASED AROUND BY THESE PUPPETS ALMOST NONSTOP.
THEY'RE EVEN AFTER ME ABOVE-GROUND......
IF IT WEREN'T FOR EXHAUSTION NULLIFI-CATION, I'D HAVE DROPPED DEAD BY NOW!!
EXPAND MY SEARCH RADIUS, MARK PUPPETS, AND RUN...... RINSE AND REPEAT.
EVENTUALLY, I FIGURED OUT THERE ARE ELEVEN PUPPETS IN TOTAL.
I CAN'T BELIEVE SHE MADE TEN MORE!!

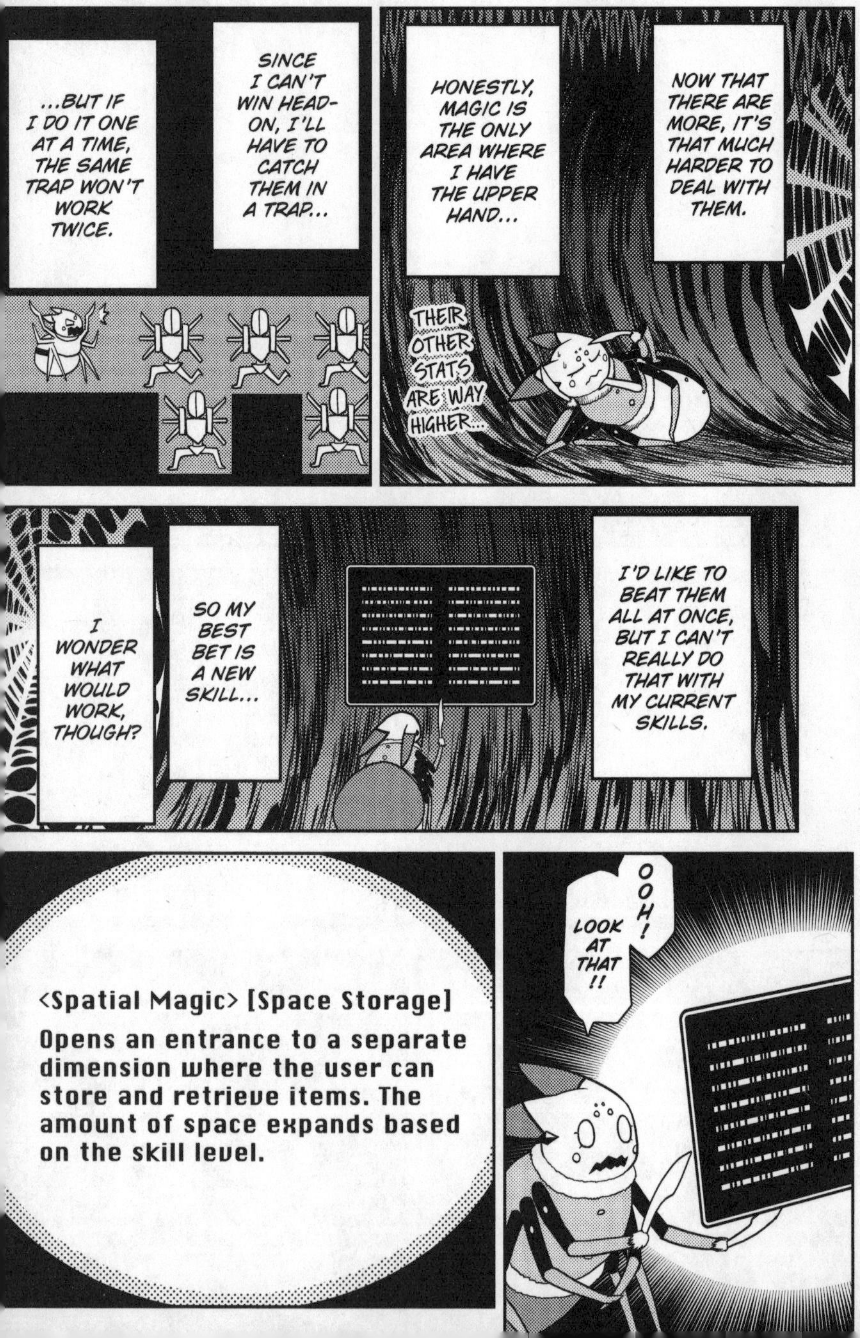
NOW THAT THERE ARE MORE, IT'S THAT MUCH HARDER TO DEAL WITH THEM.
HONESTLY, MAGIC IS THE ONLY AREA WHERE I HAVE THE UPPER HAND...
THEIR OTHER STATS ARE WAY HIGHER...
SINCE I CAN'T WIN HEAD-ON, I'LL HAVE TO CATCH THEM IN A TRAP...
...BUT IF I DO IT ONE AT A TIME, THE SAME TRAP WON'T WORK TWICE.
I'D LIKE TO BEAT THEM ALL AT ONCE, BUT I CAN'T REALLY DO THAT WITH MY CURRENT SKILLS.
SO MY BEST BET IS A NEW SKILL...
I WONDER WHAT WOULD WORK, THOUGH?
OOH!
LOOK AT THAT!!
<Spatial Magic> [Space Storage]
Opens an entrance to a separate dimension where the user can store and retrieve items. The amount of space expands based on the skill level.

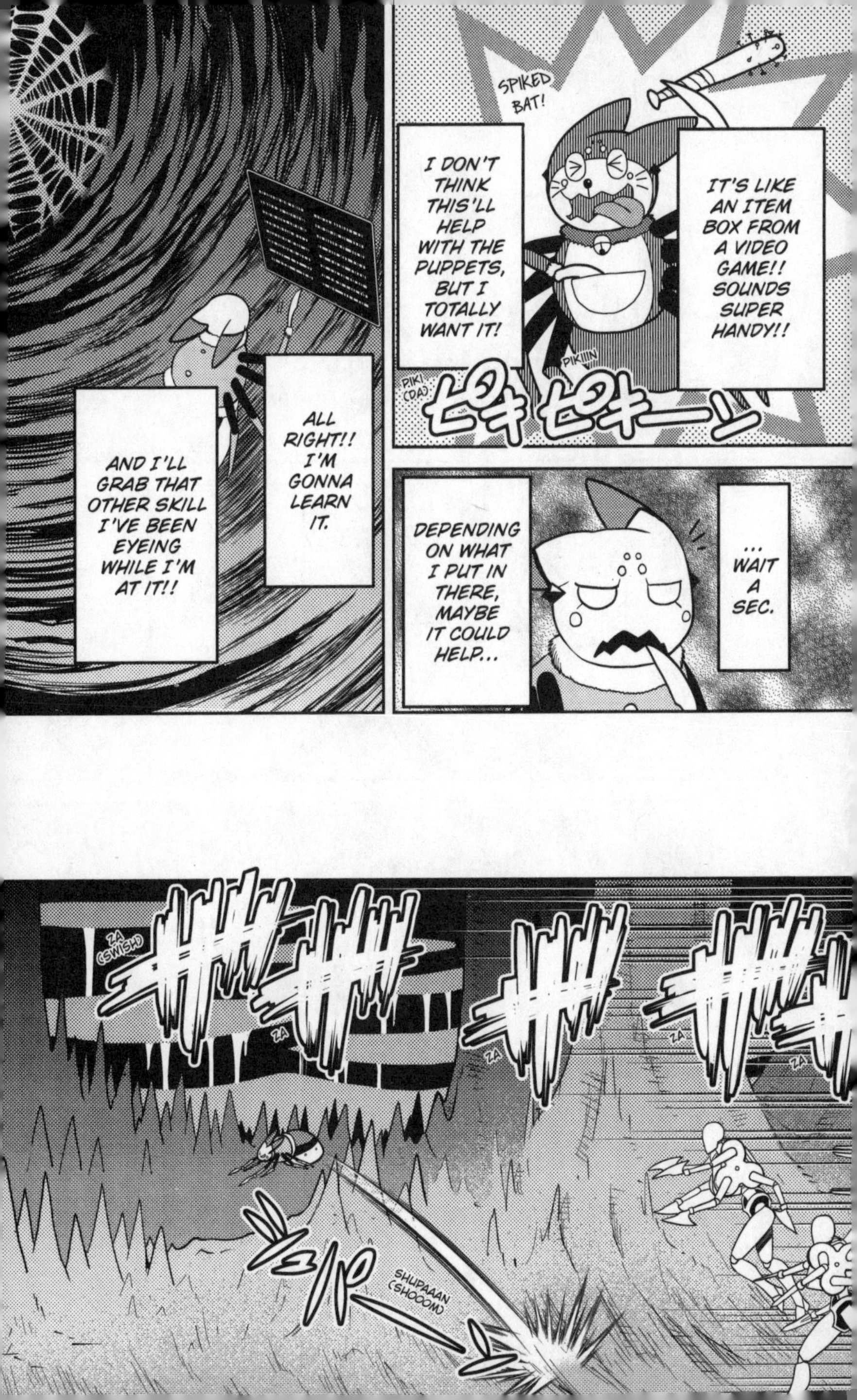
IT'S LIKE AN ITEM BOX FROM A VIDEO GAME!! SOUNDS SUPER HANDY!!
SPIKED BAT!
I DON'T THINK THIS'LL HELP WITH THE PUPPETS, BUT I TOTALLY WANT IT!
PIKIIN
PIKI (DA)
ピキ ピキーン
... WAIT A SEC.
DEPENDING ON WHAT I PUT IN THERE, MAYBE IT COULD HELP...
ALL RIGHT!! I'M GONNA LEARN IT.
AND I'LL GRAB THAT OTHER SKILL I'VE BEEN EYEING WHILE I'M AT IT!!
ZA
ZA
ZA
ZA (SWISH)
SHUPAAAN (SHOOOM)

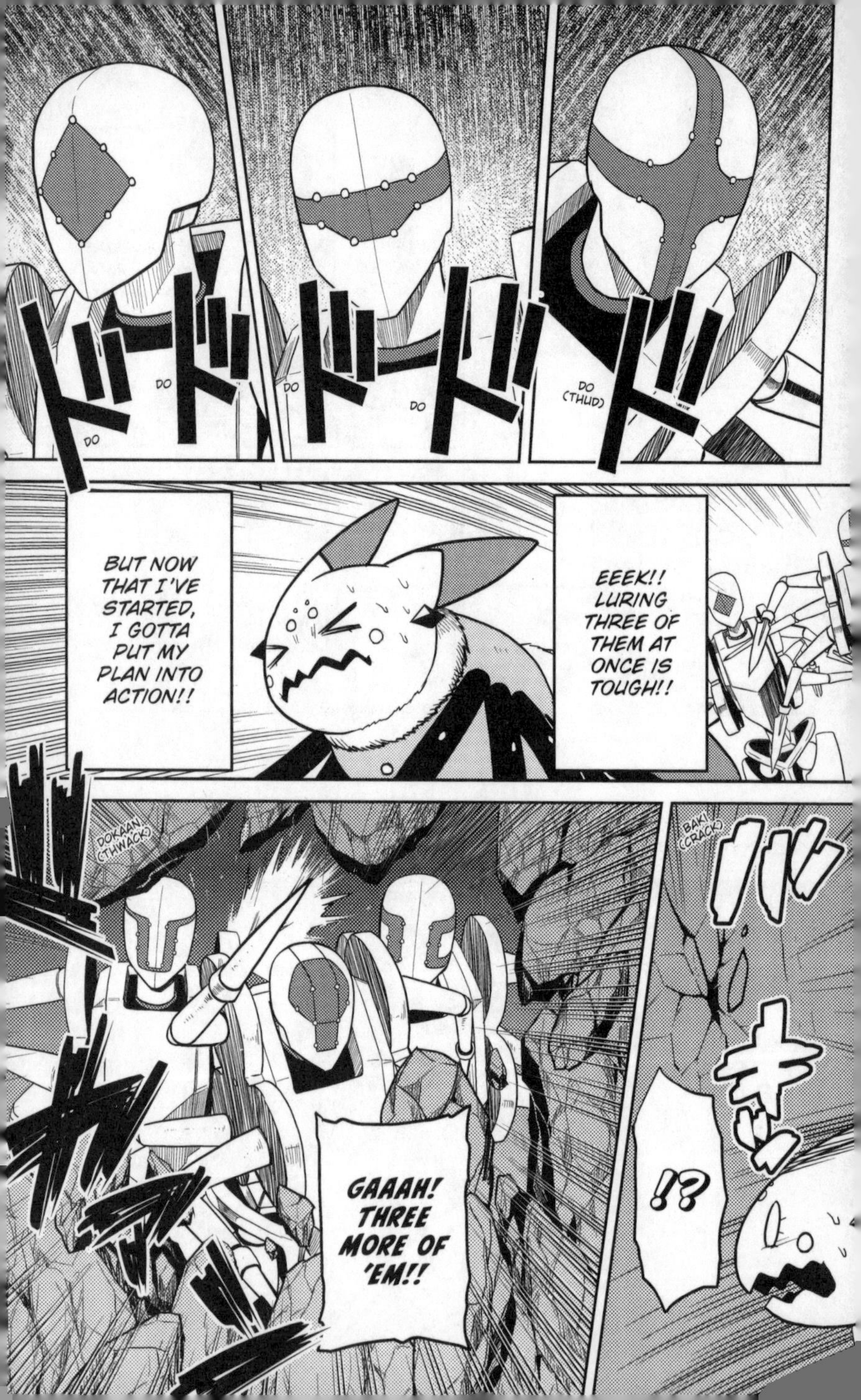

DO (THUD)
DO
DO
DO
DO
EEEK!! LURING THREE OF THEM AT ONCE IS TOUGH!!
BUT NOW THAT I'VE STARTED, I GOTTA PUT MY PLAN INTO ACTION!!
BAKI (CRACK)
!?
DOKAAN (THWACK)
GAAAH! THREE MORE OF 'EM!!

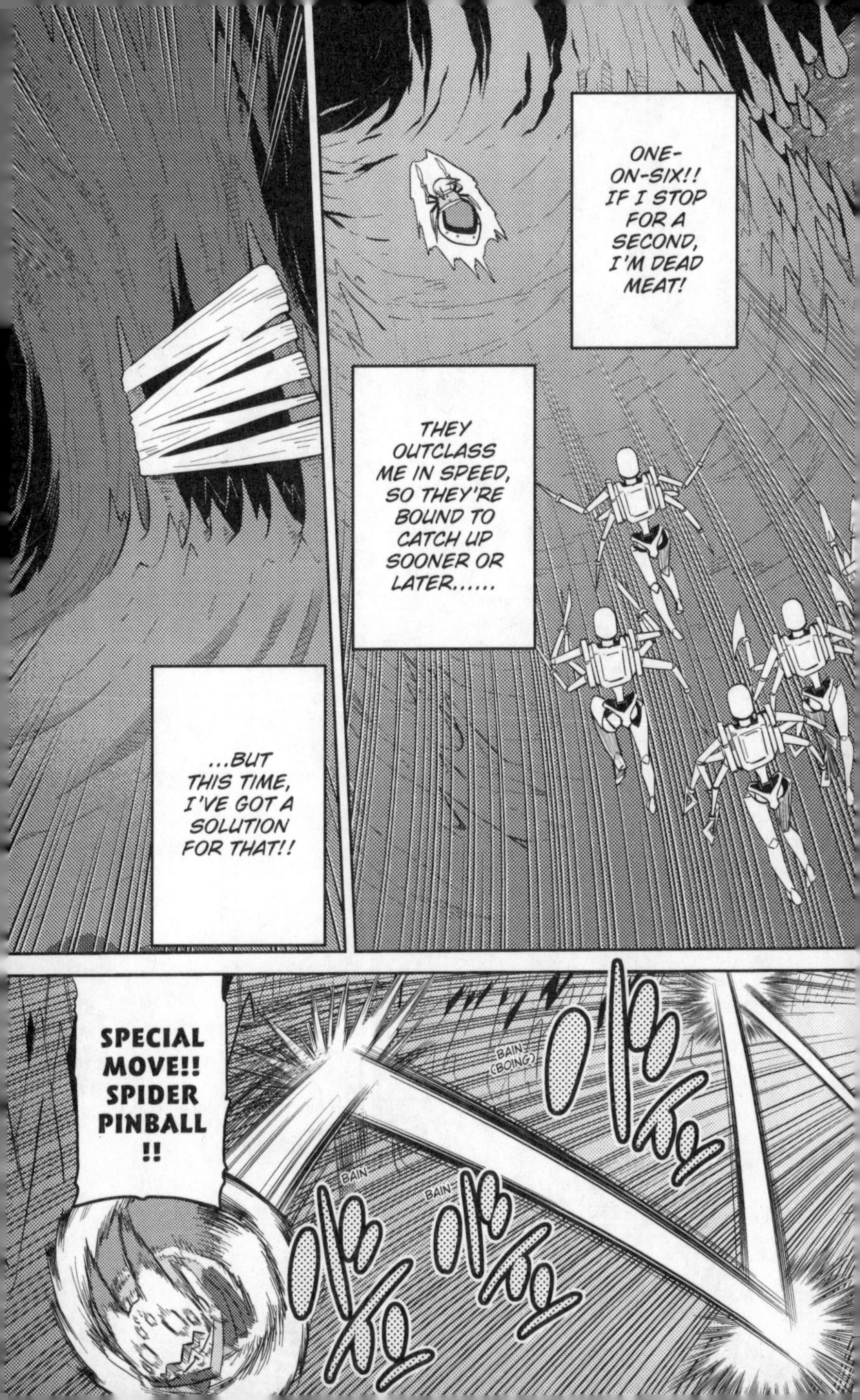
ONE-ON-SIX!! IF I STOP FOR A SECOND, I'M DEAD MEAT!
THEY OUTCLASS ME IN SPEED, SO THEY'RE BOUND TO CATCH UP SOONER OR LATER......
...BUT THIS TIME, I'VE GOT A SOLUTION FOR THAT!!
SPECIAL MOVE!! SPIDER PINBALL !!
BAIN (BOING)
BAIN
BAIN

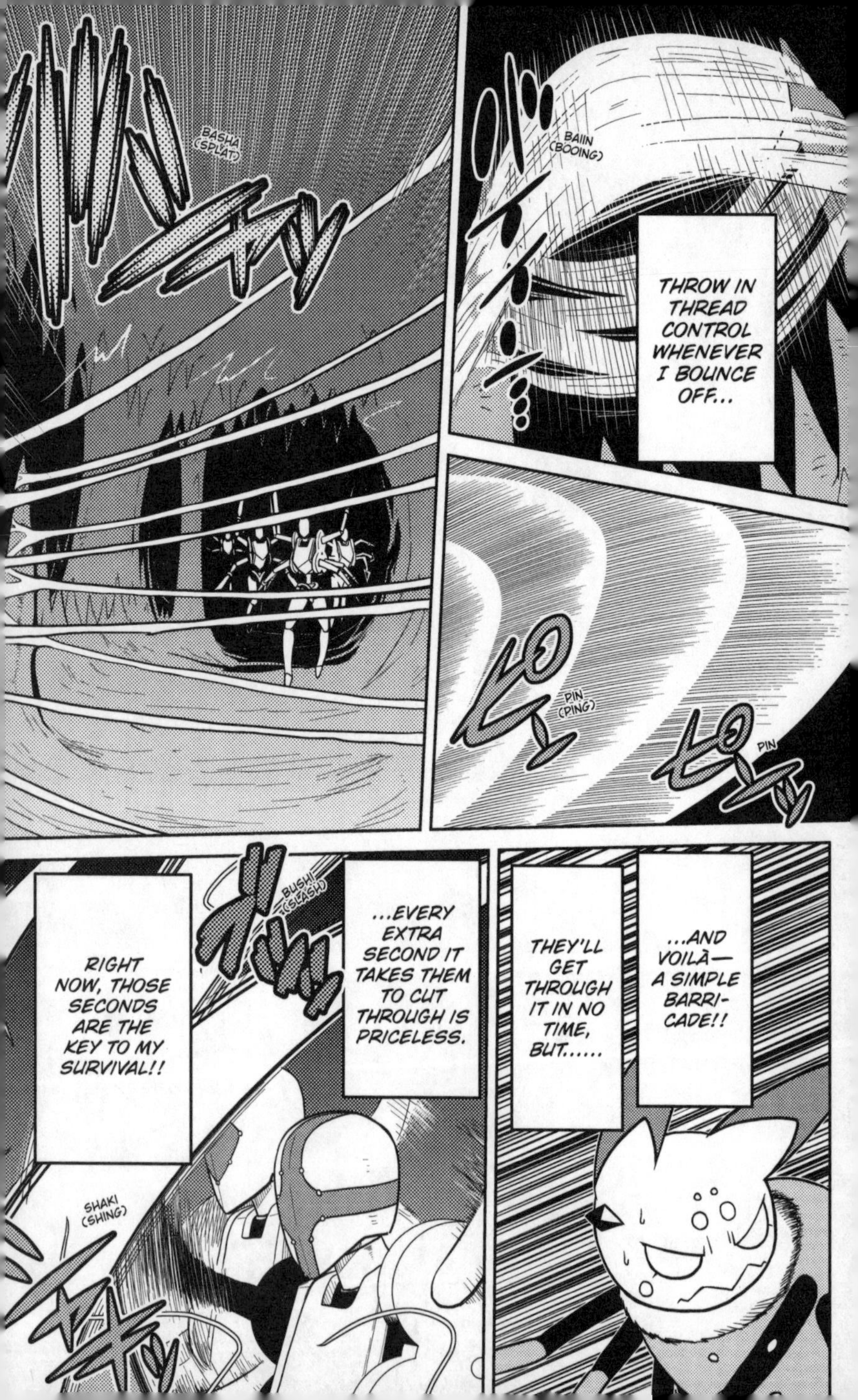
BAIIN
(BOOING)
THROW IN THREAD CONTROL WHENEVER I BOUNCE OFF...
PIN
(PING)
PIN
BASHA
(SPLAT)
...AND VOILÀ— A SIMPLE BARRI-CADE!!
THEY'LL GET THROUGH IT IN NO TIME, BUT......
...EVERY EXTRA SECOND IT TAKES THEM TO CUT THROUGH IS PRICELESS.
BUSHI
(SLASH)
RIGHT NOW, THOSE SECONDS ARE THE KEY TO MY SURVIVAL!!
SHAKI
(SHING)

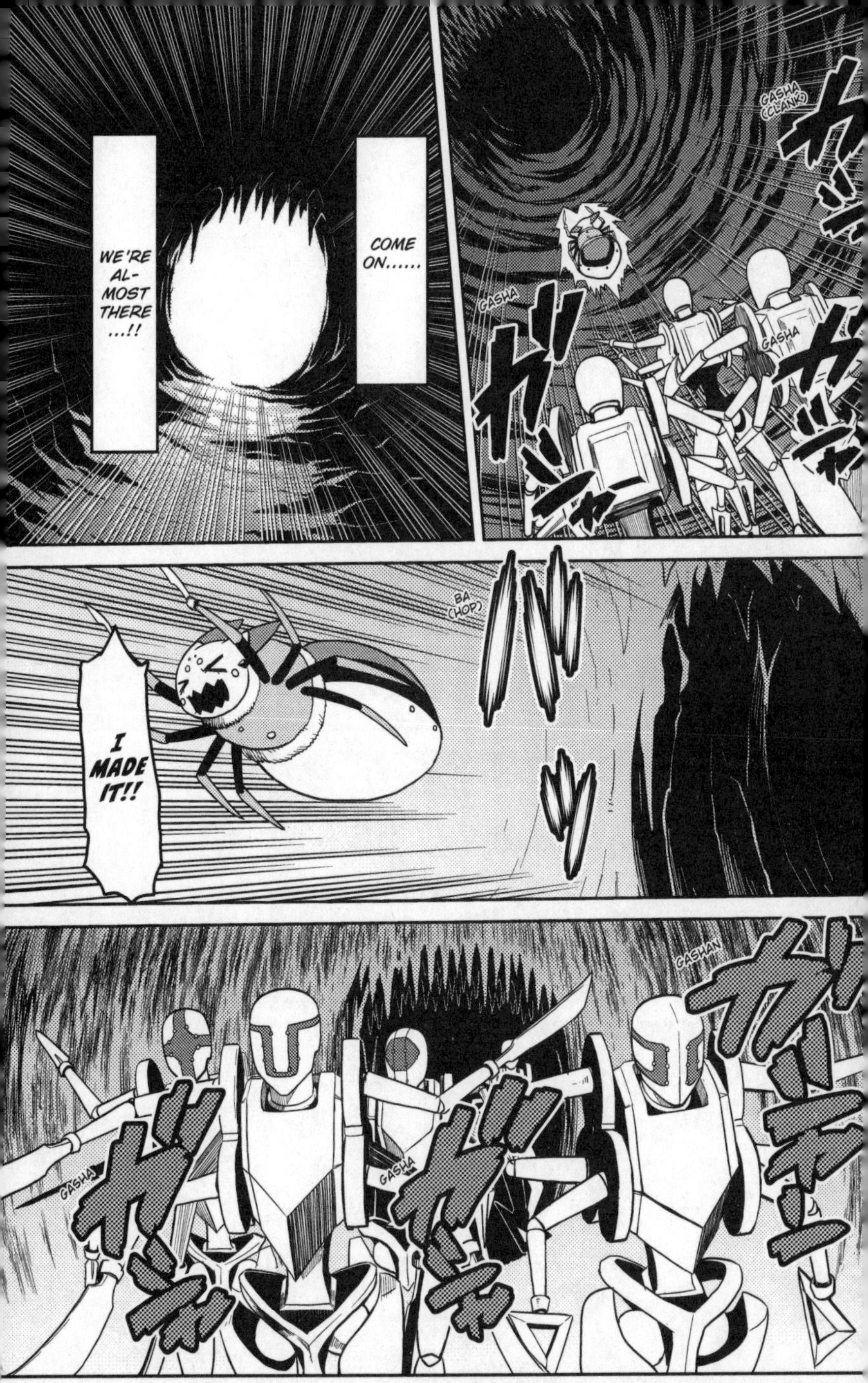
COME ON......
WE'RE AL-MOST THERE ...!!
GASHA (CLANK)
GASHA
GASHA
BA (HOP)
I MADE IT!!
GASHAN
GASHA
GASHA

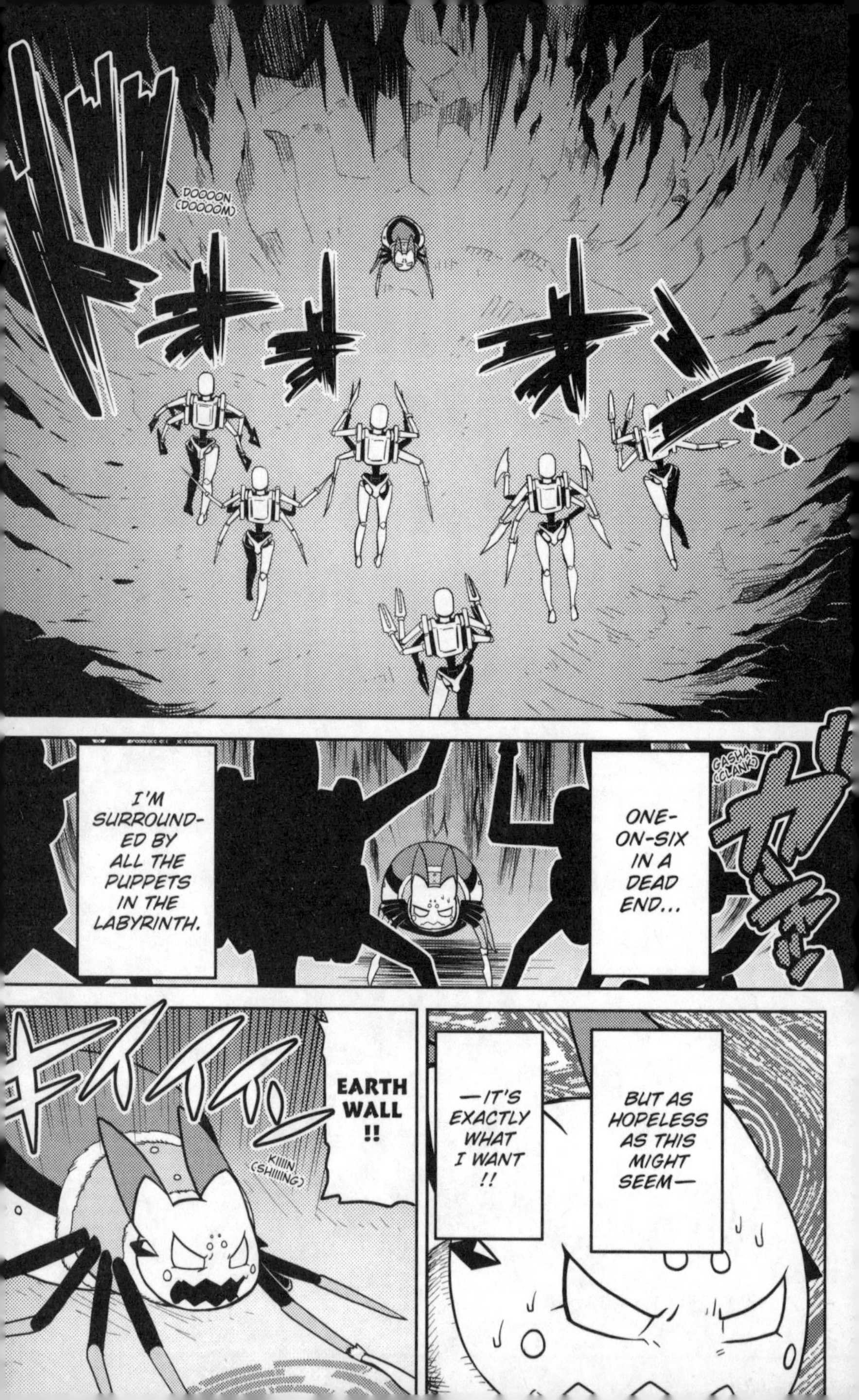
DOOOON (DOOOOM)
GASHA (CLANK)
ONE-ON-SIX IN A DEAD END...
I'M SURROUNDED-ED BY ALL THE PUPPETS IN THE LABYRINTH.
BUT AS HOPELESS AS THIS MIGHT SEEM—
—IT'S EXACTLY WHAT I WANT !!
EARTH WALL !!
KIIIN (SHIIIING)

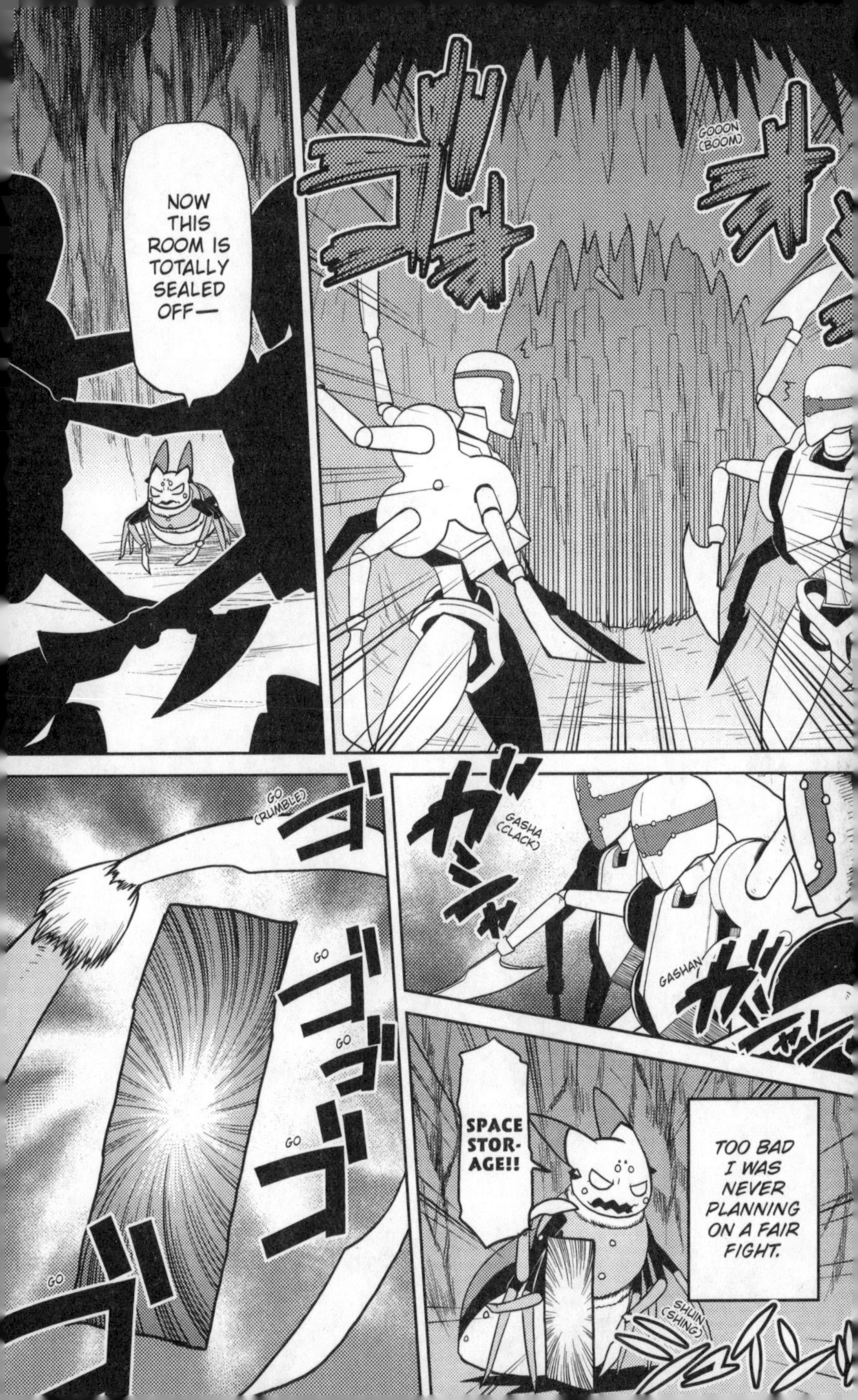
GOOON (BOOM)
NOW THIS ROOM IS TOTALLY SEALED OFF—
GASHA (CLACK)
GASHAN
TOO BAD I WAS NEVER PLANNING ON A FAIR FIGHT.
SPACE STORAGE!!
SHUIN (SHING)
GO (RUMBLE)
GO
GO
GO
GO

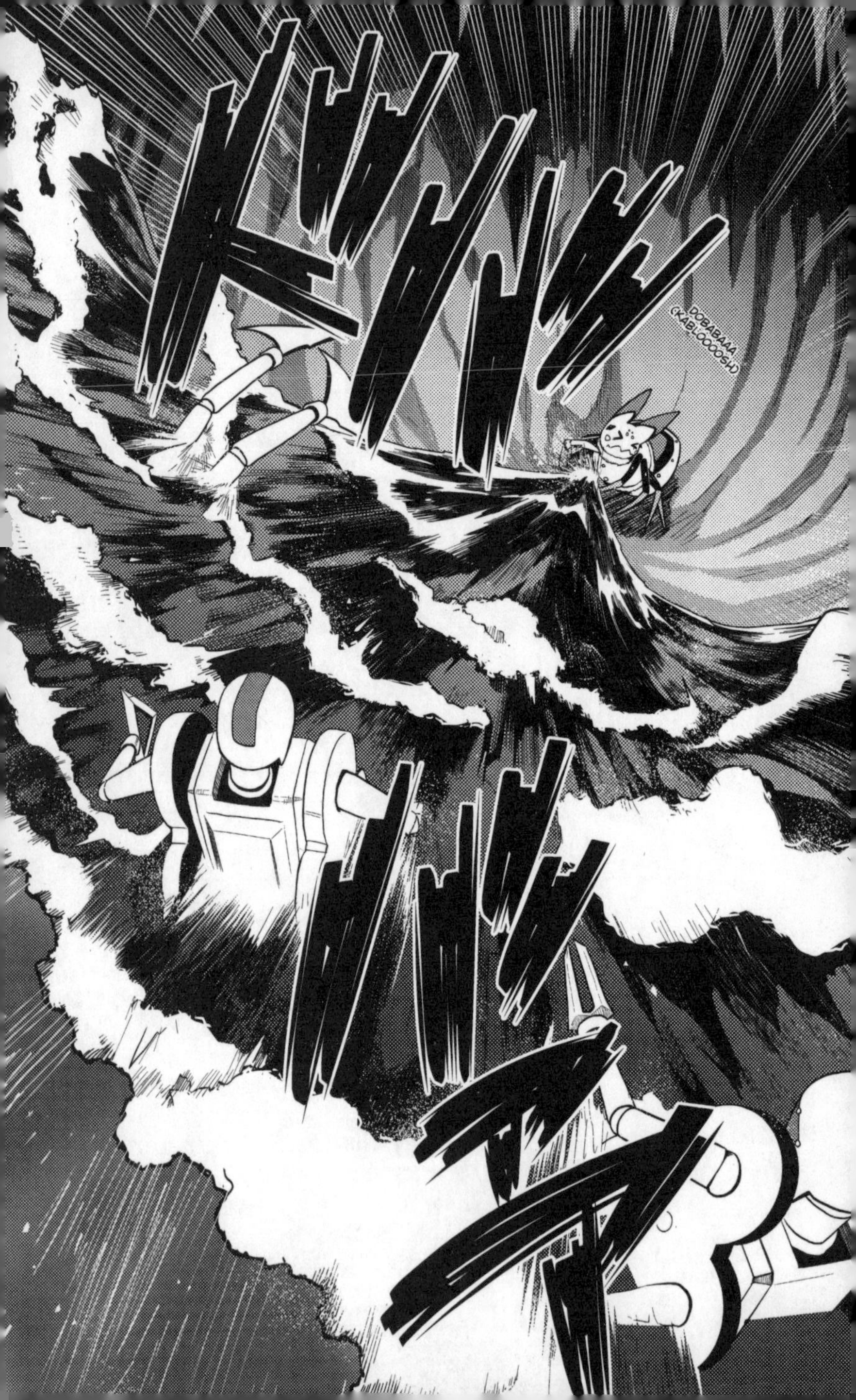
DOBABAAA
(KABLOOOOSH)

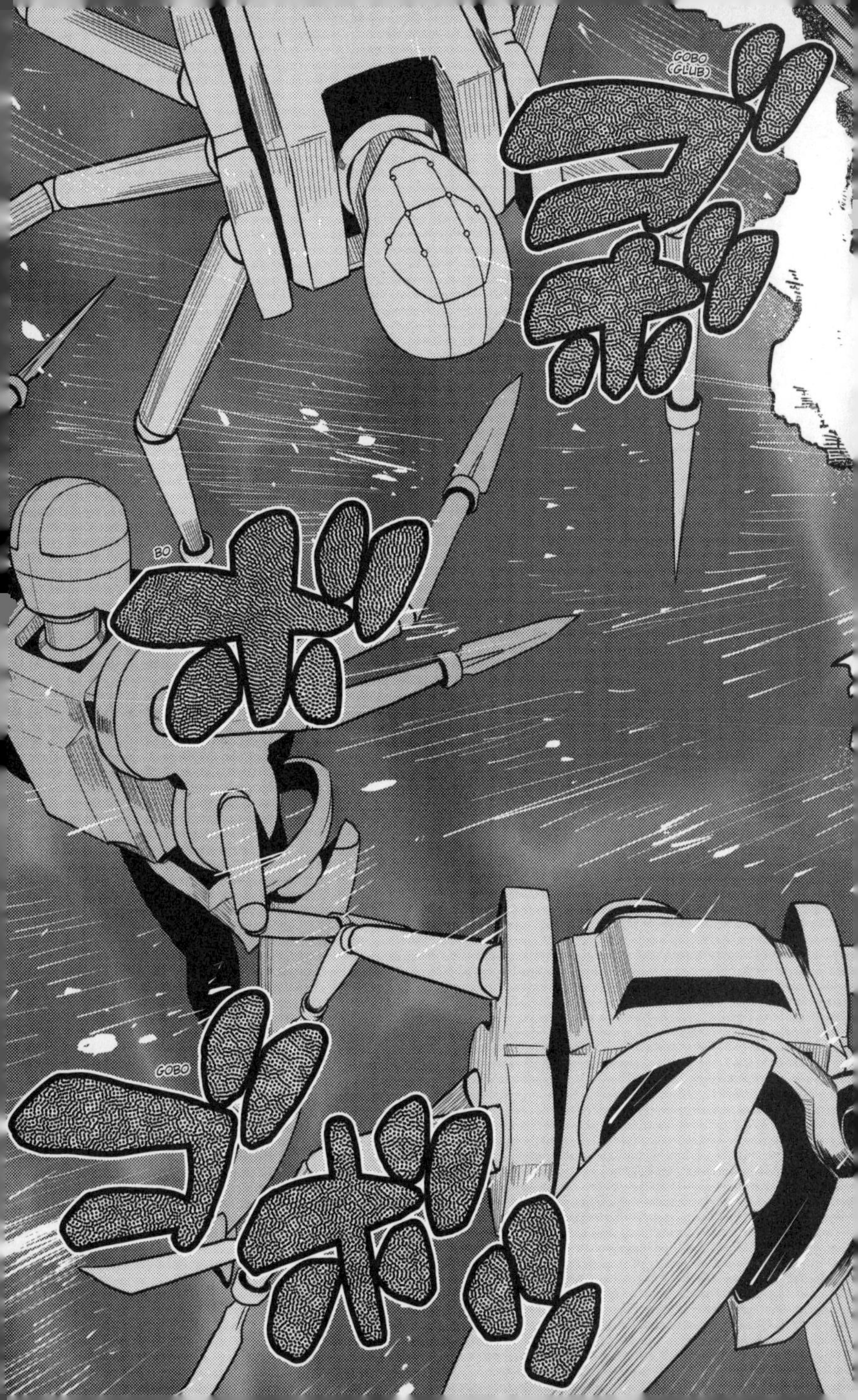
ゴボ
GOBO (GLUB)
ボ
BO
ゴボッ
GOBO

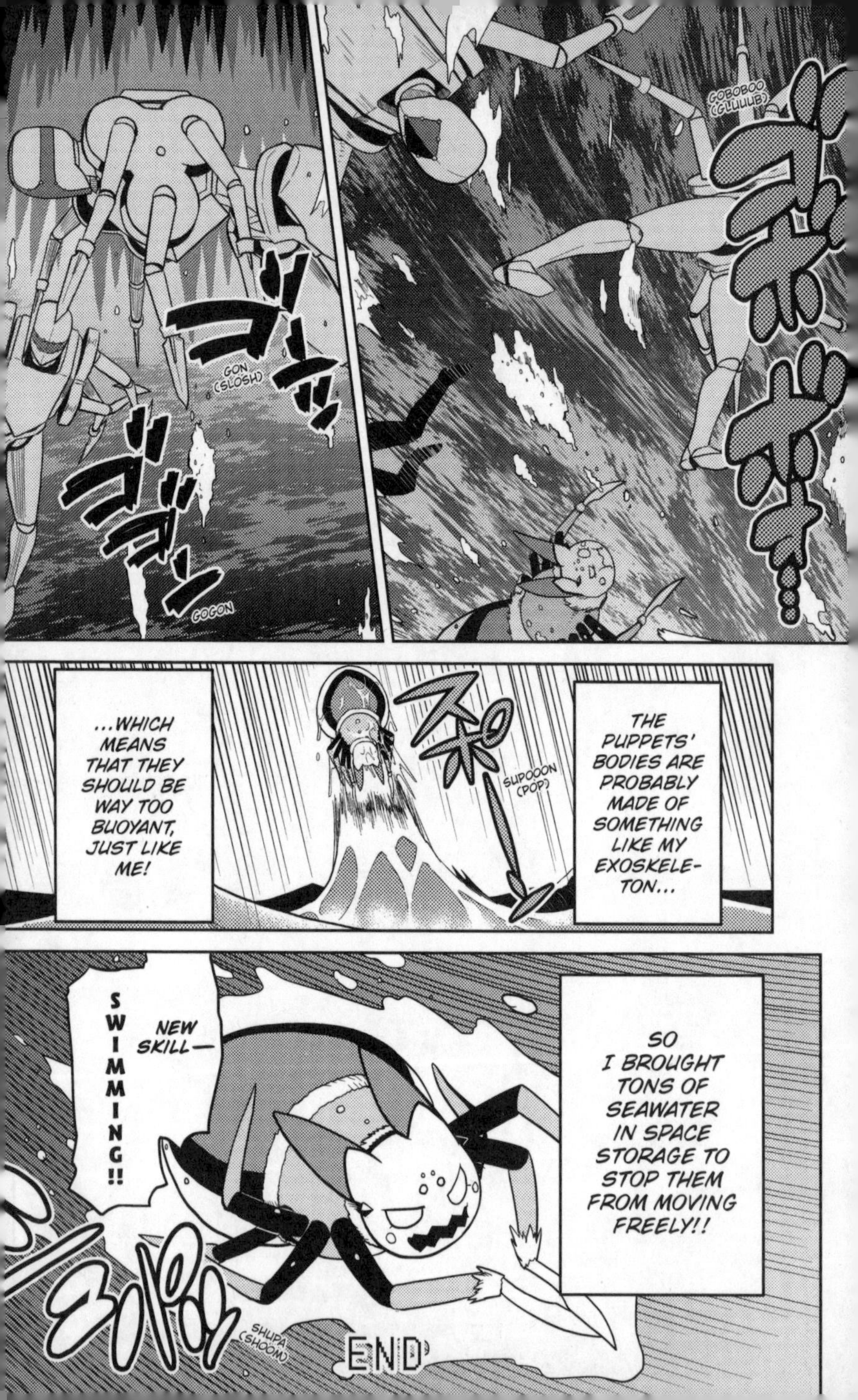
GOBOBOO (GLUUUB)
GON (SLOSH)
GOGON
THE PUPPETS' BODIES ARE PROBABLY MADE OF SOMETHING LIKE MY EXOSKELE- TON...
SUPOOON (POP)
...WHICH MEANS THAT THEY SHOULD BE WAY TOO BUOYANT, JUST LIKE ME!
SO I BROUGHT TONS OF SEAWATER IN SPACE STORAGE TO STOP THEM FROM MOVING FREELY!!
NEW SKILL—
SWIMMING!!
SHUPA (SHOOM)
END

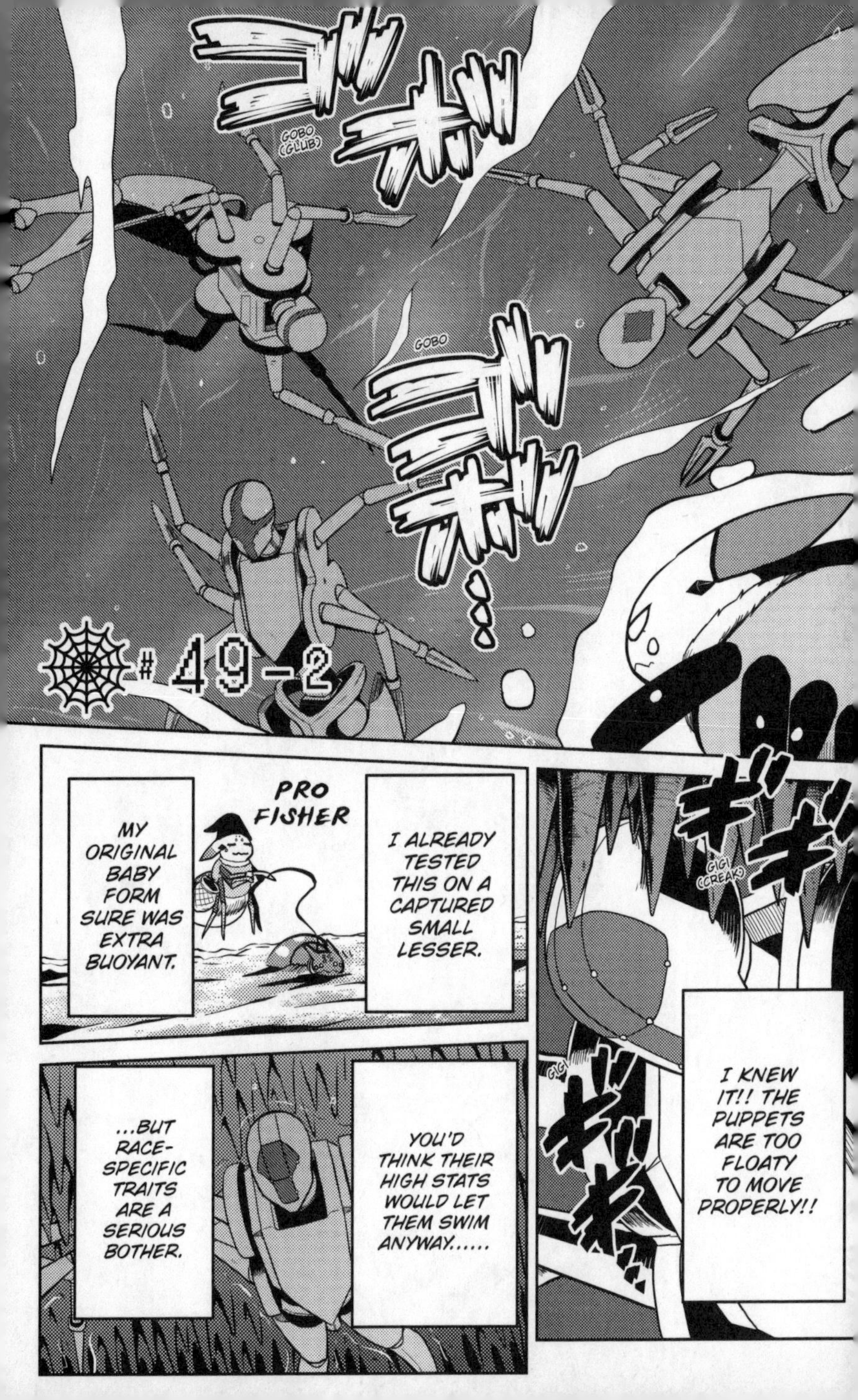
GOBO (GLUB)
GOBO
49-2
GIGI (CREAK)
GIGI
I KNEW IT!! THE PUPPETS ARE TOO FLOATY TO MOVE PROPERLY!!
I ALREADY TESTED THIS ON A CAPTURED SMALL LESSER.
PRO FISHER
MY ORIGINAL BABY FORM SURE WAS EXTRA BUOYANT.
YOU'D THINK THEIR HIGH STATS WOULD LET THEM SWIM ANYWAY......
...BUT RACE-SPECIFIC TRAITS ARE A SERIOUS BOTHER.

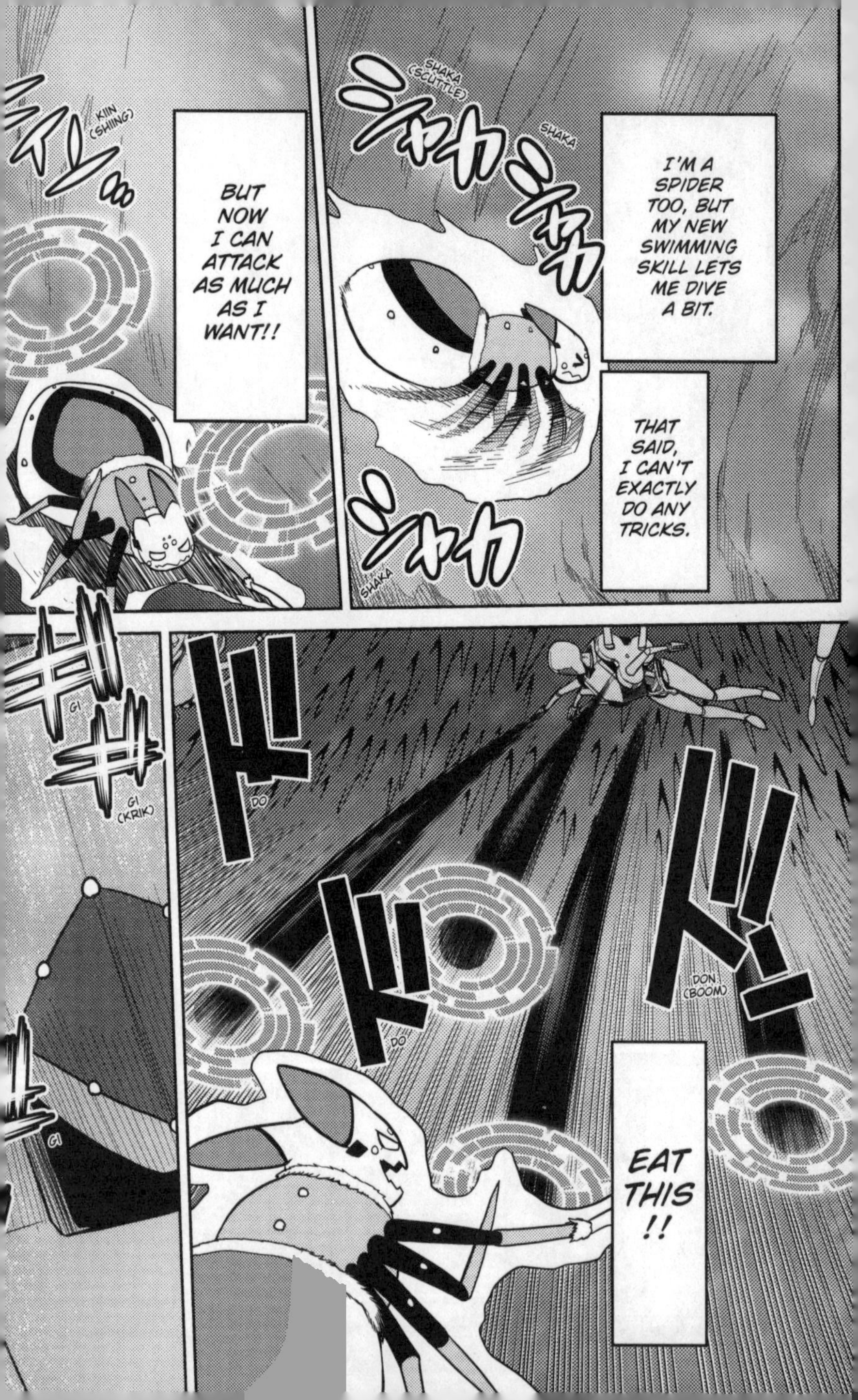
SHAKA (SCUTTLE)
SHAKA
I'M A SPIDER TOO, BUT MY NEW SWIMMING SKILL LETS ME DIVE A BIT.
THAT SAID, I CAN'T EXACTLY DO ANY TRICKS.
SHAKA
KIIN (SHIING)
BUT NOW I CAN ATTACK AS MUCH AS I WANT!!
DON (BOOM)
DO
DO
EAT THIS!!
GI
GI (KRIK)
GI

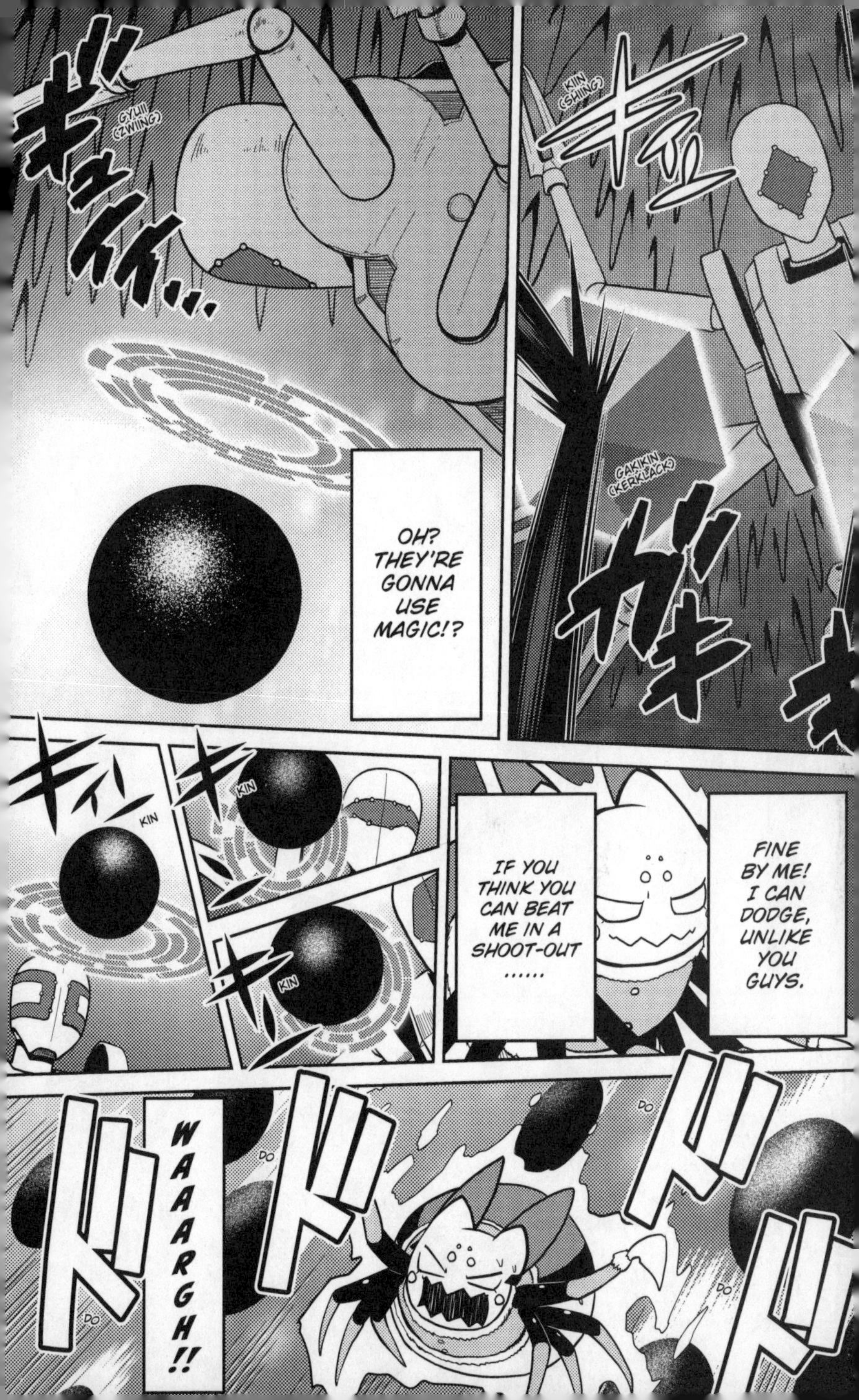
KIIN (SHIING)
GAKIKIN (KERKLACK)
GYUII (ZWIING)
OH? THEY'RE GONNA USE MAGIC!?
FINE BY ME! I CAN DODGE, UNLIKE YOU GUYS.
IF YOU THINK YOU CAN BEAT ME IN A SHOOT-OUT ......
KIN
KIN
KIN
DO
DO
WAAAARGH!!
DO
DO

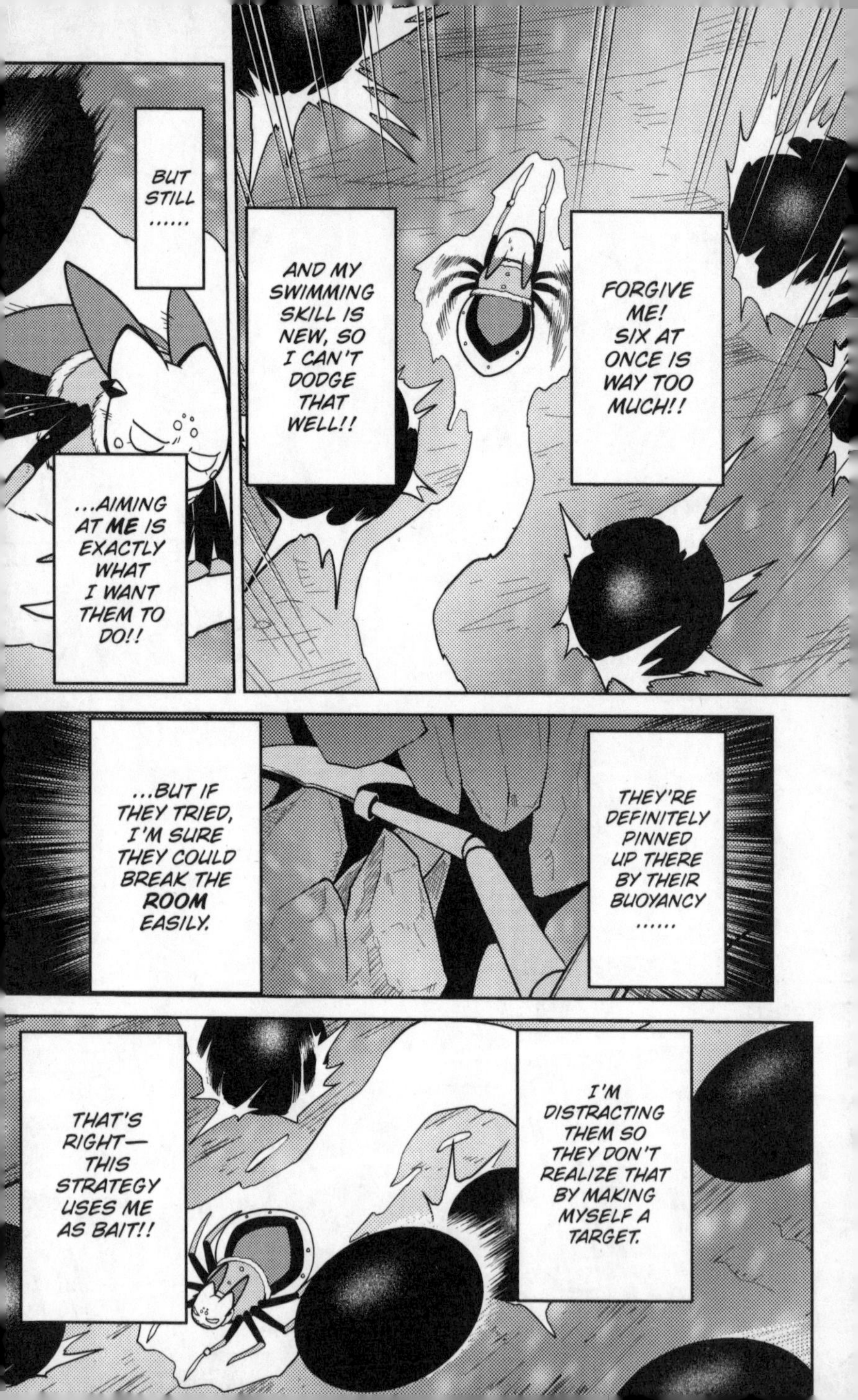
FORGIVE ME! SIX AT ONCE IS WAY TOO MUCH!!
AND MY SWIMMING SKILL IS NEW, SO I CAN'T DODGE THAT WELL!!
BUT STILL......
...AIMING AT **ME** IS EXACTLY WHAT I WANT THEM TO DO!!
THEY'RE DEFINITELY PINNED UP THERE BY THEIR BUOYANCY......
...BUT IF THEY TRIED, I'M SURE THEY COULD BREAK THE **ROOM** EASILY.
I'M DISTRACTING THEM SO THEY DON'T REALIZE THAT BY MAKING MYSELF A TARGET.
THAT'S RIGHT—THIS STRATEGY USES ME AS BAIT!!

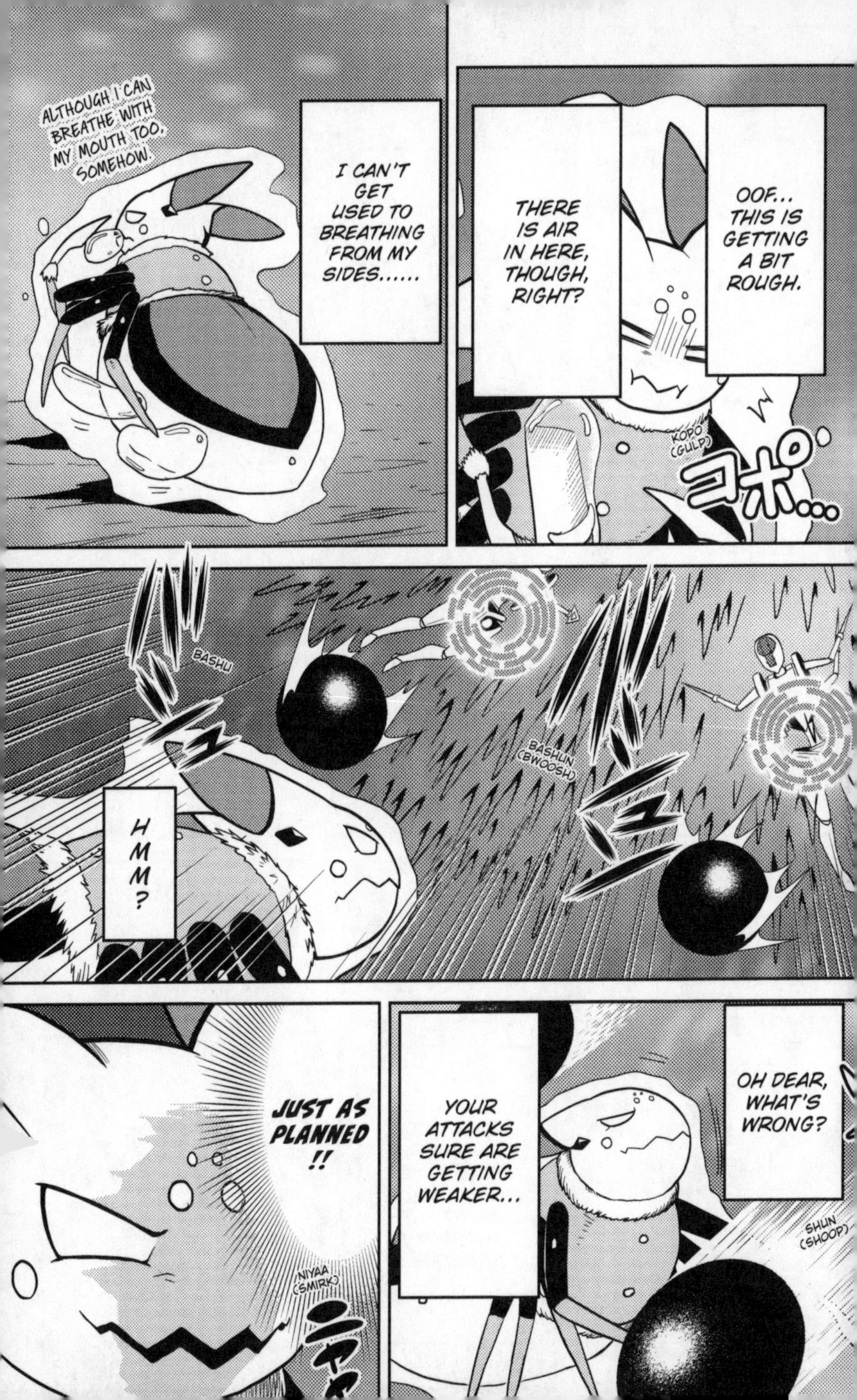
OOF... THIS IS GETTING A BIT ROUGH.
THERE IS AIR IN HERE, THOUGH, RIGHT?
KOPO (GULP)
コポ…
I CAN'T GET USED TO BREATHING FROM MY SIDES......
ALTHOUGH I CAN BREATHE WITH MY MOUTH TOO, SOMEHOW.
BASHUN (BWOOSH)
BASHU
HMM?
OH DEAR, WHAT'S WRONG?
YOUR ATTACKS SURE ARE GETTING WEAKER...
SHUN (SHOOP)
JUST AS PLANNED!!
NIYAA (SMIRK)

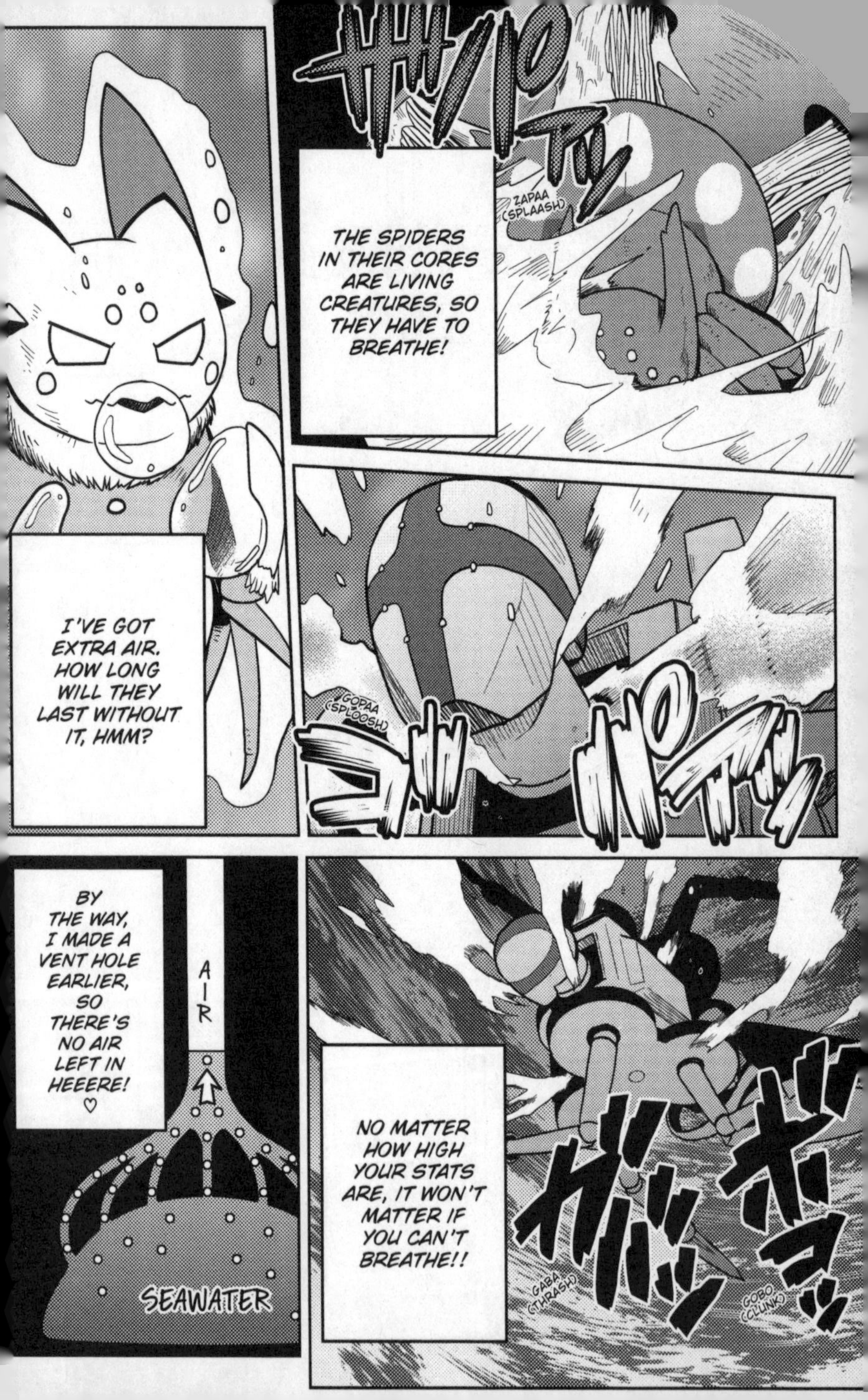
ZAPAA (SPLAASH)
THE SPIDERS IN THEIR CORES ARE LIVING CREATURES, SO THEY HAVE TO BREATHE!
GOPAA (SPLOOSH)
I'VE GOT EXTRA AIR. HOW LONG WILL THEY LAST WITHOUT IT, HMM?
NO MATTER HOW HIGH YOUR STATS ARE, IT WON'T MATTER IF YOU CAN'T BREATHE!!
GOBO (CLUNK)
GABA (THRASH)
BY THE WAY, I MADE A VENT HOLE EARLIER, SO THERE'S NO AIR LEFT IN HEEERE! ♡
AIR
SEAWATER

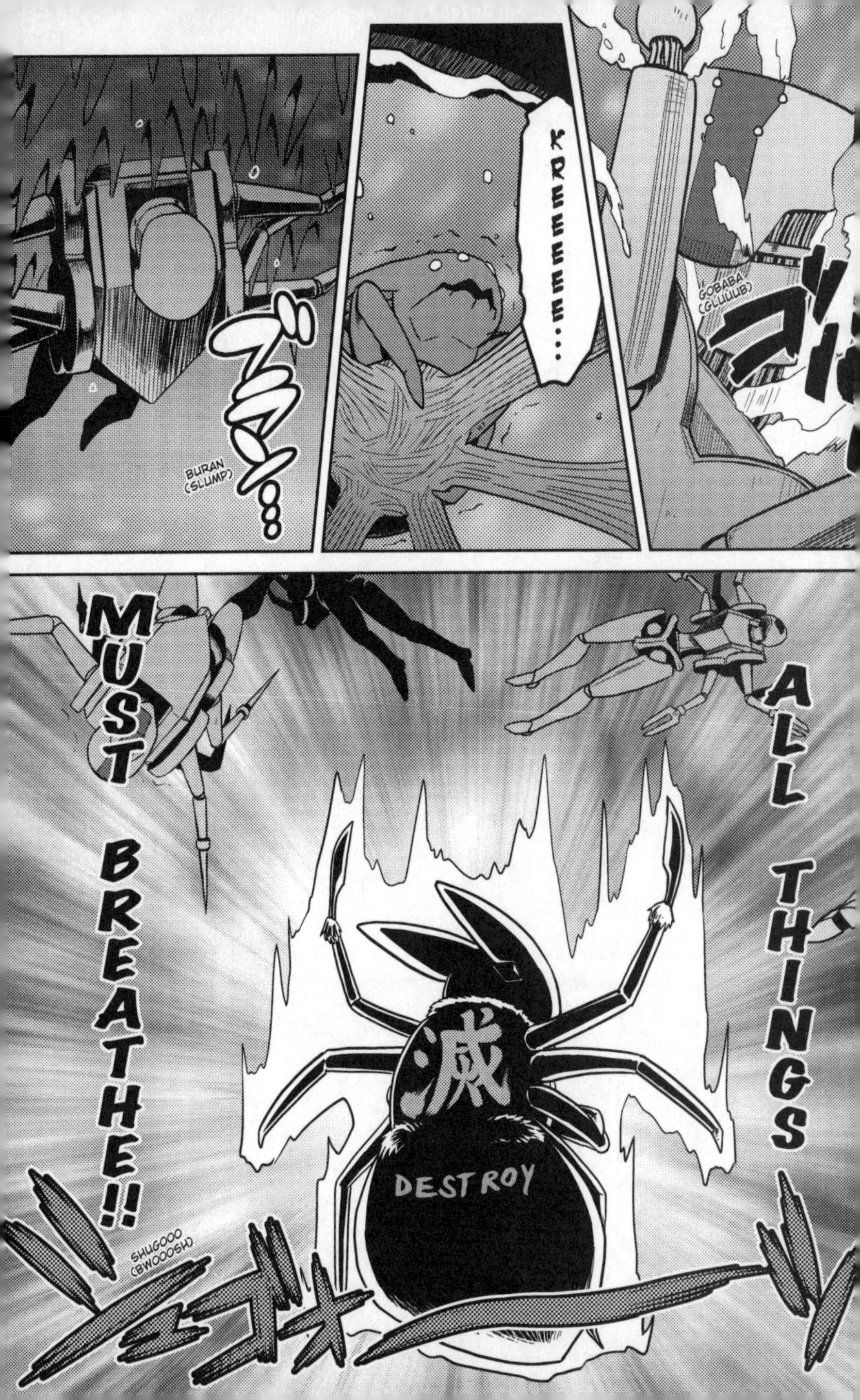
GOBABA (GLUUUB)
KREEEEEE...
BURAN (SLUMP)
ALL THINGS
MUST BREATHE!!
DESTROY
SHUGOOO (BWOOOSH)

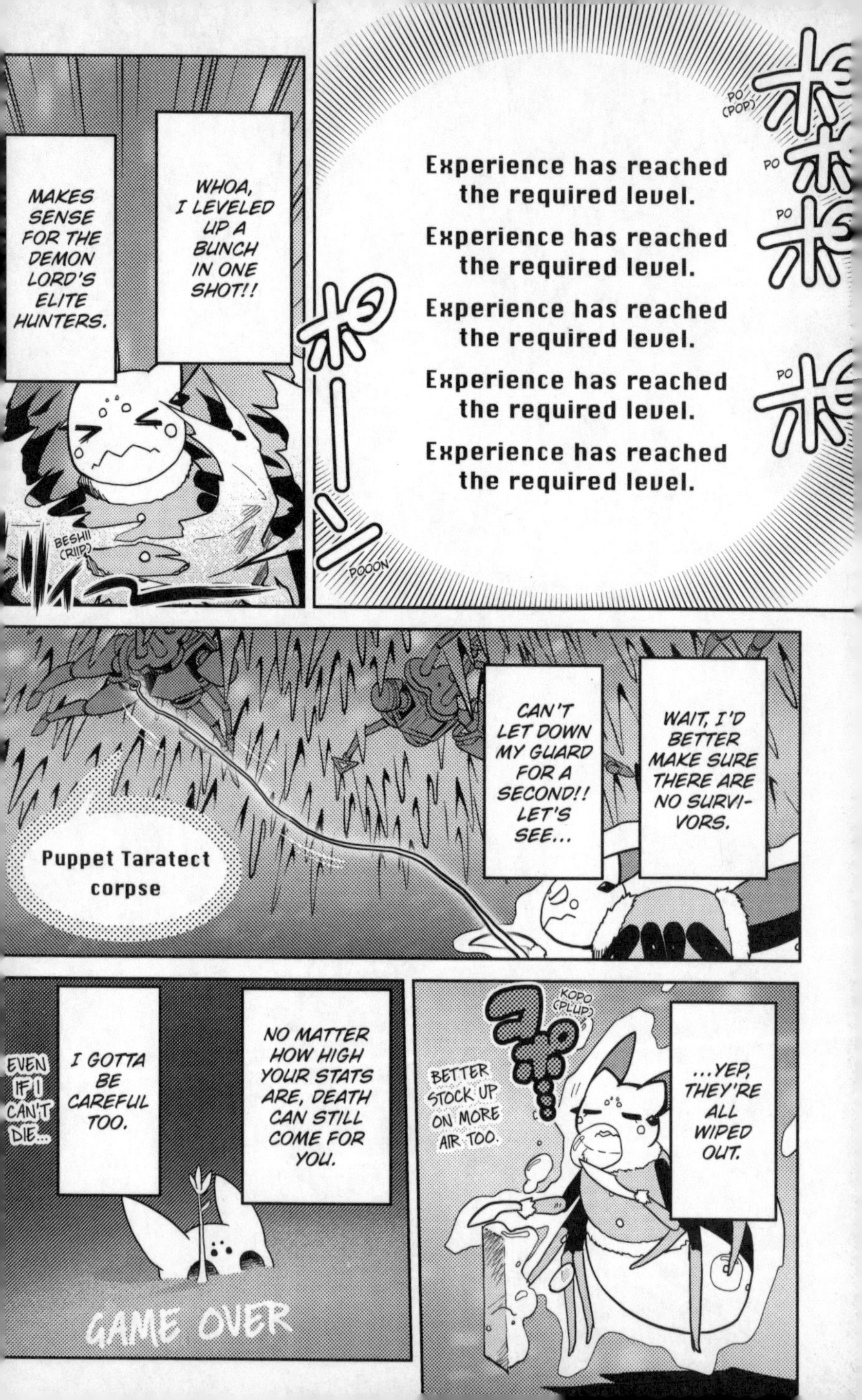
PO (POP)
PO
PO
PO
Experience has reached the required level.
Experience has reached the required level.
Experience has reached the required level.
Experience has reached the required level.
Experience has reached the required level.
POOON
WHOA, I LEVELED UP A BUNCH IN ONE SHOT!!
MAKES SENSE FOR THE DEMON LORD'S ELITE HUNTERS.
BESHII (RIIP)
WAIT, I'D BETTER MAKE SURE THERE ARE NO SURVI-VORS.
CAN'T LET DOWN MY GUARD FOR A SECOND!! LET'S SEE...
Puppet Taratect corpse
KOPO (PLUP)
...YEP, THEY'RE ALL WIPED OUT.
BETTER STOCK UP ON MORE AIR TOO.
NO MATTER HOW HIGH YOUR STATS ARE, DEATH CAN STILL COME FOR YOU.
I GOTTA BE CAREFUL TOO.
EVEN IF I CAN'T DIE...
GAME OVER

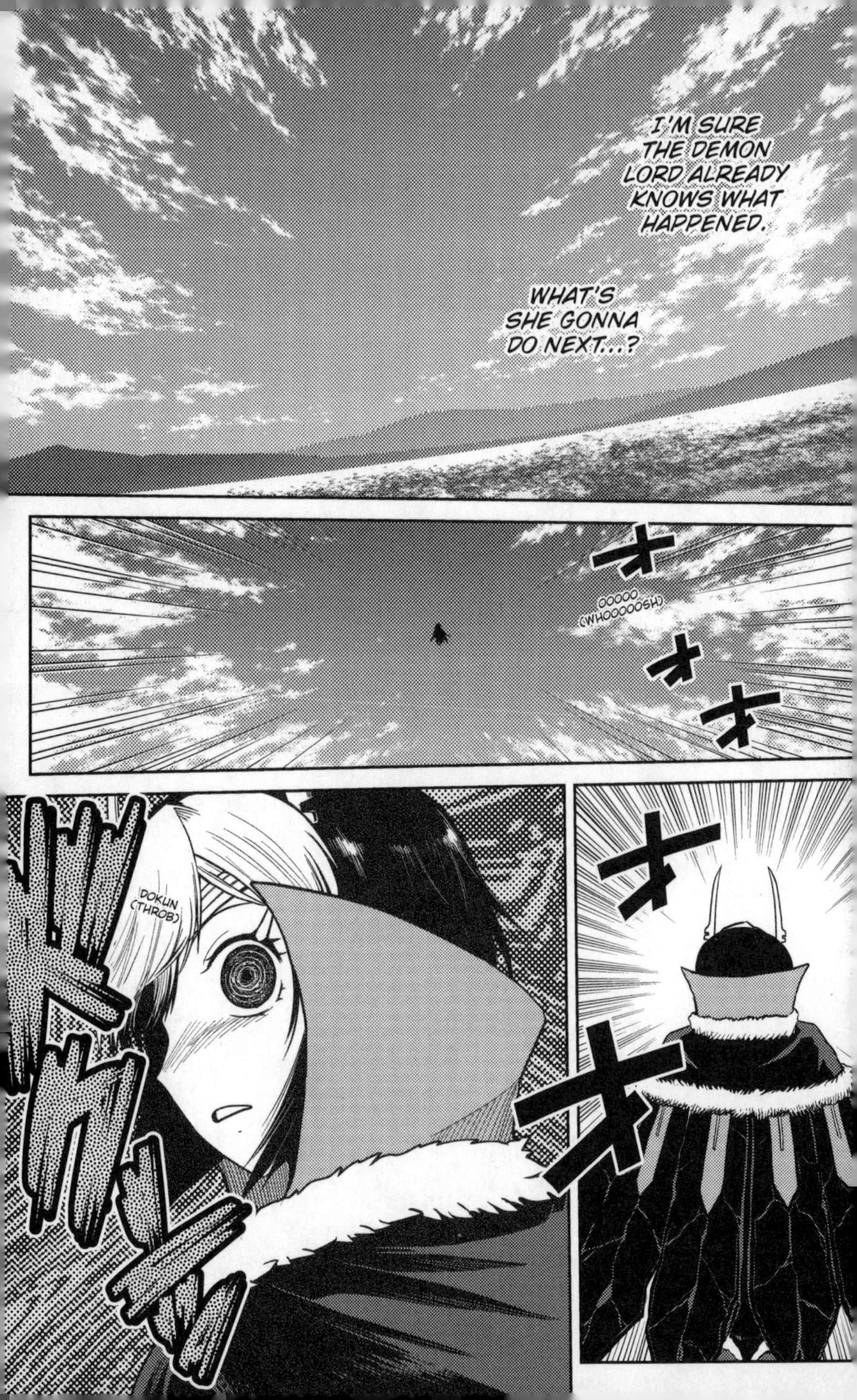
I'M SURE THE DEMON LORD ALREADY KNOWS WHAT HAPPENED.
WHAT'S SHE GONNA DO NEXT...?
OOOOO (WHOOOOOSH)
DOKUN (THROB)

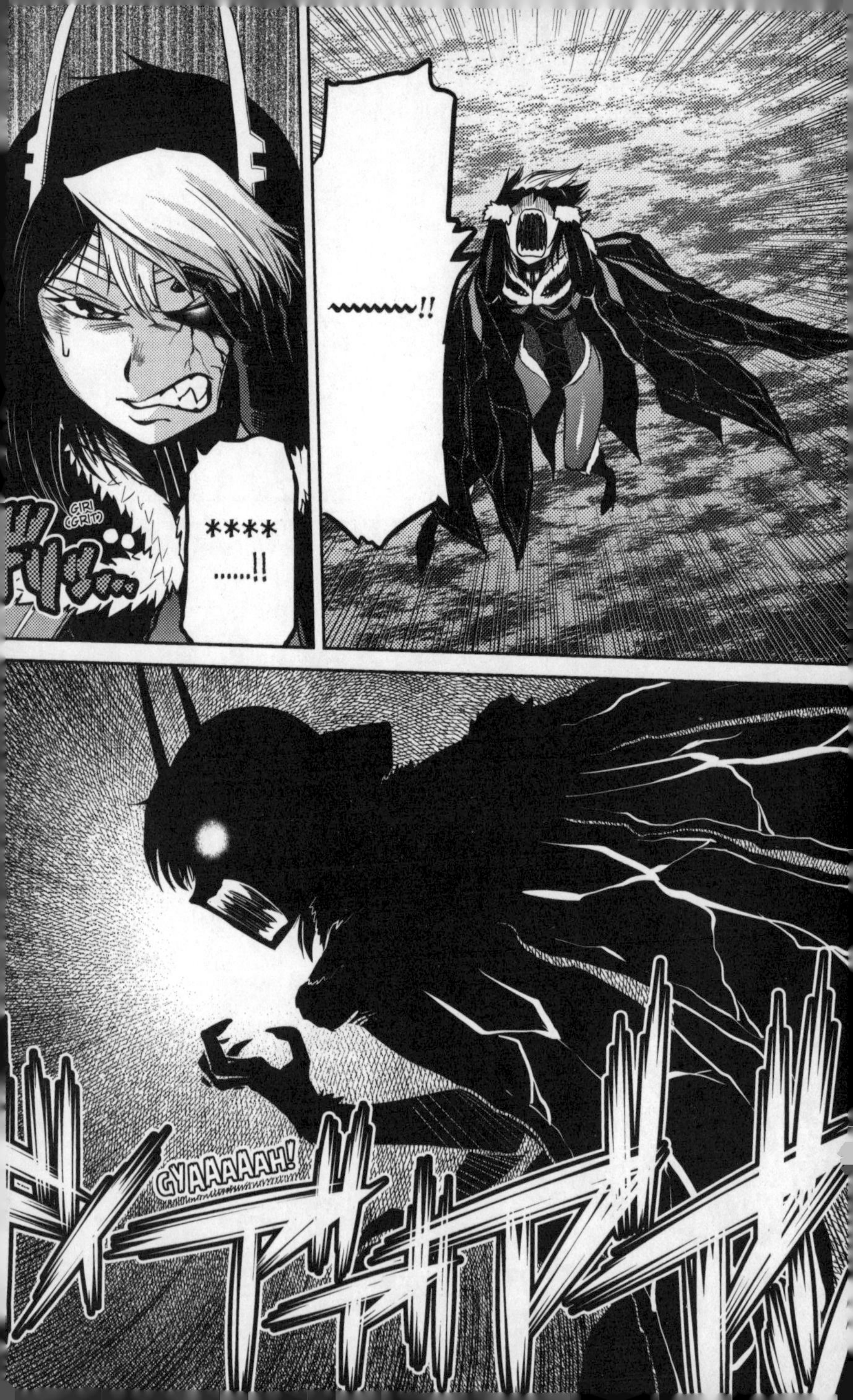

****
......!!
GIRI (GRIT)
GYAAAAAH!

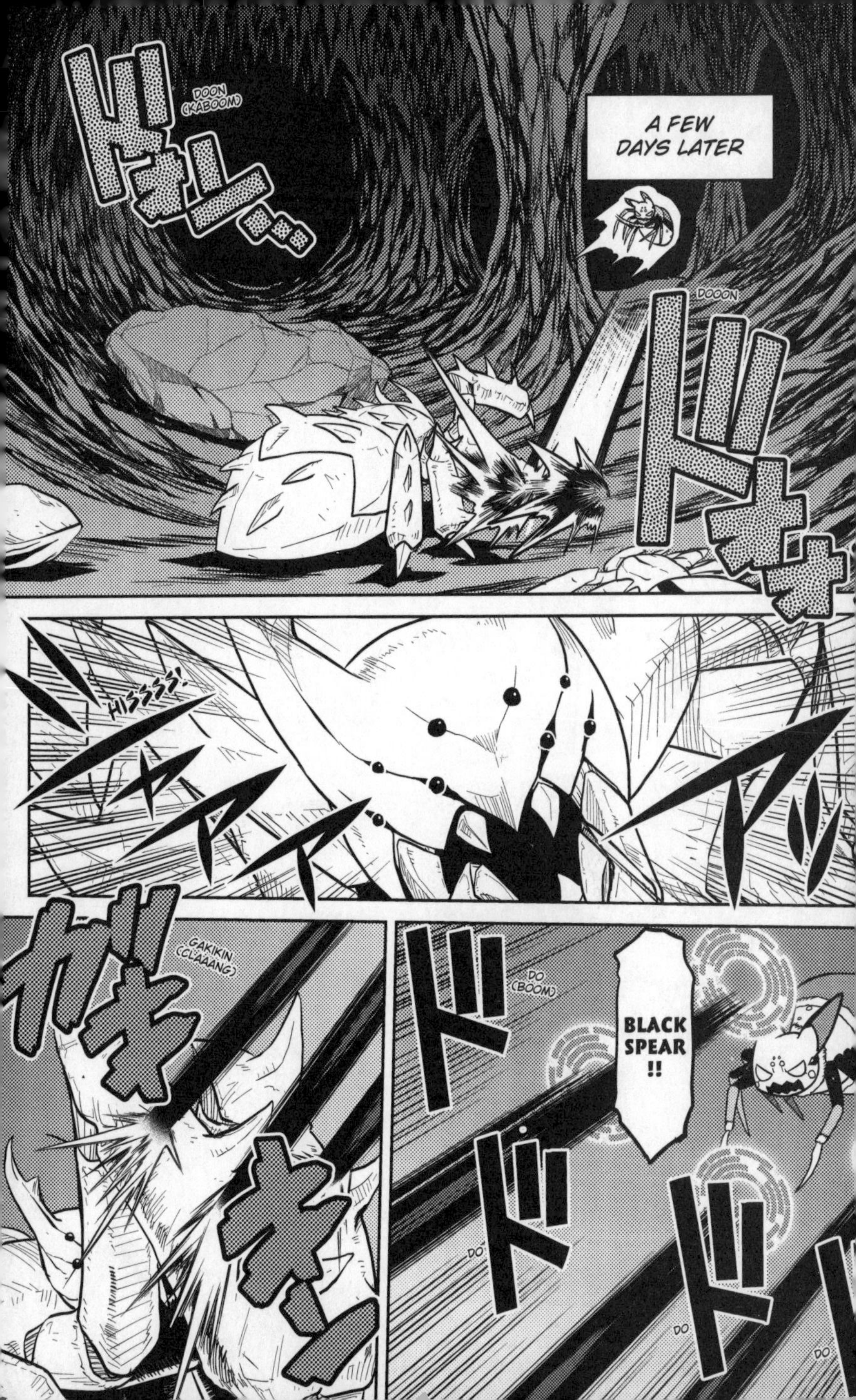
A FEW DAYS LATER
DOOON
DOON (KABOOM)
HISSSSS!
BLACK SPEAR!!
DO (BOOM)
DO
DO
DO
GAKIKIN (CLAAANG)

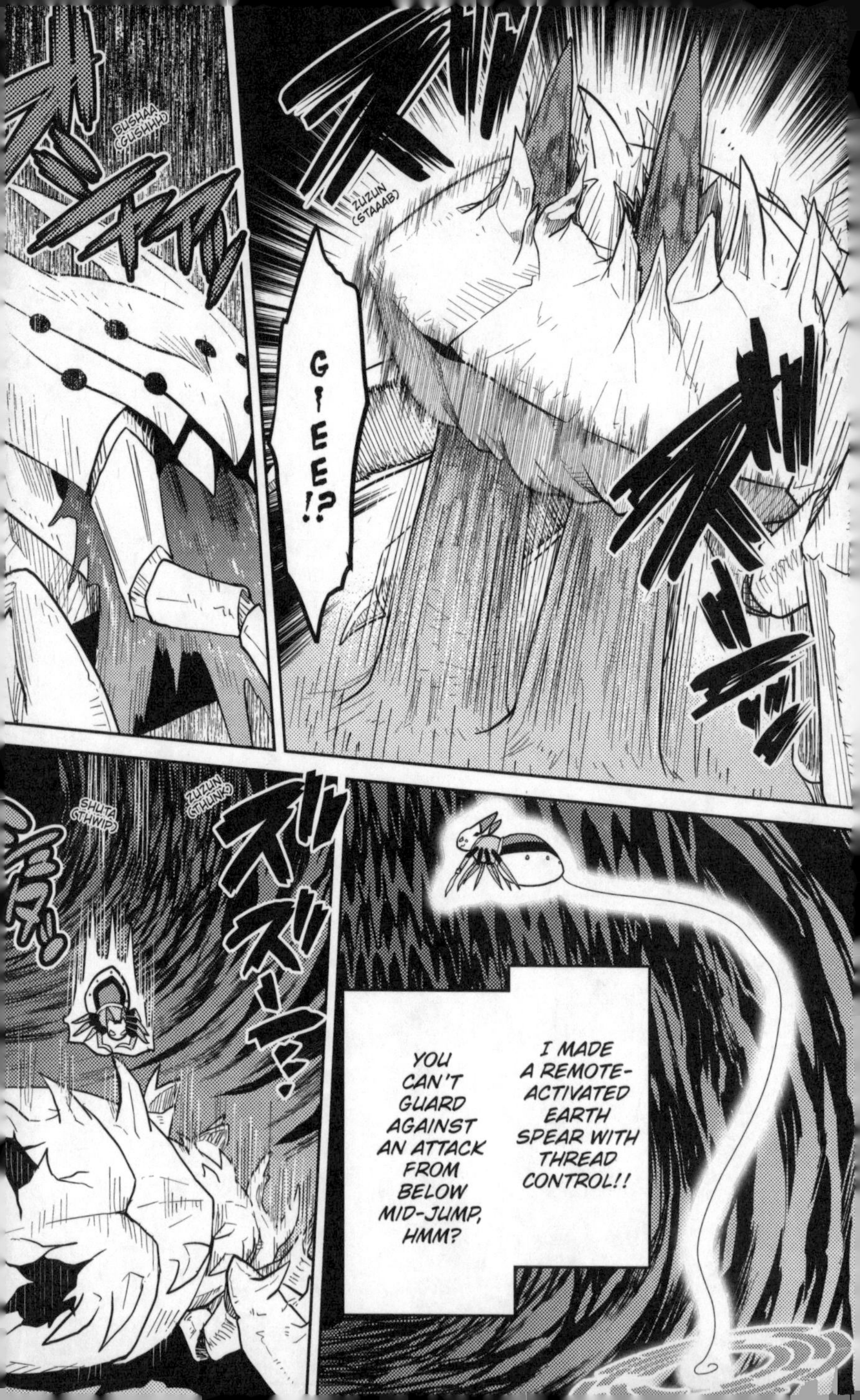
ZUZUN (STAAAB)
GIEE!?
BUSHAA (GUSHHH)
I MADE A REMOTE-ACTIVATED EARTH SPEAR WITH THREAD CONTROL!!
YOU CAN'T GUARD AGAINST AN ATTACK FROM BELOW MID-JUMP, HMM?
ZUZUN (THUNK)
SHUTA (THWIP)

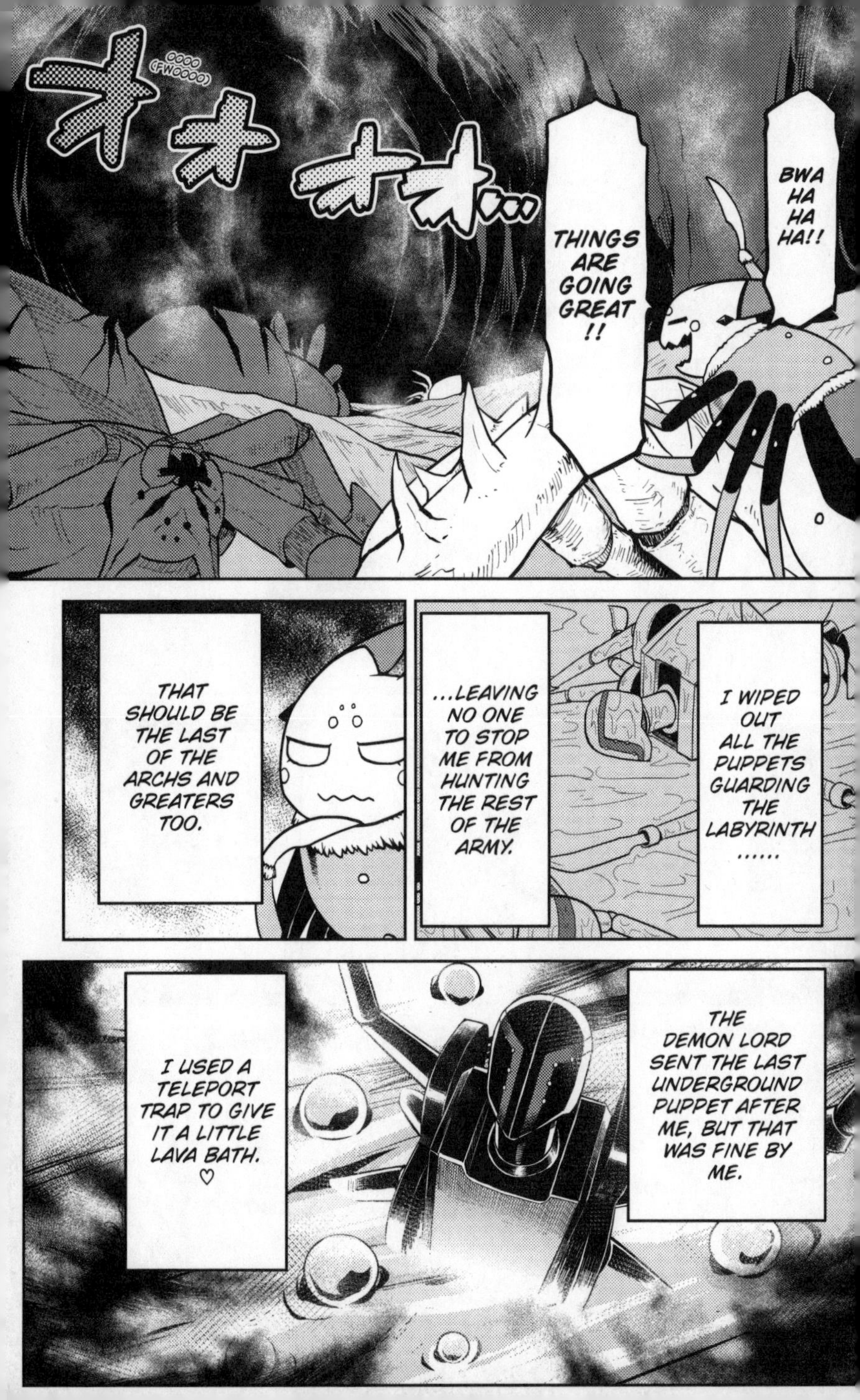
BWA HA HA HA!!
THINGS ARE GOING GREAT!!
OOOO (FWOOOO)
I WIPED OUT ALL THE PUPPETS GUARDING THE LABYRINTH......
...LEAVING NO ONE TO STOP ME FROM HUNTING THE REST OF THE ARMY.
THAT SHOULD BE THE LAST OF THE ARCHS AND GREATERS TOO.
THE DEMON LORD SENT THE LAST UNDERGROUND PUPPET AFTER ME, BUT THAT WAS FINE BY ME.
I USED A TELEPORT TRAP TO GIVE IT A LITTLE LAVA BATH. ♡

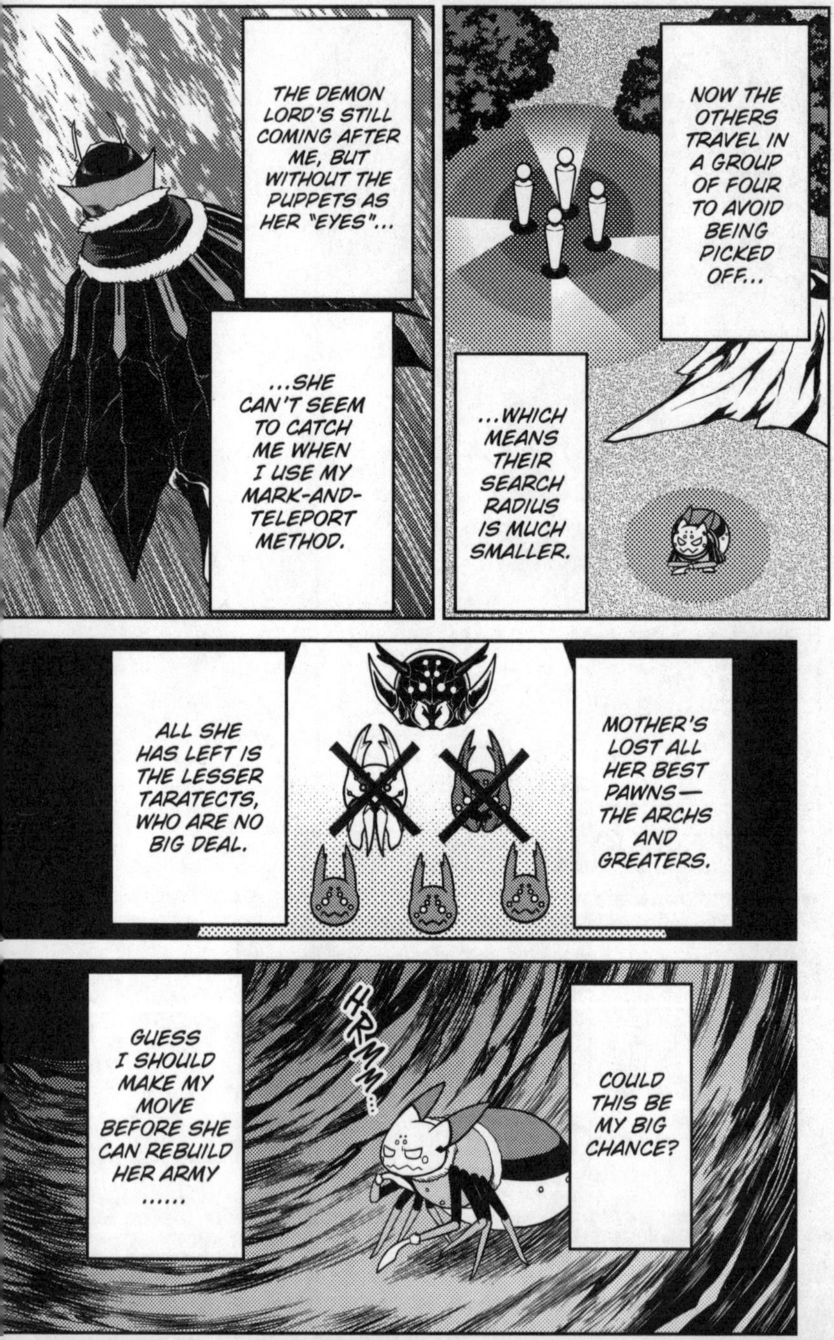
NOW THE OTHERS TRAVEL IN A GROUP OF FOUR TO AVOID BEING PICKED OFF...
...WHICH MEANS THEIR SEARCH RADIUS IS MUCH SMALLER.
THE DEMON LORD'S STILL COMING AFTER ME, BUT WITHOUT THE PUPPETS AS HER "EYES"...
...SHE CAN'T SEEM TO CATCH ME WHEN I USE MY MARK-AND-TELEPORT METHOD.
MOTHER'S LOST ALL HER BEST PAWNS—THE ARCHS AND GREATERS.
ALL SHE HAS LEFT IS THE LESSER TARATECTS, WHO ARE NO BIG DEAL.
COULD THIS BE MY BIG CHANCE?
HRMMM...
GUESS I SHOULD MAKE MY MOVE BEFORE SHE CAN REBUILD HER ARMY ......

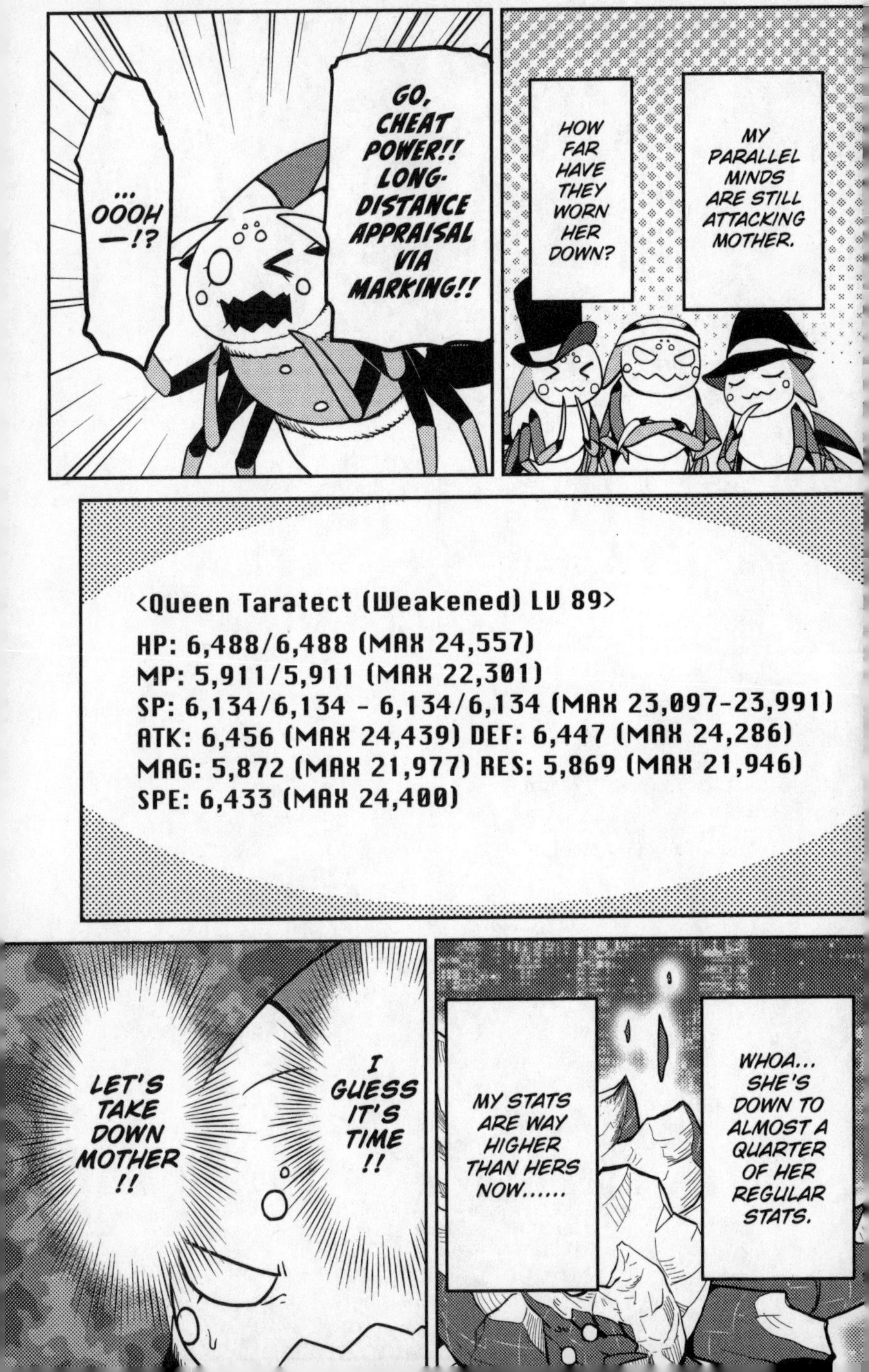
MY PARALLEL MINDS ARE STILL ATTACKING MOTHER.
HOW FAR HAVE THEY WORN HER DOWN?
GO, CHEAT POWER!! LONG-DISTANCE APPRAISAL VIA MARKING!!
...OÖOH—!?
<Queen Taratect (Weakened) LV 89>
HP: 6,488/6,488 (MAX 24,557)
MP: 5,911/5,911 (MAX 22,301)
SP: 6,134/6,134 - 6,134/6,134 (MAX 23,097-23,991)
ATK: 6,456 (MAX 24,439) DEF: 6,447 (MAX 24,286)
MAG: 5,872 (MAX 21,977) RES: 5,869 (MAX 21,946)
SPE: 6,433 (MAX 24,400)
WHOA... SHE'S DOWN TO ALMOST A QUARTER OF HER REGULAR STATS.
MY STATS ARE WAY HIGHER THAN HERS NOW......
I GUESS IT'S TIME!!
LET'S TAKE DOWN MOTHER!!

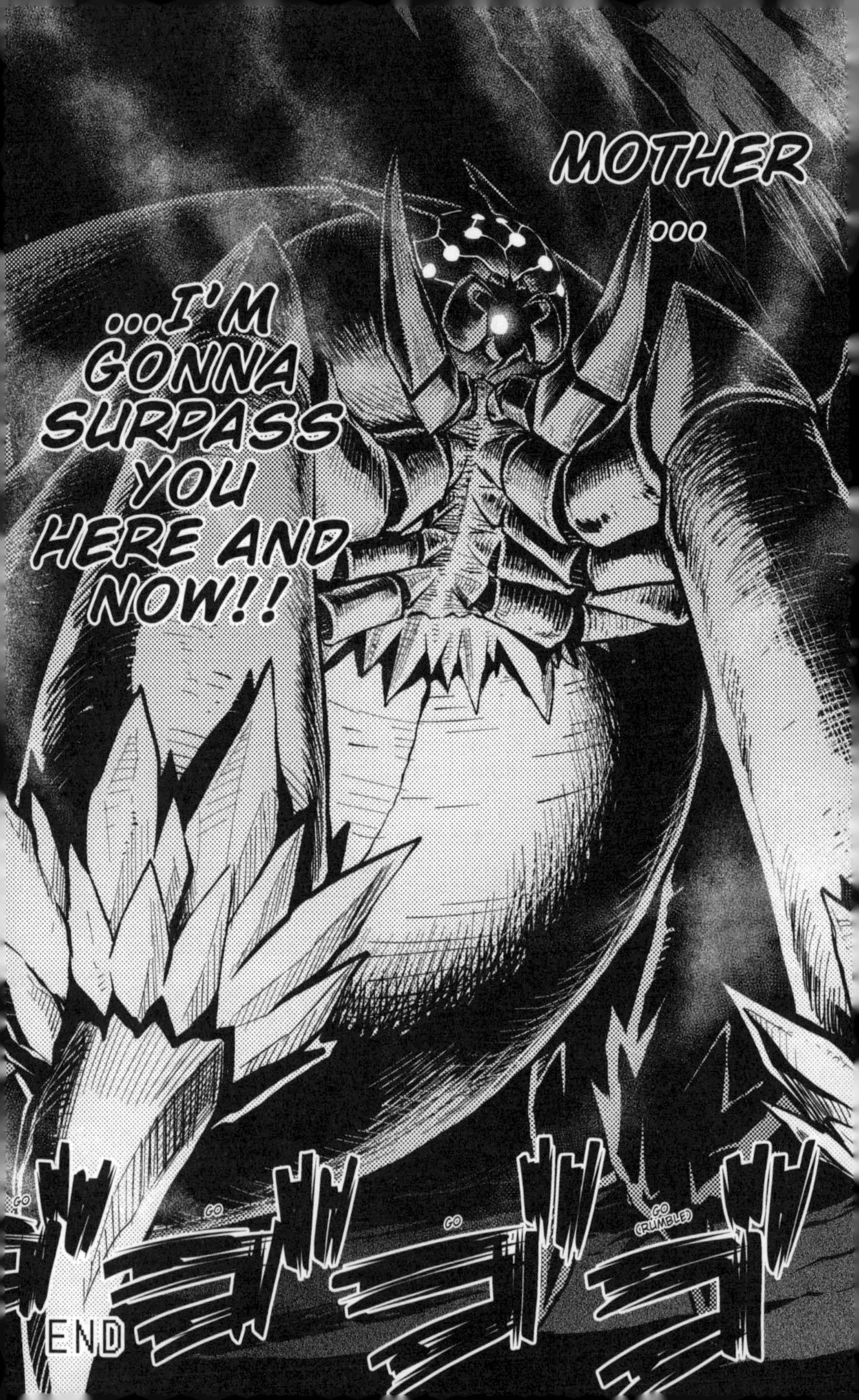
MOTHER...
...I'M GONNA SURPASS YOU HERE AND NOW!!
GO GO GO GO (RUMBLE)
END

So I'm a Spider, So What?

so I'm a **Spider**, so What?

AFTERWORD

ORIGINAL CREATOR:
OKINA BABA

HELLO, I'M OKINA BABA, THE AUTHOR OF THE *SPIDER* NOVELS.

LAST VOLUME, WE FINALLY MADE IT OUTSIDE! ONLY TO HAVE TO TURN AROUND AND GO RIGHT BACK IN.

THUS BEGINS A NEW LIFE OF POPPING IN AND OUT OF THE GREAT ELROE LABYRINTH.

I GUESS ALL SHUT-INS END UP WANTING TO GO BACK HOME WHENEVER THEY END UP OUTSIDE...

WELL, NOT IN THIS CASE!

I DON'T THINK MOST SHUT-INS WOULD GO ON A BEACH VACATION OR ANYTHING LIKE THAT.

NO SELF-RESPECTING SHUT-IN WOULD ACCEPT THE IDEA OF RUNNING AROUND THIS CRAZILY!

I SHOULD KNOW, SINCE I'M ONE MYSELF.

THIS YEAR, LOTS OF PEOPLE HAVE BEEN INVOLUNTARILY EXPERIENCING THE SHUT-IN LIFE, BUT MY BASIC LIFESTYLE HASN'T CHANGED ONE BIT...

IT SURE IS NICE BEING ABLE TO WORK AT HOME.

BUT THAT ALSO MEANS I CAN'T USE ANY OF THIS AS AN EXCUSE FOR SLACKING OFF WORK.

GOSHDARNIT!

ANYWAY, YEAH, I'M DOING JUST FINE.

PLEASE MAKE SURE YOU ALL TAKE CARE OF YOUR HEALTH TOO.

AND PRAY FOR THE HEALTH OF KAKASHI-SENSEI!

CONGRATULATIONS ON VOLUME 9!

I REALLY LIKE THE DEMON LORD'S SEXY-COOL OUTFIT. 🙂

8/2020 輝竜 司 TSUKASA KIRYU

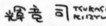

STAFF LIST

The author

ASAHIRO KAKASHI

Assistants

TERUO HATANAKA

REIICHI MASAKI

HIROTSUGU FUJIWARA

Design

R design studio

(Shinji Yamaguchi, Yuwa Tojo, Chie Ooshima)

You're reading
the wrong way!
Turn the page to read
a bonus short story by
So I'm a Spider, So What?
original creator,
Okina Baba!

Wouldn't the tides end up ebbing and flowing in a crazy-fast cycle or something?

I thought maybe I could use Professor Wisdom to calculate that, but then I was like, what would be the point? And then I realized, there'd be no point!

Thinking about stupid stuff like that is the whole problem with drifting in the ocean.

There are way bigger problems than that?

Yeah, no kidding...

[The End]

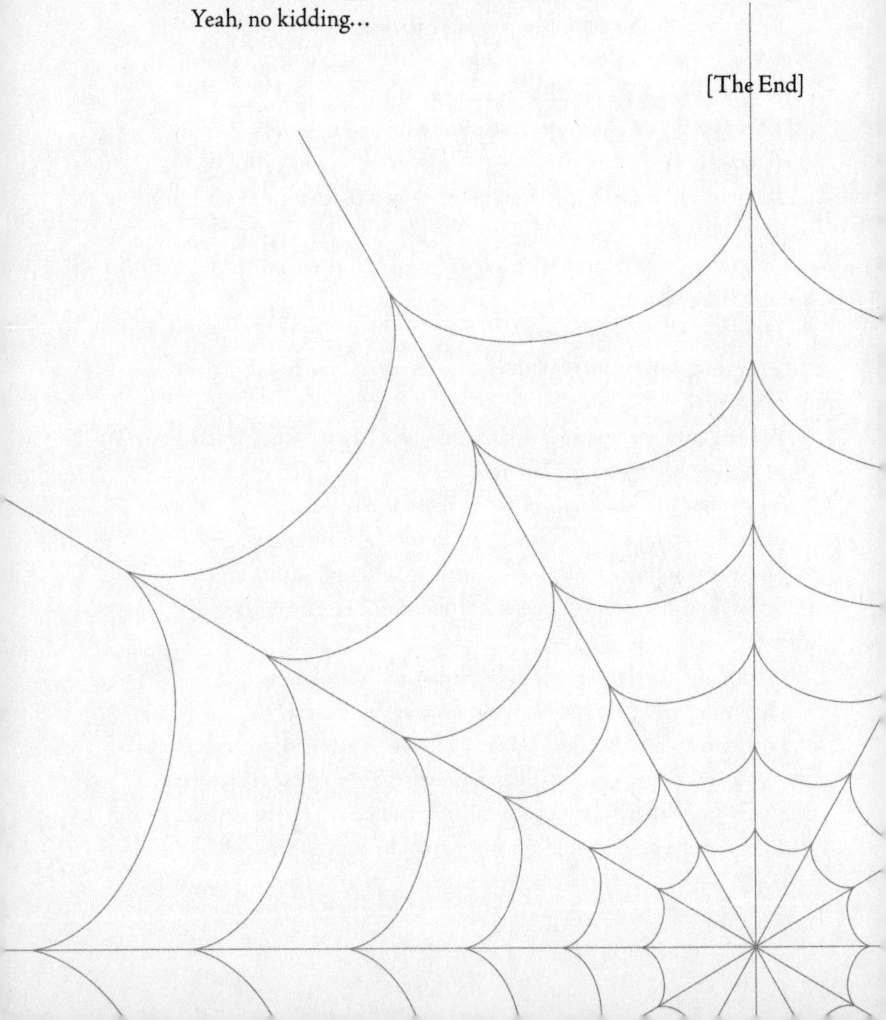

Since this is a fantasy world and all, the sky looks totally different from back on Earth.

I don't know tons of constellations and stuff, but I did look for the North Star, the Summer and Winter Triangles, and other basics like that. I didn't find a damn thing.

But the moon really caught my interest.

Or rather, the moons. There are more than one!

Wow! It really is a parallel world!

Well, I guess that's not all that surprising.

There are planets like Jupiter with tons of moons, so it's not really too unusual.

If anything, there might even be some worlds that don't have a single moon.

So looking at all those moons got me thinking. What are the tides like in this world?

Huh? Are the moons pretty?

I'm more about function than aesthetics, so you're asking the wrong spider.

Who's got time to be all fancy about moon viewing when you're a floating head in the ocean? Not me!

A disembodied head can't be fancy about squat!

Anyway, the ebb and flow of tides are influenced by the moon, right?

So if there are multiple moons, what happens to the tides exactly?

Yeah, I know. It's kind of a pointless question, but it's the first thing that came to mind.

I was floating on the waves in the ocean and all, y'know?

How was I not gonna think about tides at that point?

I definitely remember tides being a phenomenon caused by the push and pull of the moon, so what happens when there's more than one?

Does that mean there's way more pushing and pulling on the waves...?

Kinda seems like it would get super complicated.

So I'm a Spider, So What?
The Moon Is Beautiful
Okina Baba

White sand.

Crashing waves.

It's the beach!

When I think of the beach, for some reason, I end up picturing a paradise for annoyingly happy couples, but the ocean here is a paradise for water wyrms and dragons instead...

What kind of god-awful place has tons of Araba-class water dragons just hanging around?

And I spent several days floating in that very ocean as just a head, pretending to be a piece of seaweed.

Luckily, even as a disembodied head, I could still use magic, so I was able to beat the water wyrms and flee from the water dragons effectively.

And when I wasn't dealing with those clowns, I just let the waves carry me along.

Thanks to Professor Wisdom, I was able to keep track of my location, so I didn't get lost at sea or anything.

That's Professor Wisdom for ya.

So.

When you're drifting at sea for days on end, you get bored sometimes.

I mean, it's not like the water dragons and stuff were coming at me nonstop...

So I had tons of time to think about stupid nonsense while I was bobbing along on the waves.

I found a lot of ways to entertain myself, like looking up at the stars at night.

So I'm a Spider, So What? 9

Art: **Asahiro Kakashi**
Original Story: **Okina Baba**
Character Design: **Tsukasa Kiryu**

Translation: Jenny McKeon 🕷 Lettering: Bianca Pistillo

KUMO DESUGA, NANIKA? Volume 9
© Asahiro Kakashi 2020
© Okina Baba, Tsukasa Kiryu 2020
First published in Japan in 2020 by KADOKAWA CORPORATION, Tokyo.
English translation rights arranged with KADOKAWA CORPORATION, Tokyo, through TUTTLE-MORI AGENCY, INC.

English translation © 2021 by Yen Press, LLC

Yen Press
150 West 30th Street, 19th Floor
New York, NY 10001

Visit us at yenpress.com
facebook.com/yenpress
twitter.com/yenpress
yenpress.tumblr.com
instagram.com/yenpress

First Yen Press Print Edition: April 2021
Originally published as an ebook in January 2021 by Yen Press.

Yen Press is an imprint of Yen Press, LLC.
The Yen Press name and logo are trademarks of Yen Press, LLC.

Library of Congress Control Number: 2017954138

ISBN: 978-1-9753-2423-0 (paperback)

10 9 8 7 6 5 4 3 2 1

WOR

Printed in the United States of America

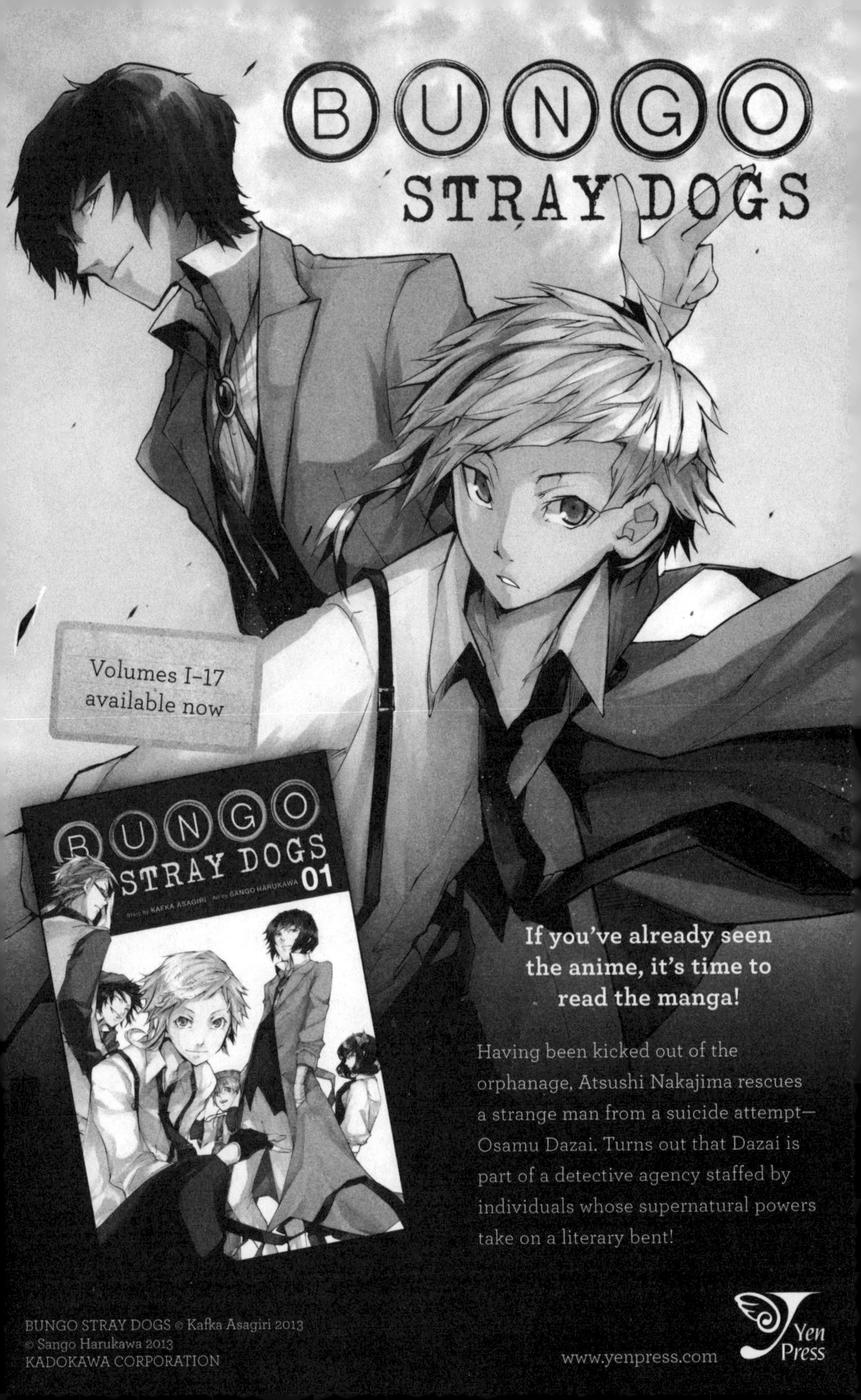
BUNGO
STRAY DOGS
Volumes 1–17
available now
BUNGO
STRAY DOGS
01
Story by KAFKA ASAGIRI Art by SANGO HARUKAWA
If you've already seen
the anime, it's time to
read the manga!
Having been kicked out of the orphanage, Atsushi Nakajima rescues a strange man from a suicide attempt—Osamu Dazai. Turns out that Dazai is part of a detective agency staffed by individuals whose supernatural powers take on a literary bent!
BUNGO STRAY DOGS © Kafka Asagiri 2013
© Sango Harukawa 2013
KADOKAWA CORPORATION
Yen Press
www.yenpress.com

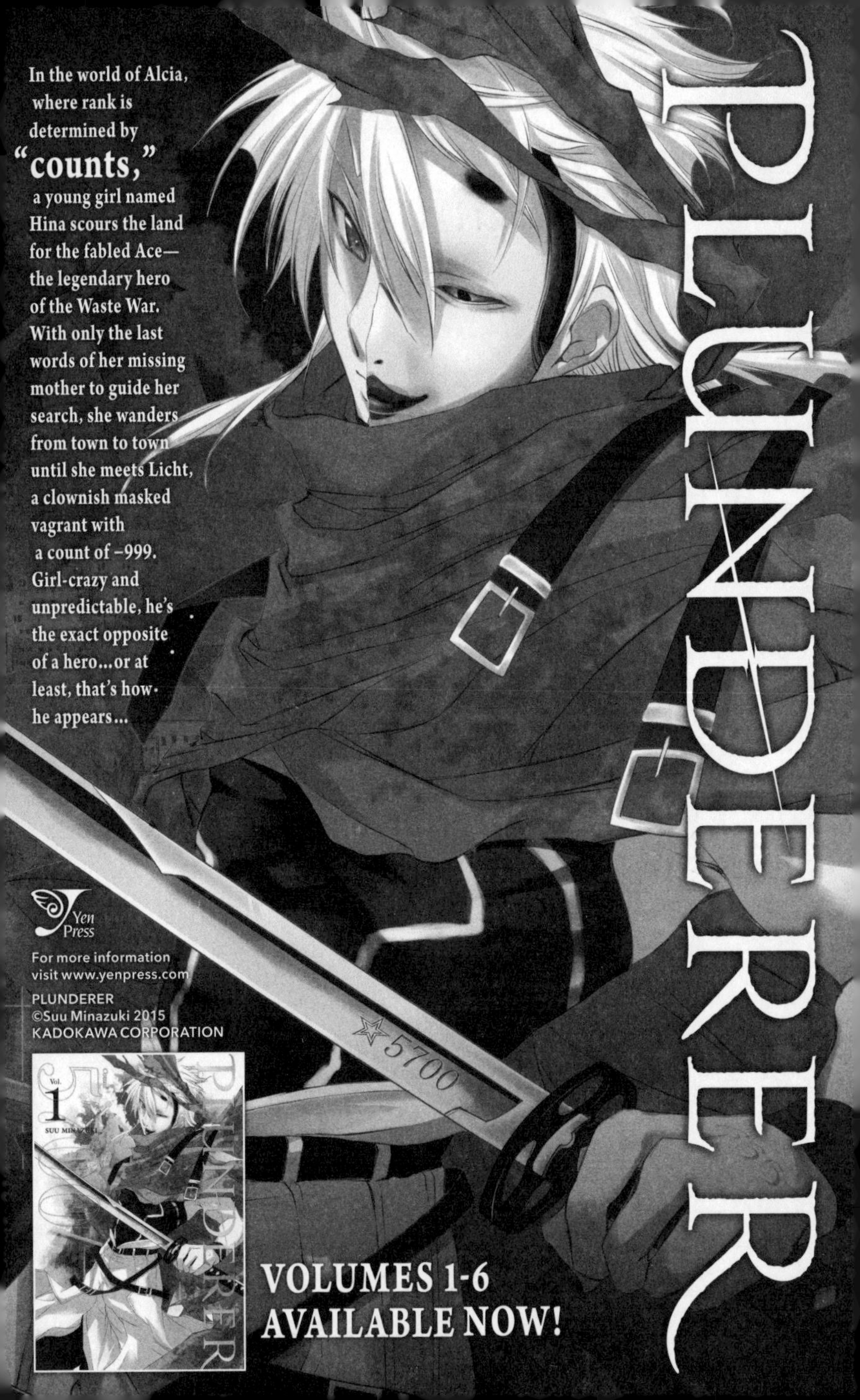
PLUNDERER
In the world of Alcia, where rank is determined by
"counts,"
a young girl named Hina scours the land for the fabled Ace—the legendary hero of the Waste War. With only the last words of her missing mother to guide her search, she wanders from town to town until she meets Licht, a clownish masked vagrant with a count of –999. Girl-crazy and unpredictable, he's the exact opposite of a hero...or at least, that's how he appears...
5700
Yen Press
For more information visit www.yenpress.com
PLUNDERER ©Suu Minazuki 2015 KADOKAWA CORPORATION
Vol. 1
SUU MINAZUKI
PLUNDERER
VOLUMES 1-6
AVAILABLE NOW!

From the *New York Times* bestselling author of *Durarara!!* comes a
light novel series full of n

BACCANO!

VOLUMES 1-15 AVAILABLE NOW

WWW.YENPRESS.COM

"BACCANO! © RYOHGO NARITA ILLUSTRATION: KATSUMI ENAMI
KADOKAWA CORPORATION ASCII MEDIA WORKS"